TECHNOLOGICAL LAG AND INTELLECTUAL BACKGROUND

Technological Lag and Intellectual Background

Problems of Transition in East Central Europe

Edited by

JÁNOS KOVÁCS
Institute of Economics
Hungarian Academy of Sciences

Dartmouth

Aldershot • Brookfield USA • Singapore • Sydney

Published by
Dartmouth Publishing Company Limited
Gower House
Croft Road
Aldershot
Hants GU11 3HR
England

Dartmouth Publishing Company
Old Post Road
Brookfield
Vermont 05036
USA

British Library Cataloguing in Publication Data
Technological Lag and Intellectual
Background: Problems of Transition in East
Central Europe
    I. Kovács, János
    338.9270943

Library of Congress Cataloging-in-Publication Data
Technological lag and intellectual background : problems of transition
    in East Central Europe / edited by János Kovács.
        p.   cm.
    Includes bibliographical references.
    ISBN 1-85521-642-6
    1. Europe, Eastern–Economic conditions–1989-. 2. Technology-
-Economic aspects–Eruope, Eastern. 3. Research, Industrial-
-Europe, Eastern. 4. Economic development–Effect of education on.
    5. Post-communism–Europe, Eastern. 6. Europe, Eastern–Social
conditions–1989- I. Kovács, János, 1926- .
    HC244.T412   1995
    338.947–dc20   94-46888
                                                                    CIP

ISBN 1 85521 642 6

Typography and graphics: T. Zimler
Printed and bound in Great Britain by Ipswich Book Co. Ltd., Ipswich, Suffolk

CONTENTS

PREFACE

The difficulties faced by the economics in transition are among the largest and most embarrassing faced by the Western world - and induced by central and eastern Europe. These countries hoped that by abandoning state planning they would achieve a rapid and sustained improvement in their standard of living, with help from the West. The experience initially has been the reverse; output has fallen rapidly and unemployment has soared. Not surprisingly they feel considerable dissatisfaction and there is some considerable criticism of the role of the West.

In the West's defence, the probability of the change had been so small that few had studied it and there are few people who doubt the long-run benefit. The question of the short and medium-term costs remains. Any structural change involves the waste of existing resources. Existing factories and knowledge are found to be redundant. Creating their replacement is both costly and time-consuming. The extent and distribution of the redundancy and the costs vary with the speed and sequencing of the reforms that are undertaken.

This book relates to just one area of resource loss, namely that in highly skilled personnel involved in scientific research and development. This area is particularly important, as prima facie it is a source of comparative advantage for these countries, which have developed strong educational systems to a high level. In this respect they did not appear to lag the West significantly.

In the ensuing chapters the authors consider why this stock of knowledge and skills is not as advantageous as it might appear and address the question of how it might be harnessed more effectively to produce new goods and services and increase competitiveness.

However, the immediate problem is that this stock of human capital is depreciating rapidly for three main raisons: emigration, transfer to other occupations, incoherence of existing knowledge to new needs of industry and society. In part this is a simple function of the market system. Redundant assets by definition have a low value in their existing use. Since non-market solutions like banning emigration or bonding people to remain in their current employment are not appropriate, market responses are required. The most obvious is to retrain such people so their knowledge can be more relevant.

Since these people are highly qualified much of this can be domestically generated. However, it is also clearly an appropriate role for western scientists. An interesting question addressed in the book is where that advice should be applied - in universities, in the research departments of firms or in special technology transfer institutions.

Professor Kovács and his team are to be congratulated, not merely because they have been able to make the transition themselves - Hungarian academic traditions in economics has always recognised this need - but because they have identified this need and been successful in securing a research grant to study it under the European Union's co-operation program ACE through the COST mechanisms (a jumble of acronyms to conjunct with).

COST covers the whole field of scientific collaboration among the European countries, not just the European Union. The member countries choose the projects in which they wish to collaborate. Most are in the natural sciences but six are in social sciences. The action of which this Hungarian project forms part is entitled somewhat cumbersomely 'The Evolution of Rules for a Single European Market'. It is looking at six specific issues in the formation of the single market, one of which is the process of adjustment for central and eastern European countries.

The papers in this book stem from a conference organised by János Kovács and his Hungarian colleagues as their contribution to the COST action. I was delighted to be able to participate myself as chairman of the Management Committee and welcome the opportunity to commend the resulting book to the reader.

David G. Mayes
Reserve Bank of New Zealand

ABOUT THE AUTHORS

BANAI, Miklós
    Managing Director
    Multiratio Ltd.
    Budapest

BERTRAND, Olivier
    Co-ordinator professor
    CEREQ
    Paris

BONIFERT, Donát
    Scientific adviser
    Foundation for Market Economy
    Budapest

DALLAGO, Bruno
    Professor of Economics
    University of Trento
    Trento

EHRLICH, Éva
Professor of Economics
Insitute for Word Economy of HAS
Budapest

FÖLDESI, Tamás
Professor of Law
Eötvös Loránd University
Budapest

GOLDPERGER, István
Managing Director
ECOLAB Ltd.
Budapest

KARPINSKY, Andrzej
Professor of Economics
Committee for Future Studies "Poland in XXI century"
in Polish Academy of Sciences
Warsaw

KIGLICS, István
Chief Counsellor
Ministry of Finances
Budapest

KOVÁCS, János
Professor of Economics
Institute of Economics, HAS
Budapest

KOZMA, Tamás
Professor of Pedagogics
Director of Hungarian Institut for Educational Research
Budapest

LUKÁCS, Béla
Scientific adviser
Central Research Institute for Physics
Budapest

MAJOROS, Pál
  Professor of Economics
  College for Foreign Trade
  Budapest

MASON, Geoff
  Professor of Economics
  National Institute of Economic and Social Research
  London

MAYES, David
  Chairman of COST A7 Management Commettee
  Co-ordinator Professor
  National Institute of Economic and Social Research
  London

MOLNÁR, György
  Research Fellow
  Institute of Economics, HAS
  Budapest

NYERS, Rezső
  Member of the Parliament
  Professor of Economics
  Former director of Institute of Economics, HAS
  Budapest

SEREGHYOVÁ, Jana
  Professor of Economics
  The Economics Institute, Academy of Sciences of the Czech Republic
  Praha

SIPOS, Aladár
  Professor of Economics
  Former director of Institute of Economics, HAS
  Budapest

TARJÁN, Tamás
  Senior Research Fellow
  Institute of Economics, HAS
  Budapest

TERK, Erik
Professor of Economics
Director of Estonian Institute of Future Studies
Tallin

TÍMÁR, János
Professor of Economics
Budapest University of Economics
Budapest

VIRÁG, Ildikó
Senior Research Fellow
Institute of Economics, HAS
Budapest

WAGNER, Karin
Professor of Economics
Wissenschaftszentrum
Berlin

INTRODUCTION

In the past few years there has been an abundance of literature on the transformation of the former socialist countries. A host of economists, sociologists, politologists, researchers and journalists write, talk and discuss it. 'Transitionology' has become a new type of science and some of its slogans (e.g. the catching up of East Europe with Europe) have become outworn by now. It is unavoidable that with the succession of processes short term problems, timely and unsolved issues force their way into the focus of attention. The failure to solve them pushes the long term strategic approach into the background or gives way to wishful thinking which is a marketable product in politics.

This volume of essays can be regarded unusual in this regard. It focuses on more or less neglected long term processes and strategic questions. Before describing the research program behind this publication and giving a short review of the studies in this volume it is worth calling the attention of readers interested in the transformation of the former socialist countries to some problems related to the twofoldness of short term and long term points of view.

There is another twofoldness of content, which is somewhat parallel with the twofold approach, due to the twofold goal of East European transformation: the transformation of the social structure, the building of the institutions of the market economy and multiparty democracy on the one hand and the considerable reduction of the lag in relation to the West (Western Europe in this context) on the other hand. There is a fairly widespread opinion that expects the automatic fulfilment of the second goal after the realization of the first one, so analyses made in this spirit concentrate mainly - sometimes solely - on the building of the market economy.

I think the problem is more deeply rooted since our lag goes back several centuries rather than a few decades only. From the point of the so called socialist countries the seemingly unified market economy in fact presents several varieties and possibilities. It is not all the same which version is chosen in the course of the transition or, to put it more precisely, which version takes shape due to our frequently unconscious activities. Besides the daily activities attention should be paid so that in the process of tackling the problems of structural transformation the chances of catching up will not be lost. This is an unnegligible interest not only of the countries directly involved but from the point of the prospects West European integration as well. If the Eastern part of the continent becomes a peripherical appendage to Western Europe, its 'Latin America', whole Europe may lose its position in a world of globalizing regions.

This global approach leads us to another important problem related to transformation. The political discussions about transformation are dominated by local standpoints which are also influenced by day to day matters: participants both from the West and the East apply an approach that is based on their conditions and current tasks awaiting solution and the two types of approach contradict each other accordingly.

It often seems that it is only Russia that is really important for the West in the whole East European region, and that the 'in-between' East-Central European region is negligible due to its size. This limited approach is partly justified by the extraordinary importance of Russia in matters of security and naturally by the size of the potential Russian market. This feeling is further strengthened by the fact that it looks as if the satisfaction of the increased Western interest is the task of the transitionologist-turned sovietologists. We intend to tinge this picture with this volume as the studies basically deal with the problems of East-Central Europe providing some outlook on the Baltic states as well. The bringing together of the standpoints of the two regions, which we consider a necessity in the long run, may be eased by including in this volume the works of such Western authors who do not view the problems through the eyes of sovietologists.

Beyond making up for a long felt need, this approach is justified by the in-between character of the East-Central European region mainly in the sense of the level of development and structure of the society rather than in the sense of geography. All these countries are closer in development to the advanced countries than the successor states of the former Soviet Union (except the

Baltic states). This situation may enable them to perform the role of a sort of bridge in the process of globalization. If the integrating Europe is not able to integrate the East-Central European region, there is no chance of tackling the problems of Russia either.

The coupling of the short term and long term aspects in the East European transition manifests also in the fact that the transition is marked by a certain continuity while fundamental social and economic changes are taking place. There have been several cases when there was a sort of inertia inherent in the changes of the economic system and we do not belong to the optimists who believe that our catching up with the western technical level, productivity and competitiveness or approaching the average western living standards is only a matter of a few years. At the same time we hope that the often landslide like changes during the transformation will not completely destroy our genuine values rooted in the past, just because of the inertia inherent in the long term processes.

It is a specific feature of the East-Central European region that in most places the transformation was preceded by a reform process combining central planning and efforts aimed at building a market economy. The duration and depth of the above largely differed in the different countries but we believe that these reforms were most fundamentally accomplished in Hungary. Consequently if we are optimistic to a certain degree concerning the chances of catching up, it is based on the surviving effects of the advantageous processes that were launched earlier.

We believe that the adaptability of a society depends on the human factor above all. The experiences of the two world wars show that the production capacity could be restored relatively soon if the economy had the workforce able to apply the suitable technics. This region possesses deeply rooted European cultural traditions, an above-the-average educational system on the basis of which there is a very productive research system, the effect of which can be seen in the structure of the society. As an output of the high quality educational system, a society dominated by the middle class and technocracy came into being, which emphasizes the specific European character of the region.

It was to our pleasure that the above described approach and ideas of our research team gained the support of the COST program of the European Community, when this formerly West European scientific program was expanded to East Europe. In this way we received the possibility to include our activity in the West European research on the topic of the Single European Market and to organize a conference under the title of this volume in Budapest at the end of January 1994 with the financial support of the

COST project. This volume contains the texts and the discussions-related additions to the addresses at the conference in an edited form.

The core of the team organizing the joint research which served as basis for the conference is made up of Hungarian economists; this explains the relatively larger number of studies dealing with the processes in Hungary. The studies contributed by researchers from the neighbouring former socialist countries convince us however that despite major differences in detail the fundamental processes take place in a similar manner, raising similar problems in the countries of the region.

Due to the nature of the transition process now under way this conference could not close or summarize the research done so far, it should rather be regarded an important milestone in the research process. I would like to refer to a publication by the same publishing house in 1990, titled Economic Planning in Transition, which was compiled right before the transition. The authors were partly the same and the book dealt, from a slightly different aspect, with the role of long term regulators as decisive elements of economic movements in relation to the profoundly changed place and role of planning. That volume was also the product of an international group of researchers and already at the time of its publication, in totally different historical conditions, the importance of the cooperation and the joint movement towards Western Europe of the East-Central European countries emerged - principally that of Czechoslovakia, Hungary and Poland. This possibility is still open and their historical traditions and economic interests point to the importance of it.

✦

This volume consists of five parts. Part I deals with different aspects of the transition-crisis, principally with the aim of providing a comprehensive analysis of the current situation. The essay by Rezső Nyers analyzes the problems of overall recession connected with the transition. The continuity of the transition rooted in the past is represented by Rezső Nyers in his person since he was the main initiator and father of the 1968 economic reform in Hungary and he had a considerable role in the preparation of the present transition. It is more than mere coincidence that this volume begins with his study.

The following three lectures concentrate on the events of the past four years and the possibilities for development in relation to the main sectors of the economy. Donát Bonifert gives an analysis of the structural causes behind the enormous industrial recession. Concerning Aladár Sipos's study I would emphasize the notion which questions the necessity of the extent of agricultural recession and in connection with that he deals with the shortcomings of the agricultural policy. It is in this field where the harmful effects of decision making built on wishful thinking and non consideration of the actual processes in the society can most clearly be seen. Éva Ehrlich's study gives a comprehensive picture of Hungarian infrastructure. In the former decades it was the production infrastructure which was the most backward field of the socialist economies, constituting the biggest obstacle to further development. After the transformation the extraordinarily important telecommunication and trade network showed a fast development.

Part II makes an effort to evaluate the extent of the lag behind the West in production and technology with special view of Research & Development as the main tool of increasing competitiveness. The studies by Molnár and Tarján focus on the apparent paradox that parallel with the several decade-long lag in productivity Hungary has a workforce and R&D base that are of high quality compared with the existing technical level. This fact could provide comparative advantages in the catching up process in comparison, for example, with the South European region. However the erosion of the R&D network began in the transition process and gathered speed because of short term fiscal considerations and this certainly does not ease catching up.

The outcome of the debate over the future role of research and development in the former socialist countries is somehow in harmony with the opinions expressed by the study of two western authors, Geoff Mason and Karin Wagner, who, when comparing English and German corporate competitiveness, come to the conclusion that technological transfer is the decisive element in competitiveness on the market. The ensuring of this depends on the innovative abilities of the workforce both in the internal and outside transfers and this means more than mere R&D capacity. Their conclusions provide important lessons for Eastern Europe as well.

The studies of Andrzej Karpinski and Jana Sereghyová on the technical level and technical background of the Polish and Czech economy do in fact reinforce the Hungarian experience. The only difference is that it looks as if Sereghyová's assessment of the Czech situation is somewhat more positive and more optimistic as far as catching up with Western Europe is concerned. She may be right when she applies this assessment to the state of the Czech industry. Judgment on this is left to the reader. I want to add that Karpinski is not very pessimistic either, at least as far as the start of the catching up process is concerned. In conclusion we can say that the assessments of the opportunities of the three countries do not considerably differ. The differences in the answers may depend on the research attitudes of the authors.

The studies in part III examine the role of foreign trade in the development of the situation and possibilities of the economy. The essays written by Pál Majoros and István Goldperger deal with foreign trade in Hungary. The two authors wholly agree on one thing, namely that the eastern markets have lost their importance only temporarily and that the rearrangement of the proportions in the direction mentioned earlier does not at all justify the abandonment of the former Soviet markets. They both believe that grave political mistakes by the government also had a part in this. Godperger, who formulates his opinion in a harsher manner, uses an economic policy approach whereas Majoros applies more statistical data from a more theoretical angle. Both studies, especially that of Goldperger, underline that the changes in the structure of foreign trade have an influence on the structure of the skilfulness of the workforce partly directly, partly indirectly through its effect on production.

The report by Erik Terk about Estonia convinces the reader that the problems of the Baltic states are not solely of political or military nature. Gaining independence does not automatically bring about economic independence if a country is tied by thousands of threads to the powers of the region that it has just seceded from politically. Despite the relative economic development the exorbitant price of secession and a certain degree of subsequent social disintegration may considerably slow down the integration of the Baltic states and Europe.

The title of part IV, 'Educational System: Key to Development' rightly expresses an opinion that the development of the educational system is of utmost importance from the point of the future. Hungary had a developed system of education and training earlier as well, but we are aware that in the present transition and integration process it has to be adapted to the new requirements generated by the new conditions. Three studies have been included to provide assessment of the Hungarian educational-training system. The essay by Tamás Kozma reflects the position that globalization sets new requirements for the educational system. János Tímár concentrates on the increased needs due to the changes of the structure of the economy whereas János Kovács and Ildikó Virág focus on the tasks set by the Hungarian social structure and the employment situation. The question keeps arising in the public and among experts as to how the Hungarian educational system can be brought in line with the western one, or to put it more practically, how it is possible to issue diplomas recognized in the West without the Hungarian educational system losing its good traditions. The solution requires that the divergence of the two systems be revealed.

Concerning the different vocational training systems, the study by one of the French experts in this field enlightens that moving closer to the western model is complicated by the fact that there is not a unified system in the West either. In analyzing the differences of the different (Anglo-Saxon, French, German and East European) systems he reveals the recently manifested integration tendencies that the West has recently shown.

Finally about part V. Although the members of the research teams from the East and the West are all economists, we could not ignore the effects exerted by the overall cultural background, the legal environment and social traditions on the development of the economies and on the way the problems of the region can be brought into one unified framework. The effects of the Soviet-type system on the East-Central European region in the last 50 years have been dealt with by Bruno Dallago with special emphasis on the role of the state. The author is a longtime expert of Hungarian economic reform and he is also at home in the East-Central European developments. Being an outside spectator he may give a more objective picture than those who are directly involved in the processes.

The study by Miklós Banai and Béla Lukács reviews the catching up efforts in the Carpathian basin throughout a time span of several centuries. Tamás Földesi describes the recent changes of the Hungarian legal system and shows how quickly the West European standards in human rights are approached in Hungary.

The integration of East Europe with the West brings about the conflict of the different cultures and traditions to a certain extent. In order not to exaggerate the problems in this regard (although we started on the assumption that it cannot be underestimated either) we were looking for an example for comparison, an example which may well seem to be too far away from our situation. This is why we included the study of István Kiglics in the materials of the conference as it demonstrates how a thousand years old culture is able to include and to use in its own manner the western production and technical culture.

✦

In conclusion I would like to express my thanks to the Management Committee of the COST A7 research project for their support. Their participation and remarks have meant a great contribution to our activity. I owe my special thanks to chairman of the Management Committee Professor D. G. Mayes, who had a decisive role in enabling us to join in a Europe-wide international research network. The participation of COST action secretary Tuija Partonen was of immeasurable importance, who helped us to find our way on a new terrain, in the jungle of the administration of the European Community.

As I have already mentioned this book is the result of team work. My earnest thanks are due to my closest colleagues György Molnár, Tamás Tarján and Ildikó Virág, who most contributed to the success of the project.

János Kovács
Professor of Economics

PART I
CRISIS AND TRANSITION:
THE MAIN SECTORS OF
HUNGARIAN ECONOMY

1 The economic strategy of Hungary in the grasp of the transformation and recession

Rezső Nyers

The change of the system in East-Central-Europe

Eastern-Europe ceased to exist in 1989 in terms of politics as well as economy. It was not by chance that the Central-European and the Balkan states as well as East-Germany had already seceded from the integration before the collapse of the Soviet Union as the economies and cultures of these countries have always differed from that of imperial Russia. It was also self-evident for East Germany to turn its back on East-Central-Europe following the German reunification. There is no way back to the revival of the cooperation that existed for forty years. Parallel to the growing independence of the East-Central-European region, the former cooperation mechanisms between these countries have disappeared. With the Soviet planning coordination abolished, their mutual cooperation has become disordered and the basic elements of market connections (financial network, company relations, legal framework) are being implemented very slowly. The question is still open: will these countries get closer to the European Union by using the opportunities of cooperation or by seeking individual opportunities?

The transformation in East-Central-Europe is characterised by two simultaneous processes: a new economic environment (new ownership structure and market institutions) is built while, on the other hand, the economy is in an acute and serious recession. The reasons for the latter are hard to clarify because the side-effects of the reforms are mixed with the loss of the Eastern markets and some mistakes in the Government's policies.

The market trends are different from what was prognosticated by the governments whose hasty measures are unacceptable for the entrepreneurs while the population does not get from either side what it expected. These factors are shaping the unique East-Central-European political climate which of course has a counter-effect on the economy.

The group of the 'Visegrád countries' (Hungary, Poland, the Czech Republic and Slovakia) has made more progress in reforming their markets; they started their reforms earlier and under more favourable circumstances and their financial situation is also more balanced. Of the successors of ex-Yugoslavia, only Slovenia could keep pace with these countries. The Balkan states, i.e. Albania, Bulgaria and Romania started their reforms later, under less favourable circumstances and they still struggle with the hardships of the start. Besides the different development levels of the national markets and the least compatible legal systems, there is a very low capital transfer within the area with more than 120 million population, the information and commodity exchange is slow and the economic resources are not united. Four years ago, the political parties that seized power reckoned with a quick change of ownership and they planned to base the entire economy on market principles by the middle of the decade and were prepared to consummate the process by joining the European Community by 1995. Today, it is clear that the process of full-scale transformation that was estimated to last half a decade will in fact take a decade.

The economic recession is deeper and more lasting than it was anticipated. Recession was not unexpected as the growth stopped already in 1989-1990. However, both the politicians and the economists were unprepared for the crisis that actually broke out.

In four years, the GDP has decreased by 20 per cent in the Visegrád-group, by 30-40 per cent in the Baltic states and by 50 per cent in the small Yugoslavia and Croatia. Investments decreased even faster than the GDP and unemployment rose to double digit figures. The inflation rate was curbed in the Visegrád-group at 20-30 per cent but it ran out of control in all the other countries. The economic policies ensuring a balanced growth have not been found yet in any of the countries in the region and they probably should get more international support for this.

Transformation and recession in Hungary

Among the centrally planned economies, Hungary had the strongest orientation towards the West in the 80's, and even so, the transformation process started in 1989 has been going on with unexpected and painful shock-effects. Among these, one has to mention the total collapse of the ex-Soviet market, the 22 per cent decrease in economic output that has lasted for four years now, the 18 per cent unemployment rate, the controlled but still high 22-23 per cent inflation rate. The year of stabilization announced by the Government will be shifted from 1993 to 1994 but also its realization is doubted; the modest optimism of the Government is surrounded by the pessimism of entrepreneurs and consumers. Nevertheless, the transformation process continues despite its uncertain conditions.

Pursuing the policy of the period 1987-89, the Government in its economic strategy focused on the requirement that the transformation should be implemented while maintaining secure foreign exchange relations. To achieve this, efforts were made to reduce the deficit in the balance of current payments, to draw in foreign working capital and to accumulate sufficient foreign exchange reserves. These efforts produced full success between 1990-92.

There was a slight positive balance in current payments, the annual level of incoming working capital rose from USD 200 million to 1.4 billion. Around 50 per cent of the capital invested in the East-Central European region flew to Hungary. However, the majority of this was not spent on new developments but on acquisitions of existing Hungarian assets. The foreign exchange reserves of the central bank increased from USD 1.1 billion to 6 billion by the end of 1993 which is equal to seven months' total imports. However, the export volume significantly decreased in 1993 and the slight positive balance turned to a deficit of USD 3 billion. Although this can be financed under the present circumstances, total debts will grow by at least USD 0.5 billion and the prognoses for 1994 forecast USD 1.5-2.0 billion deficit. There is no chance of growth this year and the protection of the external balance will be given priority.

The Government started the privatization process very ambitiously as one of the main means of the transformation of the economy. The first phase, started in 1987, was finished in 1990. It was characterized by spontaneous privatizations (to public limited and limited liability companies) and management-initiated acquisitions were most frequent. The second phase was implemented between 1991-92 by establishing the State Property Agency (SPA) and enacting relevant laws and with the debate on 'centralisation vs. decentralisation'. Although central programmes were less successful, the transfer of ownership was very considerable in this period. The third phase started in 1993 when new techniques were introduced, the permanent state property was separated and transferred to the management of holding companies while the domestic privatization demand was enlivened.

How far has ownership restructuring proceeded by the means of market sales? It is hard, almost impossible, to evaluate the progress, we have only few data from the SPA and a general analysis of the procedure from the Privatization Research Institute.

According to expert estimates, in the middle of 1993 the share of fully privatized companies (where private ownership is full or in majority) is 26.5 per cent and it is 35.8 per cent if partially privatized companies are also considered. If we also take into account small private enterprises and foreign investments outside the privatization process, we can assess the share of the private sector around 50 per cent in the economy today and within that, 15-17 per cent is the participation of the foreign capital. Mass-scale privatization is slowly getting to an end but it may last until the end of the decade with less improvization, in a more decentralised manner, better harmonized with crisis management, parallel to the reorganization of state-owned companies and the development of technologies.

The Privatization Research Institute has arrived at the remarkable conclusion that privatization cannot be efficient if implemented hastily, by the means of shock-therapy, it cannot solve alone the structural problems inherited from socialism, no immediate improvement in profitability can be expected from the transfer of ownership and the positive effects will be felt only later. In summary, privatization cannot be the main tool for combating recession.

The most conspicuous consequence of the recession and the decreased economic performance is the tilted balance of the state budget, which has caused an acute and grave deficit and accordingly growing internal state debts.

Although the transfer expenditures of the state budget have increased in four years from 18.5 per cent of the GDP to 21 per cent, this is not the only cause for the considerable tilt of the balance but this was also due to the missing state revenues because of the decreased economic outputs, the increasing debt service and because of the black economy out of state control which has grown to 30 per cent according to estimates. As a result of the above factors, the deficit of the state budget grew in four years from 2 per cent of the GDP to 8 per cent while internal state debts increased from 58 per cent of the GDP to almost 80 per cent of the same.

The severe position of the state budget seriously burdens the entire economy because financing the deficit drains domestic financial resources from investments instead of the state making infrastructural investments to spur economic growth. All in all, one can say that no structural reforms other than some partial corrections and modifications have been implemented in the state budget. No wonder this area refrains rather than activates the economic transformation.

If we ask how successful the Government's economic policies were in the grasp of the transformation and the dangers of the recession, the realistic answer is that it was sometimes successful sometimes unsuccessful. Progress has been made in the transformation of the ownership and institutional structure, the management of the foreign exchange sector has been basically successful, while on the other hand, the Government failed in the stabilization of the real processes of the economy (production, turnover, investments). This failure is reflected in the unbalanced state budget and the deterioration of the balance of payments that reappeared in 1993. The conclusion is therefore justified that the economic policy is not consistent enough in principal areas.

Either the ownership reform has negative effects on the real sphere or the state budget on the lending or vice versa, or the trade interests collided with the foreign exchange rate policies, or the debt management with interest rate policies. Very often, the decision-makers were too late to recognize the intersection points of the correlating effects and eventually it is the micro-sphere of the economy that suffers from these faults, the recession has become too deep, the balance of payments is too fragile and the predictability of enterprises is limited.

The situation of enterprises and the influence of the EC

The participants of the economy as well as the interest representation organizations almost fully agree on the importance of economic relations with the European Community as well as on the strategic goal of getting full membership in it. Community relations account for about 50 per cent in the foreign trade of Hungary, the ex-socialist countries have a share of 25 per cent, the OECD countries outside the EC have 20 per cent and the developing countries have 5 per cent. Therefore, the growth of the Hungarian economy largely depends on the intensity of the relations with the EC and the OECD countries. No doubt, the Hungarian Government displayed great activity in diplomacy: it succeeded in raising the existing relations with the EC and OECD to a higher level of associated membership. Nevertheless, there are serious doubts in the Hungarian society concerning the future of these relations, especially the Brussels integration, in two main aspects:

- *Firstly* because although the Hungarian institutional framework is getting closer to the European model, at the same time, the economic performance is lagging more and more behind the average of the EC even if only the less developed members are considered. To be able to join the Community, Hungary should produce an annual growth of 5 per cent parallel to a 2-2.5 per cent assumed growth in the EC. This can be very much doubted regarding the internal resources of growth of the present Hungarian economy.

- *Secondly* because while the intentions to improve relations are very strong on the Hungarian side, there are serious concerns that the 12 EC countries - and the new ones admitted meanwhile - will not in fact be very eager to take measures to improve the Visegrád-group countries to the level required for EC membership. There is a lot to be done by the applicants but much should be done also by the member states: open their markets to Central-Eastern-Europe, including partly such protected markets as steel, textile, chemical and agriculture because 45 to 55 per cent of the exports of the Visegrád-group is composed of these products.

A further question arises: can the Hungarian economy meet the requirements of EC-membership if it could not simultaneously develop its alternative economic opportunities (i.e. with developed countries outside the Community, the Eastern-European region and the Third World)? Obviously, without appropriately diversified external relations, the development of the domestic market would be more uncertain, the comprehensiveness within the common market would be weakened and the subsidizing needs of the economy in relation to the Community would increase. Another open question is whether and how the associated countries may profit from the future development of the external trade and technological relations of the Community. If we can, we could be better partners of the Community but if not, our membership would be made more difficult to achieve.

For the Hungarian companies, the Common Market is hardly more than one of the important external markets while for the Government it is hardly more than a question of economic diplomacy. These are very important but not enough for the future. Under the current information flow, companies and interest representation organizations do not have in-depth information other than the concrete trading conditions or they receive such in-depth information too late. To improve this situation, better cooperation is required (among others also in this area) in the triangle of the Government, entrepreneurs' associations and the Chamber of Economics. The superficiality of current relations are well reflected by the negotiations held in the Interest Reconciliation Council which are inappropriate both in depth and in exactness, or for example the preparation of the new law on the chambers when it turned out only in the Parliament that there are totally opposite views on the topic.

The survey prepared in September 1993 by the Hungarian Chamber of Economics and the Economic Research Institute provides a fairly clear picture on the opinions and intentions of the managements of companies in the given situation. In this study, the managements of 1,200 companies expressed their expectations on privatization, the economic development, the constraints of growth, their competition strategy and their positions on the EC market. The value of this survey is enhanced by the fact that a similar survey was prepared in 1992 so that the changes can be retraced.

The answers reflect weakening expectations concerning the privatization. 42 per cent of the companies reckoned with privatization by involving foreign partners in 1992 while this ratio fell to 25 per cent in 1993. A greater portion of companies are looking for domestic owners and one third of them wants their own management to acquire ownership. They consider the privatization process too slow while more and more of them indicate that the transfer of ownership does not offer the solution to their basic problems (capital, technology, market).

The expectations in the industry, trade and services concerning economic development are more optimistic while those in the agriculture, transport and building industry are pessimistic. The companies reckon with a constant 24 per cent inflation rate for 1994 in contrast to a more optimistic forecast of the Government. They do not hope for improving credit conditions either as most of them estimate the cost of loans around 25-30 per cent. The majority of companies judged their export opportunities favourable in 1992 while they now judge it rather unfavourable for 1993.

Regarding the constraints of growth, 65 per cent of the companies - irrespective of their size, ownership structure or industrial branch - regard insufficient domestic demand as the primary constraint to growth. They place lack of capital as second (33 per cent) and the lack of demand on external markets as third (19 per cent). At a very high proportion (70 per cent) of companies, there are financial difficulties hindering expansion. In general, there has been no improvement in the lack of capital compared to last year.

The unpredictably changing behaviour of the State in the areas of legislation, fiscal and monetary policies also hinders growth and at the same time decreases competitiveness. For most of the companies, current financing and the management of current assets is the hardest task and the area that needs the greatest improvement. The domestic credit conditions are unfavourable therefore more and more companies are seeking opportunities for foreign loans. They think that capital increase is possible almost exclusively with a foreign partner although their expectations in this aspect have weakened compared to last year.

By the end of 1993, the expectations of entrepreneurs concerning Western markets have become smaller because within the overall 25 per cent decrease of exports, the exports to the EC fell more rapidly: by 33 per cent. On the other hand, only 20-30 per cent of the persons questioned judged themselves adequately informed, competitive and prepared enough in connection with the EC. 16 per cent of those questioned believe that the EC membership will bring about losing markets for the company while another 16 per cent cannot yet evaluate the consequences of the future membership. The expectations in connection with the EC of smaller ventures as well as those with foreign ownership are more optimistic both in terms of expanding markets and the integration opportunities.

In conclusion, it follows from the above that the Hungarian economic policy should be revised both from strategic and development aspects and it should be re-programmed in the light and shadow of the experiences of the past period.

Data on the situation of the Hungarian economy

Table 1.1
The distribution of foreign trade by relations, 1993 (in %)

	Export	Import
European Community	46.6	42.1
EFTA	14.2	18.5
Developing countries	5.5	4.6
Ex-socialist countries	25.6	25.2
OECD, others	8.1	9.6
Total:	100.0	100.0

Table 1.2
The volume indices of production (1980=100%)

	1980	1989	1992	1993
Industry	100.0	115.0	76.2	77.2
Agriculture	100.0	106.7	76.2	60.0
Commodity transport	100.0	111.4	54.7	50.0
Revenues of tourism	100.0	565.2	1400.0	-

Table 1.3
The main items of the central budget
in HUF 1 billion and in the % of the GDP

	1990	1991	1992	1993	1994
Revenues	1105.9	1120.8	1364.3	1293.6	1369.1
% of the GDP	52.9	48.6	49.1	48.0	-
Expenditures	1089.2	1294.9	1586.8	1504.4	1637.7
% of the GDP	52.1	56.1	57.1	56.0	-
Subsidies	184.7	151.0	139.4	110.8	97.6
% of the GDP	8.8	6.5	5.0	4.9	-
Transfers	387.4	488.5	695.7	604.0	560.9
% of the GDP	18.5	21.2	21.0	21.0	-
Balance	1.4	-114.1	-199.5	-210.8	-329.6
% of the GDP	0.0	4.9	7.1	8.0	8.0

Source: OECD Economic Surveys, MNB Year-Books

Table 1.4
Foreign capital - investments in Hungary in USD million

1988-1990	807
1991-1992	2617
1993	1400
Total	5024

Source: MNB 1993.11-12. Monthly Report

Table 1.5
Annual changes in the real economic sphere

	1990	1991	1992	1993	1994
	% change compared to the previous year				
Real GDP	-3.5	-11.9	-5.0	-2.0	1-3
Total consumption	-2.7	-5.3	-2.6	-2.0	-1-0
-Individual consumption	-3.6	-5.8	-2.5	-2.0	0
-Social consumption	-2.6	-2.7	-3.0	-2.0	-1
Gross investments	-15.0	-11.6	-7.5	-5.0	5-10
Export volumes	-4.1	-4.0	+1.5	-15.0	2-5
Import volumes	-5.2	+5.5	-7.6	+12.0	3-6
Consumer price index	28.9	34.8	22.8	23-24	16-19
	Projected to the GDP in %				
Budget balance	-0.5	-4.9	-7.1	-8.0	-8.0
Gross investments	22.0	20.8	18.9	18-19	20-22
Household savings	11.0	12.7	10.4	8.0	7.0
Current balance of payments	+1.3	2.9	+0.8	-3.0	-7.0

Source: OECD Economic Surveys, MNB Year-Books

Table 1.6
Factors hindering the activities of the company*

	State majority	Domestic private	In foreign ownership	Total
Foreign market limits	26.95	41.55	44.57	36.40
Domestic demand and opportunities	73.46	60.44	62.86	65.31
Organisation difficulties	27.16	29.42	24.58	26.56
Lack of capital, financial difficulties	77.57	74.53	43.43	70.60
Insufficient information	6.58	7.76	8.56	7.33
Keen competition	32.71	34.20	39.42	24.75
Unpredictable government measures	11.11	25.45	21.14	18.97
Organisational uncertainties	17.91	3.78	5.14	10.13
Other	9.06	6.17	11.43	8.79
Total	282.51	283.30	261.13	266.84

*   More than one factor could be named.

Source: The Survey of the Hungarian Chamber of Economics and the Economic Research Institute Plc on the intentions and opinions of companies, September, 1993

Table 1.7
On the anticipated development of the Hungarian economy
(by ownership types)

	State majority	Domestic private	In foreign ownership	Total
Significantly improve	0.00	0.20	0.57	0.17
Slightly improve	19.14	22.27	23.43	21.25
No change	27.78	22.07	29.14	24.76
Slightly deteriorate	39.09	37.52	33.71	38.11
Significantly deteriorate	13.57	17.50	12.57	14.82
No answer	0.42	0.44	0.58	0.89
Total	100.00	100.00	100.00	100.00

Source: The Survey of the Hungarian Chamber of Economics and the Economic Research Institute Plc on the intentions and opinions of companies, September, 1993

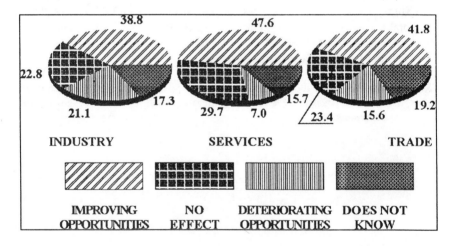

Figure 1.1   The affect of EC-membership on enterprises (by sectors, in %)

Source: The Survey of the Hungarian Chamber of Economics and the Economic Research Institute Plc on the intentions and opinions of companies, September, 1993

Table 1.8
Measures planned to improve technology*

	State majority	Domestic private	In foreign ownership	Total
Investment, licence, know-how	6.17	6.36	8.57	6.76
Major investment	13.17	16.70	23.43	16.37
Minor development projects	61.93	39.05	55.43	59.12
Development of cooperation	26.96	35.98	33.71	31.92
Close-down of outdated facilities	30.66	19.88	20.57	24.27
Involvement of a new investor	36.83	20.08	13.14	25.33
Other measures	28.62	20.23	16.00	18.89
No development is planned	18.92	27.12	24.58	26.38
Total	223.26	185.40	195.43	209.04

*   More than one measure could be named.

Source: The Survey of the Hungarian Chamber of Economics and the Economic Research Institute Plc on the intentions and opinions of companies, September, 1993)

Table 1.9
Factors hindering the activities of the company[*]

	State majority	Domestic private	In foreign ownership	Total
Foreign market limits	26.95	41.55	44.57	36.40
Domestic demand and opportunities	73.46	60.44	62.86	65.31
Organisation difficulties	27.16	29.42	24.58	26.56
Lack of capital, financial difficulties	77.57	74.53	43.43	70.60
Insufficient information	6.58	7.76	8.56	7.33
Keen competition	32.71	34.20	39.42	24.75
Unpredictable government measures	11.11	25.45	21.14	18.97
Organisational uncertainties	17.91	3.78	5.14	10.13
Other	9.06	6.17	11.43	8.79
Total	282.51	283.30	261.13	268.84

*   More than one factor could be named.

Source: The Survey of the Hungarian Chamber of Economics and the Economic Research Institute Plc on the intentions and opinions of companies, September, 1993

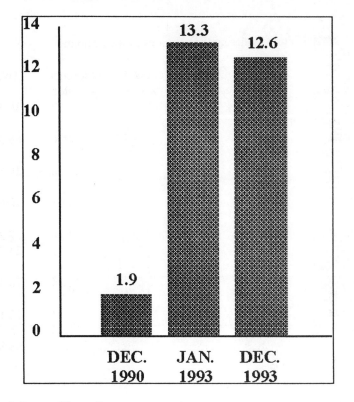

Figure 1.2   Unemployment rate

Source: MNB 1993.11-12. Monthly Report

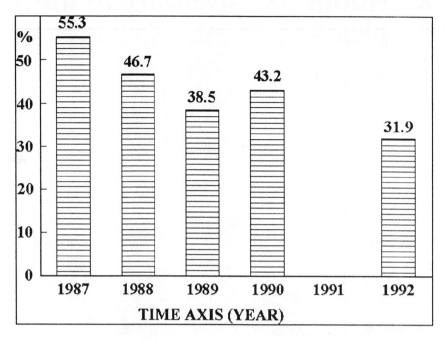

Figure 1.3   Debt service projected to the export of commodities and services

2 Hungarian industry in the process of transformation

Donát Bonifert

The technology level of the Hungarian industry at the end of the eighties was mixed: there were in it world-level, medium and obsolete technologies. Within its structure, we could find areas to be developed and areas to be cut down. During the last decades new products and technologies appeared which can be the basis of further development but there remained a large number of obsolete areas unfit for development, often within the same technology line.

In the mid-eighties structural changes were started in metallurgy: within steel production the share of the oxygen converter process and of continuous casting increased although it is still behind the international level. Within engineering relatively up-to-date capacities appeared in precision mechanics, in the production of office machines and computers, and in machine tool production. Chemical industry became a leading industry, with modern and medium level capacities and sometimes with competitive products. Pharmaceutical industry is an appealing area to foreign capital too - although the technology level of its production capacities is mixed.

Light industry produced mostly for domestic demand but the bulk of its export went to Western markets. Its technology level is mixed. Furniture industry was on medium level, a part of the capacities of paper industry were in the mid-eighties on world level, but the other part of it was obsolete. The larger part of textile capacities was rendered obsolete by the recession of the eighties, at the same time it also had some high-level, automated machinery.

In food industry modern technologies were created and modern packaging technologies were also introduced.

It the nineties the situation deteriorated. Wear and tear of production tools increased as did the average age of machinery. The share of new products within sales is below 50 per cent, i.e. extremely low. The share of products produced under licence was not more than 10 per cent during the last five years.

It is a healthy phenomenon however that the share of automated machinery grew and after 1988 machinery import was channelled to Western markets (although import did not serve as much the implementation of new technologies as the day-to-day operation of existing equipment).

The lack of resources, the general recession set back R&D activity to a minimum level, enough only for stagnation. There is a danger that due to the collapse of firms, the lack of domestic capital, the reluctance of foreign investors and the dragging of the process of transformation, R&D activity will definitely die away.

Scientific-technical cooperation and innovation relationships with the technical - scientific centres of the world were established in the seventies and the process speeded up in the second half of the eighties. An intelligent stratum of professionals did arise which was able to learn and operate modern technologies. After the change of the political system, new possibilities in this area appeared: the COCOM was abolished, scientific-technical agreements were concluded with major developed industrial countries, in 1991 an Association Agreement with the EC was signed. In 1991 Hungary was admitted as member of the COST program, in 1992 as member of the EUREKA program and in the PHARE program too R&D cooperation had a prominent role right from the start. The serious recession of the industry had an impact on the situation of individual research and development institutions. The number of such institutions decreased, as has the number of their employees. Their financial resources were curtailed.

The lack of priorities within the regulatory system and its incalculability caused problems. Research and development firms have no outlook even for a whole year. A decentralised regulatory structure capable of tracking down economic processes is still lacking as are its legal preconditions. Thus e.g. there are no non-profit organizations, investment and risk capital funds, there is no Law on Innovation etc.

There are less possibilities for sale of research findings since such purchases are no more subsidized. Parallel with the decrease of own resources, credit lines too were curtailed. Under the existing regulatory system, there are no tools which would stimulate development.

The impact of privatisation on R&D is not positive. Foreign proprietors do not rely on the domestic R&D capacities, rather they try to transform them into a service background of industry. The government's role in privatized innovation activities is not clear as yet.

Mobility for high level intellectuals has increased, brain-drain is intensifying.

The transfer of R&D results into production is endangered by the lack of resources, potential sponsors are not ready to take risks. Under the changed economic framework it is dubious whether past research findings can be used.

Let us overview the process of transformation in the Hungarian industry, the present state of the process and within it the state of changing ownership relations, organizational changes, the changes in employment and in the performance of the industry.

The centralized system of control changed considerably under the 1968 Hungarian reform. At that time firm managers obtained larger autonomy, which could not be repealed even under recurring political backlashes. From the early eighties larger room was given to small ventures, a large part of state firms were detached from the ministries and worker-employee self-management was introduced. Under this system managers could feel like real owners. The process of creating a preponderantly private property based market economy was started even if slowly in the first part of the eighties. At the time of the change of the system, in 1989 and 1990 the process was speeded up considerably.

In theoretical problems of *privatization*, the professional opinion was more or less uniform even before the political changes. Its essentials are that during the transformation preference should be given to privatization against payment.

The idea of free or low-price distribution of state assets (so-called 'people's shares') was rejected on two accounts: for one thing such kind of privatization does not create knowledgeable, responsible proprietors, for the other due to the high level of government debt one could not do without privatization income.

After the change of the political system there were keen battles around the principles and actual solutions of privatization. The political idea was raised that privatization against payment does not make it possible for large strata of society to become proprietors, which makes the government unpopular. From an economic point of view the need of budgetary income results in overdetermination and a further problem is that privatization is not attached to the solution of structural problems and to suitable reorganization programs. Therefore the conditions for a non-market, subsidized distribution of assets were created (employee share ownership programs, subsidized credits). Due to the income needs of the budget, the importance of selling to foreign investors grew and measures were taken in order to solve structural and reorganization problems.

Nevertheless, dissatisfaction with Hungarian privatization did not subside. The original principles were challenged, turned out to be unfeasible, haphazard solutions appeared in practice. After purchasing the few high-value firms, the amount of foreign investments went back and domestic demand is not enough to buy the whole of state assets to be privatized. Partly due to this and partly due to other causes the state's propensity to privatize diminished. The state tries to keep a larger share of assets.

Before changing the ownership relations, one had to *change the organizational structure of industry.* Firms to be privatized could not cope in their original form with requirements against market actors: their size was not commensurate with their profile, their structure was not satisfactory, their ability to adapt was insufficient. Under the spell of the market one had to increase the number of market actors and basic changes had to be implemented in the size structure of production units.

To this end, measures were taken to speed up organizational changes, firms were compelled to incorporate themselves, plants trying to split away were encouraged. As a result by 1992 30 per cent of state assets went over to the company form. A peculiar feature of the transformations is that in 1990 in most cases they brought with them a change in the proprietor due to the participation of foreign capital. From 1991 however the larger part of transformations was formal, did not involve a change in the proprietor and this process continued well into 1992. Organizational decentralization did not result always in abolishing monopolies, nay in certain cases firms in monopolistic positions were sold to foreign proprietors, producing much debate and criticism (see e.g. the sale of the vegetable oil industry).

All in all, in a few years the number of industrial organizations grew considerably. In 1988 there were only 1,143 state firms and 1,582 industrial cooperatives in the country, the total number of organizations being 2,725. The number of cooperatives was higher already at that time than the number of state firms but their role in the economy, their share in production was smaller. Cooperatives had a 10 per cent share in industrial production and a 14 per cent share in employment. The share of cooperatives in capital invested was negligible.

In the middle of 1993 there were already 14,600 production units in industry, i.e. their number grew six-fold within five years. Under this process the strongest was the growth of smaller organizations. Whereas in 1988 the number of industrial units employing less than 300 people was a mere 2,000, by 1993 their number grew to 14,000. Within this figure the number of units employing 20 people or less was 9,000. A large part of them were recently established ventures. At the same time the business role of small organizations is still minimal: organizations with 20 people or less employ a mere 3 per cent of industrial workers and produce 5 per cent of industrial output. At the same time organizations with more then 300 employees employ 75 per cent of industrial workers and produce 80 per cent of industrial output.

The change of property relations and privatization was slow in Hungary during the last three years since the change of the system.

According to data of the State Property Agency, up to the end of 1992 10-15 per cent of state assets were transferred into companies and 10-15 per cent were given to privates. A small part of assets was given to other market actors such as local governments.

By the end of 1993 30 per cent of state assets were sold and according to government information privatized firms contribute 50 per cent to GDP. According to the scant data we have at our disposal the situation is similar in industry: by the end of 1992 10 per cent of capacities were given to privates. Since that time the share can have approached 30 per cent. We have to take into account that considerable capital has flown into the country as new investment which also adds to the private sphere. According to published data of the State Property Agency and the government, up to the present USD 6 billion came into the country as foreign investment. USD 1.4 billion from this was privatization income to the budget.

The progress of privatization within industry was uneven. In food industry 25-30 per cent of previous state assets were given to privates, whereas in other industries, in chemical industry e.g. the share of privatized assets (mainly to foreign capital) might be 5-10 per cent. According to my estimates 5 per cent of those employed in industry work for partly or totally private firms. Even if we add those working for new private ventures we can say that a mere 10 per cent of employees of industry work for private firms.

Foreign capital played a considerable role in domestic privatization both in 1990 and 1991 but due to the small size of the undertaking its share within domestic capacities is still minuscule: according to some estimates it amounts to 8 per cent of transferred property.

The main problem is that foreign capital was not geared primarily towards additional investment, even less to technology development. A few exceptions apart (e.g. the two car factories established with Japanese and German capital) foreign capital mainly tried to acquire stable market share, monopoly positions and well-in-demand real estate. Its contribution to domestic production capacities and entry of foreign markets was small.

As a result, privatization in the last 2-3 years did not contribute either to the fighting down of the crisis or to the solution of structural problems. After buying up the few healthy firms or plants, the inflow of foreign capital went back in 1992 drastically. According to specialists of the State Property Agency, sales to foreigners will be moderate in the future.

At the same time domestic demand, capital accumulated through domestic savings is meagre and its growth is unlikely considering the low level of performance and income. Therefore there is a fear that the privatization process will get stuck or be pursued through aggressive methods.

Reviewing the number of those employed by industry we can estimate the contribution of industry to unemployment.

In the eighties some 1.5 million people were employed by the industry. This is 33 per cent of the country total.

By the end of the eighties industrial employment went slightly back: it was 1.4 million, i.e. 30 per cent of total employment. Reduction of employment in the period 1981-91 did not cause unemployment. In this period not only industrial employment decreased, since due to demographic causes the national supply of labour went back by 250 thousand (4 per cent). At the same time the number of the active labour force diminished too, by 400 thousand, (8 per cent). At the end of the period 1-2 per cent unemployment appeared. By 1993 it surpassed the level of 10 per cent. By that time industrial employment went below 1 million, which meant 27-29 per cent of total employment in the economy - as opposed to the previous 33 per cent.

By early 1993 industrial employment diminished more rapidly than total employment. According to my estimates half of the 600 thousand unemployed are those previously employed by industry or young people not replacing those pensioned from industry.

The output of the industry went back considerably in the period 1988-1992. The size of the recession in these few years is approaching 40 per cent. The largest drop occurred in 1991: at that time it was 19 per cent, in the previous and the following years (in 1990 and 1992) 10 per cent.

The decrease of output hit different branches of industry to different extents, resulting in a structural change. The share of extraction within industry fell somewhat and that of metallurgy considerably. There was equally a fall in the share of engineering and within it in vehicles, electrical machinery and telecommunications production. The share of instrument and food production grew however. A part of changes points towards modernization (lower share of extraction and metallurgy and higher share of instruments) but a part of them is contrary to modernization (the growth of share of food processing, the large fallback of modern telecommunications).

This unprecedented fallback in industrial production - and overall performance of the national economy - are according to domestic and foreign specialists: structural problems and the collapse of export to Eastern (former CMEA) countries. But if we look at the facts we find it otherwise.

Hungarian industry - and the whole national economy - functioned previously at a medium level of development, with the same structural and incentive problems without even a small fallback in output. Structural changes, changing property relations, activity of enterpreneurial strata in the early nineties ought to have propitious impact on the performance of industry. Domestic structural problems cannot therefore be the cause of the recession.

Loss of export to Eastern markets cannot be the cause of recession either, considering that:

- Direct export sales constitute only 23-25 per cent of industrial production. If we take into account its indirect impact, export still cannot influence more than half of the industrial production.
- Losses suffered on Eastern markets could be countervailed by offensive on Western markets. The share of Eastern markets was smaller in the early nineties than previously. Whereas in 1980 55 per cent of total Hungarian export was heading to Eastern markets, the figure in 1989 was 47 and in 1990 33 per cent. Export to developed industrial countries has risen from 35 per cent in 1980 to 60 per cent in 1990. The change of the export orientation was a fact in 1990, without causing serious recession.
- Industrial output performance is year by year similar to domestic sales and not to export figures. The cause of the 1990 and first of all the 1991 - industrial and macroeconomic - recession is somewhere else, namely in the monetary restriction started in 1988 and applied up to 1992. In 1988 - referring to different factors - a large amount of money was siphoned off the economy by cancelling credit contracts and repealing credits. As a result, firms had liquidity problems, became indebted to one another, and the volume of this mutual indebtedness steadily grew. It caused first sales, then production problems and eventually resulted in the fall of output.

In 1991 the restrictive monetary policy was abandoned and supply of money was adapted to real economic processes and to inflation. It is highly probable that this is the cause behind the recession being stopped this year.

The question here arises *how industrial production and its technology level will develop in coming years?*

In the short run - if there are no restrictive measures similar to those of 1988 - industrial production will slowly grow and this growth will stabilize. My argument for this statement is that the fallback in industrial capacities was much less than the fallback of output. In Hungarian industry in last years capacity reserves were accumulated and this may result in propitious demand in stable growth. A sign pointing towards this direction is that in 1993 - after the stagnation of the year 1992 - output of industry will grow by some 3 per cent.

Our conclusion about the existence of excess capacities is based on the fact that investment in industry went back only by 10 per cent in the period 1988-91 whereas production by 40 per cent. Similarly, industrial employment was reduced by less than the industrial output.

Despite recovery in industry, the *foreign trade balance of Hungarian economy* largely deteriorated in 1993. Our present knowledge is insufficient to find out what role the decrease of industrial export might have had in that. It is an undeniable fact that industrial export has decreased somewhat since the beginning of this year and import - first of all import of machinery and equipment from the developed countries - increased. This might be the first signs of a recovery but also the result of the high inflation of the forint since the late eighties which was not followed by a matching devaluation. At the same time world market recession - first of all recession in Western Europe - has an undeniable impact, too.

Another question is whether transitory recovery based on the use of excess capacities will be followed by a *stable recovery based on technology development?*

The conception of industrial policy prepared by the Ministry of Industry and Trade reckons with present processes - sale of surplus capacities, crisis management, stabilization - continuing up to 1995. This view is corroborated by the already mentioned abandoning of the restrictive course in 1992 and the parallel starting of a reorganization policy which involves large subsidies given to firms in difficulties. The conception forecasts stagnation or a small increase in the volume of production in this period. In 1992 and 1993 these endeavours were successful.

From 1996 the conception of industrial policy forecasts 4-5 per cent growth secured through the development of competitive industries. Among these industries the conception mentions the following:
- production of agricultural and food industrial machines
- certain areas of machine tool and energy generating machinery production
- production of electrical machinery and instruments
- electronics

- pharmaceutical industry
- furniture and paper industry
- individual firms in cotton and apparel industry.

Between 2000 and 2010 qualitative changes based on competitive advantage will occur according to the conception of industrial policy in the following areas:

- food economy (biotechnology, food processing, production of agricultural machines, freezing industry, production of food industrial machines)
- certain elements of health systems (pharmaceutical industry, production of medical instruments, design and construction of hospitals as part of complete medical systems, medical aids and ingredients)
- certain phases of aluminium production (new modes and structures of use)
- production of vehicle parts and assembling of vehicles (electronics, natural and artificial leather products, production of plastics and paints)
- furniture and apparel industry.

The conception ranges among industries to scale down:

- extraction;
- metallurgy;
- steel industry;
- precision instruments (from 1995);
- telecommunications (from 2000);
- construction materials (from 1995);
- microelectronics (from 1995).

In the area of *state industrial policy* the conception provides for the following:

- change in the organizational structure;
- direction of privatization;
- regional crisis management.

Within the change of organizational structure, the industrial policy of the State is aimed at:

- support given to corporate units trying to split away;
- strengthening of the sector of small and medium-sized firms;
- antitrust actions.

Of the many small ventures created in the Hungarian industry in the last years, the majority are working with minimum capital and workforce (less than 20 people). The regional breakdown of small ventures is uneven. Supply with technology in this sphere is scant, there are not many ventures whose technology and products would be on world level.

In the coming one to two years, organizational changes will not be as rapid as they were in the past 2-3 years. Within a few years the main elements of a market-economy firm structure will probably arise and in the second half of the decade a market-directed, slow and gradual organizational development will characterize Hungarian industry. By that time government interference - based primarily on direct proprietary decisions - will be replaced by market effects.

The conception of industrial policy thinks the increase of privatization investment by foreigners to be desirable. Restrictions will be made only in a narrow range. It is in the interests of the industrial policy and the national economy to attract leading multinationals of the world into Hungary. The Ministry of Industry and Trade tries to contribute to this process by business diplomacy, foreseeable industrial policies and suitable protection of industrial activities.

It is a requirement against the privatization of industry that the production of consumer goods and production cultures representing national professional-intellectual assets should not be sold out to foreigners. Among them we find production of household machines, household chemicals, research-development institutes.

The necessity of crisis management arises from the fact that crisis phenomena in Hungarian economy have structural manifestations. Government interference is unavoidable if we want to alleviate the harmful impacts of the crisis (unemployment, foregone income, irrational destroying of production resources). At the same time we have to reckon with the limits to government interference: on one hand we have to secure that the orientation given by the market be not distorted, on the other we have to reckon with the limits to government expenditure.

It would not be proper to rely during crisis management on financing of loss. For regional and branch-level crisis management we need the renewal of productive and human infrastructure. We have to apply the tools of regional development and employment policy and have to deploy complex regional crisis management programs, systems of professional and branch-level subsidization. Company-level programs of structural adaptation have to be assisted by privatization and reorganization. To this effect the following tools are conceived:

- reduction of debt through monetary tools if it is only they that cause problems, otherwise the firm has liquid markets;
- payment for public debt, and for arrears to public utilities by credit whose collateral is the firm's assets and real estate;

- an institutional system for bankruptcy-avoiding agreements, the dampening of the self-generating impact of bankruptcy and reorganisation campaigns;
- stabilization and development studies and strategies based on corporate screening;
- protection of markets and industries;
- working out a system of government procurement (a suitable step of business diplomacy would be attachment to the government procurement codex of GATT);
- the creation of regional development partnerships which would contribute to crisis management through revealing resources, coordinating funds and activities, working out development actions, providing market information.

Hungarian industry is - despite the serious problems of the past years - 'well and strong' and if the government policy is suitable it can start coming up to West-European partners. To this end we have at our disposal capacities created in the seventies and eighties, under the soft dictatorship, which are partly satisfactory partly suitable for further development, and educated, flexible, relatively cheap labour. Many domestic firms are already cooperating with industrial firms of developed countries and are ready to comply with their requirements. In the coming years, the Hungarian industry will be an appealing investment area, cooperative partner and a bridgehead of expansion towards the sooner or later recovering Eastern markets.

3 Technology development in Hungarian agriculture: results and problems

Aladár Sipos

1. Introduction

In Hungary the agricultural sector has - even in international comparison - an outstanding role both in the economy and foreign trade. At the beginning of the 90s around 17 per cent of the Hungarian GDP was generated by agriculture employing 18 per cent of the labour force. Hungary - due to its climatic and ecological endowments plus expertise - has a huge agro-potential which made the country one of the leading agricultural exporters in Eastern Europe. Consequently, Hungary had a yearly surplus of USD 2 billion in its agricultural trade in 1991 and 1992, highly needed for balancing external payments and servicing outstanding debts.

2. The output of Hungarian agriculture

If we want to measure the impact of technology development on agricultural production *one possible approach* is to relate changes in *output* to changes in input. The data in Table 3.1 show that in the period 1960-90 the growth of production in former CMEA countries was the highest in the sixties. In this period the average yearly rate of growth was the highest in the Soviet Union - almost 4 per cent. Next came Hungary with its 3.5 per cent average yearly growth. In the following decade the position of agriculture changed in these two countries profoundly. From 1970 to 1980 Hungarian agriculture with its above 4 per cent rate of growth far surpassed the other CMEA countries and became a world leader in this respect. According to calculations of the CSO as to the volume of per capita agricultural production (measured in corn equivalent) Hungary was the *third* in Europe already in 1969. She kept this place in the following decade. In the subsequent ten years however Hungarian agriculture too got into difficulties and as a result production stagnated. Striking is the two-decade long fall in the performance of the Bulgarian agriculture too.

Table 3.1
Rate of growth of gross agricultural production (%)

Period	1961/65-1969/71	1971-1980	1981-1988
Country			
Bulgaria	3.4	1.1	0.4
Czechoslovakia	3.0	2.6	1.7
GDR	1.6	1.7	2.4
Hungary	3.5	4.1	0.8
Poland	1.8	0.4	2.4
Yugoslavia	3.1	2.9	0.6
Soviet Union	3.9	1.2	1.0

Sources: Economic Research Service, US Department of Agriculture, World Agricultural Trends and Indicators, 1970-88, Statistical Bulletin Number 78. 1990., Indices of Agricultural and Food Production for Europe and the USSR Statistical Bulletin Number 635.

The main role in the increase of agricultural production had increased *average yield* since arable land diminished continuously. Average yield of wheat and maize is shown in Tables 3.2 and 3.3 whereas data on milk per cow is given in Table 3.4. It turns out from the table that the highest yields in wheat and maize production were attained by GDR, Czechoslovakia and Hungary. The other CMEA countries were far behind, particularly the Soviet Union. Similar was the situation in milk production with the only difference that the highest yield in this area was produced by Hungary.

Table 3.2
Average yield of wheat (kg/ha)

Year	1960	1970	1980	1985	1990	1992
Country						
World total	1,210	1,510	1,880	2,190	2,558	2,553
From this:						
Common Market	2,270	3,050	4,490	4,660	4,807	4,520
Hungary	1,680	2,130	4,860	4,830	5,040	-
Bulgaria	1,900	2,290	3,970	2,870	3,947	3,632
GDR	3,480	3,560	4,380	5,290	5,732	-
Poland	1,690	2,320	2,600	3,430	3,727	3,027
Romania	1,220	1,450	2,840*	2,380	3,333	2,197
Soviet Union	1,060	1,530	1,600	1,550	2,264	2,020
Czechoslovakia	2,310	2,930	4,500	4,930	5,153	-
USA	1,760	2,090	2,250	2,520	2,661	2,650
Canada	1,420	1,790	1,740	1,770	2,277	2,087

* with rye
Source: CSO statistics and FAO Quarterly Bulletin of Statistics, 1993. Nr.1.

Table 3.4
Milk per cow (kg)

Year	1960	1970	1980	1985	1990	1992
Country						
World total	-	1,838	1,976	2,077	2,063	2,028
From this:						
Common Market	-	3,348	3,901	4,026	4,120	-
Hungary	1,863	2,250	3,704	4,531	4,949	5,043
Bulgaria	1,444	2,211	2,656	3,017	3,354	2,981
GDR	2,669	3,160	3,407	4,376	4,820	-
Poland	2,122	2,456	2,812	2,984	3,061	3,040
Romania	1,368	1,607	1,960	2,071	2,105	1,618
Soviet Union	1,779	2,110	2,143	2,254	2,614	2,222
Czechoslovakia	1,862	2,565	3,185	3,756	3,989	3,369
USA	-	4,421	5,203*	5,911	6,673	7,002
Canada	-	3,259	3,857*	4,762	5,780	5,348

* Data on 1979.
Sources: Narodnoe hosjajstvo strán chlenov SEV-a 1981; Mezőgazdasági
Statisztikai Zsebkönyv 1945-1975 and 1990; Magyar Statisztikai Évkönyv
1990; FAO Quarterly Bulletin of Statistics 1993.2.sz.; A mezőgazdasági
termelés főbb adatai nemzetközi összehasonlításban (1975-1989)
STAGEK

Table 3.3
Average yield of maize (kg/ha)

Year	1960	1970	1980	1985	1990	1992
Country						
World total	2,030	2,440	3,090	3,770	3,718	4,044
From this						
Common Market	3,290	4,920	5,810	6,490	6,992	4,789
Hungary	2,500	3,380	5,320	6,290	4,500	-
Bulgaria	2,360	3,740	3,580	3,070	2,877	3,833
GDR	2,350	2,750	4,490	5,530	7,076	-
Poland	2,690	2,350	3,540	4,300	-	-
Romania	1,550	2,120	3,390	4,920	3,172	2,046
Soviet Union	1,930	7,800	3,170	3,210	3,852	2,029
Czechoslovakia	3,040	4,090	4,690	5,440	6,144	-
USA	3,420	4,540	5,710	7,410	7,468	8,247
Canada	-	-	5,590*	5,580*	6,586	7,333

*   The average of the previous five years.

Source: CSO statistics and FAO Quarterly Bulletin of Statistics 1993. No.1.

The above data signal a very dynamic increase of output in the seventies. The growth of output continued in the eighties but it was much weaker than in the previous decade.

The above facts should be stressed here because they prove that technology development has to serve actual economic objectives. In Hungary - as in other CMEA countries too - this objective was the increase of production. Therefore development periods or programs were judged by the output volume. This attitude was particularly strong in Hungary in the seventies but we find it sometimes with more recent projects too.

3. The most important inputs of agricultural production

In a broad outline the major inputs of agricultural production are the following:
- arable land;
- labour;
- implements and;
- information.

The latter is often left out from practical analysis since it is not easy to express it exactly in quantitative terms. Taking this fact into account we now turn to the analysis of changes in the major input elements of agricultural production.

Arable land

It is an important characteristic of Hungarian agriculture that a large part (ca. 70 per cent) of the territory of the country is arable. Agricultural land area steadily diminished in the past - even if at different speed. See the information in Table 3.5.

Table 3.5
The breakdown of land area in Hungary

	1980		1985		1988		1989	
	1000ha	%	1000ha	%	1000ha	%	1000ha	%
Plough-land	4,734.7	50.9	4,697.5	50.5	4,712.0	50.7	4,712.7	50.7
Garden	291.4	3.1	338.7	3.6	338.3	3.6	329.3	3.6
Orchard	138.4	1.5	103.5	1.1	94.9	1.0	94.3	1.0
Vineyard	167.8	1.8	153.6	1.7	142.2	1.5	140.3	1.5
Grass	1,294.2	13.9	1,246.5	13.4	1,209.8	13.0	1,197.3	12.9
Agricultural area	6,626.3	71.2	6,539.7	70.3	6,497.3	69.8	6,483.9	69.7
Forest	1,610.3	17.3	1,647.9	17.7	1,678.3	18.0	1,688.2	18.1
Reeds	7.7	0.4	39.7	0.4	40.2	0.4	40.6	0.4
Pond	25.3	0.3	25.9	0.3	26.5	0.3	26.7	0.3
Productive area	8,299.8	89.2	8,253.2	88.7	8,242.3	88.6	8,239.4	88.6
Non-productive area	1,003.8	10.8	1,050.1	11.3	1,060.8	11.4	1,063.6	11.4
Total area	9,303.6	100.0	9,303.3	100.0	9,303.1	100.0	9,303.0	100.0

Source: Mezőgazdasági-Élelmiszeripari Statisztikai Zsebkönyv, 1990

The decrease of agricultural land within the period examined is considerable: more than 2 per cent. Even more striking is the change if we compare the present state with earlier ones. The decrease is:

4.6 per cent compared to 1975

6.0 per cent compared to 1970

7.2 per cent compared to 1965 and

10.1 per cent compared to 1960.

Within agricultural production the most important for plant cultivation is plough-land. Its decrease up to 1989 was:

relative to 1985: + 15,200 ha (+0.3 per cent)

relative to 1980: - 22,000 ha (-0.5 per cent)

relative to 1975: -265,000 ha (-5.6 per cent)

relative to 1970: -333,500 ha (-7.1 per cent)

relative to 1965: -371,800 ha (-7.9 per cent)

relative to 1960: -597,100 ha (-12.7 per cent)

We can see that the last years apart there was a permanent decrease in the area of plough-land. What is striking: in the period investigated the decrease of plough-land was always larger than the decrease of total agricultural land area.

One can prove with similar data that the growth of output cannot be explained by growth of arable land, i.e. in the period investigated growth in agriculture had to be of an intensive type.

Labour

As with arable land agricultural labour too is decreasing as a percentage of total labour 'all over the world'. The relevant data for former CMEA countries are included in Table 3.6. It turns out from the table that in the last 30 years the number of people employed in agriculture and their share within the total of those actively employed gradually diminished. Thus we can state that the growth of agricultural output could not be caused by an increase of labour employed either.

When looking at agricultural employment we have to take into account that in former socialist countries the bulk of agricultural farms pursued industrial and other activities too which is not the case for industrial countries. This was characteristic first of all for Hungary where in the eighties an increasing part of production and income of agriculture was provided by auxiliary activities. If we take this fact into account we obtain that in 1989 in Hungary not 17 but only 11.7 per cent of those actively employed were engaged in agricultural activities.

Table 3.6
The share of agricultural employment within total employment (%)

Year	1960	1970	1980	1985	1990
Country					
Hungary	37.7	24.0	19.5	20.0	17.0
Bulgaria	55.0	42.0	33.3	20.4	19.3
GDR	17.0	12.0	9.6	10.3	10.6
Poland	43.0	38.0	30.4	28.1	26.4
Romania	65.0	52.0	47.2	28.5	27.9
Soviet Union	39.0	32.0	16.4	19.1	18.6
Czechoslovakia	24.0	16.0	10.3	12.4	11.5
USA	8.0	4.0	4.0	3.1	2.9
Canada				5.0	4.1	3.4

Sources: Mezőgazdasági szövetkezetek gazdálkodása a számok tükrében, TOT, 1976; Statisztikai Évkönyv, KSH, 1991.; Nemzetközi Statisztikai Zsebkönyv, KSH, 1987 and 1991.; Narodnoe hosjajstvo stran chlenov SEV-a 1981 and 1986.

Implements

The results of scientific and technical revolution are most tangible with fixed assets and tools employed in agriculture. Therefore if we want to analyze provision with tools of production we have to insist - beyond quantitative data - also on qualitative characteristics. (Let us mention that a similar problem arises with the already mentioned inputs too.)

As to the mechanization of agricultural work the data on engines are worth mentioning. We present data on the most important kinds of engines namely tractors, combines, lorries and special trucks. It turns out from Tables 3.7 - 3.10 that quantitative growth is palpable with all the three kinds of tools as is the growth of average capacity. (Similar is the case with lorries and combines, with the former it was the ton kilometer per unit, with the latter the throughput that has increased.)

Let us mention that beyond quantitative growth qualitative changes were most palpable with agricultural machines. The general increase of the technology level is characterized by the following:

-    mechanical loss caused by the use of machines has decreased,
-    operation principles and technological solutions more adapted to biological requirements appeared resulting in lower biological loss,
-    universality and adaptivity has increased, new elements were added to machine systems and thereby the conditions for putting together an optimal machine park have improved.

Table 3.7
Tractors (in thousands)

Year Country	1960	1970	1980	1985	1990
World total	12,521.3	15,329.5	21,741.7	24,898.5	26,554.0
Hungary	41.0	68.4	55.5	55.3	49.0
Bulgaria	25.8	53.6	62.0	55.2	53.0
GDR	70.6	148.9	144.5	158.0	173.0
Poland	62.8	230.9	646.1	853.2	1,185.0
Romania	44.2	107.3	146.6	184.4	127.0
Soviet Union	1,122.3	1,977.5	2,561.5	2,774.7	-
Czechoslovakia	74.9	136.4	136.7	137.1	139.0

Sources: Narodnoe hosjajstvo stran chlenov SEV-a 1981.
Nemzetközi Statisztikai Évkönyv, 1989.
Nemzetközi adatok a mezőgazdaságról, AGROINFORM, 1969.
Mezőgazdasági és Élelmiszeripari Zsebkönyv, 1990.
Mezőgazdaság és Élelmiszeripar 1992. AKII.

Table 3.8
Combine for cereals (piece)

Year Country	1960	1970	1980	1985	1990
Hungary	4,167	11,773	14,071	11,885	10,000
Bulgaria	7,042	9,340	9,682	8,491	7,813
GDR	6,409	17,911	13,582	16,383	17,461
Poland	3,120	13,968	39,302	56,186	60,853
Romania	17,577	45,241	39,341	49,804	-
Soviet Union	497,222	622,644	722,088	828,352	826,757
Czechoslovakia	6,326	16,433	17,771	19,533	20,606

Sources: Narodnoe hosjajstvo stran chlenov SEV-a 1981 and 1986.
Mezőgazdasági és Élelmiszeripari Zsebkönyv, 1990.

Table 3.9
Lorries and special trucks in agriculture (piece)

Year Country	1960	1970	1980	1985	1990
Hungary	3,023	14,339	28,704	33,240	32,000
Bulgaria	-	22,079	23,421	25,352	26,250
GDR	9,312	27,186	51,590	54,584	57,490
Poland	4,010	15,232	55,586	43,583	49,310
Romania	-	19,772	28,306	31,917	34,870
Soviet Union	761,100	1,137,700	1,693,500	1,986,800	2,085,110
Czechoslovakia	9,675	21,537	61,666	75,348	87,150

Sources: Narodnoe hozjajstvo stran chlenov SEV-a 1981. and 1986.;
Mezőgazdasági és Élelmiszeripari Statisztikai Zsebkönyv, KSH 1990.

Table 3.10
Nominal traction power per hundred ha ploughland, garden, orchard and
vineyard (kW)

Year Country	1960	1970	1980	1985
Hungary	18.0	41.5	56.9	66.0
Bulgaria	15.7	39.4	71.0	70.3
GDR	36.8	98.3	136.0	153.0
Poland	9.0	37.5	127.0	183.0
Romania	12.8	43.6	65.6	86.8
Soviet Union	16.5	37.5	63.3	75.4
Czechoslovakia	32.3	80.0	125.0	138.0

Source: Narodnoe hosjajstvo stran chlenov SEV-a 1981 and 1986.

('Optimal' means in this respect quantitative and qualitative composition of the set of engines and processing machines which makes it possible to perform all the production tasks within optimal biologic-agrotechnology time constraints in the quality requested so that:

-       unit costs of machine use;
-       unit costs of investment in machines; and
-       unit costs of labour be minimal.)

Similar requirements might be formulated against other kinds of tools of production. The conclusions are similar: mechanization of agricultural production, its provision with tools of production has improved in the period investigated parallel with agricultural output.

The data demonstrate that in Hungarian agriculture in the period investigated dynamic growth of output was attained before the background of permanently decreasing arable land and labour and an improving provision with tools. The question here arises: how can one explain that as an overall result of the above mentioned tendencies the volume of agricultural production increased by more than 200 per cent? Certainly provision with tools has a prime importance but it could not in itself countervail the decrease of arable land and labour and result in a large quantity increase.

Beyond the measurable quantitative elements one has to refer to the importance of qualitative changes since:

-       parallel with the decrease of arable land there was a drive for better land utilization;
-       decrease in the number of workers was seconded with a rising professional level;

-        the quantitative growth of tools of production occurred on a palpably
         higher technology level.

Within the dynamic system of the above mentioned changes there was a transfer mechanism embracing the whole agricultural production which - through sensing and processing changes in factors, through decision and control induced the above mentioned results. *The backbone of this mechanism was the complex technology development of agriculture.*

4. The interpretation of technology development within agriculture

In our world we experience a dynamic flow of scientific achievements. Their implementation too is much more rapid than was in the past. New activities never heard of in the past have appeared. These statements remain true even if at the time of writing this study there are events both in world and in domestic politics which cause uncertainties. More than that: there are areas (first of all in military technology) which obtain - precisely due to these events - larger publicity. (Think about the experiences of the man in the street during the Gulf War who could see the high level and modernity of military equipment. There are of course more peaceful signs of scientific research bringing practical results.)

In these results, an undisputable role was played by specialization which can be perceived both in research-development work and in practical adaptation. One cannot deny however that parallel with exaggerated specialization there are *interdisciplinary* endeavours (both in science and application). As a result of them one can synthesize the multiple components of a wider problem area. This synthesizing activity is important from the point of view of our present topic since the social-economic integration of technology development in agriculture requires that we minimize the risk of agricultural production becoming the racing track for well-compartmentalized specialists. There is a potential danger that R&D specialists, propelled by their 'conviction' develop their special area in a self-contained way, independent of social and economic interests and neglecting the harmony between production factors of agriculture.

Seeing the impact of exaggerated specialization it is justified to forecast in a synthetic way the development of science, technology and economy - at least in the area of technology development of agriculture. The above mentioned synthetizing activity is required in the following areas:

-        area of technology
-        area of economy
-        area of society.

We will deal with the problems of individual areas in later parts of our study. First let us have an overview of interpretations of technology development.

Technology development aims at improving the efficiency of production. It is a complex technical-economic category *whose content is the improvement of economic indicators and its method is the steady modernization of agricultural production, harmonized improvement of production processes and the employment of new (improved) tools and materials.*

In my view technology development in agriculture is a steady, complex and purposeful innovation activity which causes quantitative and qualitative changes in the elements of agricultural production (land, labour, production tools) *and as a result of which we can pursue agricultural production at a higher level and more efficiently.* Since the horizons of classical agricultural production are widening, the borders of technology development in agriculture are shifting too. Successful technology development requires that it embrace the whole of the chain of innovation: from research and development work up to the sale of the end product.

From the above mentioned characteristics let us elaborate only one: *complexity.* A whole range of practical examples demonstrates that in the absence of harmonization of factors of development the advantages cannot be realized. *The site of technology development is the site of the product path. That means it is basically a microeconomic activity which has however macroeconomic linkages and aspects.*

If however we lay the stress on social economic linkages and embedding we should *enlarge somewhat the term* and investigate impacts in wider ranges. Thus technology development would include tasks of vertical and/or horizontal extension of production, change of profile, environmental protection etc.

5. The dominant substantive elements of technology development

As a result of our past deliberations and the nature of technology development we can characterize the dominant substantive elements by main branches of agricultural production.

Plant cultivation

The rise of average yield in plant cultivation was caused by the increased potential productive capacity attained in the last two-three decades. The aims of genetic improvement are generally the following:
- to increase the potential productive capacity
- to improve quality
- to increase resistance
- to diminish fluctuation in yield.

The increase of potential productive capacity was with the most important plants successful and followed by cyclic change of variety. (See the data in Tables 3.2 - 3.4.)

It should be mentioned when looking at average yield data that plants are also grown on land unsuitable from an ecologic point of view (the figure is 30 per cent for Hungary). Thus growing within favourable conditions resulted in yield far surpassing the average. The increase of potential yield capacity did not always result in improved efficiency.

One could not *rationally diminish costs of production*. It is well known e.g. that with cereals a large part (65-75 per cent) of costs of production are the costs of chemicals and of machine work. Genetic improvement was geared towards varieties better adapted to machine work. Progress in the area of reaction to chemicals was much weaker. As a result producers used higher than optimal quantity of fertilizer and pesticide - with all its consequences (first of all environmental damage).

There were efforts to reduce this waste but they were usually 'suppressed' by efforts to increase quantity. In the past 30 years it was - a hidden - slogan of state policy that we should produce more at whatever cost!

According to specialists - and also proved in the last years - the main bottleneck of raising average yield was *water*. According to calculations average rainfall available is enough to grow 1.6 tons of organic mass per hectare. One fourth of it is root, the remaining 1.2 tons falls on grain and straw. It would have been desirable to gear the work of genetic improvement towards sorts with short, thin but strong stalk, few or no leaves (generic breeding). Such sorts can better utilize rainfall and nutritives. It is a task for the future to develop plants of early growing sorts optimal from the point of view of production and utilization of organic material and thus from the point of view of production costs.

Great effort was made to improve the quality of main plants. This was the case first of all with cereals where the main goal was to increase protein content. The so-called protein-wheat is already introduced in general growing practice but with other quality indicators there has been much less progress. It is a big problem that up to the recent past *quality of the produce was not an important indicator*. Only in the recent past were *procurement prices made contingent on quality* stimulating thereby producers to look also at quality and not only at quantity.

Plant physiology and plant protection

There has been no substantial progress in practical use of the results of plant physiology. This is the explanation why there was no considerable attention directed towards the micro-element content of soils. In the focus of producers was the ever increasing quantity of NPC, and the need for micro element replacement was neglected.

Similar is the case with hormones. Only in last years did we encounter a conscious - even if sporadic - use of these materials.

The development of plant protection was assisted by a dynamically developing chemical industry producing ever newer compounds and combinations. Unfortunately the breeding of resistant sorts is not given due importance even if both economic and environmental factors stress their role. Besides that certain plant diseases cannot be cured by chemical plant protection due to time and technical constraints. Growing resistant sorts will have a decisive role in the foundation and development of complex plant protection technologies in the near future.

Soil management

In plant cultivation one of the main factors of increasing yields is the effective increase of productivity of soils by increased *nutrient replacement* (quantity and quality of nutrients introduced). Distinct importance here are both *organic manures and chemical fertilizers*.

In the area of the use of organic manure proper handling of traditional manure produced by animal breeding and of diluted manure is only partially solved. Only 1/2-2/3 part of organic manure is used. As a result the area under organic manure was between 5-15 per cent. In 1989 in Hungary only 6.1 per cent of arable land was under organic manure. Quantity used in the seventies was below the level of previous years and in the eighties it steadily decreased. In 1989 e.g. the volume of organic manure used was 2,342,000 tons. As a result on average 36 tons of organic manure was applied to 1 ha. According to former conceptions the use of fertilizers in plant cultivation was determined by the realistic target of growth of production. Today we already know that producers are 'directed' by cost and price relations towards rational (or forced?) use of fertilizers. On the actual data see Table 3.11.

Table 3.11
Fertilizer use per ha ploughland, garden, orchard and vineyard in active agent
(kg)

Year	1960	1970	1980	1985	1990
Country					
World total	19	42	80	87	91
From this:					
Common Market	126	214	232		
Hungary	29	150	262	253	127
Bulgaria	36	159	205	209	173
GDR	188	319	325	329	350
Poland	49	162	244	230	104
Romania	8	67	113	146	107
Soviet Union	12	47	84	109	106
Czechoslovakia	95	230	334	337	255
USA	37	82	113	103	97
Canada			43	51	45

Sources: Narodnoe hosjajstvo stran chlenov SEV-a 1981.
        Nemzetközi Statisztikai Évkönyv, 1989.
        Mezőgazdasági Statisztikai Zsebkönyv, KSH 1972, 1974, 1990.
        Mezőgazdaság és Élelmiszeripar 1992, AKII.

Measures were taken to better adapt the regional distribution of fertilizers to needs and to soil characteristics. An important step forward is the larger role given to liquid fertilizers and to fertilizer application differentiated according to the different layers of the root zone. There was an important progress in the eighties in the transportation, handling, storage and distribution of fertilizers.

The characteristics of agrotechnology

In plant cultivation the most important novelties are often those of agrotechnology. The main domestic areas of agrotechnology - beyond those already mentioned - are the following:
-       regional distribution of different plants
-       crop rotation
-       soil protection, water management, soil improvement
-       progress in soil cultivation and last but not least
-       research into the conscious development of these factors and changes in the attitude of professionals.
    As far as the regional distribution of individual crops is concerned, there have been no considerable changes despite the fact that a need for it was

expressed for a long time by the professional community. No cultivation districts for main crops and sorts were formulated based on scientific and practical experiences. The lack of regional specialization has repercussions on the structure of production in individual farms. In Hungarian economy diversification is much stronger than specialization. In this context the problem of crop rotation arises. Although foreign and domestic experiences revealed unequivocally that systems based on the rotation of two or three plants are optimal monoculture still prevails in several regions.

The preservation and increase of the productivity of soils requires huge amelioration work on vast areas year by year.

In the near future great stress will be laid on complex amelioration and concentration of finances available since in the past these were areas much neglected. One should further pursue the implementation of chemical ameliorators (sprinkling with lime). On soils with adverse mechanical characteristics, materials improving physical properties should be applied.

There has been much effort in the area of soil cultivation both as regards the mode of cultivation and engines and machines used. The aim is invariably to reduce the energy consumed by soil cultivation.

We have already hinted at the topic of plant protection. In Hungary the agricultural use of chemicals is on such a level that it increasingly causes environmental problems. That is why beyond the use of chemicals not damaging the environment and not harmful for human health one should increasingly rely on preventive biological and agrotechnical processes.

The analysis of individual areas of plant cultivation and gardening is not the task of the present study. We called your attention only to the most general factors, mentioning possible problems and perspectives. Our approach to animal breeding will be similar.

Branches of animal breeding

The undeniable quantitative growth notwithstanding there were many problems in animal breeding in the last 30 years. One could not integrate the whole range of breeding - propagation - production - processing - sales so that each phase be subsumed to market needs.

Genetics, new species

The tendencies and endeavours of plant improvement can be recognized in animal breeding too. Unfortunately in the most important branches, namely cattle and pork work of amelioration was not successful in providing a sound basis for the tasks of production in the period ahead. One should further raise the level of breeding work. By relying on biotechnology processes and adapting to the requirements of the market, by better definition of the objectives of use one should in the future better utilize genetic capacities.

In our present situation we have to reformulate the task of a previous generation of geneticians, namely that animal populations suitable for 'industrialised' breeding should be created. New species should be more resistant to different illnesses and propagation troubles.

In line with market needs one should select meat producing sorts against the propensity to fat. One should engage in the future more closely in worldwide genetic cooperation since no country can in today's world keep the genetic quality of its animal stock on world level merely by self-reliance.

One should make advance in the objective method of species evaluation and in the improvement of fodder plants.

Animal physiology, animal health

Despite the many results of research into animal physiology one still does not know with several species the range of adaptation tolerance. (This is not primarily a physiological problem. It is rather practical: the efficiency requirement often had an effect contrary to the biologically-physiologically optimal production environment.) To mention a special problem of physiology steps made in the area of detoxicating carrion and processing them into fodder are still not definitive. Similarly one should go on with the research and development work in the area of technical background of animal health (washing and disinfecting machines, fastening equipment, laboratory instruments for rapid analysis etc.).

Prevention of contagious disease should be intensified all the more since in recent years we had considerable commercial loss due to unexpected animal health problems.

Foddering, fodder economy

In the last decade our accumulating physiological knowledge made it possible to improve the efficiency of *fodder transformation*. This was realized partially through new methods of fodder preparation. Its methods (flaking, granulating, heating, steaming etc.) have been diffused right after their development.

Preservation and storage of fodder is still cumbersome and involves *much waste*. At the same time there is much complaint against the quality and stability of mixed fodders produced according to different recipes. There are 'evergreen' problems in this area which should be solved in the future. These are:

-    the utilization of agricultural by-products (stalk, straw, sugar-beet head etc.) as mass fodder;
-    utilization of industrial by-products, the solution of physiological, organizational, economic and technical problems in this area;
-    the increase of yields;
-    more efficient use of meadows and pastures;
-    breeding technologies.

In the development of *breeding technologies* there were many different endeavours and solutions in past decades. This was the result of factors motivating technology development such as:

-    maximal utilization of capacities of the animal stock;
-    elimination of production uncertainties due to different outside effects.

In future one should rethink - in line with all that was said in the above - the content and criteria of 'industrial breeding'. Several factors justify the replacement of oversized farms with rational size ones. There are many partial problems with every species of animal whose enumeration is not the task of the present study.

An insecure future after a difficult decade

As a result of the above mentioned growth of agricultural production, agriculture was a *success industry* in Hungary. By Eastern-European or Eastern-Central-European measure, Hungarian agriculture of the last three decades was successful, nay the most successful industry. At the same time when analyzing the functioning of the industry we can see that the success meant first of all the growth of gross production. It contributed to the easing and abolishing of quantitative shortage and made possible - beyond an unprecedented in Eastern-Europe level of supply on the domestic market - an agricultural export whose importance for the equilibrium of the national economy was large and increasing.

At the same time qualitative features of development were not without problems. Growth of production went hand in hand with deteriorating efficiency of resource use. (One has to stress particularly the strong decrease in capital efficiency up to the early eighties.) At the same time a polarized plant structure was created which included both large and small farms and in which large farms excelled in waste of capital whereas small farms in waste of labour. *As a result of these structural distortions a vulnerable production structure and a one-sided market orientation arose.* All in all we can say that in Hungarian agriculture from the mid sixties a peculiar form of development, more efficient than in other Eastern-European countries did arise resulting in a higher level of activity and stimulation but at the same time considerable structural distortions remained and were reproduced. The consequences of these distortions resulted from the mid seventies increasingly in smaller income production by agriculture and from the second third of the eighties in stagnation of basic agricultural activities. Elements of a *latent crisis* accumulated in the eighties.

After the change of the system previous hidden crisis increasingly *turned into an open one*.

Consequently the roots of the crisis of Hungarian agriculture should be searched for in the *previous development path*. A scientific analysis of the agricultural policy of the past three years unequivocally reveals that policy did not react on the intensifying problems.

For want of a suitable strategy, transition *accumulates tensions and uncertainty* is general. There are serious sales problems, liquidity problems, decrease of production is a steady phenomenon as is the loss and consumption of assets. Investment went back radically, the state of biological and technical capacities is deteriorating. A wide range of cooperatives and food industrial firms are threatened by bankruptcy and liquidation. A large part of those working in agriculture did not earn even the official minimum wage and the number and share of agricultural unemployed is rapidly increasing. Intellectuals leave the industry in large numbers.

Rapid decay of agricultural organizations and agricultural production began in 1991. The decrease of so-called auxiliary activities was even stronger than the decrease of agricultural production proper. In 1992 the volume of gross production by agricultural organisations was less by 41 per cent, that of agricultural production by 28 per cent than in 1988. The trend continued well into 1993. The seriousness of this decrease of production is demonstrated by the fact that as a result of World War II. between 1938-39 and 1946-47 gross production of agriculture decreased by 43 per cent, which is only marginally more than the decrease of output in the last five years.

The decrease of net production (GDP) was less than that of gross production. This is the result of more than rational economy with materials. The material content of production decreased by 10 percentage points, from previous 60 per cent to 50 per cent. There was a further decrease in the nutritive content of soils. In 1992 the effective substance content of fertilizer used per hectare was 29 kgs, less than the data for 1950 (30 kgs). The anyway low level of organic manure use further decreased. Producers tried to economize on seeds, on soil cultivation, on fuel, on fodder. Almost half a million hectare arable land remained untilled.

Within animal husbandry the size of the stock decreased with every major species. Shortage of production largely contributed to the radical decrease of agricultural export in the first half of 1993.

Characteristic of the Hungarian agriculture is the permanently *low level of income*. Profit per value of assets, per cost or per total revenue was much less with agricultural organizations already in the eighties than in other branches of the economy. In 1991 loss surpassed HUF 20 billion, in 1992 HUF 35 billion.

Low level of income, coupled with insecure organizational framework and bad outlook for return reduced the investment resources of agriculture to a minimum. The share of the industry within total investment went back to 1.5-2.0 per cent (1.5 according to CSO, 2.0 according to the Ministry of Agriculture).

Now it has been a long time that one cannot speak about development in agriculture any more. Investments a decade ago did not cover (in real value) the obsolescence of equipment. Average age of machinery used on large farms is more than 10 years. Machines are in the last third of their life-cycle. Particularly critical is the situation with tractors, reaper-threshers and self propelled harvesters. Taking into account the high level of capacity utilization wear and tear is on a critical level.

The technological state of machinery in private farms is still worse since they use preponderantly discarded machines of large farms or used machines bought abroad. Specialists fear that in the import of machines for private farms and in commerce with used agricultural machines the situation experienced with passenger cars will be reproduced. After used cars Hungary will be the cemetery of used agricultural machines too.

For development first of all financial resources are needed. The problem is not which bank to choose for credit but whether it is worth while taking credit and how to pay it back. Guaranteed prices offered by the government for five agricultural products for the year 1994 are extremely important from the point of view of security of production and income earned. Wheat, maize, cattle, pork and milk give 55 per cent of gross production of Hungarian agriculture. The question only is to what extent guaranteed prices take into account the costs of production.

Finally we have to mention that the number of those employed in agriculture decreased in the 1988-92 period by 300 thousand people. There was no similar decrease of employment in any other branch of the economy. At present the number of those whose employment in agricultural organizations was discontinued is put at about 200 thousand.

In agricultural production in 1992 8-9 per cent of the employed worked. This ratio is similar to that of Western-European countries. (The average for the EC is about 7 per cent.) A further decrease is likely in Hungary since in the first half of 1993 the number of those employed in agriculture further decreased by one fourth and - considering the perspective and income earning capacity of agriculture - one cannot assume that these 75 thousand people became self-employed farmers. It is much more likely that a large part of them became unemployed.

6. Summary and conclusions

The practice of the last thirty years in technology development of Hungarian agriculture is noteworthy because it transgressed in certain of its elements the 'follow-up paradigm'. Agricultural growth had an unparallelled dynamism if compared to countries with similar political systems.

The originality of the system 'faded away' gradually since the late seventies and by now the problems of technology development in agriculture are similar to those of other branches of the national economy.

In the present income position of agriculture it is not possible to replace the antiquated machinery within a short time. Therefore one should study the Western idea of Low Input Sustainable Agriculture. It is not an extensive type agriculture. Rather it might be called intensive since part of material resources is made good by intellectual investment. The main objective is to avoid the decay of natural environment at previous levels of production.

One of the most exciting problems in this area is *how to go on* with technology development of agriculture.

The special characteristics of agriculture, the relative inelasticity of supply, slow return on investments require even in an organic economic system that an agricultural policy, a scenario for agricultural development be developed. Producers need - beyond market signals - clear indications from the government about the future agricultural system, about structural changes. Even more important is such information in the period of transition to market economy.

The lack of an outline of the future commanding at least a minimum of national consensus makes the actors of agricultural market insecure. If there are no clear signposts intelligible even for less educated agricultural producers, then a cautious behaviour will prevail among them. Credibility problems too might reoccur: if market actors think everything is possible, programs announced are too general, do not seem to be sincere (are often changed and without consequence) then deep-going transformation and modernisation will be shunned.

Agricultural society needs not only a logical, self-contained snapshot on present situation but also an agricultural policy conception, a system of means and ends which would - beyond its consistence - include the ways of how to implement such rational, agreed-upon future structures.

I would stress three cardinal elements of such an agricultural development scenario: on the one hand there is the role to be played by agriculture in the national economy, second there should be a clear idea about the market (the social market economy), finally we ought to have an idea about the structure of agriculture.

1. The macroeconomic role: One should determine what performance is required by economic policy from agriculture in the post-transition period. Consistent forecasts about output, export-import, income, employment and budgetary flows ought to be made.

2. Agricultural market, social market economy. It is important that a conception of agricultural market policy be worked out. As for its principles, one should determine the role of government in the regulation of agricultural market; the possibilities and constraints of collective self-regulation; the operation of resource and product markets; the role of social considerations. The eventual marketization of ecologic factors also has a bearing on the market framework of agriculture.

3. The structure of agricultural production. Beyond initiating transformation of property relations - which process should be speeded up in order to attain a settlement satisfactory for all concerned - one should work out the foundations of a long-term conception of agricultural (land) property. In our opinion under the actual circumstances only a pluralistic ownership structure (which would rely both on - at present only imaginary - family farms, on part-time farming and on large farms) is viable. A forecast of the future agricultural structure might be the basis of the regulation of the agricultural farm. Without government regulation these processes may generate adverse social-economic consequences. One should stress the importance of giving preference on the long run to young entrepreneurs who already have (or are ready to acquire) professional knowledge. One should think about the regulation of land ownership: under the property reform there is an increased need for regrouping plots and it is in our prime interest to obtain as a result a competitive land structure. Passivity, 'staying apart' for agricultural policy is not 'market conform'. An active stance is indispensable for a functioning market economy to arise.

One should stress that the transitory period ahead of us has to be qualitatively different from the longer-term perspective of transformation. The consistence of the main agricultural policy objectives requires that short-term objectives and development paths be different from the long-term. The short-term scenario is in certain respects a predetermined one whereas in a longer perspective we have a wider margin for sequencing and choosing among objectives at our disposal. In the short run one should make compromises, harmonize the requirements of feasibility of day-to-day operation with those of deep-running irreversible change, all built on the conditions of the present situation (product structure, capital etc.).

Finally let me mention two preconditions of successful choice among and harmonization between objectives. On the one hand it is indispensable that all the relevant interests be taken into account when determining objectives. On the other - and this is attached to the previous one - agricultural policy objectives ought to be human, ought to mobilise rural society and offer a perspective for individuals and families.

If these requirements are not fulfilled, large-scale transformation will harm the interests of large segments of rural society, intensify the conflicts within rural society. All this, parallel with increased industrial unemployment and a long-term stagnation of the national economy might have unforeseeable consequences. In this unfavourable case, large agricultural *strata* might challenge the legitimity of transformation and this would lead to a tragic disequilibrium in society.

4 International tendencies, infrastructure and services in Hungary

Éva Ehrlich

The study was prepared in the first version as part of the research project led by Éva Ehrlich: 'The role of infrastructure and services in the modernization of the economy'. This version is a compact one adapted to the needs of project COST A7.

The heritage of the remote and the recent past in Hungary

Our international investigations embracing more than 100 years (1860-1983)[1] outlined two historical types of development in the industrialization and infrastructural development of developed market economies:
-        the preceding type[2] and
-        the parallel type.[3]
   In the 19th century the latter, the parallel type was characteristic of the majority of market economies.
   In Hungary from the middle of the last century up to the beginning of the present the development of infrastructure preceded that of industry: first of all with sewage, the canalization of riverways, transportation, railway and attached telegraph, telecommunications, with the establishment and steady widening of trade, and the banking network and urbanization.
   The Trianon Treaty (1920) reduced Hungary's territory to one third. This smaller Hungary was in a particularly favourable situation concerning

infrastructure: the infrastructural level (primarily in the sectors of transportation and telecommunications) improved considerably, since in the annexed regions the infrastructure was less developed than in the remaining regions. The inherited concentration on the capital (Budapest) and the radial structure of the railway and road network further intensified. As a result East-West and North-South connections within the transport system remained underdeveloped in spite of the territorial reduction. We should mention that concentration on the capital was characteristic not only for transportation but also for industry, higher education and bureaucracy.

In the period between the two world wars - similar to the majority of Western-European countries - the parallel development of industry and infrastructure continued.

The development type characterizing the Soviet Union since its formation and the socialist countries imitating Soviet industrialization after World War II was totally different from the types mentioned above. Adapting to this pattern reconstruction of infrastructure after World War II in Hungary was equivalent to the reproduction of the pre-World War II technology level and structure. The infrastructural networks were rendered operational and served for a long time and still in some respects serve the Hungarian economy and society. The development of infrastructure and services was almost totally abandoned for 10-15 years after World War II both in Hungary and in the other former socialist countries.

In Hungary at the end of the forties, by also adopting the Stalinist model of industrialization, the private sector in services - wholesale and retail trade, repair and maintenance etc. - was nationalized. Services and institutions previously attached to the market (business and financial services, banks etc.) were abolished or adapted to the requirements of the planned economy. Later the forced increase of industrial (mainly heavy industrial and military) output led to the gradual wearing out and decay of infrastructural networks and services which caused serious trouble in production and also in everyday life. As a result an infrastructure-development policy targeted at the most acute shortages was developed in socialist countries. This model which was also characteristic of Hungary despite considerable development in some infrastructural and service areas from the late sixties, is called the 'follower type' of infrastructure development.[4]

We summarize in Table 4.1 the international levels of infrastructure and services for the years 1960-1983.[5]

Table 4.1
Ranking and scores of infrastructure in 27 countries, 1960-1983*

Ranking of countries in 1983	1960		1983	
	Rank	Scores	Rank	Scores
Denmark	5	68	1	74
Sweden	2	75	2	69
USA	1	82	3	68
Switzerland	4	70	4	66
Finland	15	45	5	66
Norway	6	64	6	66
FRG	11	51	7	64
Japan	17	42	8	64
Canada	3	72	9	64
Netherlands	9	55	10	63
Australia	7	64	11	63
France	14	47	12	59
Belgium	10	54	13	58
Italy	18	39	14	58
United Kingdom	8	62	15	58
Austria	12	48	16	55
Greece	23	29	17	54
GDR	13	47	18	50
Spain	20	33	19	47
Czechoslovakia	16	43	20	45
Bulgaria	21	33	21	43
Hungary	19	34	22	43
Poland	22	32	23	40
Portugal	24	28	24	37
Yugoslavia	25	26	25	36
Romania	26	23	26	33
Turkey	27	10	27	22

*   See Appendix for the details.

Source: Ehrlich, É. (1990)

From Table 4.1 the following conclusions for Hungary might be drawn:
- The relative level of the whole of Hungarian infrastructure was in 1983 much higher than in 1960. This 'catching up' is in line with international tendencies.
- Among socialist countries Hungary's position improved. Whereas in 1960 the infrastructural level of Hungary was exceeded by the GDR by 38 per cent, that of Czechoslovakia by 26 per cent, by 1983 the gap was reduced to 16 per cent in the case of the GDR and to 5 per cent of Czechoslovakia.
- Infrastructural development in Hungary was not sufficient enough to keep her place among the countries of the world. From among 27 countries Hungary was 19th in 1960 and 22nd in 1983. In market economies in this period the rate of growth of infrastructure and services was much higher than in Hungary and inter-country differences concerning the above diminished.
- Whereas in the 23 year-long period from among South-European countries Italy, Spain and Greece caught up with the infrastructural level of Western-Europe, Hungary's relative level lagged behind. Thus in 1983 from among the market economies only the level of Portugal and Turkey was lower than that of Hungary.

In infrastructural areas figuring in the international survey Hungary's scores for the years 1960 and 1983 are summarized in Table 4.2. In international comparison the least developed infrastructural fields in the whole period were telecommunication, followed by transportation and in 1960 by housing. Relatively developed compared to the average Hungarian level are the health sector, education and culture in both years and housing in 1983.

Table 4.2
Scores of Hungary's main infrastructural areas in 1960 and 1983

Infrastructural areas	Number of scores in	
	1960	1983
Transportation	15	24
Telecommunications	10	16
Housing supply and household equipment	24	61
Health service	63	62
Education and culture	56	52

Source: Ehrlich, É. (1990)

In 1983 individual infrastructural areas of Hungary occupied the following places in the international rank order: telecommunications 24th, transportation 22nd, housing and health 21st, education and culture 17th.

The main characteristics of the Hungarian economic policy and practice were:

- the neglect of infrastructure and services in proportion to productive sectors (first of all heavy industry and the defence industry),
- the development of infrastructure and services based on the residual principle,
- production-centred attitude and practice within the infrastructural and service sector which neglects direct relations between the service-provider and the client and the fine structure of networks and services[6] required for this, i.e. general dispreference of the consumer and the service sphere,
- in several areas the almost exclusive financing through budgetary redistribution,
- the dominance of monopoly organizations, the preference of large organizations and large consumers against small organizations and small consumers,
- artifically low prices,
- the lack of markets and competition.

The above characteristics together resulted in infrastructure and services lagging behind the productive sectors of the economy, the needs of society and those of population. The deficiencies in services are present almost everywhere.

The underdevelopment of infrastructure and services was enhanced by the fact that education and health were free, culture, passenger transport and housing highly subsidized, an important achievement in itself compared with the pre-World War II level and at the development level of Hungary. As a result of gratuity (or strong subsidization) needs grew abruptly. High level long-term satisfaction of enhanced needs could not be provided for under the existing economic circumstances.

The need for services was also enhanced by the method of Stalinist industrialization. This industrialization attracted within 4-5 years one and a half million people into towns. Heavy and defence industry-centred, low technology level (relative to developed market economies), environment-destroying production and institutional structures generated their own demand for services (and infrastructure).

Chronic shortages, tensions and distortions, ill-conceived 'fire-extinguishing methods' accumulated and were constantly reproduced.

When we stress the general validity of the picture outlined above we also have to mention that there was a healthy change in the handling, by the economic policy, of infrastructure and services from the end of the sixties. As a result of aggravating shortages, troubles and a reform spirit for an 8-10 year period (1968-78) the previous practice of dealing only with acute problems and development according to the residual principle seemed to have been abandoned. The prime role of the standard of living for the political stability of the country pushed Hungarian economic policy towards a satisfaction of service needs, compensation for shortages, and the development of infrastructure and services.

In certain areas of services (catering, housing, tourism, trade, passenger transport, repair) the general standard of the supply in Hungary was on a higher level than in other socialist countries. This was due to the fact that in labour-intensive services service activity as a secondary or tertiary occupation (white, grey and black market) expanded from the second half of the seventies and by the eighties a sizeable private sector[7] had developed in the service sector alongside the government sector. At the end of the eighties the entry of small private firms intensified in the areas of personal, business, and financial services.

This phenomenon of the eighties, the growth of private sector organizations reduced service shortages and considerably improved the level of supply, helping a rapid and flexible adaptation to needs. Despite this, government offices and decrees were, even at the end of the eighties, ambivalent towards the private sector, compelled it to a 'transitory existence' and hindered, restricted its activity in many respects.[8] Although in 1988-89 parliament adopted laws favourable to the private sector (e.g. the Law on Partnerships, the Law on Transformation) the private sector's role in services was marginal even in 1989 in spite of the rekindling of the entrepreneurial spirit.

In the area of services the most important changes among Eastern-Central-European countries occurred in Hungary. Here the process was started in which the development of infrastructure and services became a part of economic policy and business initiatives.

The improvement showed up in Hungary in a larger concentration of investment and labour resources in service sectors. One can see from the data of Table 4.3 that among the Eastern-Central-European countries Hungary already ranked first with respect to the share of investment[9] allocated to infrastructure (services) in 1980 (49.1 per cent) and even more in 1989 (54.8 per cent)[10]. The employment share of infrastructure was equally high in 1989.

Table 4.3

Share of services in the Eastern Central European countries, 1970-1992
(Total = 100%)

	1970	1980	1985	1989	1990	1991	1992
				Investment			
GDR	32.4	34.0	35.5	30.8	-	-	-
Czechoslovakia	47.1	43.5	40.0	40.2	41.1	44.0	...
Hungary	41.6	49.1	52.7	54.8	59.3*	62.7	65.4
Poland	41.0	46.3	49.6	47.4	51.8	57.6	56.9
Bulgaria	36.0	42.7	40.8	39.2	37.5	40.1	...
Romania	31.7	30.5	28.6	34.4	32.2	33.2	30.0
				Employment			
GDR	37.0	37.6	38.1	39.1	...		...
Czechoslovakia	33.6	37.3	38.7	39.4	41.1	41.8	...
Hungary	30.4	36.6	37.8	41.7	43.9	45.7	49.1
Poland	27.5	30.7	32.8	35.6	36.9	37.5	39.3
Bulgaria	25.3	31.8	32.8	35.4	36.7	38.9	...
Romania	19.3	25.6	25.5	26.0	27.5	30.3	29.9

* Investment and modernization inclusive.

Sources: CMEA yearbook 1990.
Statistical Yearbooks, 1990, 1991, 1992.
Hungary 1992: CSO Department of Macroeconomic Statistics.

Despite the important developments at the end of the eighties (and continuing today) the main characteristic feature of the Hungarian infrastructural network is the rundown, obsolete, dysfunctional state of physical assets and one can still experience a quantitative shortage of infrastructural and service networks.

A large section of the railway network is not fitted with safety equipment, and their capacity is well below the international norms; 50 per cent of the rolling stock is more than 21 years old; half of the nations roads are not wide enough, half of the roads in general have a substandard working load. At the same time the number of passenger cars is increasing by 9-10 per cent yearly, that of lorries by 5-5.5 per cent; 49 per cent of passenger cars, 35 per cent of lorries, 40 per cent of buses are more than 10 years old; only a small part of vehicles are fitted with a catalysator; and the majority of rural roads have not been developed. The water and sewage network is decrepit, a large part of public utilities 80-100 years old. A large part of outlet water in the public sewage system is not treated either mechanically or biologically. At the end of the eighties towns are seriously contaminated - primarily in heavy industrial centres - the air is dirty and the noise is excessive. In many small villages water is unhealthy. At the end of the eighties a large number of urban flats and buildings in the state property sector (primarily in old towns and in the central districts of Budapest) were in a poor state, because of the neglect of maintenance and repair. Energy is not suitable for the complete electrification of households and the large-scale use of modern household appliances. 44 per cent of Hungarian settlements are attached to the international long-distance dialling network. At the end of the eighties more than 100 thousand people have been waiting for years (some of them for decades) for a telephone line. Certain exchanges and a large part of the telephone network were physically run down at the end of the eighties; 50 per cent of the still operating 1,700 exhanges are totally outdated, manual exchanges are ripe for replacement, 90 per cent of them operating only in day time hours.[11]

Human infrastructure networks too are characterized by decay, wear, shortage and waste.

The Hungarian health sector for example did not utilize the although still inadequate but increasing resources at its disposal; small sums were spent on the preservation and improvement of the health infrastructure. Public utilities and sanitary engineering were not maintained. As a result, according to an authoritative survey 16 per cent of the building stock requires reconstruction, 25 per cent maintenance, and 70 per cent of the machinery and instruments of health institutions (50 per cent of X-ray diagnosis equipment) are old fashioned and 37 per cent technically outworn. Health institutions are crowded, the number of hospital beds being raised by crowding more beds into old rooms.[12]

As the above examples show, in the last two decades with larger infrastructure developments only the filling in of holes, repair and modernization was connected.

For present-day Hungary regional differences were characteristic even before World War I. These differences were considerably reduced after the late fifties and primarily after the sixties but they are still perceptible.

In the majority of Hungarian counties there was an important infrastructural development in the sixties-seventies, which slowed down in the eighties. The relative level of the infrastructure of Hungarian counties for the years 1970-1985 is given in Table 4.4.

Table 4.4
Ranking and scores of infrastructure in the Hungarian 19 counties, 1970-1985

Ranking of counties in 1985	1970		1980		1985	
	Rank	Scores	Rank	Scores	Rank	Scores
Baranya	1	83.0	1	87.0	1	84.8
Győr-Sopron	2	80.3	2	83.2	2	84.0
Veszprém	3	80.0	3	82.5	3	82.2
Zala	8	71.1	7	79.1	4	82.1
Vas	5	77.0	4	81.7	5	80.6
Csongrád	4	78.8	5	81.1	6	80.1
Somogy	7	73.3	8	77.4	7	78.4
Heves	13	67.9	9	74.8	8	78.3
Komárom	6	75.2	6	80.4	9	77.0
Tolna	10	69.1	10	73.3	10	75.4
Borsod	11	68.7	11	72.8	11	74.1
Hajdú-Bihar	15	65.0	12	72.1	12	72.6
Nógrád	12	68.3	14	70.4	13	72.1
Szolnok	14	66.6	15	69.3	14	72.0
Békés	16	64.1	16	68.2	15	70.7
Bács-Kiskun	17	62.5	17	67.2	16	70.5
Fejér	9	70.9	13	71.8	17	70.3
Szabolcs-Szatmár	19	55.6	18	60.9	18	63.7
Pest	18	56.0	19	58.3	19	57.3

Sources: 1970: VÁTI (1982)
1980-1985: Incze, Zs. (1988)

One can read from the data that country levels converged and that infrastructure and services are still most developed in Western-Hungary, in Transdanubia bordering Austria, as they were in the past. After World War II together with these most developed Transdanubian counties, heavy and defence industry centres of Northern-Hungary (Borsod-Abaúj-Zemplén county), energy producing counties (Zala and Heves) and Hajdú-Bihar in Eastern-Hungary caught up. At the same time from among the Transdanubian counties Fejér lagged behind and approached the infrastructurally least developed Eastern-Hungarian county Szabolcs-Szatmár-Bereg.[13]

Regional differences in infrastructure are still greater if we investigate it along the dimension of settlement size (town, village). Such an investigation revealed[14] that complex infrastructural supply is a privilege of city-dwellers. The problem surfaced in the regional development plans of the mid-eighties when parts of towns became crowded, shortages intensified and smaller settlements became depopulated.

As a result of the power and political set-up of the economy and society, an attitude and practice favouring centralization and hostile toward grassroots, spontaneous, individual action became prevalent. There is a dominance of hierarchical, radial networks, lacking horizontal, ring-like links and cooperation. This attitude and practice is clearly visible in the transport network, in links between Budapest and county centres, and in contacts between county centres and towns and villages. Everywhere there is a lack of horizontal, two-way, mutual relationships in networks and services. For example the development of postal services one-way (top down) and radial communication systems (radio, tv, relay stations) have a clear priority over horizontal, two-way contacts such as the telephone.[15] Within the overall low level of telephone supply there was a 7:1 difference in the supply of Budapest and rural districts in 1990.[16]

In the regional distribution of investment an important role was played by political and economic pressure on central party and government organs and leaders up to the end of the eighties. Influence and personal prestige led in many instances - as it did in other spheres of the economy - to inefficient, irrational infrastructural investment, to ill-conceived 'development and modernization'. Such kinds of 'development' often consumed large resources without easing the concentration of networks, tensions and shortages in different areas.

The first four years of the change of the system[17]

It is well-known that contrary to general and Hungarian expectations (illusions) the first years of economic transition meant for Hungary - just like the other former socialist economies - a deep recession, deeper than that of the 1929-33 crisis.

Here we do not go into the outside objective causes of this recession (the collapse of the CMEA market, world market recession, protectionism), the special characteristics of individual countries (economic, social and human factors important for the transition to the market economy, readiness for change) and their differences, government failure etc.[18]

It is important to note however that in Hungary the first years of transition had already brought considerable changes in infrastructure and services. The most important changes and shifts in our opinion are the following:

1. Recession in infrastructure and services was much smaller than in the whole of the economy.[19] Whereas between 1989 and 1993 the GDP and its domestic use receded by 20-22 per cent, industrial production by almost 30 per cent, agricultural production by 33 per cent, gross investment by 23 per cent, retail trade and catering by 19 per cent, the decrease in the aggregate output of services was only 3 per cent. The considerable decrease in the productive sectors and the small decrease in the performance of services (coupled with a relatively larger increase of service prices[20]) resulted in a growing share of services in the composition of the GDP and in employment. As a result the share of services in Hungary is now approaching the share in market economies at a similar level of development. The share of services in the GDP grew from the 1989 51 per cent level to 62 per cent by 1992 and from 41.7 per cent to 49.1 per cent in employment.

Within the largely heterogenous aggregate of services the the growth was most dynamic in infrastructural networks and services necessary for the establishment of a market such as financial, banking and business services and telecommunications. Infrastructural networks attached to the market (banks, financial institutions etc.) have expanded unabated since 1988 with a slight decrease of services performed due to the drop of needs.

2. The ownership and organizational structure of the economy and within it infrastructure and services is radically changing. In the whole of the economy, but particularly in the service spheres state property is decreasing and private property (bought or created with either foreign or domestic capital) mixed (state and private) property and local government property are expanding.

The share of private property within the economy is demonstrated by the fact that - according to estimates - 8 per cent of the employed worked for the private sector in 1989 and almost 30 per cent in 1992.[21] The share of the state sector in employment diminished from 71 per cent in 1989 to below 60 per cent by the end of 1992. We have to take into account however, the hidden economy attached to the private sector which is put by certain estimates at 10-15 per cent in 1985 and 25-30 per cent in 1992. If we also take this fact into account we obtain the result that in 1992 the state sector only accounted for slightly more than half of the Hungarian economy (in 1989 the share of the state sector was almost 2/3).[22]

There are two main forms of the spread of private property in Hungary: on the one hand there are the recently established and mushrooming private ventures (business organizations, partnerships, private entrepreneurs) on the other the sale of state property in different forms.

a)   The number of business organizations based on private property and of individual entrepreneurs multiplied in the last four years. Whereas in 1989 almost 4500 business organizations (partnerships) were registered, in the first half of 1993 the figure was already 80,000. The number of registered individual entrepreneurs was 320,000 at the end of 1989, and 610,000 at the end of 1992. By September 1993 2/3 of business organizations were active in some type of service sphere. More than 89.3 per cent of these business organizations employed less than 20 people (50.3 per cent employed less than 11 people).[23] It is a remarkable fact that the share of business organizations active in real estate, leasing, in - mainly private - business services amounted in September 1993 to 18 per cent of the total number of business organizations.[24]

The majority of registered individual entrepreneurs work as sole ventures or ventures with a small number of employees, i.e. as self-employed[25] and/or as an entrepreneur of necessity.[26] A large part of small venturers and the self-employed pursue their private venture activity parallel with their main occupation.[27]

In one-person ventures and in partnerships without legal personality the breakdown of active, full-time wage earners according to industries is as shown by Table 4.5. It appears from the data of the table that the self-employed[28] (construction and agriculture excluded) are engaged primarily in the service sectors (trade, transport, personal and business services).

Table 4.5

The number of active wage earners in partnerships without legal entity on 1 January 1993[a]

Branch of the economy	Active wage earners total	From this		Total	Share in national economy
		At partnerships without legal entity[b]	At individual entrepreneurs[b]		
Industrial	1119.9	35.3	149.5	184.8	16.5
Construction	255.8	15.9	78.9	94.8	37.1
Agriculture and forestry	391.9	2.4	123.5	125.9	32.1
Transportation	272.5	6.1	62.8	68.9	25.3
Post and telecomm.	75.2	0.3	-	-	-
Trade	574.5	30.9	213.9	244.8	42.6
Water management	51.9	0.1	-	-	-
Other productive activity	17.1	1.4	-	1.4	8.2
Personal and business serv.	223.1	15.0	37.1	52.1	23.4
Health and cultural serv.	636.2	2.3	2.7	5.0	0.8
Public serv., admin. & other	249.4	2.2	-	2.2	0.9
Total national economy	3867.5	111.9	668.4	779.9	20.2[c]

Notes: a   Calculations based on the balance of labour of CSO 1. January 1993. Table 2.2. (p. 12.)
　　　　b   With employees and family help.
　　　　c   Average.

Source: Laky, T. (1994).

With the increasing number of different types of private ventures (organizations, small producers, service providers, self-employed) the size structure is changing not only in manufacturing but in services too. The 'upside down' pyramid characterizing the size structure in Hungary and other former socialist countries (few small and medium-sized and many large units)[29] is increasingly done away with: first as a result of the rapid growth of small (and less so of medium-size) organizations of the service and also of the manufacturing sphere[30] the reverse pyramid is increasingly turned upside down.

b) Every country differentiates between small- and large-scale privatization. Small-scale privatization is the privatization of trade, catering, tourism, construction and personal and industrial services. Small-scale privatization attempts to divide the administratively created centralized state (local council) monopolies into relatively small units (shops) and the autonomous, functional smaller units thus created (e.g. small plants) are given into private ownership (rent in the case of premises). Large-scale privatization means breaking the monopoly position of large, monopolistic firms and giving them into private (national, foreign or mixed) ownership.

In the service sphere small-scale privatization has been more or less completed. As a result, in the wholesale and retail trade, in repair and maintenance, in dry-cleaning etc. the previously existing huge regional monopolies were divided and passed into private ownership. This process had already begun in 1987, before the change of the system. Concerning industrial and service cooperatives: a large part of them have been transformed under the Law of Transformation of 1988 (share warrants were issued). Others were transformed into joint-stock or limited liability companies or were liquidated.

The ownership structure of infrastructure and services was different in individual sectors:

- Energy, gas and water supply, the railway and road network is - and very probably will remain - as state or local government property. In the road transport of goods and passengers private ownership will become dominant.
- In telecommunications the state monopoly was dismantled: 30 per cent of the shares of the only large state property firm (MATÁV Rt.) was given into foreign ownership in December 1993 under a telecommunication concession. The law provides for the privatization of telephone services if certain conditions are met whereas the basic telephone trunk lines will remain state property. By winning radio telephone concessions, foreign firms (with the participation of Hungarian capital) enter the Hungarian radio telephone market.

-       Some two decades ago, with the assistance provided by preferential
        credits, private housing construction accelerated in Hungary. In the
        second half of the eighties some 60-70 per cent of housing
        construction (first of all in cities) was undertaken privately (with
        government credit). At the end of the eighties only 30-35 per cent of
        the housing stock was state property. This share will further diminish
        in the years of the change of the system since there is a continuous
        process of the sale (at preferential prices)[31] of state and local
        government flats to private owners.
-       With government (ministry) licence private schools can be set up at
        every level of public education (basic, medium and high)[32]; up to the
        present only a few private schools have been established. School
        buildings originally in church property and nationalized after World
        War II are given back to the church in a 10 year-long process where
        the churches concerned and local governments have to reach some
        compromise.

In the sphere of health[33] the private sector has already appeared (privately
owned consulting rooms, private clinics, full or part-time private practice of
physicians and dentists in state owned polyclinics). 95-98 per cent of
hospitals, polyclinics and nursing homes are state property (or more precisely
the property of the Health Insurance Self-government,[34] which was separated
in 1993 from the state but has no assets as yet[35] and whose authority is not
quite clear).

In the sphere of banking, insurance and finances, state property is still
dominant. Privatization of the 5 large commercial banks will start later this
year. In addition to this, several small, mixed ownership (foreign and
domestic) banks and financial institutions, and also some private insurance
firms were set up.

Almost the whole of business services are done (asset evaluation, brokering,
consulting firms etc.) by privately owned firms (the larger firms are foreign).
There is a large number of participants in this area and many of them are
prosperous. In recent years private (mixed or Hungarian) property appeared
and became dominant in the sphere of business services.

3. In the changes in property relations and the organization of infrastructure
and services, in services assisting market creation, in the modernization of
infrastructural networks and in the creation of new ones, and in the spread of
private foreign capital, credit and financing by large foreign banks have an
important role. Total foreign direct investment in Hungary amounted in 1988-
93 to USD 6 billion[36] which is more than 40 per cent of all the foreign
capital[37] invested in Central-Eastern-European (formerly socialist) countries.

30 per cent of foreign direct investment went into service sectors[38]: 11 per cent into financial services, 9 per cent into trade (foreign and domestic), 7 per cent into hotels and office buildings, and 3 per cent into transport and communication (not considering large national projects which are later dealt with separately).

There was a sudden increase in the number of mixed property (foreign and Hungarian) firms. Whereas in 1988 there were only 104 joint ventures in Hungary, in 1989 there were 1,114, and 16,810[39] in the first three quarters of 1993, 30 per cent of them were active (according to their main activity) in services (finances, trade, transport, communication, hotels, tourism etc.).[40] Foreign capital per joint venture[41] indicates that:

-    joint ventures in services have a lower capital stock than those in production[42];
-    their strategy is 'gain market with small risk: small investment, high return, market presence'.

A new phenomenon is that since 1991 Hungary is not only a capital importer but also - even though by small amounts - a capital exporter. In 1989 the creation of 78 joint ventures with Hungarian capital was registered abroad, in 1990 159, in 1991 367, in 1992 398. Thus by the end of 1992 1,002 such joint ventures were registered. Most of these ventures deal with barter and the retail trade (whether established in former socialist or in market economies).

In the past four years large international banks supported the modernization of transportation and the development of telecommunications with USD 940 million credit.[43]

The Hungarian government in the last three years created special funds, separate from the budget (Road Fund, Telecommunications Fund) to keep infrastructure functioning, to make up more rapidly for shortages, to develop and modernize these funds (e.g. the costs of roadbuilding included in the price of gas) by automatically securing the financial resources necessary for maintenance, development and modernization. The range of mixed-financing (state, local government, foreign and domestic investors) has widened.[44]

4. We ought to mention separately the turn in the development of Hungarian telecommunications. Although in the last 3-4 years per capita GDP decreased considerably, there was a large increase in telephone line density (main lines per 100 inhabitants): whereas in the eighties telephone main-line density grew at a rate of 4.5 per cent yearly, in the last 3-4 years the rate of growth attained the level of 9.6 per cent. As a result of this accelerated quantitative development Hungary's lag behind market economies at a similar level of development has been reduced. The quantitative shortage still existing is demonstrated by the fact that there are still 690,000 applicants (of this 265,000 in Budapest, 425,000 in the countryside) who have been waiting for years (sometimes for decades) for a line.

A qualitative change has been brought about in recent years by extending a modern, digital trunk line network. As a result all information systems can also be implemented and operated in Hungary which are available in developed market economies.

In December 1993 the natural monopoly Hungarian Telecommunications Corporation (MATÁV Rt) was privatized. The privatization tender was won by Deutsche Telecom and Ameritech. 60 per cent of the sum paid for a 30 per cent share in MATÁV Rt serves telecommunication development purposes, 40 per cent was paid into the central budget. There are promises that in 1996 a telephone line can be obtained (with all the attached services) within half a year, in 1998 within two weeks. It is certain that by first reducing, than abolishing the telephone shortage, by establishing a modern digital network, by providing all the modern information services and improving quality in the whole spectrum of telecommunications the competitiveness of the national economy can be improved and its appeal to foreign and domestic investors will be enhanced.

Although the monopoly of privatized MATÁV Rt over the digital trunk line will remain, in the case of services provided through this network its monopoly position will already erode in 1994. In the case of services provided through the network tough competition will arise.

In recent years regional differences in the telephone supply have diminished somewhat but they are still important. This is demonstrated by Table 4.6. The data of the table shows that the difference between the telephone supply of the capital and that of other towns was 1:2 in 1992, that between towns and the countryside 1:3, finally that between Budapest and the countryside 1:7.

Table 4.6
Telephone main lines per 100 inhabitants in Hungary, 1992

	Population		Main lines		Main lines
	1,000 inhabit.	%	1,000	%	density
Budapest	2,100	20.3	539	41.8	25.7
Cities	4,200	40.8	578	44.8	13.8
Rural areas	4,000	38.9	174	13.4	4.4

Source: Statistical Yearbook of the Hungarian Post Office, 1992.

In the above we have outlined only the most important changes which have occurred since the change of the system in the field dealt with here. The description shows that everything is in a flux, in a transitional state. Changes and shifts demonstrate that infrastructure and services were a stabilizing factor for the shrinking economy, that in certain infrastructural and service areas there was considerable progress, and that former quantitative shortages have been eased or abolished. It appears from the changes outlined above that quantitative development was strongest in the institutional system of the financial sector, in low capital-intensity services and in telecommunications. In other infrastructural and service areas the positive impact of the changes in ownership structure, in the diversity of ownership forms and with it the intensification of competition and organizational reshuffling are less perceptible.

During the rule of the first freely elected Hungarian government no comprehensive strategic program for the economy has been developed. Only half a year before the expiration of its mandate (at the end of 1993) did they begin to develop, in a hurry, the long term (up to 2000 or 2005) concept of transportation and telecommunications (radio, television and post included). The development program of transportation was completed by early 1994. The work on the development concept of telecommunications, radio, television and post was halted by the minister in April 1994 after the first variant was ready in March 1994. For want of a macroeconomic strategy and of comprehensive development programs at branch level investment into transportation and telecommunication was a mere reaction to compelling shortage situations.

To support my opinion just mention one single fact. In 1993, on the proposal of the government parliament adopted the Act on Telecommunications. I think it was a serious mistake by the ministry and the government that parliamentary adoption of the Act on Telecommunications (and of MATÁV Rt privatization, and other concessions) preceded the working out and adoption of a telecommunications strategy. In my opinion the Act on Telecommunications should have been preceded by a telecommunications strategy shaped in a professional debate and then adopted unanimously. Since this has not happened, a paradox and awkward situation has arisen in Hungary: the telecommunications strategy has to be adapted to the already passed Act on Telecommunications. Even the modification of the Act on Telecommunications cannot be ruled out (maybe this would be the better solution).

But all is not lost that is delayed as the saying goes. I think the most important task of the new government to be elected in 1994 during the first 100 days of its rule would be to work out a macroeconomic strategy[45]. This could provide the basis for longer term development concepts for infrastructure and services.

There was an important increase in the number and activity of financial institutions, banks, insurance companies and other financial organizations and institutions necessary for the market economy (broker, consulting, asset evaluating etc.). However, their appropriate functioning is hindered by several factors. Such factors are: lack of capital, slow development of the infrastructural network necessary for the rapid fulfilment of international and domestic financial transactions, the constant delay of the much heralded giro-system, the lack of qualified specialists, the dominance of state property in the banking sphere, the delay in privatization, and oligopoly in the insurance sector.

Hungary is a small open country at a medium level of development, exporting 30-35 per cent of its output, with considerable tourism, and a central location between East and West. The country's inclusion in the international division of labour, raising its productivity and competitiveness, requires its infrastructural networks and service to be developed in harmony with the countries of the European Union and the neighbouring former socialist countries struggling with similar problems and dilemmas.

Appendix

The method was worked out in the early seventies[46] with the aim of determining relative levels and their change in time for the whole infrastructure and its main areas over the last 100 years.

In order to quantify the infrastructural level we assembled a set of indicators.[47] The method used to quantify relative levels synthesizes physical indicators of this international data base.

We calculated relative level indicators from physical indicators in five infrastructural areas. The indicator of infrastructure as a whole is obtained by averaging the indicators of the five areas.

The relative level of infrastructural development is measured by scores. The highest value of a physical indicator in the year of the comparison is considered to be 100 and scores for other countries range between 0 and 100. What follows from the relative level of individual countries is the arithmetic average of these scores. 100 score relative level means a fictitious country who has the largest value with every physical indicator. The score of individual countries is the infrastructural level of the individual country as a percentage of the level of the fictitious country.

The primary role of the scores is to determine relative infrastructural levels of countries. In addition to that the change of relative levels can also be traced: a change in the scores shows that in the given period the infrastructural level of two countries converged or diverged, whether a country caught up with another one etc. It follows from the nature of the method that the scores are not suitable to measure the dynamics of the infrastructural level of individual countries relative to themselves.

One should stress that the set of physical indicators assembled is hardly able to reflect differences in the quality of services. Similarly, they do not reflect differences in the state of infrastructure (whether it is maintained or rundown). As a result, ill-maintained, obsolete infrastructures and countries with such infrastructures obtain better values in the comparison than the true situation deserves, contrary to countries with a high level, well-maintained infrastructure.

As all international comparisons, this too has a far larger error margin than national statistics have. Our scores and rank orders built on them thus only approach reality.[48]

Bibliography

Árvay, J., Lenotti, K. et al. (1993) *Database*. Hungarian Statistical Office. Prepared in the framework of the 'Eastern and Central Europe 2000' European Community Project. Manuscript. Forthcoming in 1994.

Árvay, J., Vértes, A. (1994) *A magánszektor és a rejtett gazdaság súlya Magyarországon (1980-1992)* (The private sector and the hidden economy in Hungary, 1980-1992). Summary. GKI Gazdaságkutató Rt., Budapest.

Csáki, Gy. (1993) *Foreign direct investments and joint ventures in Hungary: a basic issue of transformation towards market economy*. Study prepared for JETRO. Budapest. 17 December, 1993.

Csernok, A., Ehrlich, É. and Szilágyi, Gy. (1972) 'Hundred Year of Infrastructural Development: An International Comparison.' *Acta Oeconomica*. Vol. 9. No. 1.

Csernok, A., Ehrlich, É. and Szilágyi, Gy. (1975) *Infrastruktúra. Korok és országok, 1860-1968* (Infrastructure. Ages and Countries, 1860-1968). Kossuth Könyvkiadó. Budapest.

Csizmadia, M., Ehrlich, É. and Pártos, Gy. (1984) 'The Effects of Recession on Infrastructure'. *Acta Oeconomica*, Vol.32. No.3-4.

Ehrlich, É. (1978) 'An international comparison of infrastructural development' in Levcik, F. (ed.), *International Economics-Comparisons and Interdependences.* Springer-Verlag, Wien-New York.

Ehrlich, É. (1985) 'Infrastructure' in Kaser, M.C. and Radice, E.A. (eds.), *The Economic History of Eastern Europe, 1919-1975,* Clarendon Press, Oxford.

Ehrlich, É. (1990) 'Nemzetközi összehasonlítás a szolgáltatásokról, 1960-1983' (International comparison of Services, 1960-1983) *Gazdaság,* No.1.

Ehrlich, É. and Révész, G. (1993) *Present and a feasible future in Hungary,* 1985-2005. Manuscript. Forthcoming.

Ehrlich, É. and Révész, G. (1994) 'Várakozások és valóság' (Folyamatok 1989-1993 között) (Expectations and reality. Processes between 1989-1993). *Közgazdasági Szemle,* No.3.

Fleischer, T. (1988) *Az ellátottság terjedése a településhálózaton* (The spread of supply in the network of settlements). Institute for World Economics of the Hungarian Academy of Sciences. Manuscript. Published in 1992. Comitatas. Dec.

Fleischer, T. (1989) *Egy környezet- és szolgáltatásorientált gazdaságfejlesztési modell vázlata* Prepared for the Institute of Transport Sciences. Manuscript. Published in 1992: Gyorsjelentés, az építési piac tájékoztatója. No.12.

Incze, Zs. (1988) *Magyarország megyéinek infrastrukturális színvonala, 1980-1985* (Infrastructural levels of the counties in Hungary, 1980-1985). Institute for World Economics of the Hungarian Academy of Sciences. Manuscript.

Laky, T. (1987) 'Elosztott mítoszok - tétova szándékok' (Myths evaporated - vacillating intents). *Valóság,* No.7.

Laky, T. (1994) *A vállalkozók és a vállalkozások az 1990-es évek kezdetén* (Entrepreneurs and ventures in the early nineties). Manuscript.

Major, I. (1993) *Infrastruktúra-fejlesztés és gazdasági növekedés* (Development of Infrastructure and the Economic Growth). Institute of the Hungarian Academy of Sciences. Manuscript.

Orosz, É. (1993) *Two possible scenarios for health care* Prepared for the Project titled 'Eastern and Central Europe 2000' for the European Community. Manuscript. Forthcoming.

Petschnig, M.Z. (1994) *Örökségtől örökségig* (From Heritage to Heritage). Századvég Kiadó, Budapest.

Révész, G. (1986) 'On the expansion and functioning of the direct market sector of the Hungarian economy'. *Acta Oeconomica,* 36. No. 1-2.

Schamschula, Gy. (1994) *Magyarország 2000-ig* (Hungary up to 2000). Kráter Műhely Egyesület, Budapest.

Statistical Bulletin 1993/3 (1994) KSH. Budapest.

Schweitzer, I. (1982) *Vállalatméret* (Size of Enterprise), Közgazdasági és Jogi Könyvkiadó, Budapest.

VÁTI (1982) *A magyarországi megyék infrastrukturális színvonala* (Infrastructural levels of the Hungarian counties). Várostervezési Intézet (VÁTI). Vol. 1-2-3-4.

Notes

1   Csernok, A., Ehrlich, É. and Szilágyi, Gy. (1972) and (1975); Ehrlich, É. (1978); Csizmadia, M., Ehrlich, É. and Pártos, Gy. (1984); Ehrlich, É. (1990).

2   In this type of development infrastructure far preceded modern industrialization. Therefore the process of modern industrialization in several European countries at the end of the 18th and at the beginning of the 19th century could be based on an infrastructural base created in former social-economic formations. The most characteristic examples of this development are England, The Netherlands and Belgium.

3   In this development type the development of industrialization and infrastructure proceeded from the first third of the 19th century in parallel, instigating one another. The most characteristic example of this type is the United States.

4   Csernok, A., Ehrlich, É. and Szilágyi, Gy. (1975).

5   We are working on an international comparison of infrastructure and service levels for the nineties. Although the calculations have not been completed as yet, one can already see that the place of Hungary in the international rank order did not improve in the period 1984-90 but very probably deteriorated (like that of other former socialist countries).

6   Fleischer, T. (1989).

7   2/3 to 3/4 of Hungarian families are attached in one way or another to the so-called second economy, agricultural small scale production on household plots included. Work done in the second economy is the equivalent of full time work of one and a half million people (30 per cent of the total of actively employed). Half of the activity in the second economy is agricultural, a further 25-30 per cent service and some 20-25 per cent industrial (Révész, G. [1986], Laky, T. [1987]).

8   E.g. changing rules of taxation, administrative regulations, the difficulties of buying material, machinery and parts on both the domestic and the foreign market, the long time needed for obtaining different licences etc.

9   The share of infrastructure in investment was 30 per cent in the fifties - below a very high rate of accumulation. This share approached by the mid-seventies 50 per cent and by 1989 - with a considerable yearly fluctuation - 55 per cent. When evaluating this fairly high percentage we have to take into account that from 1978 the investment to GDP ratio diminished abruptly: the 33 per cent share of net

accumulation in 1978 decreased to 24 per cent by 1979, to 14 per cent by 1982 and to 11-12 per cent by the end of the eighties. Source: Statistical yearbooks and publications, CSO, Budapest. Thus the relatively high share of infrastructure within investment signified a modest growth in volume.

10   In the share of the service sector in employment there was a turnaround in the seventies. This was the first period when labour was acquired by this sector - unlike all the other socialist countries - not from agriculture but increasingly from industry. In Hungary in the seventies the decrease of the number and share of industrial employment had already begun. Since the growing service sphere took up an unlimited number of workers released from other sectors (if we also take into account the workforce employed by the second economy) full employment (or more precisely overemployment) remained.

11   Source: different propositions by the Planning Office, Hungarian Statistical Yearbooks, the unofficial conception of the Ministry of Transport, Telecommunication and Water Management from March 1994 called Közlekedés 2000 (Transport 2000).

12   Orosz, É. (1993); Ehrlich, É. and Révész, G. (1993).

13   The unfavourable position of Pest county (excluding Budapest) is caused by the proximity of Budapest. Although the infrastructure of Budapest serves Pest county too, it is conspicuous that its catchment area lacks even basic infrastructural networks of its own.

14   Fleischer, T. (1988).

15   Fleischer, T. (1989).

16   Ehrlich, É. (1993).

17   I used for the evaluation ideas from the studies Ehrlich, É. and Révész, G. (1993) and (1994); and Major, I. (1993).

18   See more on this in Ehrlich, É. and Révész, G. (1994).

19   Macroeconomic indicators of the economy are the following:

Table 4.7
Macroeconomic indicators of the economy
(previous year = 100 %)

Year	1990	1991	1992	1992/1989
GDP produced	96.5	88.1	95.5	81.2
of this:				
industry	92.1	81.9	94.1	71.0
agriculture, forestry	95.1	91.8	86.3	75.5
services	103.1	94.4	99.1	96.9

Note: Preliminary data.
Sources: 1989-91: Árvay, J., Lenotti, K. et al. (1993).
        1992: Statistical Bulletin 1993/3 (1994) KSH, Budapest

20   Changes in the consumer price index are the following

Table 4.8

Changes in the consumer price index*

	Total	Services
1990	128.9	-
1991	135.0	141.9
1992 I-IV quarter	123.0	126.0
1993 I-III quarter	122.8	123.2

*   corresponding period of the previous year = 100

Source: Statistical Bulletin 1993/3 (1994). KSH. Budapest.

21   This datum includes organizations in a majority or totally private ownership after the privatization of state organizations and the transformation of cooperatives. (Ehrlich, É. and Révész, G. [1993] and [1994]).

22   A research report from the end of 1993 presented GDP including the estimated output of the hidden economy. Breakdown of this 'extended GDP' according to form of property is as follows:

Table 4.9

Data of the 'extended GDP'

	1980	1985	1989	1990	1991	1992
State sector	83	79	74	70	63	50
Domestic private sector	17	21	26	29	34	42
Private sector foreigners	0	0	0	1	3	8
Total	100	100	100	100	100	100

The report was submitted to the Blue Ribbon Committee formed by Canadian, American and Hungarian specialists. See Árvay, J. and Vértes, A. (1994).

23   Source: Statistical Bulletin 1993/3 (1994).

24   Source: Statistical Bulletin 1993/3 (1994).

25   We have to differentiate between entrepreneur and self-employed due to the differences in their behaviour. See more on this in Laky, T. (1994).

26   With the spread of unemployment all over the world entrepreneurs of necessity are people without a job or income, thereby compelled to start a venture.

27   Their vanguard is constituted in both industry and services by craftsmen and retail traders. Their activity does not require knowledge obtained through a several years long training. Several of these activities do not require any capital. Among the self-employed we find people whose activity requires special knowledge, an own shop, special machinery, equipment, i.e. considerable capital. The majority of the self-employed are satisfied if they can keep their business, their family and themselves with the work of one person. Under favourable conditions real ventures emerge and entrepreneurs, who growth-oriented and ready for change arise from their ranges (Laky, T. [1994]).

28   The figure of self-employment is a reliable indicator of economic development within broad ranges. In 1990 in EFTA countries and in the United States the share of self-employed in total employment from industry and services was 7-8 per cent, in the 12 countries of the European Community 13 per cent, in Italy and Greece 20 per cent, in Spain and Portugal 15 per cent. The share of self-employment in Hungary (20 per cent at the beginning of 1993) was in line with the

present development level of the country. (Source Employment in Europe [1993], quoted by Laky, T. [1994] p.25.)

29   Schweitzer, I. (1982).

30   Favourable changes in the size structure of manufacturing are the result of three related processes two of which are related to services. On the one hand the international tendency whereby service activities ready to adapt to changing needs broke away from manufacturing (and from agriculture) appeared in Hungary too. On the other hand monopoly positions are dwindling away: large manufacturing organizations and former service firms are split into smaller units. Finally part of the survival strategy and of asset hiding manipulations of former subsidized huge production firms is to give autonomy to their viable smaller units and secure conditions for their survival.

31   A large part of housing estate buildings in state, cooperative and/or local council property need expensive repair. When privatizing flats in these blocks, a low price and downpayment is offered to compensate for the large investment these assets require.

32   On medium level special training has been given on two channels up to the recent past. On the one hand it was done in high schools within the state educational system and on the other in large, state owned firms. Since 1/3 of current state own manufacturing plans went bankrupt (a few successful large manufacturing firms passed into foreign ownership) large state firms struggling with financial problems, insecurity of the environment and a fighting for survival discontinued training for their workers. With the shrinking of the economy and the spreading of unemployment (12 per cent in 1993) the government started a so-called active employment policy by teaching new trades and providing for further training courses etc.

33   A dual structure is characteristic of the Hungarian health sector and its most serious problem. The 'official' state health sector was intermingled with a semi-legal private sector within state institutions, based on tips. Tips are general. This is a tacit agreement between the state, the health sector and the population. (See more on this in Ehrlich, É. and Révész, G. [1994] p.171.)

34   The Law prescibes that the government has to give assets to the Health Security Self-government to the value of HUF 300 billion. It is not clear as yet what these assets will be, how, when, or in what form the transfer will materialize.

35   The leading organ of the health insurance self-government has 30 voting members from the employer, and 30 from the employee side. The responsible committees of parliament and the government have a non-voting member of each these bodies.

36   The development of direct foreign investment in Hungary is shown by the table below:

Table 4.10
The development of direct foreign investment in Hungary

Period	USD million
1972-84	40
1985-86	70
1987	80
1988	430
1989	550
1990	900
1991	1700
1992	1641
1993 up to June	651
Total	6062

Source: Csáki, Gy. (1993) p.20.

37   Whereas in the first half of 1993 per capita foreign investment in Hungary amounted to USD 600, in Slovenia to USD 300, in the Czech Republic to USD 180, in Slovakia to USD 100, in Poland to USD 50. 29 per cent of direct foreign investment came from the USA, 20 per cent from Germany, 14 per cent from Austria, 7 per cent from France, 6 per cent from Italy, 5 per cent from Japan, 4 - 4 per cent from the Netherlands and the United Kingdom, 11 per cent from other countries. (Csáki, Gy. [1993] p.20.)

38   Source: State Property Agency. Quoted by Csáki, Gy. (1993) Appendix 9 and p.21.

39   Petschnig, M.Z. (1994) p.178.

40   Source: State Property Agency.

41   See Petschnig, M.Z. (1994) p.178.

42   In the first half of 1993, 15.7 per cent of joint ventures in the manufacturing industry accounted for 35 per cent of the capital, 54 per cent in trade and repair accounted for 17 per cent of the capital. Csáki, Gy. (1993) Appendix p.4.

43   In the last four years the Ministry of Transportation, Telecommunication and Water Management raised the following credits from large international banks:

Table 4.11
Credits from international banks of Ministry of TTWM

Creditor	- Area	Amount*
IBRD	Transportation.I.-II.-III.	284
IBRD	Telecommunication I.-II.	220
EBRD	Road I.	26
EBRD	Telecommunication I.	122
EBRD	Radio teleph. (Westel)	10
EBRD+IFC	Telecommunication	60
		30
EIB	Road	62
EIB	Air transport	25
EIB	Telecommunication I.	100
Total		939

*   USD million

Source: Schamschula, Gy. (1994) p.64.

44   They finance the transport corridor linking Budapest with Vienna and Europe (M1 highway, Hegyeshalom-Budapest railway modernization), the further development of the highway network, the accelerated electrification of railways, and the modernization of the rolling stock. (Schamschula, Gy. [1994] p.547-58.)

45   As all the important parties produced before the 1994 elections more or less detailed programs for development, the ruling parties of the future - whoever they may be - already have a strategy at least for the period of their mandate.

46   Csernok, A., Ehrlich, É. and Szilágyi, Gy. (1972).

47   Magdolna Csizmadia (Central Statistical Office) took part in the selection of indicators for 1980. She performed calculations necessary for the international comparison for 1980 and took part in the evaluation of results for 1960 and 1980.

48   Detailed description of the methods see Csernok, A., Ehrlich, É. and Szilágyi, Gy. (1975).

PART II
TECHNOLOGICAL LEVEL, COMPETITIVENESS AND R&D

5 Productivity lag and intellectual background

György Molnár - Tamás Tarján

1. Introduction

The productivity lag between Hungary and Western Europe amounts to about 15-20 years. The problem, however, is even more profound: the backwardness is not simply a matter of productivity or technology but that of the global economic and social structure.

The backwardness as compared to Western Europe is not of a recent origin. As far as the social structure is concerned Hungary levelled the western standard in the late 15th century for the last time, and even at that time with some 'simpler tissue', or with 'some differences in degrees' only[1]. Since then it has developed (or sometimes stagnated) together with the other East-Central-European countries as an in-between region between the West and East. *From this perspective,* socialism was simply an experience encompassing the whole society which aimed at escaping from the deadlock, eliminating backwardness.

But socialism itself has proved to be a deadlock. After a first period of rather fast development, the economy got stuck in a crisis, so that backwardness has even been aggravated. This has been true not only in quantitative but also in structural terms: while the socialist system managed to eliminate some feudal features and brought about an industrialization of great importance, on the other hand the infrastructure and the service sectors remained very heavily underdeveloped (that, we emphasize once more, is not simply a problem of economic development but that of the social structure). On the other hand two elements of the infrastructure partly for political-ideological reasons were preferred, so that shortly after the Second World War the build up of the schooling system and the research and development network (and in this way accumulation of some kind of intellectual potential) started to develop at a fast rate.

In recent years the countries of the region had for the first time, in a long while, a gleam of hope to join the main stream of development, and to get closer from the periphery to the centre. The adherence of Hungary (and more generally the East-Central-European region) at some time in the future to the Single European Market represents first of all a means necessary to this achievement. All these considerations justify that -especially in the first phase of our research work - we should deal with the long-term processes instead of short-term details of technical nature of the adherence to the Single European Market.

2. The development of Hungarian productivity on an international scale

We cannot go back to the 15th century with time series but from the middle of the previous century we have got more or less reliable data.

In the last third of the past century, up to the end of World War I for some 50 years Austria and Hungary formed a common Monarchy. Both countries have lost the two World Wars. They are similar as to their area and population. The area of Austria is 90 per cent of that of Hungary, its population 70 per cent. Both countries are poor in natural resources. Hungary has good endowments for agriculture whereas Austria had considerable industrial potential already under the Monarchy. Hungary was the bread-basket of the Monarchy. This division of labour was favourable for Austria. It was not in the interests of Vienna for Hungary to be strong in industry. Thus during the Monarchy in Hungary it was first of all agriculture and industries connected with it that developed. In the second half of the past century Hungary surpassed Austria as to agricultural production and the 72 per cent lead of Austria in productivity (measured by per capita GDP) has diminished to 44 per cent (see Table 5.1).

Table 5.1
Per capita GDP in the Austro-Hungarian Monarchy in 1850-1913

	in 1850		1911-1913 average	
	Austria	Hungary	Austria	Hungary
Per capita GDP (in crown)	107.0	62.2	517.0	360.0
Share of (in per cent)				
agriculture	57.0	81.7	33.7	64.0
industry and extraction	27.8	11.5	46.7	25.8
trade and communication	15.2	6.8	19.6	10.2
Total	100.0	100.0	100.0	100.0

In the period between the two World Wars, development of Austria and Hungary was more or less parallel. After World War II Hungary entered the road of socialism. Following the Soviet model it started a forced industrialization. Since this overlapped the post-war reconstruction period, the economy produced spectacular results up to the early sixties when the possibilities for extensive development were definitely exhausted. At that time the country experimented with introducing market elements in the economy. As a result, the development of Hungarian economy was more favourable than the average of the other socialist countries but by the eighties it turned out that this is still not enough since the lead of Austria compared to Hungary - measured by purchasing power parity (PPP) per capita GDP - increased from 41 per cent in 1975 to 85 per cent in 1980, 113 per cent in 1985 and 144 per cent in 1990 (see Figure 5.1 and Table 5.2). Let us remark that in Figure 5.1 the Hungarian data are adjusted with PPP while in Table 5.2 they are not. Therefore in Figure 5.1 the Hungarian time series decrease from 1975 while in Table 5.2 the Hungarian data increased during this century.

Beside the historical reasons comparison with Austria is relevant for Hungary since Austria is another country trying to join the Single European Market (even if from a better starting position).

We shortly (only on Figures) present two more comparisons. Comparison with Finland is important (beyond the remote kinship) because it is another small European country like Austria and because both are contiguous with the former CMEA and aspiring after membership in Unified Europe. Finland is particularly interesting for us since it had a strong economic relationship

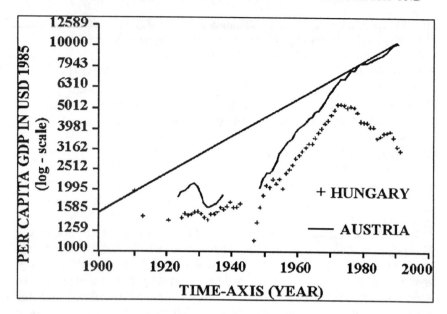

Figure 5.1 Comparison of Austria and Hungary

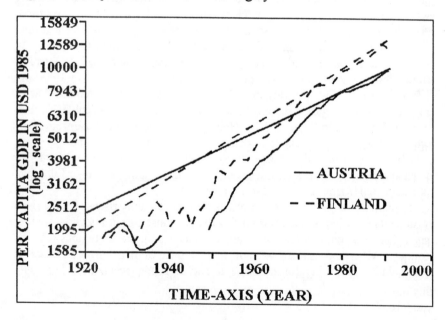

Figure 5.2 Comparison of Austria and Finland

with the Soviet Union and profited from this relationship much more than Hungary did and could precede even Austria (see Figure 5.2).

Italy is important for us since North Italy had strong ties during its history with Austria and produced in the last 15 years spectacular results (see Figure 5.3). Important is also the fact that in Italy for a long time one third of GDP was produced by the black economy. It is the same with Hungary.

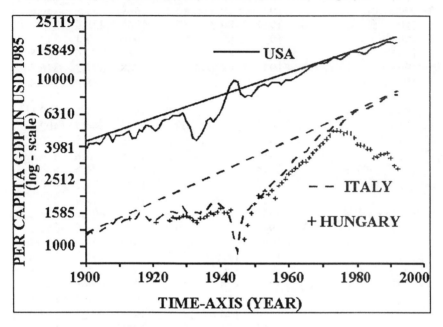

Figure 5.3 Comparison of USA, Italy and Hungary

How many years are we behind Austria?

In 1990-91 a wide ranging international comparison project was completed - under the leadership of George F. Ray, a scientific adviser to the London based National Institute of Economic and Social Research - to reveal how large the technological lag of former Eastern-European socialist countries[2] is. The research project concentrated on the state in 1989 in smaller CMEA countries similar to Hungary. Research workers from Bulgaria, Czech Republic, Slovakia, Poland and Hungary participated. When we were starting this research project we did not anticipate the rapid collapse of the statistical systems of CMEA and the Eastern-European countries.

Table 5.2
The volume of national product and national income
in Austria and Hungary in the 20th century[*]

Year	A	H	Year	A	H	Year	A	H
1900	-	49.4	1931	91.7	85.7	1962	210.2	234.0
1901	-	-	1932	82.3	81.6	1963	218.7	247.1
1902	-	-	1933	79.5	79.4	1964	231.9	256.6
1903	-	-	1934	80.2	86.6	1965	238.6	257.8
1904	-	-	1935	81.8	87.2	1966	252.1	278.1
1905	-	-	1936	84.2	91.5	1967	259.6	300.8
1906	-	-	1937	88.7	97.7	1968	271.2	316.3
1907	-	-	1938	93.2	95.5	1969	288.3	341.4
1908	-	-	1939	-	100.4	1970	308.8	358.1
1909	-	-	1940	-	107.9	1971	324.6	379.6
1910	-	-	1941	-	100.6	1972	344.7	402.6
1911	-	-	1942	-	101.2	1973	361.5	430.9
1912	-	66.2	1943	-	106.3	1974	375.8	456.0
1913	97.5	-	1944	-	-	1975	374.5	484.6
1914	-	-	1945	-	-	1976	391.6	498.9
1915	-	-	1946	-	-	1977	409.4	534.7
1916	-	-	1947	-	61.2	1978	409.6	556.2
1917	-	-	1948	-	80.3	1979	429.0	562.2
1918	-	-	1949	100.0	100.0	1980	441.5	557.4
1919	-	-	1950	112.4	119.4	1981	440.3	571.8
1920	-	-	1951	120.2	138.5	1982	445.0	586.1
1921	-	56.0	1952	120.5	136.1	1983	453.8	587.3
1922	-	-	1953	125.2	152.8	1984	460.1	601.6
1923	-	-	1954	136.0	145.6	1985	471.3	593.2
1924	86.4	-	1955	151.1	157.6	1986	476.9	598.0
1925	92.2	65.2	1956	158.8	139.7	1987	486.3	623.1
1926	93.7	78.8	1957	168.1	171.9	1988	505.1	619.5
1927	96.6	74.7	1958	175.1	181.4	1989	525.2	612.3
1928	101.1	78.0	1959	179.9	193.4	1990	539.2	592.7
1929	102.6	84.8	1960	194.9	211.3	1991	547.8	533.2
1930	99.7	87.6	1961	205.3	220.8	1992	556.0	509.2

Notes: A   Austria, GNP/GDP
        H   Hungary, NNP/NMP
        *   1949 = 100
        GNP   Gross national product
        GDP   Gross domestic product
        NNP   Net national product
        NMP   Net material product

Sources: Mitchell (1975); KSH(a); OECD (1993)

Now we know that this was a last minute effort at measurement.

The research included the most important industrial technologies introduced in developed industrial countries after World War II. We investigated the latest so-called 'high-tech' production systems and products, energy production and consumption, international patenting and research and development.

As a final conclusion of the research we estimated the technological lag of Hungary's industry behind that of Austria to be 15-20 years. This is an average for the industry, the figure is larger in heavy industry and smaller in light industry. Our research did not include agriculture, food industry and services. In service sectors the lag is probably larger than in most industrial sectors.

How many years are needed for catching up?

We know that to answer this question is very difficult even if strong simplifications are allowed. An answer like 'to eliminate a 20 years long lag requires 20 years' is overly simplified. The correct answer is much more complicated.

First of all we have to be clear about what we think to be catching up with Austria, since Austria too will develop in the meantime. Therefore, first we have to estimate the development of Austria 10-20 years ahead. This is not an easy task either. A much easier goal would be e.g. to reach in 2000 the 1989 level of Austria (shooting at a motionless target) than to say that the difference between purchasing power parity per capita GDP between Austria and Hungary should not be more than 30 per cent (shooting at a manoeuvring target). Catching up with Austrian productivity level (0 per cent difference) does not seem to be a realistic target for the immediate future. We assumed a 30 per cent productivity advantage for Austria since this was the best ratio during the history of Austria and Hungary – reached about the time when World War I was breaking out. (Between 1911 and 1913 the Hungarian per capita GDP was exactly 70 per cent of that of Austria, see Table 5.1.)

Jánossy (1966, 1971) when analyzing post-war reconstruction periods formulated a relatively simple relationship for the time path of the quantity of production. The law can thus be formulated for the classic case of reconstruction period: if economic growth up to the war was unabated, the logarithm of time series data on the quantity of production for the periods before the war and after the reconstruction period will fall under a so-called trend-line which by definition is a straight line connecting the outstanding quantities of production plotted on logscale. In other words: economic reconstruction does not terminate when the production reaches the level before the war, but rather lasts up to the time when the output reaches the level which might have been attained in a given year if the war had not occurred at all. Jánossy saw the reason of this that in a reconstruction period the human capital as a production factor has a preponderant role over that played by technology. Knowing this law we might have avoided many economic policy errors during post-war reconstruction[3]. These errors were caused by extrapolating the short-term tendencies of a transitory reconstruction period.

The question arises immediately whether the present catching up process could be conceived as a Jánossy-type reconstruction period. In a loose interpretation it certainly can. During the 65-year long period up to World War I and the two decades between the two world wars Hungary's economic development was more dynamic than that of Austria. This market-based development was halted first by World War II then by the socialist experiment. Since 1989 Hungary (but also the whole Eastern-European region) has been struggling to establish a market economy and catch up with Western-Europe. If we are facing a Jánossy-type reconstruction period then during the post-1989 reconstruction (catching up) the trend of economic development from 1850 to 1973 should prevail.

Relying on Jánossy's theory we could say the only chance for Hungary is to reach again the trend-line already reached before World War I and for a few years in the early seventies.

The 'only' remaining question is when we will reach this Hungarian 20th century trend-line parallel with the Austrian[4]. The almost one hundred years long time series of Austria and Hungary justify the general opinion that reconstruction periods after wars bring abrupt recovery whereas after the trough of the business cycle growth comes slowly. In our opinion the present crisis - although it is not a purely economic crisis - will be similar in this respect to economic crises. Bródy in his forecast for the period 1992-2004, based on long (68 years) time series sketches such a future[5].

Let us depart from the optimistic but realistic assumption of Bródy that by 1999 we can attain the purchasing power parity real per capita GDP of the year 1989 and afterwards the Hungarian time series will grow at its top 20th century rate of 5 per cent. Then we can attain our 1910 and 1970 relative position to Austria in 2025 the earliest. This result can be read from Figure 5.4 which is a continuation of Figure 5.1 to 2030 and a parallel shift of the trend-line of the fifties and sixties (with growth rate of 5 per cent in the post-war reconstruction period) into the starting point of the 1989 real per capita GDP (assumed to prevail in 1999).

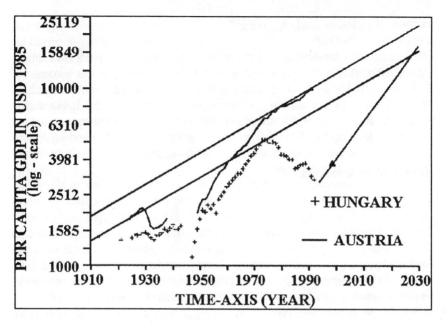

Figure 5.4 Forecast up to 2030 for Hungary

During our train of thought it was assumed that we are facing a case of Jánossy-type reconstruction period. Of course this is the optimistic scenario of the possible future development, which requires hard preconditions to be held. From these conditions the most important is the maintaining and further development of the accumulated human capital. If these conditions do not prevail, one can take as probable that a considerably more unfavourable scenario would be materializing, which in the best case would mean a development parallel with that of Austria, and would perpetuate our relative backwardness and impede any genuine integration to the Single European Market.

One important element of the human capital, the educational system, is treated by other papers of the workshop. Another element, the R&D, is in closer connection with the production process. Now, we are going to deal with the state of this field.

3. The situation of R&D before 1989

The accelerated development of the research and development network which began after World War II lasted in some East-Central-European countries until the early 80s while in others it ended in the mid or late 80s. As a result of this, the ratio of researchers and engineers employed in the R&D sector related to the economically active population has reached and even exceeded that of highly developed countries. This is shown in Table 5.3 and on Figure 5.5 attached thereto which depict the situation after 1970, failing appropriate data from the previous period[6].

The relative number of researchers and engineers employed in the R&D sector grew dynamically further in the 80s almost everywhere in the world but significant restructuring can be observed on Figure 5.6. From our point of view, the most important change is that the relevant index uniquely started to decrease in the second half of the 80s in Hungary. At the same time, Hungary still occupies an outstanding position if compared to its development level.

We get a similar picture if we compare material expenditures instead of direct human expenditures. Table 5.4 presents the proportion of R&D expenditures within the GNP.

In 1975 Hungary was the first of all countries! After this the Hungarian index started to fall while in all other countries (with the exception of the South American countries shown in our table) the ratio was growing. Figure 5.7 compares the data of 1975 and 1989 (where the appropriate value was missing we took the data of the year nearest or we calculated the average on the basis of the growth trend). We can establish from Figure 5.7 that, despite the regression, Hungary still occupied an outstanding position among the ranking of countries in 1989.

As we have seen, these R&D expenditures are very high in Hungary if compared to the relative level of GDP. Many critics say that it was senseless to develop the Hungarian R&D sector so intensively because its results were not sufficiently reflected in the overall economic development. However, this view does not take into account the fact that the entire, so called socialist, economy was operating with low efficiency and that is why it got into a general crisis by the end of the 80s. On this basis, the argument that expenditures were not in line with the results is true for any other sector of the economy.

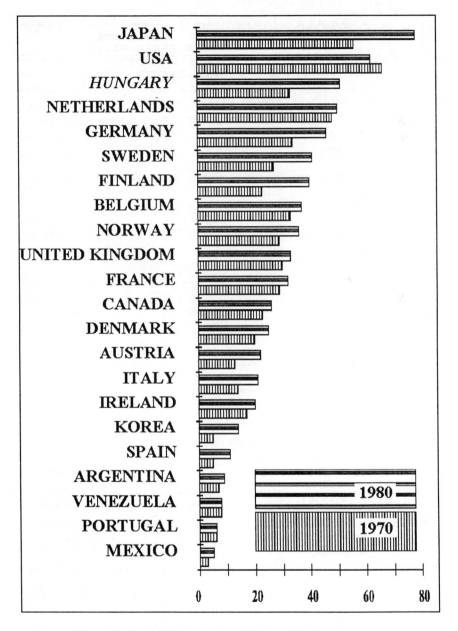

Figure 5.5   Ratio of R&D scientist, 1970 and 1980
             (Based on Table 5.3)

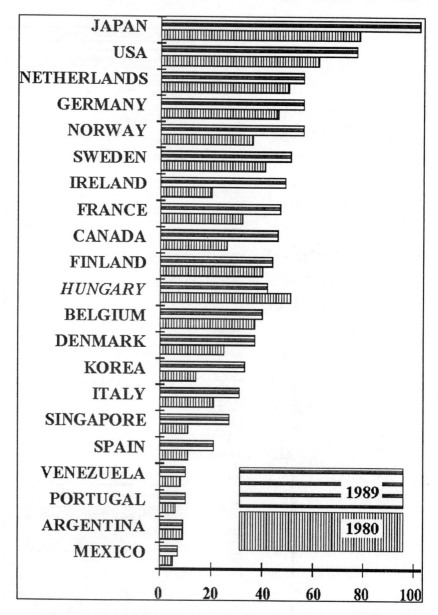

Figure 5.6   Ratio of R&D scientist, 1980 and 1989
               (Based on Table 5.3)

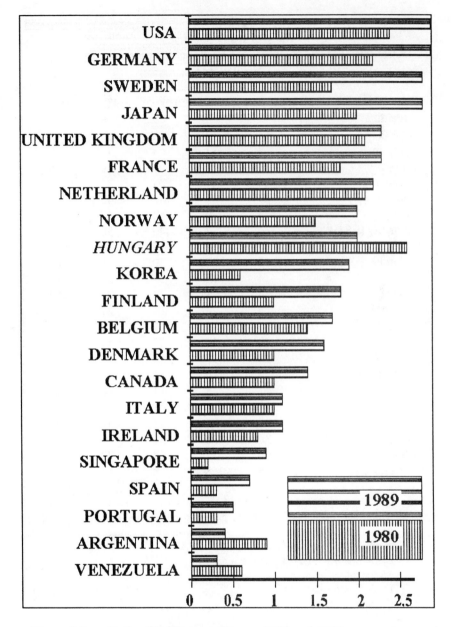

Figure 5.7   Ratio of R&D expenditures, 1975 and 1989
              (Based on Table 5.4)

Table 5.3
Ratio of R&D scientists
(R&D scientists and engineers per 10,000 of the economically active
population[a])

	1970	1975	1980	1985	1989
Argentina	7	8.	9	9	9
Austria	13	17	22	23	-
Belgium	33	37	-	37	40
Canada[b,c]	23	22	26	30	46
Denmark	20	21	25	31	37
Finland	23	31	40	45	44
France	29	30	32	42	47
Germany (FRG)[b]	34	37	46	50	56
Hungary	**29**	**39**	**46**	**46**	**42**
Ireland[b]	17	22	20	28	49
Italy	14	18	21	27	31
Japan[b]	56	73	78	91	102
Korea[b,d]	5	8	14	27	33
Mexico	3	5	-	7	-
Netherlands[b]	48	46	50	56	56
Norway	29	39	36	47	56
Portugal	6	5	6	8	10
Singapore[b]	-	8	11	20	27
Spain	5	6	11	12	21
Sweden[b]	27	36	41	50	51
United Kingdom[e]	30	30	33	-	-
USA[b]	66	57	62	72	77
Venezuela[d]	8	8	8	10	-

Notes:

a   If data are not available for the given year then we used the data of the nearest available year. Number of scientists and engineers is in full time equivalent.
b   Excluding scientists of social sciences.
c   Methodological changes after 1980.
d   Excluding military R&D.
e   Excluding higher education.

Source: Computations based on different volumes of *UNESCO Statistical Yearbook* and *ILO Yearbook of Labour Statistics*.

Table 5.4
Ratio of R&D expenditures
(R&D expenditures in the percentage of GNP[a])

	1970	1975	1980	1985	1989
Argentina	0.9	-	0.6	-	0.4
Austria	0.6	0.9	1.2	1.3	-
Belgium	0.9	1.4	-	-	1.7
Canada[c]	1.3	1.0	1.3	1.5	1.4
Denmark	0.8	1.0	1.2	1.3	1.6
Finland	0.7	1.0	1.2	1.5	1.8
France	2.0	1.8	1.8	2.3	2.3
Germany (FRG)	1.9	2.2	2.4	2.5	2.9
Hungary	**2.1**	**2.6**	**2.3**	**2.2**	**2.0**
Ireland[c]	0.6	0.8	0.8	0.9	1.1
Italy	1.2	1.0	0.8	1.3	1.1
Japan[b,c]	1.9	2.0	2.4	2.8	2.8
Korea	0.5	-	0.7	1.5	1.9
Mexico	0.1	-	-	0.6	0.2
Netherlands[c]	2.1	2.1	1.9	2.1	2.2
Norway	1.1	1.5	1.3	1.6	2.0
Portugal	0.2	0.3	0.4	0.5	0.5
Singapore[c]	-	-	0.2	0.5	0.9
Spain	0.2	0.3	0.3	0.5	0.7
Sweden[c]	1.4	-	2.0	3.0	2.8
United Kingdom[c]	2.4	2.1	2.2	2.2	2.3
USA[d]	2.7	2.4	2.4	2.6	2.9
Venezuela[b]	0.1	0.6	-	0.3	-

Notes:
a   If data are not available for the given year then we used the data of the nearest available year.
b   Excluding military R&D.
c   Excluding or only partially containing higher education.
d   Excluding R&D investment of private sector.

Sources: Different volumes of *UNESCO Statistical Yearbook.*

Another consideration in this respect is the special importance of the accumulated human capital. Later we will return to this subject.

We believe that under the given circumstances the quality of Hungarian R&D activities is relatively high and its basic problem has always been to translate and integrate the results in the production. Although there are no appropriate indices to measure the direct output of R&D activities, we can still use best the number of patents despite certain problems. Table 5.5 shows three data sequences related to the number of patents projected on 100,000 population in 1989.

Table 5.5
Patent statistics

	granted to residents[a]	secured abroad[b]	granted in the USA[c]
Austria	16.7	43.0	5.25
Belgium	6.8	24.6	3.93
Canada	4.6	15.1	7.55
Denmark	4.8	33.4	4.31
Finland	14.1	39.4	4.65
France	15.7	43.3	5.62
Germany	26.4	91.7	13.57
Hungary	**13.3**	**16.0**	**1.22**
Ireland	0.7	8.0	1.84
Italy	7.5	15.6	2.25
Japan	43.7	41.5	16.45
Korea	1.8	-	0.37
Mexico	0.1	0.1	0.05
Netherlands	5.3	60.9	7.18
Norway	6.0	21.7	3.00
Portugal	0.8	0.3	-
Spain	4.4	2.4	0.34
Sweden	23.8	78.2	9.92
UK	8.3	30.1	5.42
USA	18.0	27.7	20.37

Notes:

a   Average annual number of patents granted to residents per 100,000 inhabitants, 1986-89.

b   Number of patents secured abroad per 100,000 inhabitants, 1989

c   Number of patents granted in the USA by country of origin (per 100,000 inhabitants), 1989.

Source: The World Competitiveness Report 1991.

Hungary occupies quite a good position as regards the number of registered domestic patents. It reflects unequivocally our financing difficulties that we are much farther behind if considering the number of patents secured abroad although our performance is still not negligible. In order to analyze the third column of Table 5.5, that is the number of patents granted in the USA, it is worth highlighting the above said financial difficulties.

In the case of the developed countries, several authors[7] found high correlation between the R&D activity of these countries and the number of their patents registered in the USA. We have to treat this index with greater caution in the case of East-Central-European countries. Following Ray[8], let us mention some of the special limitations applicable to East-Central-European countries: lack of convertible currency; the general lack of financial incentives on behalf of the institutions authorized to proceed; legal problems in connection with the proprietary rights of inventions and finally the USA was not considered an important market for these countries and this fact also prevented them from registering their patents there. If we take into account all these factors, the values found in Table 5.5 do not seem so small any longer.

Briefly summarizing the situation developing by the time of the political changes in 1989-90, the development level of Hungarian R&D activities was high if compared to the overall development of the country, the relative expenditures in this sector were closer to those of highly developed countries than to those of similarly developed ones. The results of R&D activities were lagging behind the expenditures but the efficiency of the sector was still higher than that of other sectors of the economy. At the same time, at the end of the eighties R&D expenditures started to slowly erode.

4. Changes after 1989

After 1989 all significant political forces, economic experts of all parties have pointed out R&D as one of their highest priorities. Unfortunately statistical data are only available up to 1992 and even those available are not consistent with the data before 1989[9], but it may be unequivocally stated that the R&D instead of receiving the priority promised has become a stepchild. Data in Table 5.6 prove this statement.

The workforce employed in R&D (in full-time equivalent) diminished by 43 per cent between 1989 and 1992, the staff of the research and development workers decreased by a somewhat less percentage (40 per cent). Thus the number of scientists and engineers employed in R&D amounted to only 0.29 per cent of the economically active (employed) population. (The decrease in the relative indicator is somewhat smaller than that of the absolute value, because the open unemployment, which was practically non-existent in 1989, reached 8 per cent at the beginning of 1992 and 13.2 at the end of 1992.) Let us remember Figure 5.6: this value is somewhere around that for Singapore in 1989.

The diminution hit most the research-development units in the enterprises (integrated with the production). Almost 60 per cent of these research centres were dissolved in the course of the three years, the number of the research workers and engineers shrunk to one third of the former number. As an outcome of the process, one fifth only of the total research staff worked with enterprises. The diminution of the research staff was least pronounced in higher education, where it was only ten per cent. (But it should be said that in our experience the ratio of research to teaching activities is overestimated by the statistics.)

Table 5.6

Change of some Hungarian R&D indicators between 1989 and 1992[a]

	Level in 1992
Workforce employed in R&D[b]	57
Researchers[b,c]	60
Number of R&D units in enterprises	42
Researchers in enterprises	33
in higher education	90
in R&D institutes	68
Researchers in technical sciences	45
Researchers in electronics and comp. tech.	28
R&D expenditures	45
R&D capital expenditures	41
R&D expenditures in enterprises	35
Expenditures for basic research	90
for applied research	56
for experimental development	31
Number of inventions registered at home	44
abroad	47
Number of patents granted at home	54
abroad	72

Notes: a   1989 = 100
        b   In full-time equivalent.
        c   R&D scientists and engineers is abbreviated to *researchers*.
Source: KSH[a]

The almost total breakdown of research activities in enterprises was not paralleled with the reappearing of the most important technological research in other areas. When investigating the structure of the research staff basis according to scientific disciplines, we see that the number of scientists and development engineers in the field of technical sciences decreased by 55 per cent, that is well over the average. The situation is even worsened by the fact that this diminution is not selective. Beside metallurgical research - the regression of which could be seen as justified - the greatest reduction (72 per cent!) was experienced in electronics and computer technology. The researchers in chemistry, transportation and communication and in the food industry were in a relatively more favourable position.

Even more important was the reduction in research spending. As we have seen, the share of the R&D in the GDP was 2.0 per cent in 1989, and reduced to 1.1 per cent in 1992. This is around the level for Ireland (see Figure 5.7). Meanwhile the GDP decreased by ten per cent. In real terms thus the R&D spending fell to 45 per cent of that in 1989[10].

The decrease in spending hit very forcefully also the research-development departments of the enterprises. It shrunk to 35 per cent in real terms. Within total R&D expenditures the investment outlays were even more reduced, by almost 60 per cent. In this respect the situation was worst in the R&D institutes, where the value of the investment outlays shrunk to one fourth.

It is worth considering the allocation of the spending according not only to organizational structure but also according to the level of the research activity. Spending for basic research was the least reduced, only by ten per cent in real terms, that for applied research by 44 per cent, while for experimental development 69 per cent. (Perhaps this is the only field where some sign of reassurance can be seen: the rate of the reduction itself had been slowing down in the course of time, in 1992 it was already only 10 per cent.)

As we have seen, spending in the enterprise research was reduced to a somewhat lesser extent than that in the experimental development. It results from this that the research projects having more direct links to production were reduced in the non-enterprise research centres too. These research activities were formerly attached mainly to the so-called 'socialist big enterprises', if not always in formal terms (because the research centre belonged to the ministries), but in every case in the content of the research activity. Almost without exception, these big enterprises had to face a deep crisis, in part already before the change of regime. In the course of managing the crisis one of the first steps was almost everywhere the liquidation of the units which were not profitable in the short run, and the R&D departments usually fell into this category.

When privatizing these big enterprises the only solution is almost exclusively a foreign investment, because of the low level of the domestic capital supply. Thus the attitude of the foreign investors to the development of the existing R&D capacities would be worthy of a closer examination. The experiences are extremely mixed; most of the investors seem to be interested in the reduction. In several cases what the investors wanted to buy was the market share rather than the production capacity of the firm. Most frequently the investor introduces its much higher organizational, accounting and marketing practices (together with the equipment needed) while employs its own cast-off technology in the production. Very infrequent are the cases when the investor brings true high-tech to the plant and exploits the existing R&D capacities.

In the case of research institutes and academic research centres statistics show a staff reduction of a lesser extent. With respect to higher education one factor which brings some bias into the data has already been mentioned, but there exists another, more important consideration. For statistics take account only of the employment status. According to some estimates, however, about 30 per cent of the highly qualified research workers practice abroad. It is too early yet to say how many of them remain definitely abroad and how many will return, but in our opinion - based partly on personal experience - the prospects are very bad.

One of the expedients for the research workers becomes superfluous in the domestic R&D emigration. A second way out is the career change. A significant part (one third by some estimations) of the successful entrepreneurs has formerly been a successful graduated professional (not necessarily research worker, of course). Many of them have found employment in banks or hold government office. This is not surprising at all, for innovative capacity is not limited to a specific area, it can be exploited in several fields. This process holds a positive element, since the new Hungarian middle class can be crystallized around them.

What makes the phenomenon dangerous in the long run is the counterselection. It became clear from the preceding that the research spending has decreased to a greater extent than the research staff. This is reflected in the income of the research workers, while the income levels of entrepreneurs, businessmen, government officers with similar qualifications increase at a much higher rate. As a result, the most mobile, the best qualified leave first the research career or remain there, but become engaged in money-earning activities on the basis of contracts (incidentally helping their institutions to survive), which are hardly connected to any research activity.

Existence of this risk is supported by some data on the results of the R&D: in the course of the selected three years the number of the inventions registered at home and abroad has fallen back to half (44 resp. 47 per cent); the number of patents granted at home diminished to 54 per cent, those patented abroad fell to a 72 per cent level.

There is another consideration which should be mentioned by all means. This is the technological and R&D assistance by several institutions of the developed industrial countries. While from a political point of view the engagement seems to be unequivocal, short-term economic interests drive in the opposite direction. A frequent, not too important but characteristic manifestation of this is the fact that an important part of the assistance provided by non-profit organizations serves to meet the travel and other costs for experts and managers of the country which gives the assistance, ignoring the real needs of those to be assisted. What involves much graver consequences is that the joint research projects and the financial assistance provided to them very often serve only to set the stage for selecting and enticing the most talented Hungarian scientists. Moreover the number and share of the joint research programs has also diminished significantly in these years. While the number of the research themes studied in Hungary decreased to hardly more than half of the earlier number, the share of the international co-operation has fallen from 9.2 to 5.8 per cent.

5. Some conclusions

If simply the reasonable selection of R&D strategy were at stake, then this would not necessarily be a problem from the point of view of our development. It would seem to be a regular development that after many years of isolation, of a partial COMECON-autarchy, we have to change from an autonomous technological development to a follower-type one. In our opinion the real importance of all that was said above lies in the fact that the breakdown of the R&D potential built up in last decades seriously threatens the possibility of a rather fast, reconstruction-type development. We can take as probable that the best prospect before us – instead of catching up – will be a development parallel to that of Austria starting from our *present position*, which perpetuates our relative backwardness and impedes the genuine integration into the Single European Market.

Maybe it would be not too far-fetched if we return to the Middle Age, about the above-mentioned 15th century. Europe was then getting away from the first great crisis of feudalism by means of an expansion connected with the great discoveries, a development of the exporting industries and a vast capital export, which were necessarily accompanied in the East by an increase of the agricultural production, the institutionalization of the second serfdom and the stoppage of the urbanization.

We are convinced that an analogue solution would not secure any way-out for the problems of Western Europe. We think that an even greater integrated market would be necessary in order to preserve competitiveness, and the most obvious direction to enlarge this market leads through East-Central-Europe.

References

Bibó, I. (1946), *The misery of the small Eastern European countries* (in Hungarian), Új Magyarország, Budapest. Republished in *Selected studies of István Bibó* (in Hungarian), Magvető Publishing House, Budapest, 1986.

Bibó, I. (1947), 'The development of the Hungarian society and the significance of the change in 1945' (in Hungarian), *Válasz*, Vol. 7. No.6. Republished in *Selected studies of István Bibó*.

Bródy, A. (1992), 'Hungarian economy at the turn of the millennium. A forecast for the years 1992-2004' (in Hungarian), *Közgazdasági Szemle*, No.10 pp. 954-970.

Jánossy, F. (1966), *The trend-line of economic development and reconstruction periods* (in Hungarian), Közgazdasági és Jogi Kiadó, Budapest.

Jánossy, F. (1971), 'The trend-line revisited' (in Hungarian), *Közgazdasági Szemle*, No. 7-8 pp. 841-867.

Kovács, J. and Molnár, Gy. (1993), 'State and future alternatives of Hungarian R&D', Paper presented at the WAITRO International Seminar, Sofia, Bulgaria.

Patel, P. and Pavitt, K. (1987), 'Is Western Europe losing the technological race?', *Research Policy*, Vol. 16.

Ray, G. F. (1991), *Innovation and technology in Eastern Europe*, National Institute of Economic and Social Research, Report Series Number 2., London.

Soete, L. - Wyatt, S. (1983), 'The use of foreign patenting as an internationally comparable science and technology output indicator', *Scientometrics*, vol. 5.

Szűcs, J. (1983), *Outline of three historical regions of Europe* (in Hungarian), Magvető Publishing House, Budapest.

Tarján, T. (1993), 'Hungary's economic growth relative to Austria in the XX century' (in Hungarian), *Közgazdasági Szemle*, No. 9 pp.815-22.

Statistical sources

ILO, *Yearbook of Labour Statistics,* Geneva, 1972,..,1991.

KSH(a), *Statistical Yearbook 1989, 1990, 1991, 1992.* Central Statistical Office, Budapest (in Hungarian).

KSH(b), *Scientific research and experimental development, 1990,* Central Statistical Office, Budapest (in Hungarian).

Mitchell, B. R. (1975), *European Historical Statistics 1750-1970,* The MacMillan Press Ltd., London.

OECD (1993), *National accounts. 1960-1991. Main aggregates.* OECD Publications, Paris .

The World Competitiveness Report 1991, IMD, Lausanne and World Economic Forum, Geneva,1991.

UNESCO, *Statistical Yearbook,* Paris, 1970,..,1992.

Notes

1   Bibó, I. (1946, 1947) and Szűcs, J. (1983).
2   Ray, G.F. (1991).
3   Jánossy, F. (1966) p. 23-4 and 80.
4   Tarján, T. (1993).
5   Bródy, A. (1992) p. 966.
6   The socialist countries have interpreted the subject of research and development in a much wider sense than the Western standards. Many activities have been classified here which are considered elsewhere as normal development activities. As for Hungary, this statistical distortion was eliminated at the beginning of the 80s. We have corrected accordingly all previous Hungarian data presented here. Because of these statistical problems we present only the Hungarian data in our tables. Nevertheless, we believe that our qualitative statements are also applicable to some of the other countries of this group.
7   For example Soete, L. and Wyatt, S. (1983); Patel, P. and Pavitt, K. (1987).
8   Ray, G.F. (1991) p. 107.
9   Unfortunately, even the statistics after 1989 are not perfectly coherent. Most recent (up to 1992) data published in 1994 have retrospectively modified several figures. This is the reason why we are forced to deviate from our data published by Kovács and Molnár (1993).
10   We remark that when computing real values - failing other adequate data - we had to use the general GDP deflator. The inflation rate estimated by this method hit more heavily the R&D activity than the average economy, since e.g. while in 1991 the average price increase was 25.6 per cent, the prices went slightly down in agriculture and yet the prices in agriculture hardly affect the R&D outlays.

6 High-level skills, knowledge transfer and industrial competitiveness

Geoff Mason and Karin Wagner

1. Introduction

In recent years a series of international comparisons carried out at the National Institute of Economic and Social Research in London have highlighted the important links between relative performance in manufacturing and the quality and utilization of human capital inputs in Britain and other Western European nations[1]. However, attention has primarily been focused on the negative impact of Britain's relative deficiencies in intermediate-level - craft, supervisory and technician - skills. As yet little systematic attention has been paid to the extent, and possible consequences for industrial performance, of differences between Britain and other advanced industrial nations in the proportions of the workforce holding much higher-level qualifications.

In the present paper we seek to redress this neglect by reporting on a detailed comparison of the supply and utilization of professional engineers and scientists in Britain and a key competitor country, namely, Germany[2]. Anglo-German differences in this category of high-level skills were expected to be of considerable interest given the evidence of sharp disparities between the two countries in technological performance. For instance, long-term comparisons of manufacturing investment in R&D point to a relatively slow rate of growth in the average share of profits which British firms are willing or able to invest in innovative activity (Patel and Pavitt, 1987). Furthermore, as Figure 6.1

shows, if we take individual country shares of patents granted in the United States as a measure of innovative 'output', Germany first overtook Britain in the early years of this century and since then, with the exception of the two periods immediately following defeat in war there has been a continued upward trend in the German lead. By 1992 the total volume of German patenting in the US was some three times greater than that of Britain. In a detailed study of US patent data, Patel and Pavitt (1989) have shown that, while the German advantage applies to a wide range of industrial sectors, its lead is greatest in automobiles mechanical engineering and basic chemicals; Britain compares somewhat more favourably in aircraft, pharmaceuticals and food and tobacco.

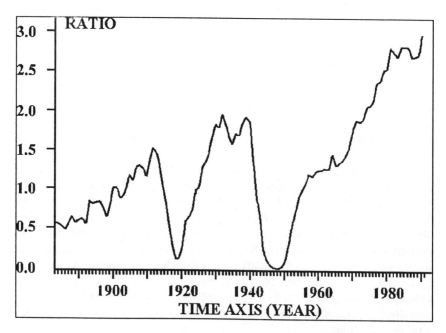

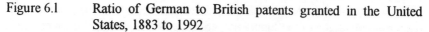

Figure 6.1   Ratio of German to British patents granted in the United States, 1883 to 1992

Source: Data supplied to Science Policy Research Unit by the US Patent and Trademark Office

In this context, the central aim of this paper is to examine the contribution of high-level skills to innovative performance and relative competitiveness in Britain and Germany, with a particular emphasis on the role of 'knowledge transfer' institutions in developing links between manufacturing enterprises and the academic science base. The term 'knowledge transfer' is preferred here to the somewhat narrower concept - which it nonetheless embraces - of 'technology transfer' in order to highlight the two-way flow of ideas and knowledge between industry and the science base, and also to focus attention on the expertise and experience associated with individual engineers and scientists as well as on firm-specific technology and know-how.

The structure of this report is as follows: in Section 2 we draw on a recent comparison of matched samples of British and German establishments in the chemicals and engineering industries to assess the mix of skills which companies need to respond effectively to competitive pressures to speed up the rate of new product development and innovations in production processes. Section 3 examines the extent to which high-level skills and knowledge, in particular, contribute to innovative performance and to industrial competitiveness. Section 4 relates changes in the employment mix of post-graduate engineers and scientists and bachelor degree graduates in each country to increasing technical uncertainty in the innovative process. In Section 5 we compare the institutional design of 'knowledge transfer' activity in the two countries and discuss the role that knowledge transfer institutions play in enhancing industrial competitiveness. Section 6 summarises our main findings and discusses their implications for policy-makers in Britain.

2. Innovation and the skill mix

In keeping with the research methodology developed in earlier National Institute comparisons, detailed information on Anglo-German differences in workforce qualifications and training was gathered primarily through visits to matched samples of establishments in selected branches of manufacturing in each country. These visits were supplemented by detailed statistical investigations and a series of meetings and telephone discussions in each country with experts in universities, independent research organizations and industry trade associations.

Two contrasting industries were chosen for investigation: chemicals, in which Britain is generally regarded as performing well compared to Germany, and engineering in which Germany is known to enjoy substantially higher average levels of productivity and competitiveness. In all some 30 production plants and eight separate research centres were visited in the two countries, focusing on the following main product areas:

Chemicals: paints & industrial coatings; specialised intermediates
Engineering: vehicle components; specialised high-speed machinery.

The establishment visits were all carried out between December 1992 and July 1993. In each case extensive semi-structured interviews were carried out with technical and personnel managers and in many cases it was possible to hold shorter interviews with (or leave written questionnaires for) individual professional engineers and scientists as well. In all but one establishment in each country the visits included direct observation of the work taking place in production and technical support departments.

In both Britain and Germany a majority of companies we visited were under growing pressure to improve the quality and performance of their products and shorten product lead-times while simultaneously having to compete on price as well. This 'double squeeze' was particularly common in the vehicle components sector where a relatively small number of large end-users seek to pass on the cost pressures resulting from their own intensely competitive battles for market share, but we heard of similar pressures in many of the machinery and chemicals plants as well.

An inherent feature of the specialized high-speed machinery sector is that each individual machine, or very small batch of machines (rarely more than four or five at a time), has to be made to precise customer-specific requirements, with the manufacturer's responsibility typically extending to installation and commissioning of the equipment in customers' factories as well. This customization of the machinery is now increasingly combined with efforts to improve its performance in respect of a range of factors such as speed, reliability, energy efficiency, quietness and compactness.

The pace of change is such that, for example, in some branches of the industry average machine speeds have increased tenfold over the last 20 years. In general terms the pressure to innovate is sustained by the certain knowledge that competitors in world markets are working on the same problems and by increasingly tight product specifications sought by customers, for instance, guarantees of reduced lifetime maintenance requirements for the machines and/or an enhanced ability for the machine end-users to make their own products with lighter, thinner materials.

In chemicals as well there was evidence of a growing pressure to innovate to meet more elaborate performance requirements specified by customers or to anticipate improvements in performance which might be necessary to survive in the marketplace in the future. Competitive pressure of this kind was clearest in the specialized intermediates sector whose prime function is to develop new kinds of ingredients or 'building blocks' for use by other chemical producers and, in particular, to devise cost-effective and reliable ways of achieving the frequently difficult chemical transformations required.

However, even in the ostensibly more straightforward paints and surface coatings sector, several producers in both countries reported facing growing complexity in product specifications, for example, lacquers which needed to be able to adhere adequately to different materials under very demanding conditions. In the bulk consumer goods branch of this industry, there is strong competitive pressure on manufacturers to seek an edge in terms of product durability, coverage and other attributes while usually seeking to compete on price as well, and (as throughout the chemicals industry) a continuing need to conform with stricter environmental requirements (e.g. through development of solvent-free products or reduction of noxious emissions from production processes).

As shown in detailed comparisons of matched pairs of plants in Mason and Wagner (1994), competitive survival in recent years has also necessitated a range of process innovations and improvements to shopfloor efficiency in order to meet more stringent cost and delivery requirements. In varying degrees both the stronger and the weaker of the plants compared have invested in new, more automated capital equipment or sought to reorganize their shopfloors so as to ensure a quicker and smoother transfer of components or materials between different production processes. In both countries a majority of plant managers also reported recent measures intended to cut product waste and reduce stocks of raw materials, components and finished goods.

In general terms our observations suggest that the more successful plants (in engineering predominantly German, in chemicals both British and German) have access to a range of different kinds of skill and knowledge needed to respond successfully to competitive pressures to innovate. These skill requirements include the ability to liaise at a high technical level with customers and properly define (and anticipate) their needs. High levels of engineering and supervisory knowhow are also needed to maintain a smooth flow of production under difficult conditions, for instance, when the product mix in engineering is subject to rapid change or, in chemicals, when production of a new and unpredictable substance is being 'scaled-up' following its initial laboratory development.

Another core area of skill needs relates to market pressure to reduce the average time taken between receipt of new orders and the delivery of final products, even when the goods in question are highly customer-specific. The key to this in precision engineering, for example, is a highly flexible ('modular') design of products which maximizes the use of 'standard' components or sub-assemblies and thus enables the actual point of customization to be delayed till relatively late in the production process. Similarly high levels of design skills (and effective management of the links between design and production departments) are needed to ensure that even complicated products (or their components) are no more difficult to manufacture than they need to be.

In short, successful innovation demands a mix of management, supervisory and workforce skills from craft- and technician-level upwards and, as will be illustrated further below, this mix is one in which post-graduates have a place as well as bachelor degree graduates. In the next section we examine the contribution of high-level skills to innovative performance and industrial competitiveness in detail.

3. High-level skills and industrial competitiveness

In engineering and technology subjects, Germany produces approximately a third more PhD's per head of population than Britain and more than five times as many people qualified to Masters degree (MSc) level. This numerical advantage is heavily reinforced at bachelor degree level. In physical sciences such as chemistry and physics, the proportions of the population gaining higher education qualifications are much the same in each country but the mix of awards in Germany is more oriented towards higher degrees than in Britain.

These differences in annual flows of highly-qualified people were reflected in workforce qualification levels in the national samples of establishments described in detail in Mason and Wagner (1994). In German engineering plants technical post-graduates and bachelor degree graduates both accounted for much larger shares of total employment than in their British counterparts. In the samples of chemicals plants the employment share of technical graduates as a whole was very similar in each country but the ratio of PhD's to bachelor degree graduates was higher in Germany than in Britain.

In respect of workforce skills, Britain's relative deficiencies at graduate level and above were found (as expected) to be much less severe than those at intermediate (craft and supervisory) levels. This was particularly true of the chemicals industry where there is a very clear role in both countries for PhD chemists trained in the disciplines of experimental science who work in combination with first degree/*Fachhochschule* engineers and others with good practical skills and experience with process equipment. As shown in detailed comparisons of matched pairs of chemicals plants in each country, the above-average productivity and trade performance of this industry in Britain is closely associated with its relative adequacy of supplies of highly-qualified scientific and engineering staff.

However, in the engineering industry British skill deficiencies relative to Germany at intermediate levels appear to be compounded by those at graduate level and above. Our observations in each country pointed to close links between the German industry's greater employment of technical post-graduates and its superior performance in respect of both product and process innovations, with consequent benefits for German export competitiveness. The

German advantage was particularly marked in the high-speed machinery sector where surviving British plants have conceded market share to their German rivals in postwar decades and tend to be 'followers' in respect of technical innovation. In vehicle components, British producers have achieved significant improvements in productivity in recent years: comparable German plants still tend to be ahead in respect of process innovations and shopfloor efficiency but the German productivity advantage is no longer sufficient to guarantee their competitiveness in the face of unfavourable exchange rate movements.

In both countries we encountered very strong views among engineering managers about the virtues possessed by 'practical', 'common sense' engineers with first degrees or *Fachhochschule* qualifications. For the great majority of jobs in engineering, graduates at these levels with three or four years' experience in employment are deemed to be far more useful than newly-graduated PhD's of the same age. In Britain several managers also expressed a view of PhD's as 'academics' who were frequently reluctant to acquire practical and commercial skills and indeed often lacked social skills as well; these kinds of concerns were much less common in Germany.

The large annual output of *Fachhochschule* engineers has found ready employment in German industry for many years and people with this qualification accounted for just over two thirds of the technical graduates in our German engineering sample. University graduate engineers (with MSc-level qualifications) tend to be recruited both for their knowledge in specialist areas and for more general reasons. They are widely regarded as being more analytical than *Fachhochschule* leavers and their deeper theoretical education is expected to make them more capable of tackling complex problems. Thus in many plants visited there was a clear division of labour, for example, between research departments employing a large proportion of University graduates and *Konstruktion* (design and development) departments where *Fachhochschule* graduates were in a majority. It was repeatedly emphasised to us that both categories of staff were needed; indeed, since University graduates command higher salaries than *Fachhochschule*-leavers, German employers were very concerned to secure a 'cost-effective' mix of each type of graduate.

In Britain, there was a sharp split in our sample between plants belonging to leading companies with a long tradition of graduate recruitment and other, smaller plants for whom it has been a big step even to start employing more first degree graduates recently, let alone post-graduates. In many cases increased employment of first degree graduates in Britain was explained in similar terms to the German rationale for employing more University-diplomates, that is, the need to employ more staff able to carry out structured analysis of problems. British employers' perception of first degree graduates in these terms reflects the fact that many of them - particularly those with 'good' degrees from highly-esteemed engineering departments - may be regarded as the 'intellectual equivalents' of German University-diplomates (although they have followed much shorter courses than their German counterparts and therefore not achieved the same academic breadth or depth).

Alongside this core recruitment of first degree graduates by British engineering firms, there is a much smaller level of demand for people with MSc qualifications in specialist areas such as acoustics materials science, microwave engineering or failure mode and effect analysis. In those British plants employing MSc's, a majority of them had actually been sponsored by their employers to study for these awards some time after first taking up employment.

In both countries recruitment of newly-graduated PhD's in engineering was usually based on the relevance to company needs of individual thesis subject areas (such as hydraulics, tribology or materials science). PhD's accounted for about 10 per cent of technical graduates in the corporate R&D centres visited in Britain but were few and far between in production plants. In the German sample of establishments (only one of which belonged to a company with a detached R&D centre), PhD's represented a fairly small proportion (4 per cent) of all technical graduates but their numbers were significant in absolute terms and they accounted for a wholly disproportionate share of senior management positions. Thus, when external recruitment of German PhD's occurs at later stages of their careers, more account is likely to be taken of their overall experience and management potential than the subject of their doctoral thesis.

Although there is no automatic correspondence at individual plant level between post-graduate employment and innovative success, the bulk of our discussions and observations in the course of establishment visits point to strong links between post-graduate expertise and the ability of firms to take quick advantage of new developments in scientific knowledge. Thus, in one comparison of matched engineering plants, technical advances in complex areas such as the use of lasers were specifically identified by British research staff as a key element in their German rival's competitive advantage. Another of the plants in our German sample is regarded as a world leader in the development of electronic systems in its field of vehicle components; its success in this area has stemmed largely from high-level in-house research in close collaboration with university-based specialists. In a different branch of vehicle components, the German plant visited engaged in similar collaboration with - and recruitment of post-graduates from - a university at the forefront of research into acoustics and had achieved such breakthroughs in noise reduction that it could now offer specialist services in this field to firms in many other sectors of engineering.

The value of post-graduate expertise in key specialist areas is recognised to some extent by those leading British engineering companies which, as mentioned, employ some higher degree graduates in their R&D centres or have developed links with university-based researchers. However, these companies are hardly representative of the mainstream British engineering industry and, as said to us by one British research director, very few even of the biggest British companies have assembled the 'critical mass' of highly-qualified personnel which is necessary if sustained technical advances are to be made.

4. Changes in the employment mix of post-graduates and bachelor degree graduates

Further recognition of the contribution to industrial performance made by post-graduates in German manufacturing industry is implied by the changes in the mix of high-level qualifications which have occurred in recent decades.

As shown in Table 6.1, the number of German home students gaining University (MSc-equivalent) diplomas in engineering and technology in recent years has grown more than twice as fast as the number gaining *Fachhochschule* diplomas. This is reflected within the German mechanical engineering industry where total employment of University engineers grew by 183 per cent between 1968 and 1987 while, over the same period, employment of *Fachhochschule* graduates increased by 55 per cent. Thus by 1987 the ratio of FH to University engineers in employment stood at 2.4:1, down from 4.4:1 in 1968 (VDMA, 1988). As reported to us in the majority of plants in our German engineering sample, this development reflects a growing preference for the more highly-qualified type of engineer, not just a response to their increased availability.

In German chemicals manufacturing, the change in mix of high-level qualifications has been less dramatic. Combined employment of University-educated scientists and engineers increased by 59 per cent between 1976 and 1991 compared to 45 per cent growth in employment over the same period of *Fachhochschule* technical graduates (predominantly engineers). In 1991 the ratio of University to FH graduates was approximately 1.7: 1 compared to 1.56:1 in 1976 *(Bundesarbeitgeberverband Chemie, 1991).*

In the British engineering industry total employment of professional engineers and scientists holding at least a first degree rose by some 55 per cent between 1978 and 1988 while, over the same period, employment of technician-level engineers declined by 19 per cent and total employment fell by 36 per cent (EITB, 1989). No detailed information on trends in the industry's employment mix of first and higher degree graduates in technical subjects is available. However, some tentative conclusions may be drawn from the fact that growth rates in the numbers of home students qualifying at first, Masters and PhD levels in engineering and technology subjects were all within a range of 35-50 per cent, as shown in Table 6.1.

Although these engineering graduates of course enter employment in many other sectors of the economy apart from engineering, the rough parity in growth of output at each level suggests that the mix of bachelor and higher degree graduates employed in engineering is unlikely to have changed as sharply in Britain as in Germany in recent years. This conforms too with our earlier point that even taking on more first degree graduates has represented a major change in recruitment policy for many British engineering companies in recent years.

In the British chemicals industry, the proportion of all employees holding at least a first degree rose from 9 per cent in the late 1970's to 15 per cent in 1990 (Mason and Wagner, 1994, Section 7.2). This includes non-technical graduates as well but recent data indicate that roughly 80 per cent of all first degree graduates recruited by the industry and 90 per cent of those with higher degrees have qualified in science or engineering subjects. At present approximately one higher degree (predominantly PhD) chemist is recruited for every two first degree graduates in chemistry; for chemical engineers the ratio of higher to first degree graduates is roughly 1:9 (Chemical Industries Association, 1990-93). As in the case of engineering, trends in the numbers of home students obtaining first degrees and PhD's in chemistry between 1980-90 suggest that the mix of first and higher degrees may not have changed greatly over this period.

In the course of our establishment visits, this overall pattern of increased employer demand for technical graduates as a whole in both countries, and for holders of post-graduate (particularly MSc-level) awards in Germany, was repeatedly explained to us in terms of a greater need for staff who could tackle new and complex technical problems in an analytical way (based on theoretical understanding) rather than simply rely on past experience and trial-and-error methods of problem-solving.

This trend is perhaps best understood in the context of recent empirical work by Bartel and Lichtenberg (1987), using data for US manufacturing industry, which supports a hypothesis that demand for highly-educated workers relative to the demand for less-educated workers is inversely related to firms' experience with technologies currently in use (as proxied by the mean age of capital equipment). One of the key premises underpinning this hypothesis is that

Table 6.1

Rate of growth in numbers of home students gaining first degree and higher degree awards in science and engineering subjects in Britain and (West) Germany, 1980 to 1990
(rounded to nearest five percentage points)

BRITAIN	First Degree	Masters[a]	Doctorate
	(Percentage change, 1980 to 1990)		
Chemistry[b]	+25	+5	+20
Physics[b]	+20	+40	+35
Mathematical sciences[c]	+60	+140	+85
Engineering and technology[d]	+40	+50	+35

GERMANY	Diplom (FH)	Diplom (UNI)	Doctorate
	(Percentage change, 1980 to 1990)		
Chemistry[b]	+20	+170	+70
Physics[b]	-20	+190	+70
Mathematical sciences[c]	+260	+110	+80
Engineering and technology[d]	+50	+115	+45

Notes:

a May include a small number of other sub-doctoral post-graduate awards such as Postgraduate Diplomas

b Includes astronomy

c Includes computer science (*Informatik*)

d Excludes architecture

Sources: USR, University Statistics, Volume 2 and private communication CNAA, Annual Reports; SB, Statistisches Jahrbuch; NIESR estimates population data from OECD, Labour Force Statistics, 1992.

the productivity of highly-educated workers relative to low-educated workers is greater, the more uncertainty there is in the production environment.

As emerged from our interviews with technical managers in both countries, one of the most striking features of the modern industrial innovation process is precisely the high and growing level of uncertainty which prevails. As new problems and difficulties present themselves, manufacturers need to be able to assess whether they can be resolved by incremental improvements in existing products and/or processes, or whether some kind of radical change or breakthrough innovation will be necessary. For instance, producers of industrial coatings may be able to solve new problems simply by fine-tuning existing recipes or they may be better advised to investigate new ways of cross-linking existing polymers or even seek to develop brand new kinds of polymers. Similarly, in the vehicle components sector, a company seeking to reduce the weight of or the friction undergone by a particular product (thus increasing its expected life) needs to know whether to continue working with its existing materials or whether to explore the use of some completely different material.

A degree of technical uncertainty is of course intrinsic to the innovative process. However, such uncertainty now appears to be intensifying within many branches of manufacturing, partly because of the growing pressure (as previously noted) to solve problems of improving product performance while simultaneously reducing production costs and product lead-times, and also because of the remarkable speed of developments in science and technology in recent years. In particular, the growing use of programmable automation equipment to meet a wide variety of different customer requirements has been characterized as an information-intensive form of production with increasing resources needing to be devoted to gathering information on both the specialist needs of customers and the technical possibilities of meeting such needs (Willinger and Zuscovitch, 1988). The pace of change in this respect has increased the risk for many firms of being overtaken by competitors who employ more highly-qualified technical personnel and/or have better access to the skills and knowledge, and specialized equipment, of the external science base (universities, research institutes and consultancies, etc.).

Recent attempts to quantify changes in the extent of manufacturers' dependence on the science base have utilized direct counts of the number of scientific papers cited in technology patents granted in the US. This literature, surveyed in Narin and Olivastro (1992), has predictably found the closest links between science and technology by this measure to exist in product areas such as biotechnology and pharmaceuticals while the linkages are weakest in traditional areas of mechanical engineering and vehicle manufacture. However, detailed studies for the period between 1975-89 show a steady increase in the number of scientific citations per patent in nearly all product areas and in nearly all countries (ibid).

In addition to this apparent growth in direct use of scientific research results by manufacturers, there has also been an increasing tendency in recent decades for technological knowledge (traditionally based on practical, largely unwritten experience and knowhow specific to firms and individuals) to enter the public domain through specialist books, journals and conference papers. Hence even those firms who have no aspirations to do more than adopt innovations developed elsewhere now increasingly require the services of highly-qualified engineers and scientists in order to identify and make use of relevant information if they are to have any hope of staying in touch with more advanced competitors[3]. This point is very clearly made by Nelson and Wright (1992) who attribute much of the decline in US technological leadership since the 1960's to rapid growth in the employment of professional engineers and scientists in industrial R&D in countries such as Japan and Germany but not in Britain[4].

In short, the increased uncertainty associated with the modern innovative process points to a continued shift in the mix of manufacturing skills towards highly-qualified scientists and engineers, and within that group there is likely to be enhanced scope for the specialist knowledge and contacts possessed by post-graduates - both as direct employees of manufacturing firms and as external specialists employed indirectly on a contract basis.

5. Knowledge transfer: indirect employment of highly-qualified personnel

Many of the establishments visited in Britain and Germany had formal R&D links with external institutions such as universities and independent research institutes or consultancies. Such links reflected companies' awareness of the need for access both to the knowledge generated in the external science base and to the specialist capabilities and computing power of the equipment in use in many universities and research organisations. However, this kind of indirect employment of highly-qualified scientists and engineers was far more prevalent in our German sample of establishments than in Britain.

Knowledge transfer between the science base and industry in Germany is facilitated by various distinctive institutions devoted to that purpose, of which the most prominent are the networks of research institutes operated by the Fraunhofer and Max-Planck Societies. Between them these institutes employ some 5,300 professional engineers and scientists of whom approximately 60 per cent hold PhD's. The remaining 40 per cent are University-diplomates of whom at least half are also studying for their PhD's. At any one time these two types of institute also have approximately 3,700 visiting engineers and scientists working on a 'fellowship' basis, of whom half are PhD's and half are qualified to University diploma level. The purpose of these fellowships which last on average about six months is a continuous exchange of knowledge; about 40 per cent of visiting fellows are foreigners. The full-time scientific personnel are supported by more than 3,000 'student assistants' who work part-time to finance themselves during their PhD or University studies (Max-Planck-Gesellschaft and Fraunhofer Gesellschaft, private communications).

The two societies have very different research priorities which are reflected in their different sources of funding. The Fraunhofer Institutes are primarily oriented towards applied 'near-market' R&D and presently receive about a third of their income from 'pure' industrial contracts and another third from government-sponsored projects which are usually carried out in collaboration with industrial partners; the remaining income mainly derives from 'basic funding' provided by the federal and states governments. By contrast, the Max-Planck Institutes focus on basic and strategic research with a longer time horizon and are largely financed by public funds (Meyer-Krahmer, 1990).

This well-organized division of intellectual labour contributes to German industrial competitiveness in several different ways. For instance, given their funding structure, Fraunhofer Institutes need to 'sell' their services to industrial clients rather than wait to be approached, and one PhD-qualified Fraunhofer department manager we interviewed believed that he was not unusual in travelling as many as 60 thousand kilometres a year visiting prospective clients.

At his Institute 80 scientific staff supported by 250 'student assistants' are typically dealing with about 200 different industrial clients at any one time. Individual projects can range in length from a few months to four years and are concerned with a wide range of product and process innovations which clients need to implement in order to remain competitive and/or comply with new environmental legislation. In common with most other Fraunhofer Institutes, the great majority of clients are small or medium-sized *Mittelstand* companies whose own research facilities are non-existent or inadequate for their needs. However, about 50 per cent of turnover derives from contracts with large companies, some of them foreign-owned multinationals. Staff turnover is high (averaging less than five years) and recruitment of both their full-time research staff and their 'student assistants' by client companies is considered to be a highly important mechanism for 'knowledge transfer' *(Wissenschaftstransfer)*.

Although the Max-Planck Institutes are closer to university departments in the way they operate - and are frequently located on or near university campuses - the proportion of their funding which they are obliged to find for themselves is still significant and motivates the development of close links with private industry. For example, previous success with longer-term research projects which have ultimately borne fruit commercially now helps individual Max-Planck Institutes to organise consortia of companies willing to contribute to research funding on a five to ten year time scale - something which the companies as separate entities would hardly have contemplated. At the same time, industrial research projects at Max-Planck Institutes may also develop as a result of companies approaching them with pressing 'near-market' problems which, upon investigation, turn out to have links with more fundamental research programmes of interest to the Institutes.

As in the Fraunhofer network, the Max-Planck Institutes play a key role in preparing post-graduate students for subsequent industrial employment. Upon completion of their PhD's, former student assistants from both type of institute are highly regarded for their experience of industrial project work and for having worked in an inter-disciplinary environment. They are also well-placed to maintain or initiate contacts between their employers and technical specialists based in universities and independent institutes - and thus continue to have advance information about new research results which may take two years or more to be formally published.

Many examples of fruitful relationships between industry, universities and independent research organizations can also be found in Britain. For example, the Association of Independent Research and Technology Organisations (AIRTO) embraces some 36 contract research groups and industry research associations which together account for about 3 per cent of total R&D in Britain; about three quarters of their income derives from private industry and the remainder from various government sources (Rothwell and Dodgson, 1993). These organizations have been described in a recent assessment as 'emulating Fraunhofer Institutes in funding embryonic post-graduate schools', however, the same report suggests that increased financial pressure to engage in short-term problem-solving has restricted these organizations' ability to keep up to date with recent developments in university-based research (ibid, pp. 13-14).

Two prominent initiatives - both jointly funded by government and industry - which attempt to bridge the gap between industry and the academic research base are the LINK programme (which supports collaborative research projects) and the Teaching Company Scheme (TCS) which provides an opportunity for recent graduates and post-graduates to undertake industry-based training. Numerous other schemes have also been launched by the Science and Engineering Research Council in recent years in an effort to increase the industrial relevance of post-graduate education and training, for example, Collaborative Awards in Science and Engineering.

At their best these various initiatives have proved highly beneficial to some firms and individuals. For example, a recent review of the TCS has found that almost two thirds of programmes have 'performed well'; in some cases the scheme has even contributed to 'cultural change' in participating companies with traditional 'craft' methods of operating being largely replaced by a more scientific approach (Senker, Senker and Hall, 1993). However, the scheme is relatively small in scale and is oriented toward first degree graduates rather than post-graduates: in 1991-92 the TCS had a total of 648 individual Associate places either filled or in the process of being filled; only about a fifth of these Associates held higher degrees (TCS, Annual Report, 1991-92).

As we heard from several British companies during our visits - and as acknowledged in the recent government White Paper on science, engineering and technology (HMSO, 1993), - existing knowledge transfer schemes in Britain are widely seen as 'piecemeal' in nature and in some cases they are also regarded as unnecessarily complex in their administration. Taken as a whole they simply do not have the industrial 'reach' of German institutional arrangements for knowledge transfer, nor do they facilitate the transfer of highly-qualified people between higher education and industry on anything like the same scale as in Germany[5].

Of course, the wider incidence of knowledge transfer activities in Germany must be attributed to a very great extent to German firms' higher average rate of investment in R&D generally and (in the case of engineering, for example) their greater employment of highly-qualified technical staff who are willing and able to make good use of external knowledge sources. However, in our observation, a key feature of German institutions such as the Fraunhofer and Max-Planck networks is that their services are particularly easy for private firms to understand and seek out. The lack of similarly high-profile and easily-accessible independent research institutions in Britain has negative consequences in particular for small and medium-sized manufacturing firms.

Thus, in one British vehicle components plant we were told that the specialist steels they are now obliged by customers to use cause many problems because the new materials 'have properties that we simply don't understand'. However, although managers at this plant had thought about seeking help from external specialists, and had 'looked into' various government-supported schemes which might be of assistance, in effect they found it easier to let the problems carry on.

Another relatively small plant producing high-speed machinery was typical of British firms which have only recently set out to recruit more first degree graduates. Full-time employment of post-graduate engineers had never been considered. However, the technical director recognised the benefits of having this level of expertise 'on tap' whenever it was needed. He had recently sought (and obtained) assistance from a local university with problems caused by 'material failure' on one model in his product range. As a relatively young graduate himself he had known that universities were now under pressure to undertake consultancy work but he doubted that older managers or non-graduate managers would have been willing to seek out specialist help in the same way. He also suspected that if his local university had been unable to help him, he would have found it difficult to look any further.

Perhaps the strongest comment about the need for occasional access to highly-qualified specialists in different research areas was made by a manager at another, larger British engineering company which already has a serious research capability of its own: You don't know what you don't know - you want reassurance that you're on the right path, asking the right questions . There seems little doubt that the institutions required for this indirect industrial employment of post-graduate scientists and engineers to occur are far better developed in Germany than in Britain. In our conclusions to this paper we address some of the policy implications arising from this comparative assessment of knowledge transfer activities.

6. Summary and assessment

1. Rising industrial demand for technical graduates as a whole in both Britain and Germany in recent years, and in Germany for technical post-graduates as well (particularly those at MSc level), reflects a growing need for people who can tackle complex technical problems in an analytical way (based on theoretical understanding) rather than simply rely on past experience and trial-and-error methods of problem-solving. This growth in demand for high-level skills and knowledge derives from intense competitive pressure in many different product markets where manufacturers are obliged by their customers to achieve higher quality standards and meet ever more elaborate performance specifications while simultaneously shortening product lead-times and having to compete on price as well.

2. These competitive pressures, combined with the remarkable speed of developments in science and technology in recent years, have led to a high and rising degree of technical uncertainty: as new problems arise it is not immediately clear whether they can be resolved by incremental improvements in existing products and processes, or whether some kind of radical change or breakthrough innovation will be necessary. In consequence, even firms that aspire to do no more than adopt innovations developed elsewhere increasingly need access to the services of highly-qualified technical staff - either as full-time employees or as external specialists employed on a contract basis - in order to

be able to identify and make use of all relevant information generated by their competitors and in the external science base (universities, research institutes, consultancies, etc).

3. Given the present relatively low level of direct employment of post-graduates in many branches of British manufacturing, we suggest that some urgency needs to be given to measures to expand 'indirect' industrial employment of post-graduate skills and expertise in universities and intermediate knowledge transfer institutions. As is widely acknowledged, knowledge transfer in Britain at present is restricted in large part by the relatively low level of industrial *demand* for the existing specialized services on offer. However, our observations of the interaction between industrial firms and the networks of intermediate research institutes run by the Fraunhofer and Max-Planck Societies in Germany suggest that careful institutional reforms on the knowledge transfer *supply* side in Britain could in themselves contribute to an increase in demand.

4. Accordingly, we have recommended to the British government that consideration should again be given to the main principles underlying proposals for a new network of intermediate research institutions -named 'Faraday Centres' after the famous British scientist - which would aspire to a role similar to that played by the Fraunhofer Institutes in Germany. (CEST, 1992). However, we are mindful of the very specific national-institutional setting within which knowledge transfer organizations have thrived in Germany. In Mason and Wagner (1994), we have laid particular stress on the strong incentives for German engineers and scientists to finance themselves through long periods of post-graduate study by part-time employment as a result of the highly visible salary premia attached to post-graduate qualifications and the favourable prospects for technical post-graduates to advance to senior positions in management. The opportunities for German engineering and science students to undertake such part-time work in intermediate research institutes complete a *'circulus vitiosus'* since the experience thus gained on industrial consultancy work serves to enhance the salaries that post-graduate engineers and scientists can command after completing their studies. By contrast, in Britain most post-graduates take some years even to catch up with the salaries earned by first degree graduates of the same age and there is no evidence of post-graduate qualifications enhancing management career prospects at all. In consequence, most of the key ingredients for the projected Faraday Centres to succeed in preparing post-graduate students for industrial employment on the 'German model' are missing.

5. However, without addressing the fine detail of the original proposals for Faraday Centres, we suggest that the key merits of these proposals deserve

renewed attention: firstly, their recognition of the need for knowledge transfer institutions in Britain to be highly visible, clearly understood and easily accessible by the many firms which (as we discovered in the course of our research) could well benefit from closer links with the external science base; and secondly, the need for such a high-profile network *to complement and build on* existing successful knowledge transfer activities rather than add to the present confusing array of schemes and organisations.

6. The immediate objective in developing high-profile Centres therefore, would be to deliver a sharp boost to industrial use of research resources in intermediate institutions and universities which are at present under-utilized. To succeed in this objective, the organization and funding of the Centres would need to be tailored to British circumstances (and should only draw on foreign models for broad inspiration).

7. In the medium term, we suggest, a key aim of Faraday Centres should be to attract otherwise highly-specialized post-graduate students to gain valuable experience on a range of different industrial contracts and thus become more attractive to employers in the process. However this objective will not be achieved without a significant level of financial support by government and/or industry to compensate for the current absence of financial incentives for individuals to undertake long periods of part-time study in Britain (as implicitly recognised in the recent pilot scheme for Postgraduate Training Partnerships).

8. In the long run developments of this kind could increase industrial demand for post-graduate engineers and scientists and thus contribute to greater recognition for post-graduates in respect of salaries and career prospects. This in turn could increase the willingness of individual engineers and scientists in Britain to invest in their own post-graduate education. Any steps in this direction, however small, are likely to have positive consequences for British industrial competitiveness.

References

Atkinson, H., Rogers, P. and Bond, R. (1990), *Research in the United Kingdom, France and West Germany: A Comparison*, SERC, Swindon.

Bartel, A. and Lichtenberg, F. (1987), 'The comparative advantage of educated workers in implementing new technology', *The Review of Economic* and *Statistics*, February.

Bundesarbeitgeberverband Chemie (1991), *AT-Angestellte, Leitende Angestellte, Akademiker und Fachhochschulabsolventen in der Chemischen Industrie,* Wiesbaden,1991.

Centre for Exploitation of Science and Technology (CEST) (1991), *Attitudes to Innovation in Germany* and *Britain: a Comparison,* London.

Chemical Industries Association (1990-93), *Graduate Recruitment Surveys,* London.

Cohen, W. and Levinthal, D. (1989), 'Innovation and learning: the two faces of R&D', The *Economic Journal,* September.

Daly, A., Hitchens, D. and Wagner, K. (1985), 'Productivity, machinery and skills in a sample of British and German manufacturing plants', *National Institute Economic Review,* May.

Engineering Industry Training Board (EITB) (1989), *British Engineering: Employment, Training* and *Education,* Watford.

Gesellschaft Deutscher Chemiker (1992), *Statistik der Chemiestudiengänge in der Bundesrepublik Deutschland 1991,* Frankfurt/Main.

HMSO (1990), *Highly Qualified People: Supply and Demand: Report of an Interdepartmental Review,* London.

HMSO (1993), *Realising our Potential: a Strategy for Science, Engineering and Technology,* London.

Mason, G., Prais, S. and van Ark, B. (1992), 'Vocational education and productivity in the Netherlands and Britain', *National Institute Economic Review,* May.

Mason, G., van Ark, B. and Wagner, K. (1994), 'Productivity, product quality and workforce skills: food processing in four European countries', *National Institute Economic Review* (forthcoming).

Mason, G. and Wagner, K. (1994), *High-level Skills and Industrial Competitiveness: Post-graduate Engineers and Scientists in Britain and Germany,* NIESR Research Report No. 6, London.

Meyer-Krahmer, F. (1990), *Science* and *Technology in the Federal Republic of Germany,* Longman, Harlow.

Narin, F. and Olivastro D. (1992), 'Status report: linkage between technology and science', *Research Policy,* Vol. 21.

Nelson, R. and Wright G. (1992), 'The rise and fall of American technological leadership: the postwar era in historical perspective', *Journal of Economic Literature,* Vol. 30, December.

Patel, P. and Pavitt, K. (1987), 'The elements of British technological competitiveness', *National Institute Economic Review,* November.

Patel, P. and Pavitt, K. (1989), 'A comparison of technological activities in West Germany and the United Kingdom', *National Westminster Bank Quarterly Review,* May.

Rothwell, R. and Dodgson, M. (1993), 'The contribution which research and technology organizations make to innovation and competitiveness in UK industry', Association of Independent Research and Technology Organisation (AIRTO) Paper 93/1.

Senker, J., Senker, P. and Hall, A. (1993), *Teaching company performance and features of successful programmes*, Science Policy Research Unit, University of Sussex, Brighton.

Steedman, H. and Wagner K. (1987), 'A second look at productivity, machinery and skills in Britain and Germany', *National Institute Economic Review*, November.

Steedman, H. and Wagner, K. (1989), 'Productivity, machinery and skills: clothing manufacture in Britain and Germany', *National Institute Economic Review*, November.

Verband Deutscher Maschinen- und Anlagenbau (VDMA) *Ingenieur-Erhebung im Maschinen- und Anlagenbau 1988*, Frankfurt/Main.

Willinger, M. and Zuscovitch, E. (1988), 'Towards the economics of information-intensive production systems: the case of advanced materials', in Dosi, G. et al (eds.), *Technical Change and Economic Theory*, Pinter, London.

Notes

1   See: Daly, A., Hitchens, D. and Wagner, K. 1985; Steedman, H. and Wagner, K. 1987, 1989; Mason, G., Prais, S. and van Ark, B. 1992; Mason, G., van Ark, B. and Wagner, K. 1994.

2   Unless otherwise stated the term 'Germany' is used throughout this report to refer to the former Federal Republic.

3   As described in Cohen and Levinthal (1989), in-house R&D activity plays a key role in developing the capacity of any firm to 'absorb' relevant knowledge generated elsewhere, whether by other firms or in the academic science base. Indeed, their empirical results for US manufacturing suggest that, in some industries such as chemicals and electrical/electronic engineering, the positive incentive for firms to invest in R&D in order to take advantage of 'spillovers' of knowledge into the public domain may be strong enough to offset the negative impact on R&D arising from the inability of innovating firms to fully restrict the appropriation by others of their R&D output.

4   In more detail, since the 1960's the US, Japan and Germany (and to a lesser extent, France) have tended to 'converge' in respect of employment of professional scientists and engineers in R&D as a proportion of the workforce, and in R&D spending as a percentage of GNP; by contrast, over the same period a substantial gap has opened up between Britain and the other four countries in respect of both these indicators of R&D activity (Nelson and Wright,1992, Figures 8 and 9).

5   For detailed comparisons of the organisation of R&D in Britain and Germany which support these conclusions, see Atkinson, Rogers and Bond (1990) and CEST (1991, Chapter 7).

7 Intellectual background and the technological lag in Poland

Andrzej Karpinsky

1.

Contemporary Poland belongs to the group of European countries with relatively well developed intellectual potential. This is due to a long tradition in science and university education and the great leap forward in education in postwar Poland.

In 1992 in Poland there were 117 universities with the oldest one in Cracow, which was founded in the year 1364.

The total number of people with higher education amounted to 1.838 thousand in 1988. That is 6.5 per cent of the total adult population. One fourth of this data concerns engineers. Their total number is near 380 thousand people.

In 1991, in science and R&D activity outside of firms and factories, meaning mainly the state research institutes and laboratories, over 80 thousand people were engaged.

Together with people employed in the R&D services inside the firms and factories the total number was 130 thousand people.

From the total employment in this sector 62 thousand were self-dependent scientific workers. Among them were over 9 thousand professors active in science and R&D.

Poland has a rather well developed science and R&D structure. It is comprised of three kinds of science and R&D organizations:

-     the institutes in universities and other similar,
-     the institutes of the Polish Academy of Sciences and state institutes and laboratories connected directly with industry,
-     the R&D services in the framework of firms and factories.

What is lacking is 'venture capital' firms and organizations active in the process of transmission of science and R&D results to industrial practice on commercial basis according to market economy rules.

The number of scientific state research institutes and laboratories amounted to 371 in 1991.

In firms and factories of all kinds of ownership, R&D services employed 45 thousand people.

And what should be stressed is that the most up-to-date technologies could be put into operation by Polish specialists and engineers due to the qualifications and experience of the people involved.

In 1992, all these institutions spent on science and R&D over 7.4 billion zlotys, the equivalent of USD 540 million.

In some disciplines, Polish science made its own original contribution to world science (as in the case of mathematics, chemistry, etc). You can also find examples of the Polish contribution to new technologies, which is presented in one of the recent publications of The Polish Academy of Sciences[1].

The quality of graduates, especially of the polytechnics, is not worse than that of western countries. The gap between Poland and those countries grows more in its industrial practice.

2.

However this relatively well developed potential is in some parts mislocated and partially mismanaged.

It finds expression in two facts:

-     As a result of the former system there are too many people working in institutes and R&D bases outside of firms. It is reflected in the fact that over 60 per cent of the R&D potential is located in the intermediate sphere between the firms and the macro-level,
-     Too many people are employed in R&D services connected with old traditional branches especially in heavy industry as a result of excessive self-sufficiency (even autarchy) prevailing in the former system as well as a consequence of an obsolete industrial structure.

Hence the negative aspects of the industrial structure of Poland are high, and in some cases excessive: the proportion of traditional branches which, in developed countries, are mostly affected by a regress or stagnation in production as a consequence of falling demand. This applies to coal-mining, ship-building, railway rolling stock industry, cement, construction ceramics, agricultural machinery, sugar, and similiar industries. About 12.5 per cent of the total industrial employment in Poland has been working in these declining branches. This means that one eighth of that employment has been working in industries that are affected by a deep recession in developed countries. On the other hand, the proportion of industries which are noticeable of the highest dynamics in the developed countries is in Poland very low. As a result in the year 1992 over 80 per cent of employment in R&D was concentrated in the institutes and scientific organisations connected with heavy industry, mainly coal, metallurgy, engineering and heavy chemical industry.

The dislocation of this potential (including R&D services in firms) showed in the data of Table 7.1.

From the total amount of money spent for R&D the share of industry was 54 per cent. In the latter the greatest part was devoted to the electro-engineering industry - 57 per cent of the total outlays for R&D in industry. From that only 1/3 went for electronics. Western countries usually spend over 1/2-2/3. In the second place was the chemical industry with 18 per cent, followed by the energy and fuel-industry with 9 per cent with coal industry making up most of this.

Almost equal was the share of metallurgy 3.8 per cent of the industry total (mainly copper industry) and food industry - 3.7 per cent of the total.

Especially low is the share in production and R&D expenditures of high technology industries, which in western countries amounts to 1/4 to 1/3 of the total.

In regard to these industries, Poland is not able to modernize them without the contribution of Western firms and their technologies, in spite of the seemingly favourable conditions in the form of a developed R&D base in some of them. This is due to the past lags in their development which cannot be easily undone.

Due to retardation in development of our technology and the isolation from the world market, there is considerable technological lag in industry when compared to the western countries.

Table 7.1
Dislocation of R&D potential

	Employment in thousands in 1991		
	Total	% of the total	from which inside firms
National economy as a whole	130.179	100.0	44.800
Industry	88.744	68.2	45.351
Energy and fuel industry	7.030	5.4	5.287
Metallurgy	4.689	3.6	1.358
Electronic/engineering industry	56.831	43.7	31.205
Chemical industry	8.894	6.8	3.007
Mineral industry	1.755	1.3	320
Wood and paper industry	1.013	0.8	562
Light industry	3.479	2.7	691
Food industry	2.362	1.8	424
High-technology industries from the total of industry*	19.300	14.8	8.923

* By high-technology industries we do understand those ones that are included in this group in western countries, independently of the technological level they represent in Poland. The most often used criterion to define these industries is: employment of scientists and engineers higher than 25 per 1000 employees and the rate of R&D expenditure not lower than 3.5 per cent of the total sales. 'The Economist', 23 August 1986, Survey, p. 10.

According to a special inquiry, conducted by the experts connected with the Polish Committee for Future Studies, which was comprised of 142 industrial items in engineering and chemical industries, none of them was placing itself in vanguard to the adequate goods of western production. From the point of view of the West, the technological level of 10 goods was quite equal to medium western standards, and 132 were retarded. In the case of 91, that is 64 per cent of the total, this retardation had been assessed for more than 5 years, and from that in a considerable part the retardation was more than 10 years.

A relatively higher level from the technological point of view was shown by such goods as electrical machinery, apparatus and power machinery and equipment. But relatively great was this retardation in microelectronics and pesticides, where this technological lag was the greatest.

3.

Nevertheless the distance between Poland and western countries in science and R&D potential is still much lower than in the industrial practice and the dissemination of new technologies in industry. Typically in Poland there is a substantial gap between science and R&D base and industrial practice.

For example, according to recent data in the European Community as a whole, there were 25 persons per 10,000 of the population engaged in R&D. In Poland, it was slightly higher and amounted to 28 persons.

When speaking of employment in R&D activities, the situation of Poland is still relatively better than the cases of Ireland, Denmark, Spain, Portugal and Greece. As one western commentator stated 'Already the southern-european countries like Spain, Portugal, and Greece are almost practically empty of scientists'[2]. Poland is not in such a drastic state and such situation could and should be avoided.

Hence the problem of how to use the relatively rich number of scientists during the process of transition to a market economy is a crucial one.

We see as a condition for positive solution of this problem and better utilization of Polish Science the preservation and protection of Polish high technology industries and ensuring the survival of these industries. They as a rule represent the highest demand for scientific results and new technologies. As a result, the survival of many scientific institutions depends on this.

From this point of view, the Polish experience of the last four years is of special importance, in particular for countries in a similar position.

4.

After 1989, the opening of the Polish economy to the world market as a result of the transition to market economy created very positive progress from the point of view of modernization of the national economy and the industry as a whole, as well as some dangers and disquieting tendencies.

Among the positive consequences, one has to mention the great increase in imports of high-technology goods. According to some estimates in 1991 the total import of high-technology goods, measured in terms of real volume meaning fixed prices, increased in the course of two years by 2.2-fold when compared to 1989 and attained a level of USD 2.4 billion. For example, Poland grew to be one of the most dynamically developing markets for such goods as personal computers (PC). Imports of such goods as main-frame computers, automation devices, medical equipment, measuring and control apparatus etc. grew also very rapidly. The fastest growing was imports from EC countries. It increased 3.8-fold in the course of two years.

These increases occurred partly as a result of softening or removing the barriers created by the Coordination Committee for Exports Control (COCOM). Since January 1992 these limitations have been slightly reduced.

That opened for the Middle and Eastern European countries access to the most up-to-date western technology, although so far the influx of new technologies is still assessed as insufficient to attain a breakthrough in the technological level of industry. However after the barriers were removed, the increase in imports of foreign technology has been impressive.

It contributed to the dissemination of modern technologies in many industrial branches, first of all in food, furniture and some others industries, where the progress was most visible. They were as a result fundamentally modernized.

Free competition has forced many industrial firms and R&D units to faster innovations and better adaptation to market economy rules, and some of them did surprisingly well. This fact has been confirmed by western observers and commentators[3].

But the process had weaker sides also. The diminishing of the technological gap in the sphere of exploitation of new technologies was almost exclusively a result of increase in imports of them, but not by the increase of our own production. It was a significant down-fall because it is connected with some difficulties in the balance of payments. It is reflected in the negative balance sheets in this field which are more and more difficult to cover due to the insufficient growth in exports. In 1986 the export and import of high technology goods closed with a small surplus of USD 200 million. In 1991 the results were negative and amounted to USD 2 billion.

5.

This process was accompanied by some dangers for more technologically advanced industries in Poland.

One of the basic assumptions of the system transformation was that the market economy would eliminate first of all traditional low value added industries and firms, ineffective and uncompetitive on the market.

In reality the situation has developed in a slightly different direction and the greatest threat arises in more technologically advanced industries. Some western economists anticipated the possibility of such development. For example Paul G. Hare from the Centre for Economic Performance in the London School of Economics in a lecture concerning the Polish Industry stated: 'there is a significant danger that many firms could fail as a result of short-term liquidity problems, even when they would be perfectly capable of performing well in the longer term'[4]. Reality proved these warnings right. But they were not sufficiently taken into account.

The end-result was deep recession in high-technology industries in Poland. The deepest fall in production and deterioration of profitability affected most of the industries that are counted among the representatives of the relatively most modern lines of today's techniques. An example of this can be the data processing industry, automation, micro-electronics, and medical equipment. The production in these industries fell deeper than in the older, more traditional branches and they are now losing business.

The regression of these industries has been a result of many causes:

a) First was a breakdown in exports to the East-European markets, more than 80 per cent of production of these industries was being exported to these countries, and they were highly profitable exports. These products were competitive in this market.

b) The second one is an increase of foreign competition and the supply of products of higher quality standards. Certainly foreign products were more advanced and competitive. But on the other hand, not even a transitional period for reconstruction and adaptation to new conditions was ensured to Poland's industry. The result was a massive influx of imports from the West.

This is reflected by the high growth of 'import penetration index' especially in the field of high-technology products. The general 'import penetration index' (relation of imports to domestic apparent consumption) grew from 16.8 per cent in 1989 to 28.3 per cent in 1991. At the same time this index, in the field of high-technology products grew from 43.1 per cent in 1989 to 67.6 per cent in 1992.

The 'import penetration index' attains the highest level in areas such as shown in Table 7.2.

Table 7.2

Import penetration data

	Import in per cent of total apparent consumption = 100	exports = 100
Computer industry products	95.0	7.8-fold
Office automation	91.0	16.2-fold
Medical equipment	87.5	7.2-fold
Optical instruments	80.5	15.7-fold
Electronics and telecommunication products	65.2	13.1-fold
Aviation industry products	51.0	83-fold
Pharmaceuticals	46.3	2.5-fold
Industry automation	31.6	115-fold

c) The third cause was the way in which the process of privatization was implemented. In Poland there are two procedures used.

One is privatization through liquidation of state firms. That means the selling of specific objects of the current assets of the enterprises and is equal to asset-stripping instead of continuing the firm as an on-going business. Most often this form of privatization is directly connected with the elimination of production and the enterprises cease to exist. The second form of privatization is through selling shares of the firms or selling them as a whole without destroying the production ability.

Due to lack of potential buyers in the high technology industry in many branches the first form of privatization was dominant and the share of privatization by liquidation of whole state firms was high. For example, in the industry producing scientific instruments the whole industry was subdued to the first procedure. The measuring and control apparatus industry was affected the same way.

d) The fourth cause was a decrease in the demand for results of R&D base. Partially, this was the result of changes in the ownership structure of the industry and its privatization. The emerging new private firms did not show an interest in cooperating with domestic science and R&D institutes. At the same time, new foreign firms based their demand exclusively on imported know-how and new technologies. For example the share of private sector of industry in total money spent for buying the R&D results and technologies from Poland's scientific institutes amounted to only 1.4 per cent, when at the same time its share in total production was 31 per cent. The bulk of this outlay concerned the public sector. From the 375 billion zlotys spent in industry the private sector bought only 5.2 billion zlotys worth of R&D results and projects. It could be a transitional phenomenon. However there is a common view that the Polish small businesses so far do not know how to cooperate with science and R&D establishments. As a result, the share of high-technology industries, which are dominating in the western small businesses, in Poland is as hitherto negligible. This situation creates some threats for R&D base and raises the question whether it can survive without the protection of the state.

e) One of the causes was the underrating of the dangers for more technologically advanced industries connected with immediate and sudden opening to the world market, with leaving not enough time for adaptation processes in those industries.

It may be reflected in the fact that in the appendix of the agreement of Poland's association with the EC no place was found for protection of high-technology industries, particularly electronics. On the contrary, the focus was directed exclusively to traditional products like steel, textiles and agriculture goods. Even the existing regulations in EC for protection of 'infant industries' were not sufficiently exploited.

This resulted in a fall of employment in the high technology industries which is illustrated by the following data of the Table 7.3.

Table 7.3
Employment in the high technology industries
(thousand of people)

Employment in firms employing more than 50 persons Industry of:	1989	1992	1992/1989 (%)
Automation equipment	18.7	10.6	56.6
Computer and electronic computing data	9.5	4.8	49.0
Office automation equipment	0.1	0.2	200.0
Measurement instruments and control	21.7	14.3	65.9
Optical goods	5.9	3.2	54.2
Electronic apparatus	1.8	1.7	94.4
Medical equipment	5.4	4.0	74.1
Aviation	28.9	21.0	72.7
Electronics (incl. consumer electronics)	112.4	52.7	46.9
Telecommunication equipment	19.0	8.5	44.7
Metal-tools	29.7	20.2	68.0
Pharmaceuticals	21.0	20.3	96.7
Special chemicals	8.6	7.4	86.0

As a whole in the above mentioned industries, employment decreased from 255 thousand people in 1986 and 188 thousand in 1989 to 112 thousand in 1992. It cannot be explained by the liquidation of overmanning in these industries only, although certainly it did exist before. This occurred as a result of a decrease in production. In the data processing industries, total production volume fell by 63 per cent in 2 years (1990-1991), in the measuring and control apparatus industry by 44 per cent and in the electronic and telecommunication industry by 23 per cent.

In comparison to the 78 thousand jobs lost in those industries (in firms of more than 50 people) the private sector, in the same fields (in firms employing up to 50 people), created only 10 thousand of new working places. Thus the relation was unfavourable from the point of view of modernization of the industrial structure, and many people were left jobless.

The sharpest decline took place in the data processing industry. In 1987 12.7 thousand people worked in this industry and now only 4.8 thousand. This decrease took place although the studies prepared by western experts included the data processing industry in the group of Polish industries assessed to have chances of development and efficient competitiveness.

Almost the same was true of the microelectronic industry, especially professional one. For example, the production of integrated circuits, which is of basic importance for modernization of industry, decreased from 62.6 million units in 1989 to 13.0 million units in 1991 and 5.5 million units in 1993 and now is near to completely disappearing. The total production of semi-conductors declined from 373 million units to 79 million units.

In 1993 the situation has slightly improved. Some firms and R&D units got better results in market adjustments and grew more competitive.

6.

These difficulties in the most technologically advanced industries in Poland was accompanied by a considerable exodus of scientists from their professions. It could be illustrated by data of the Table 7.4.

Table 7.4
Total employment in science and technology development outside the firms

Year	Scientist (thousands of people)
1989	112.1
1991	80.4
1992	71.3

The loss of scientists is partially due to emigration and creates a real loss of productive forces of the society.

> 'According to different estimates during the last 10 years, 10 per cent of scientists left Poland, about 30 per cent of scientists of such specialization as mathematics, information technologies and engineers outflowed from the profession, as well about 25 per cent of chemists and biologists and 30 per cent of specialists in medical science'[5].

The further depression of more technologically advanced industries could accelerate this process and would make it more difficult to overcome the existing technological gap.

7.

This phenomenon was expressed in a broader spectrum of transitional deterioration of the Polish industrial structure as a consequence of opening to the world market.

We do understand by deterioration the substitution of more highly processed and technologically advanced goods in production and exports by more primitive goods, especially raw materials, semi-manufactures and raw materials in only shallow processing.

It is not only an economic problem or a problem of competition. It is at the same time a very difficult social problem. Because a lot of people are connected with these industries who are not only employed in those industries but also in science and the R&D base. With these industries at least 0.5 million people were directly or indirectly connected.

This social aspect is as a rule underrated by many experts and advisers. But the unfavourable development of these industries is very critically assessed by public opinion.

The further regress of these industries would be extremely harmful for Poland because:

- they represent, in some cases, considerable production capacities,
- they still possess a well-developed R&D base,
- it would dispose of experienced personnel and capable construction engineers,
- ambitions of creative circles of the society are strongly associated with these industries,
- they determine the possibilities of utilizing the intellectual potential of the country.

This is why, in spite of their present hardships, they have chances for further development in Poland, as soon as they overcome the difficulties of the process of adjustment to the conditions of changing ownerhip, from the state to the private sector. But restructuring and the possibilty of success cannot be without co-operation with the advanced industries in Western countries. Therefore as much as possible of the foreign investments and foreign aid should be channelled to these branches of industry or services which ensures the best utilization of the intellectual potential of the country.

Failure to secure such a co-operation with foreign firms and save the industries in question from further decline would result in the public becoming more dissatisfied and exasperated.

8.

Poland is now facing two options. Either we let the high technology industries with their high R&D potential erode further or restructure and utilize them. The latter requires protection of these industries. We are certainly in favour of the second option. In the long term, you cannot overcome a technological gap based only on imports. Import on a mass scale of engineers and specialists needed in science and R&D activity is at all impossible.

Therefore we cannot effectively use the intellectual potential of the country without having our own high technology industries in areas where they could be effective. Therefore fighting the technological gap requires saving worthy industries during the transition period to a market economy. In order to accomplish this, a special policy for these industries is greatly needed.

At the same time we consider that the utilization of Polish intellectual potential, which is impossible without rational development of high technology industries in Poland, is not only in favour of Poland but at the same time in favour of Europe as a whole. And on the contrary, the loss of this potential would be a loss not only for Poland, but for Europe, too.

Therefore changes in the policy towards these industries are necessary.

9.

The following conclusions can be drawn from the experience of the last 4 years of system transformation in Poland in the field of science and R&D development:

a) The Polish experience of the transition to market economy shows that the instruments of macro-economic policy alone, as a rule of financial nature, are not sufficient to ensure the proper changes in the real structure of the national economy and industry. Meaning that the dispute of macro-economic policy *versus* industrial policy seems, in this concrete case, to be solved in favour of the combination of both. However, the core of the matter in industrial policy should be not to pick winners but an attitude towards promoting high technology industries, which determine the possibility to overcome the technological gap in the economy in a long-term process.

It requires a conscious policy and strategic choices.

Therefore the most practical could be an approach recommended by the OECD in the following definition of the scientific and technology development policy:

'In a way, the process of selecting science priorities is that of the dialectic between the internal logic of scientific knowledge and that of the needs of the economy and society. The two are different in nature, but scientific research is not outside the economy or society, and the latter need science in order to develop. The task of science policy is to bring together their objectives while respecting their separate logics. Technology policy consists neither of 'picking winners' nor of leaving everything to the 'lottery of the market' but rather of promoting the development of good stables from which the largest number of winners may emerge'[6].

In this respect it is very important for the government to do research in order to determine which firms and types of industry are worth saving and which are not.

b) Accordingly the government should play a more active role in the protection and promotion of high technology industries as the main consumers of science and R&D results. In order to attain this goal, the government must actively promote the increase of demand for home scientific and R&D results. This would require some changes in taxation and crediting of foreign capital and enterprises. One function of the state should be the creation of such conditions so that the intellectually intensive industries could survive in a market economy environment.

c) The state must initiate, promote and support the introduction of an up-to-date organization and functioning science and R&D basis.

d) Special *stimula* are needed for the creation of the infrastructure for commercialization of science and R&D results and technologies according to the market economy rules. Therefore the 'venture capital' firms should be supported and common organizations, on the border between universities and industry, should be promoted. In the fields of most strategic importance - setting up of scientific - industrial consortia, with the financial participation of the government, could be useful.

e) Better protection in the international agreements is needed for the high technology industries, not only the traditional ones, as well as better use of regulations concerning the protection of 'infant industries',

f) Increasing the wages and bonification system for R&D results in the public sector is needed to stop an excessive outflow abroad from science and R&D base especially of young scientists,

g) It is necessary to utilize as much as possible chances of international cooperation in science and technology and R&D activity, and international cooperation in these industries, including assembly lines in production based on foreign parts and elements as an alternative to closing whole factories in high-technology industries,

h) In this situation very active marketing is strongly needed, from the side of scientific institutes and R&D basis oriented towards all kinds of industry, especially the private one, to overcome the weak knowledge among the new emerging firms of the possibilities of science and R&D,

i) Profound changes are necessary in science and R&D potential dislocation. The employment in R&D dominating now on the medium level outside the firms should be gradually shifted in the direction of universities on one side and R&D services in firms on the other.

In our view these measures could accelerate the process of overcoming the inherited technological gap and ensure better use of the intellectual background of the society.

The solution to the above mentioned problems would allow for a more optimistic look on the future. The lost potential can still be restored. At the same time, it indicates the crucial role of the transitional period from this point in science and technology development.

Notes

1   'Rola nauki w przebudowie gospodarki kraju', ('The role of science in the country's reconstruction'). Polish Academy of Sciences, May 1993, p. 21-22.
2   Cited after 'Forum' (Polish Weekly), 1986, no. 48, p. 3.
3   'The Economist', 23 January 1993, p. 25.
4   Paul G. Hare: 'Macroeconomic vs. industrial policy in shaping the branch and regional structure of the economy', a lecture presented in Poland, Cracow, November 1981, xero, p. 6-7.
5   'About the need of a strategic concept of Poland's development and the role of science in economy reconstruction', Polish Academy of Sciences, September 1993, p. 21.
6   OECD 'Choosing Priorities in Science and Technology', Paris 1991.

8 The technological lag and technological potential of the Czech economy and implications for its integration into the world economy

Jana Sereghyová

Already when considering the acceptance of my invitation to this conference I stressed that I am not an expert in educational issues, that my interests and expertize lie in the sphere of international economic relations. So it is from this point of view that I shall be dealing with the subject on hand, thus evaluating some of the implications of past and possible future developments of the technological potential of the economy of the Czech Republic and of the technological lag showing up here at present, for its incorporation into the world economy.

As I had the honour to cooperate with the late Dr George Ray on his book dealing with 'Innovations and Technology in Eastern Europe' I became aware that in the past - before totalitarian regimes were introduced here - not only in the Czech Republic, but also in other Central-East-European countries most important innovations of their time had been applied and some of them were even developed here. This indicates that before the communist take-over they belonged to the group of technologically advanced European countries. For the Czech Republic this assumption was confirmed also by the fact that the level of economic development it reached in the late 40's was very near to the development levels of West-European countries of similar size, beginning with that of Austria up to that of the Netherlands. Thanks to the efforts of my colleagues in Geneva, who were so kind as to look for relevant data in the archives of the Economic Commission for Europe of the United Nations, we are able to prove this.

Table 8.1

National income per capita in Central-East- and West-Europe in 1938 and 1948

(US dollars in 1938 prices)

Selected countries	1938	1948
West-European average	262	254
Norway	255	253
Belgium-Luxemburg	275	278
Netherlands	323	250
Austria	179	130
Czechoslovakia	176	195
Hungary	112	98
Poland	104	141

Source: Economic Survey of Europe in 1948, pp. 235., UN, Geneva, 1948.

As it is well known, there exists a strong correlation between the level of economic development of individual countries and their technological potential, - showing up not only in the qualification and the intellectual background of their population, but also in the efficiency and competitivity of their industry - these data can be regarded also as a proof that not only the economic, but also the technological level of the economy of the former Czechoslovakia - was very near to the all-European avarage at that time.

The damage, which more than 40 years history of being a 'planned economy' has wrought on the technological potential of the former CSFR, has not yet been evaluated in full. It is possible to assess the damage done only by indirect indices. As one of the most convincing ones is regarded the spectacular increase of the lag in economic development, which all Central-East-European countries showed up. Even when computed on the basis of the internal buying-power parity of their currencies, their pro-capita GDP amounted by 1985 only to 7,700 USD in the former CSFR, to 7,259 USD in Hungary and to 5,630 USD in Poland, which represents about 1/2 up to 2/3 of the ex-capita GDP the above mentioned 4 West-European countries reached at that time. (This was 11,233 USD in Austria, 11,925 USD in the Netherlands, 12,584 USD in Belgium and 13,826 USD in Norway[1].)

As another proof of this damage can be regarded the dramatic deterioration of the structure of exports of the former CSFR, which had been observed mainly after 1989. By the end of 1992 final industrial products participated only by 32 per cent in its overall exports, (consumer goods by 14.4 per cent and machinery by 17.3 per cent) while the remaining part of its exports was constituted mainly of semi-products, raw-materials and fuels. It has been argued that this deterioration of its export-structure is due to a large extent to trade-political and psychological barriers Czech enterprises are faced with in their trade with the West. This is actually the case with their exports of some types of consumer goods (mainly the so-called 'sensitive ones'), but the imports of machinery and of products of other 'research intensive' production lines of Czechoslovak provenance was liberalized in most market economies already in 1991. So as the main reason for this deterioration of the export structure of the former CSFR, we regard the fact that only after having reoriented its exports from 'soft' Eastern to highly demanding Western markets, the consequences of the technological lag which had developed here in past years became apparent, showing up in the poor competitivity of most of its 'sophisticated products'.

During a research project we were engaged in recently, we tried to ascertain whether and how quickly this technological lag which was observed in the economy of the Czech Republic is closing up. We came to the conclusion that in entirely domestically owned enterprises of long standing - even in already privatized ones - this process is going at a relatively slow pace. This is caused by a wide range of reasons, which we might try to clarify during our discussion. Already now I would like to stress that among them the lack of investment capital played an important role, as it reduced the possibility of installing new machinery, which is usually necessary when introducing entirely new technologies. Thus even the purchase of licences abroad - which were expected to be the main 'vehicle' to improving their technological level - remained scarce in these enterprises.

In small newly founded private enterprises -where new technologies and a 'new generation' of products was introduced already from the beginning, this process went on at a much higher pace. But the macroeconomic benefits of this phenomenon are as yet limited, as up to now such enterprises have only a very low share in overall industrial production in the Czech Republic.

The most spectacular transfers of technology were observed in some of the enterprises with foreign capital participation. But even here the size and types of these transfers differed case by case. Mainly in the chemical industry we observed some joint-ventures where the foreign investor 'brought in' an entirely new technology which led to fundamental changes in the characteristics of its products. In most other cases the technology the foreign investor made available led up mainly to improvements in the production process, as well as to an upgrading of the quality of the products of such joint ventures, but usually it showed up only in their partial innovations. Moreover, especially in the engineering industry such innovations were brought in much more frequently by the foreign investor supplying some of the high-tech components from his own plant, than by introducing their production in the joint-venture enterprise.

Hopefully, this represents only a transitory phase in the process of reintroducing the Czech industry to international trade with products produced in research-intensive branches. But at present it shows a rather ambivalent picture, as far as the revitalization of its technological potential is concerned.

In this respect we regard as alarming another of our findings: we ascertained that the 'survival scenarios' many of the fully domestically owned Czech industrial enterprises have applied in the past three years had led frequently to a downgrading of their production programs, to their reverting to the production of basic products. This often implied the dissolution of their R&D teams and sometimes even dismissals of their technicians and/or some other highly qualified employees. Similar developments were observed in some joint-venture enterprises, especially in those where the investors (foreign as well as domestic) were trying to make 'quick profits', utilizing mainly the low wage-levels established in the Czech Republic, by producing here the simplest, labour-intensive kind of goods.

Of course these behavioural patterns were not the only ones we observed. At present the development strategies of an increasing number of enterprises are already aimed at improving the technological level of their products, - either by using foreign progressive technologies or by developing innovations of their own- at achieving access to market-niches in which highly demanding customers are predominant. But it has to be conceded that in the sample of 63 enterprises whose behavioural patterns we analyzed, such enterprises were in the minority.

So it seems, that - though for different reasons, - the weakening of the technological potential of the Czech industry, which was triggered off in times of its 'command-economy' past, is still going on. To put a halt to and to reverse this process we consider to be a matter of fundamental importance not only because - if we are not successful in this - it might condemn numerous Czech enterprises for years to come to an existence 'on the bottom' of the markets on which they are operating, but also because the reversal of this process represents one of the important preconditions for the Czech Republic to remain a part of the 'developed world', for being able to enter later on into the 'big Europe', for being regarded as an acceptable partner by other member countries.

When evaluating the chances to achieve such a 'come-back' in the not-too-far future, we reverted once more to the usual comparisons of the economic and technological levels and the export structures of various countries. We ascertained that the structure of exports of the Czech Republic outlined above is very similar to that which we meet nowadays in some of the more developed developing countries, whose ex-capita GDP - which is regarded as one of the main indicators for their economic and technological level - represents less than half of that which was reached in the Czech Republic at present.

Table 8.2
Share of semi-products and raw-materials (i.e. SITC 1 - 6) in exports of the Czech and the Slovak Republic and in exports of selected developing countries in 1992
(in per cent, overall industrial exports = 100)

Argentine	53.3
Brazil	52.0
Czech Rebublic	54.9
Slovak Rebublic	60.9

Source: Trade in Commodities, U.N., N.Y. 1993.

Here we see that the deterioration of the export structure of the Czech and Slovak Republic has proceeded far beyond the lag in their development level which developed during past decades. This indicates that an improvement of this structure might be achieved even before embarking on the application of measures aimed at improving the qualification of their population, that it might be brought about mainly by establishing better preconditions for the utilization of the intellectual potential which already exists here, by fully utilizing this potential not only in production, but also in services as well as in trade.

But it cannot be denied that while aiming at developing a similar structure of production and exports as eg. their counterparts in West-European countries show at present - and taking into account the above mentioned correlation between export structures and development levels of individual countries - enterprises in the Czech Republic would obviously have a very long way to go before reaching this goal. Our assessments of the time-limit in which the Czech Republic and other Central-East-European countries might reach a similar economic level as West-European countries now indicate that this will certainly not happen in this century. This made us wonder whether these countries will have to accept in full the theorem, which insists on the fact that the technological level of each country - and thus also the structure of its production and exports - is closely bound to changes in its development level. Economic theory proves that this theorem is valid, but economic practice shows that there also exist some exceptions to this rule. In modern economic history the most spectacular of these exceptions was the development of Japan in the 60's as well as that of the NICs of Southeast Asia in the last two decades. Their 'legend' indicates that under special conditions, the economic potential of some countries may increase far in advance of their overall development level. This opened up the question whether the Czech Republic - as well as other Central-East-European countries - might not become another exception to the above mentioned rules; whether their industrial traditions - which in some cases reach back several centuries - and the rich intellectual background they have, do not represent another set of special circumstances, which would enable them to overcome the above mentioned heritage of the past at a high speed.

So as to be able to assess whether Central-East-European countries might also be capable of such a 'leap-frogging' in the sphere of structural changes and in strengthening their technological potential and their positions on world markets, we tried to get insight into the circumstances under which the spectacular successes the 'four tigers' achieved in these spheres were based. As none of us are experts in economics of the developing world, it may well be that we overlooked some important facts. Nevertheless, we would like to present our main findings here for discussion.

We came to the conclusion, that besides the extremely low wage-levels established here and the unusually high work-morale of the local population, these successes were based mainly on the following four groups of influencing factors:

First: on a very strong inflow of foreign capital. Although it 'came in' mostly as foreign direct investment, its growth was motivated not only by commercial interests; it was enhanced also by export-credit schemes and export-credit-insurance facilities which were partly financed from the state-budgets of the home countries of the investors, mainly from that of the USA, which were obviously interested in having their firms establish their presence in these countries. But also the tax-holidays and huge tax-exemptions the 'four tigers' granted to foreign investors represented a regulatory measure aimed at increasing this inflow of foreign capital.

Second: the foreign direct investments which came in were directed at first mainly into 'labour-intensive' industrial branches (especially into textiles), but already before long they became engaged also in the electrotechnical and electronics industry - being instrumental in building it up 'from scratch', bringing in lots of high techology from abroad. The fact that foreign investors at first established here mainly assembly plants or a subdelivery base for their own use - producing here the simplest kinds of semi-products or products - does not change the advantage that the build-up of these plants caused the qualification of the local population to increase at high speed.

Third: All the 'four tigers' increased dramatically their expenditures on education and research (both financed mainly from public resources), they did so even while running at first huge deficits of their state budgets. Simultaneously the regimes and rules applied by local enterprises (foreign and domestic) made employment conditional on their employees taking steps towards an improvement of their qualification.

Fourth: in the first years (decade) after this development concept was applied, all these countries kept their internal markets tightly closed, giving strong protection to their local enterprises, mainly to those established in 'research intensive' industrial branches.

Obviously, all these represent a rather exotic development strategy. But if we want to evaluate the possibility to become the 'four European small tigers' we shall have to reconsider whether the application of some - or none? - of these measures might be feasible and/or useful in our countries, whether they would help us to overcome not only the technological lag which still persists in our economies, but also numerous other 'handicaps' we will have to cope with, before being able to achieve the desired reintegration of our economies into the world economy.

Finally I would like to stress that I regard the overcoming of this technological lag, and the full use of the already existing, as well as the further strengthening of the intellectual background of our countries to be of major importance not only from an economic point of view. It is not less important for an early acceptance of our countries as equal partners in international cultural and political relations, it is conditional to our achieving similar positions among the developed market economies, which we occupied before the introduction of totalitarian regimes in our countries.

Notes

1   See Borenstein I.: 'Comparative GDP levels, Physical Indicators, Phase III.', U.N. Geneva, 1993

PART III
DYSFUNCTION AND INTEGRATION: FOREIGN TRADE IN TRANSITION

9 Opening up to world economy and the single European market

Pál Majoros

1. Understanding Hungary (and Eastern Europe)

A cornerstone in Hungarian history, 1990 was the year of social and political transition. The political change has gone off fairly smoothly, whilst economic restructuring will take a long time since every change affects interests, social conflicts deepen. Economic change is going on at different levels. *First*, a command economy has to be turned into a liberal market economy in a country that has not experienced real market forces before. *Second*, in foreign economy a constrained, overheated trade with Eastern Europe has partly to be replaced by trade with industrialized countries. Here, it must be noted that only an efficient market economy can cope with that task. Therefore, a most important *third* change is to get people to accept the set of values, rules and risks of a market economy. The paternalist ideal of state, enforced for the previous 40 years, has got to be replaced by the notion of liberal-social state. All this is going to take a long time.

In understanding Hungary we must emphasize that Hungary is a small country with an open economy. Small in terms of its populace, territory and economic performance, with open economy meaning that almost half of its GDP is derived from foreign trade.

Being a small country requires a mentality of utmost utilization of potential advantages whilst at the same time it also means being more vulnerable and exposed to changes in world economy, using realistic, rationalistic concepts in determining its economic and foreign trade policy in the face of extreme difficulties which now prevail in Central and Eastern Europe. Hungary has always been a buffer state, on the verge of two cultures with a need to decide which one to choose at any given time.

A brief historical outlook will show us that the Hungarian tribes arrived in the Carpathian basin in 895 AD. At that time the country was in the buffer zone of Christian and non-Christian Europe. Christianity became state regime in 1000 AD - it also means that the country had joined the Christian states. A slow and consolidated development followed, interspersed with conquests through which the country gained access to the sea. Although major European trade routes did not cross the country, the extraction of gold had made it a powerful economic centre in Europe.

In the 15th century, however, Muslim Turkey waged a 'sacred' war on Christian Europe. Through its geographical position, Hungary became a bulwark defending Europe. In the 16th century, the Turks occupied and held a large part of the country for 150 years. Hungary was torn in three parts: the Habsburgs dominated the western part, the Turks spread to the middle, and Transylvania was a principality dependent on the Turks. Following the Turkish occupation, the Habsburg realm was later formed into the Austro-Hungarian-Monarchy where the division of power obviously served Austrian interests. The Austrian and Czech industries were enhanced through customs tariffs and protectionism within the Monarchy, with Hungary extracting basic materials and cultivating agriculture. Also, where in Western Europe the institution of villenage (feudal serfdom) had ceased to exist by 16-17th century and in Austria by mid 18th century, in Hungary all this took place only in 1848.

At that time it was one of the least developed countries in Europe - with more developed industries, cultures west of it, and even more backward countries east and south of Hungary. Hungary had little industry. Industrial development started after 1872 when the privileges of guilds were abolished. Foreign - mainly Austrian - capital was invested in extracting and food industries. Domestic capital was involved in the process of capital accumulation only at the end of the 19th century. Here, a specific aspect of industrial development is the absence of manufactures - following the guilds large-scale industry made its appearance immediately. In the period between 1872 and 1913, trade within the Monarchy was dominant (80-85 per cent of all exports), trade with the British Empire was below 1 per cent.

Following the First World War, Hungary, a loser, was partitioned, and successor states got two thirds of the territory, half of the population and almost all of the mines of the former Hungarian Kingdom. More important perhaps, as a result of the dissolution of the Monarchy, Hungary lost its markets. Between the two World Wars, disabled Hungary experienced a very slow development.

Another date: 1934. Hungary became a chief food supplier of Hitler's Germany. (Following the world economic recession, such a market was very important.) Germany also had a growing share in Hungarian foreign trade turnover - 22-24 per cent in 1936, 50 per cent in 1939 and over 80 per cent in 1944. Hungary's fate again was bound to the German economic region. World War II brought about the destruction of half the fixed assets, 40 per cent of the national assets, a death toll of one million people and again a loss of the market. A short-lived multi-party system was followed by a political change (socialism), state ownership (a negation of private ownership), planned economy and Comecon. On the western border of the Soviet Union, Hungary's economic and trade relations were soon dominated by the Soviet Union. In the 60's 70 per cent of Hungarian foreign trade turnover was realized in trade with socialist countries (46-48 per cent with the Soviet Union). Hungary got in a state of double dependence. On the one hand, we depended on the Soviet Union for raw material (mainly crude oil) supplies, on the other hand we depended on the huge Soviet markets.

At the same time, hot debates began in the socialist countries about planned and/or market economies. It had become obvious that everything could not be planned in advance, (if it could, where would the world be?) and also that the market was not infallible (see Marx). It later became a regulated market. Theoretical debates were followed by practical changes for the first time in Hungary in Eastern Europe. In 1968, a reform process started - the liberalization of the economy. Although Hungary had a leading role, the reform process ground to a halt in the 70's mainly because the Western world, although approving of it, had, in practice, not supported the attempts at reforming socialism. Also countries of the East, Brezhnev's Soviet Union, had clearly objected to reforms. Hungary had been left alone. Attempts to modify the reform, to create a 'regulated market' failed. But there were also some favourable results, e.g. a rise in living standards in the 70's, and a restructuring of foreign trade started; by 1988 trade with socialist countries fell to 43-44 per cent (with the Soviet Union having 28 per cent). In 1989 trade with industrialized countries was on the same level as with socialist countries. That year saw the start of the global collapse of socialism. In 1990, in Hungary's foreign trade turnover, socialist (mainly Comecon) trade had a share of under 30 per cent, that of the Soviet Union amounted to under 20 per cent. 1991 witnessed the total collapse of trade with small Central and Eastern European countries. In the case of the Soviet Union turnover amounted to 10-12 per cent. In 1992-93 the Eastern European turnover has showed a slight increase, whilst trade with advanced Western Europe has been stagnating.

Hungary again seems to be moving to the eastern borderline of the west European integration. (This is how, from a western outpost of the Soviet Union, Hungary is becoming the eastern outpost of Western Europe.)

Summing it all up:

-     Industrial development in Eastern Europe started 2-300 years later than in Western Europe.
-     In Hungary (and Eastern Europe), during 120 years of industrial development, a change of ownership and markets has taken place every forty years (following the first and second world wars, then in 1989-90), making the strengthening of ownership rights, interests and management attitudes impossible. The continuity of development has been broken several times during these 120 years.
-     Borders in Eastern Europe came into being as a result of peace treaties 1919-20, Paris, so there was no territorial stability. By now, enforced borders have become sources of ethnic problems.
-     The late development did not encourage the creation of an appropriate labour culture. Nowadays, about 80 per cent of industrial workers are first or second generation. During the forty years of 'socialist ownership' a characteristic feature was: 'If something belongs to everybody, it belongs to nobody'. Owner and employee were identical, there was no real interest in the economy.
-     Management skills are also absent due to frequent shifts in ownership, although changes have occurred in this respect.

All in all, there has been no market economy in Hungary and in Eastern Europe so far, (apart from some short-lived attempts in 1890-1913, 1927-30), and the notions of market are missing from people's minds.

Obviously, the change that has already started will take a long time. The elimination of the command economy and the creation of a market economy, require relevant institutions. At the same time it is also obvious that the great chance of Eastern Europe getting into line with Western Europe has come, and on the whole international conditions are favourable, but western assistance is required to help this change.

Hungary will have to find effective ways of joining the international division of labour, to find ways of exploiting its sources of comparative advantages. It is important that we should see the possibilities and problems which may affect and influence Hungary's economic choices. That is now attempted. Namely:

- Hungary is poor in raw materials and fuels. Domestic fuels cover one third of home consumption and the formerly cheap power has to be bought at world market prices from the Soviet Union.
- Of metallic minerals there are sufficient quantities of bauxite only. There are sufficient quantities of non-metallic minerals for the building material industry.
- About two thirds of the country's territory has better than average arable land. Climatic conditions are good, so land could become a source of comparative advantage.
- Labour force is available. However, labour mobility is on a very low level for reasons of housing shortage and housing mobility. Workers are skilled on an average European level, but wages are well below West European level (another source of comparative advantage).
- Hungary is also poor in capital. The country has always been short of capital, a Hungarian capitalist class has never sprung up. Even in today's economy, domestic capital is very little (but on the increase).

During the past 40 years, official ideology has attracted western capital. Attempts at liberalization during the past few years have tried to invite foreign capital to decrease the shortage.

Technological backwardness, low productivity owing to shortage of capital are also characteristic features, but skilled cheap workforce, relative technical backwardness and good management could also become sources of comparative advantage.

Hungary's economic situation

- Foreign indebtedness amounts to USD 20 billion, the highest per head in Europe. (The rate is not so bad compared with exports.) Hungary has always paid its debts on time, and maintaining international solvency is a priority of today's government too! But at the same time, correct payments mean withdrawing net capital from the country (interests have to be paid). So Hungary, which faces a shortage of capital, suffers further withdrawal of capital. This is also why drawing in working capital is so important.
- Privatization has gone ahead (with the help of foreign capital), but the process is not fast enough.
- State budget has a permanent deficit and inner (domestic?) indebtedness is great (about USD 18 billion).
- Inflation has been growing fast since the early 80'. (See Figure 9.1.) An encouraging sign is that the monthly increase has stopped so a

reduction in the interbank interest rate became possible in October, 1991.

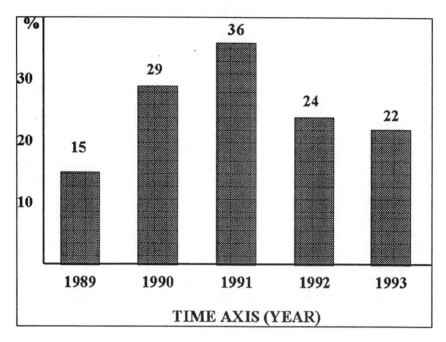

Figure 9.1   Annual inflation rate in Hungary

-    Full employment, a feature of socialism, ceased to exist since the contradictions between full and efficient employment have become more and more marked. About 14 per cent of the population eligible to work are registered unemployed and this figure is expected to increase.
-    Divided trade unions are unable to put up resistance, though bad feelings on the part of the population make the government proceed cautiously. (Today's working generation has virtually not been familiar with unemployment.)
-    Because of the technological backwardness, the raw-material and energy demand of production exceeds comparable indexes of industrialized countries by 30 per cent.
-    Poor infrastructure hinders the increase of production.
-    Ecological problems, especially air and water polluting are of major concern. (However, the source of pollution can sometimes be found in neighbouring countries.)

- Production was stagnant in the 80's, however, it decreased at the end of the decade (by 5 per cent in 1990, 10 per cent in 1991, 3 per cent in 1992, and stagnation in 1993). The decrease is particularly relevant in so-called crisis-industries like mining, iron and aluminium, metallurgy, building and building material industry. A restructuring is taking place in the economy: large-scale, overdeveloped heavy industry has always cost a lot, now attempts are being made to get rid of the least profitable ones. A major part of the Hungarian industry has been based on trade with the East, which has now collapsed. The products of these companies are not competitive on the markets of industrialized countries. Again, capital would be needed to make these companies competitive. And since there is no capital available, it is mainly these companies that are being privatized. The structure of Hungarian companies is a reason for the fall of production: under the socialist regime, to make planning easier, there were only large-scale companies. Since the early 80's, there have been more and more small-scale enterprises, but medium-scale, flexible, dynamic companies are still lacking. On the one hand, there are large-scale, inefficient state companies, on the other hand there are thousands of small business employing only a few people. The trouble is that one giant can make hundreds of small ones bankrupt.

- There are important changes in foreign trade as well. Former socialist Governments declared the policy of opening up to world economy, which means that liberal market economy should be created, capable of operating as part of, and according to the requirement and rules of the world market.

Opening up is a dual task: on the one hand it means creating a workable, competitive market economy on a world market, on the other hand it means a reorientation towards the markets of industrialized countries. The latter, owing to the collapse of the traditional, eastern markets has become an acute problem with Hungary responding fairly quickly and well. Although the volume of exports as a whole decreased, western exports have risen by 30 per cent in 1991. In 1990-92, Hungary's most important partners are the EC countries, especially Germany. Of the East European countries, Hungary has been the first to change its export pattern although the trade balance shows a slight deficit of USD 3.5 billion.

2. Hungary in the right perspective of world economy

Hungarian economic policy today is dominated by the double aspect of opening up to world economy: the formation of a competitive market economy and reorientation of foreign economy. Integration into the main trends of world development, getting into line with a developed Europe are major priorities of the Hungarian foreign economic policy.

Developed market economies are characterized by large-scale specialization and cooperation enhancing their economic development. For a small country like Hungary with an open economy, participation in the international division of labour is of utmost importance, from the points of view of both necessity and reason. Being a small country requires different scope, different priorities in economic policy, rationalities, targets, different characteristics of development. A small country cannot develop every sector of the economy, because that would mean splitting up its development resources, preserving backwardness. A small country therefore needs a well-founded economic policy, a rational, coordinated foreign economic and structural policy to achieve results on the international market.

On examining Hungary, we can see that the turbulent world economic changes of the 70's and 80's have increased the economic tensions and structural contradictions of the country. Further, the established export structure does not meet changing requirements, the terms of trade have deteriorated and national production has been devalued on the world market. Another major problem is the collapse of Comecon, our former main market. However, opening up to world economy does not simply mean strengthening contacts with developed market economies and their firms, a simple foreign economic reorientation, winding up forty years of one-sided Comecon orientation. Opening up to world economy means the ability of the Hungarian economy to adopt world market competition, regulations, incentives, rules, requirements in order to become integral part of the world economy - (but that can only be achieved by a working market economy). Opening up also means the liberalization of the economy so that the country can receive the flow of the economy, so that the country can receive the flow of goods and services as well as technical and economic know-how, information, capital and labour.

No matter how promising these objectives are, the Hungarian economic policy has a very small scope. Hungary has been living and working in a very special double relationship with the East and the West with all the characteristic structural proportions (disproportions). Therefore, Hungary needs a foreign economic policy capable of making a consistent system out of the technical challenges of the industrialized countries and cooperation with the Central-Eastern European neighbours (concerning raw material supply and outlet).

Economic policy, market economy and foreign economic reorientation have to be achieved simultaneously as these are interdependent. Liberalized foreign trade activities and the elaboration of an export orientated economic strategy are of utmost importance. A key to success may be the liberalization of imports (along with all the risks like e.g. balance of payments deficit) since it creates competition for the domestic manufacturer, helps adapt to world market competition, improves the competitiveness and export possibilities of Hungarian producers. An important achievement is the fact that, now 85-90 per cent of Hungarian imports are liberalized without a considerable deficit of the international balance of payments.

The scope of the Hungarian economic policy is restricted mostly by a considerable debt stock of the country. (The debt servicing rate amounts to a risky 40 per cent.) A basic requirement of foreign economic policy is the availability of resources to finance the debt, to maintain the liquidity of the country. These requirements limit the scope of the economic management to such an extent that the chance of modernizing the economy and the society becomes almost impossible.

Above factors make large scale direct foreign capital investment necessary in the development of economy. The much coveted economic restructuring, participation in the international division of labour, the winding up of backwardness compared to industrialized nations, the prospective lining-up are all impossible without capital. Direct foreign capital investment in Hungary in the form of economic partnerships has been possible since 1972. Laws passed in 1988 (the beginning of transition) created a stable political, legal and economic system of institutions which have made Hungary attractive to foreign investors, where foreign capital feels safe and the return on investments is adequate. Between 1989-91 the number of joint ventures has rapidly increased and the total capital investment amounts to USD 5.5 billion. In the reform process as well as the integration of foreign capital, Hungary has been first among the Eastern European countries. About 50 per cent of the capital invested in Eastern Europe has come to Hungary. (But this is just a fraction of foreign capital investments in the world economy.) Regarding the origin and size of the foreign capital, the USA, Germany and Austria take the lead. The number of firms set up with foreign capital is over 8,000, the majority with German and Austrian partners. American capital helped establish fewer firms with large basic capital while the number of German and Austrian enterprises is larger with smaller basic capital.

Direct capital investments are concentrated in industry and services. Multinationals with large capital invested mainly in industry while large numbers of joint ventures with small basic capital were set up in the commercial and service sectors. Foreign capital played a major role in the development of small scale enterprises which had been absent from the Hungarian economy, further in the change of ownership structure, in strengthening private ownership awareness.

Experience of the past three years shows that direct foreign capital investment (despite favourable effects) have not solved the problems of Hungarian economy. Capital inflow has not considerably changed the economic structure, the technical-technological level has not increased significantly, world-market competitiveness has not increased.

Hungary's chances for attracting direct capital investment are not very good. This is because the market economy and the liberalization of the economy have not been implemented yet. The low level of productive and non-productive infrastructure helping the operation of companies is also an impediment.

Now, what factors can make Hungary attractive to a foreign investor? These may be the low wage cost and an intellectual potential on average European level. Regarding its size, the Hungarian market is not really attractive and the small domestic market hinders considerable capital inflow. However, we must not forget about the huge market potential in the east. Market there is still flat but will certainly start developing after some time. (The successor states of the Soviet Union may create powerful demand.) When that market shows signs of starting to operate, investments in Hungary will become more attractive since it means producing for a much larger market. In choosing Hungary, the foreign investor is motivated by the gradual liberalization of the economy, the creation of a market economy (Hungary is first in this field in eastern Europe). Hungarian producers and businessmen know these markets and businessmen there. In the course of privatization, there is a good opportunity for foreign capital investors to acquire ownership rights in formerly Soviet market orientated big companies (and do so cheaply), to participate in improving technical-technological level. That means Hungary can become a bridge, a gate to the countries of Eastern Europe.

Hungary, on the other hand, can expect foreign capital to contribute to finances (because of the shortage of capital) and to establishing management and production on a higher level. Foreign capital means technology transfer, brings about technical improvement in other sectors of domestic economy (multiplication effect). It may create jobs and increase budget revenue. Most important, however, is the spread of a way of thinking characteristic of private ownership, which may contribute to market economy and the competitiveness of the Hungarian economy.

A very important condition of opening up to world economy is the creation of a convertible national currency, the Forint (HUF). Without that, market conditions do not operate reasonably since the money would not follow the changes of value in the world economy, the operation of the market economy would be hindered. The lack of convertibility is an obstacle to the integration into the world economy and hinders direct capital investment to help renew the economy. Conditions, advantages and risks of creating convertibility are manifold and would form the subject of a separate study. Here we must emphasize that convertibility will be the outcome of the emerging complex economic-financial links that must be settled. A supply economy is needed that stimulates entrepreneurial spirit and that operates under stable political-economic conditions (e.g. decreasing inflation etc.). Convertibility can be interpreted as a synthetic index reflecting the state and operation of the economy, the developed market conditions, the dynamic macro balance, world market integration, the economic policy and finally the inside and outside confidence in the domestic currency.

Convertibility is a sign of opening and adapting to world economy. It is through convertibility that the unity of economic and economic-political openness is achieved, it is through a convertible domestic currency that international effects can be felt without restriction in the domestic economy, this is how domestic economy becomes an integral part of the world economy.

However, opening up occurs at the cost of part of the domestic producers being pushed from the market due to practically unrestricted competition. Restructuring is a painful process since the winding up of inefficient production activities will entail the winding up of traditional trades and occupations. In its wake, there is increasing unemployment and inflation. Hungary, the Hungarian economy have started paying that price in the hope of ensuing development and prosperity.

3. Hungary and the single European market

Even from an international respect, Hungary is an outstandingly open state, highly sensitive to foreign economy. Between 1988 and 1992, Hungary has carried through a quick and successful reorientation concerning its foreign trade relations. The fruitful market reorientation and the increasing share of advanced industrialized countries in Hungarian foreign trade (which had already begun in 1968) were motivated by external forces (the cessation of the Comecon, the collapse of Eastern markets etc.), and, on the other hand, conditions for coming into market were improved by the development of a market economy and by an effective foreign trade policy (EC Association

Agreement, EFTA and CEFTA Free Trade Agreements), and also by the increasing inflow of foreign capital. During the restructuring process, the EC's importance has increased to the highest degree: by the end of 1992, more than 50 per cent of total Hungarian foreign trade activities was handled with the 12 EC member states. Hungarian-EC relations have been improving since 1988, previous discrimination was first followed by peaceful co-existence, then by a period of assistance and support. At present - according to the Association Agreement- we are a preferential country with liberalized connections, but in certain key fields (textile industry, metallurgy, agriculture, etc.) protectionist views are still dominant. It is a consequence of previous years' world economic recession that such protectionist tendencies have not declined significantly, and that our relations seem to be losing their wind since 1992 (Hungarian exports have declined by 1/3).

Being highly dependent upon external supplies of natural, technological and financial resources and markets, Hungary is structurally vulnerable. The tiny country has to integrate into the world-wide division of labour, thus opening up to world economy and the development of an export-oriented economic strategy is the essential priority of our foreign trade policy. Of course, all these bring along a need to adjust and to take risks, but there is no other choice for us.

The parallel phenomena of globalization and regionalization in world economy make it inescapable for a tiny country to throw in its lot with an economic power-centre in its own area. This economic power-centre is the EC for us. The Association Agreement was signed at a proper time (16 December 1991), since it has meant an opportunity to widen markets for both parties, and, being an asymmetric agreement, it also put Hungary at a temporary advantage. In the system of relations, we have to realize the special terms of the two participants, 'the Big and the Small'. The Big's capability to enforce its interests is many times better than that of the Small. The Small's necessity for adjustment may well lead to one-sided dependence (which we have experienced several times in the past), however, this can be avoided by adequate policies, or can be transformed into mutual (if not symmetric) interdependence. The Small has to take notice of the Big being engaged in its own internal and external problems. This is a particular issue we have to experienced recently: the EC is employed in promoting its own integration (Single European Market, monetary and economic union etc.), and with scraping through the world economic recession. Thus Central-Eastern Europe with Hungary is not ranked amongst top priorities. With the collapse of the Soviet Union the power that held together the Central-Eastern European region has ceased, leaving the region's small economies to search for new directions. Prior to this happening, the West had always aimed at separating the small Comecon member states from the Big Brother, the Soviet Union. This motivation held off with the collapse the Big Brother in 1992, and it seems as if the West's interest in the area is declining.

The most important question is whether Hungary will be able to adjust to the unified market of the EC, to the Single European Market (SEM). Due to the SEM, competition within the Community has been becoming keener and keener, but economic growth, price reduction and improvement of employment conditions are to be expected as well (Cecchini report). The improvement of competitiveness is essential to survive on such a huge market. The advantage of efficient producers and exporters will be growing at a highly increased rate, whilst all the others should reckon with the loss of market shares.

A noteworthy rearrangement of power relations between different regions and companies of the Community can be presumed, too: the large-scale capital and labour force redistribution has already been under way, and internal trade has been on the increase.

The Single Market has its contradictory effects on non-member states and companies. A positive effect of global economic growth might result in an increased need for imports, if exporters' efficiency could be improved by way of radical restructuring.

However, numerous counter-arguments may arise as well:
-      due to the global economic recession, there is no growth in 1993;
-      the price reducing effect of the single market has its impact on internal (Community) products first of all, thus increasing demand for these products at the expense of external, imported products (demand directing effect);
-      increasing internal trade may lead to strengthening protectionism against external states;
-      demand is increasing for services above all, but this is a field we are the least competitive in.

These are the circumstances that serve as a background to Hungary's adjustment to the internal transitions of its biggest trading partner, the EC. However, a country struggling with recession has severe difficulties in adjusting as its funds for restructuring are limited. A country on a lower economic development level showing a negative real growth rate cannot invest additional resources in the restructuring process. (Resource augmentation may only be possible in a case of having an economic growth rate above EC average.) The economy should find the path to growth, as growth draws capital, and capital stimulates further growth. But how could a country in recession take the first step on this path? What should this first step be? Perhaps the outline of the vision and prospects of capital-moving growth could be the starting engine. So we need an economic conception and a market that, by means of the Association Agreement, is about to open to us. A major condition to restructuring is the adjustment to EC institutes, regulations (from veterinary measures, through standards, to competition policy control). Our cultural-educational backwardness is much smaller than our technological backwardness, however, in overtaking these arrears we again have to face the problem of scarce financial resources. Initiating foreign capital might help us solve this problem, but this might result in growing economic dependence.

In the field of adjustments, the task of developing a foreign market organization suited to the new, expanded market, and conforming to technical changes of foreign trade activities are of utmost importance. Adjustment to the Single European Market covers conformity regarding technical, entrepreneurial issues and political, economical (foreign trade) policies. The fundamental function of political and economic policies is to eliminate all manner of discrimination and protectionism. The Association Agreement has abolished considerable barriers to our exports. Nevertheless, action should be taken in the field of internal economy as well: efforts should be made to develop the institutional system of the market economy. In order to do so, we have to study and examine advanced economies, institutions and practices. However, even working practices must not be adapted without criticism, as we are characterized by a very different ownership structure, and by a lower development level.

A determinative condition to adjustment is technological development in production. For this purpose, the transfer of technology should be completely liberalized, creating resources for improvement, and the role of foreign capital in Hungarian economy should be reconsidered. Since the process of modernization would be rather time-consuming without the help of foreign working capital, in my opinion, we should provide more attractive and motivating surroundings and circumstances to foreign investors. At the same time, successful adjustment is based upon market impulses, demand and expectations, so entrepreneurial conformity is the most important issue. The challenge of the Single European Market derives from the capability of Hungarian companies to make the most of opportunities arising from the Communities economic growth by providing competitive products and services.

Numerous favourable processes have begun already:

-        monopolistic positions are being eliminated, due to the increasing number of entrepreneurs and to the competition resulting from the liberalization of importation

-      information needed for our economic integration with Europe is advancing
-      the one-sidedness of our production-oriented companies is dissolving as the role and significance of trade (knowledge of the market) is realized and acknowledged.

Still there are drawbacks as well:

-      the independence of banks is not adequate yet
-      the lack of emphasis on investment operations other than loan transactions. Banks are still more willing to be 'offices' granting loans, than business venture taking risks
-      banks' capital funds are scarce, which means serious hindrance.

On the European market, everyone is measured in accordance with his abilities (and his luck to a certain extent). This market does not allow for weakness. Taking advantage of the weak is considered as a natural chance for those in higher positions.

All the above-mentioned issues have a common spring: open economies' success is dependent upon the improvement of their international competitiveness. Competitiveness determines countries', companies' opportunities and positions. The Single Market tends to intensify this competition. Taking advantage of opportunities offered by the EC is hinging upon the country's own efforts. It requires radical restructuring of the country's economic policy, the conformity of the economic mechanism to EC standards, the development of a foreign economic structure suited to the expanded market (reform of public finances, strict performance requirements, provision of a venture-stimulating economic environment etc.).

From 1993 onwards, we have to face a new kind of market with new challenges. Thanks to the Association Agreement, we have got closer to the Single Market, our adjustment is also assisted by the transforming model of economic control. However, the transformation is promising to be a time-consuming process, so the time factor of responding to the SEM is to be examined separately. In order to survive and stay on the market (with respect to the considerable exportation decline in 1993), immediate response is required in several concrete fields, and the challenge of integration should also be considered (our Free Trade Agreement is the first step towards cooperation). Hungary's adjustment to the Community began in the 1980s with the development of a market economic institution system (introduction of the two-tier banking system, value added type of taxation etc.) A minimum requirement of the adjustment is the establishment of a working, competitive market economy (this is a necessary, but not a sufficient condition), since only a market economy can integrate with the Single Market. During the establishment of a market economy, we can make use of EC memberstates' experiences; however, these must not be adapted without any regard to domestic circumstances.

A comprehensive, long-term political and economic conception is also indispensable. We must have a long-term idea, an image of the future that motivates people, and entrepreneurs, and is independent from political fluctuations, but is economically grounded, of course. A short/medium-term adjustment program should also be drawn up, as without having such a plan, there is no chance to stay in the market: we have to assess the different domains in which integration with the EC is the most advantageous for us, and what fields should deliberately be set back.

A change in entrepreneurial management attitude is necessary as well, since only companies that are the fastest and most efficient in meeting new challenges can stay in business on the SEM.

An offensive conformity is needed, that assumes market flexibility, and a comprehensive knowledge of all the special requirements of different EC regions. Moreover, on the new united market, we should not take mere requirement as a starting-point, but should proceed from existing and future demand. Putting it differently, we need to tighten bonds between production strategy and marketing. The key issues in company management will be: competitiveness, market segmentation, and marketing.

4. Conclusion

The success of Hungarian-EC co-operation turns upon the efficiency of our domestic economy. So if we aim for success, we should awaken the entire society to the consciousness of an image of working cooperation. It also should be borne in mind that technical aspects are important in the process of adjustments, but the essence of this process lies in the economy, and in the complex conformity outgrowing from it - external and internal policies, legal system, education etc. are some of the fields in which EC standards should be met. This complex process has not yet been coordinated in Hungary (many steps are left out, informing and captivating public opinion is not sufficient etc.).

An adjustment program has not yet been drawn up either, though action should have been taken even without the existence of the Single European Market. The question now is not whether Hungary can integrate with the EC, but whether we are definitively becoming a periphery, or try to approach the centre as a semi-periphery. The integration might help our nation catch up with Europe. Those being left out of the Single Market are doomed to lag behind for ever.

10 Change of the export structure in Hungary in the transition period

István Goldperger

The volume of export is about one seventh of the total output of the Hungarian economy and one third of the GDP. The changes in export highlight the position of the country in the international economy more characteristically and more significantly than any other economic feature. They reflect how the economy can join in the international division of labour and how it is assessed by the international market. This is the reason why we try to evaluate the structural reform of the Hungarian economy from the perspective of international economic relations.

I want to present 13 theses in my lecture related to the export structure, its consequences, and future plans.

1.

The most impressive and painful evidence of the deepening technological gap is the shrinking role of Hungary in the world market. This is not a new phenomenon, it results from the fact that we missed structural reform after the first oil crisis and we have been carrying this backlog ever since.

Hungary's share in the world export was 0.7 per cent before World War II. We managed to maintain this level, in fact increased it somewhat up to the beginning of the 1970s. But after 1973 this ratio started to fall and this tendency has been carried on up to now.

Table 10.1
Hungary's share in the world export, in per cent

1960	1968	1973	1980	1987	1988	1991	1993[*]
0.68	0.75	0.77	0.44	0.39	0.35	0.3	0.24

*   Estimate.
Source: From UN Monthly Bulletin of Statistics

It is worth calling attention to the fact that the line indicated by the series of numbers is similar to other data characterizing the overall output of the Hungarian economy, e.g. GDP per capita corrected by the purchase power. (See paper by Molnár György and Tarján Tamás in this volume.)

The shrinking role of Hungary in the world market is especially noticeable since the economic policy intended to open up towards the world market - although to a limited extent because of growing debts - so the share of developed capitalist countries in our foreign trade was gradually increasing since the second half of the seventies.

As we will see, expanding commercial relations did not result in organic integration but structural marginalization and an exposed outworker's role.

2.

The weaknesses of the branch and product structure of export was hidden by the high share of COMECON countries in our foreign trade for decades. The collapse of the COMECON market and the change to dollar accounting created the contradictions of the earlier structure of export and world market competitiveness obvious and rearranged dramatically the internal proportions of export into a structure indicating a lower level of development.

The most expressive indicator of weakening of export structure is the share of machines, equipments, means of transport and other investment goods in the export that decreased from 27 per cent in 1988 to 12 per cent in 1992. Increase took place in the main group of goods of industrial consumption and food products. The dynamic increase of export of industrial consumptive goods is due to sudden increase of export commission work in light industry professions (clothing). However this export activity is characterized by the fact that - although high quality products are produced - know- how and value-added activities of the exporter are not required by the commissioner so the exporter cannot obtain income enabling him to make further investments and developments.

Table 10.2
Structure of Hungarian exports in the last year of the COMECON
(current prices)

	Ruble accounting export			Non-ruble		
Year	1985	1988	1990	1985	1988	1990
Main group of goods						
Energy, electricity	0.8	0.4	0.3	5.3	3.9	3.1
Materials, semi-finished goods, spare parts	22.7	22.0	20.8	37.4	42.3	44.3
Machines, means of transport, other investment goods	46.3	47.5	43.9	14.0	12.5	11.6
Consumption industrial products	17.2	16.6	19.2	13.9	15.5	15.6
Food industry materials, livestock, food products	13.0	13.5	15.8	29.4	25.8	25.7

Source: CSO

Table 10.3
Change of the Hungarian export structure in the transitional period

Year	1988	1990	1991	1992	1993*
Main group of goods					
Energy, electricity	2.1	2.4	1.7	2.6	3.9
Materials, semi-finished goods, spare parts	33.8	37.9	38.0	35.1	37.4
Machines, means of transport, other investment goods	27.1	20.1	12.6	12.0	15.0
Consumption industrial goods	16.2	16.5	22.6	26.3	23.4
Food industry materials, livestock, food products	20.8	23.1	25.1	24.0	20.2

*   I-IX months only

The change of the export structure had an effect on the structure of production as well. In the production area branches of machine industry producing the highest added value suffered the biggest decrease (precision engineering, transportation industry). The share of metallurgy, construction and light industry increased in industrial exports.

To get a more complete picture it should be mentioned that according to 1993 data analyzed so far, the decreasing tendency of share of machinery export stopped and turned around.

However this change of tendencies took place when the total volume of export decreased suddenly and although export of most groups of goods decreased, machinery export remained the same in fact. This change of direction cannot be considered as a result of a conscious restructuring policy, it rather indicates how to find the right way from market as well as management and development point of view in the current grave crisis situation of the Hungarian economy.

Table 10.4
Industrial export structure by branches
(Comparative prices, per cent)

Branches	1988	1992	Change
Mining	1.1	0.8	-0.3
Metallurgy	12.2	15.7	+2.5
Engineering industry	46.9	35.2	-11.7
Building material industry	1.6	4.2	+2.6
Light industry	14.8	22.2	+7.4
Other industry	0.3	0.5	+0.2
Industry	100.0	100.0	-

Source: Mogyorósiné dr. Halász, Rózsa: Analysis of structural changes in industry. Ipari Szemle, 1993. No. 5. pp. 6-9.

3.

Forced restructuring of Hungarian export relations deteriorated the chances of increase of the economy and income.

The most widely known characteristic of the *structure of export relations* is a significant decrease of the share of earlier COMECON countries in the total Hungarian export. This segment of export had a shortfall in 1991 when the transfer to dollar- based accounting took place. However it is scarcely known that the share of developing countries in our export also decreased significantly, it was half the level of 10 years ago.

Table 10.5
Split of export by groups of countries in per cent

Year	1980	1989	1990	1991	1992	1993*
Group of countries						
Developed countries	35.9	49.6	59.8	69.5	71.3	67.7
Among them: EC	19.6	24.8	32.2	46.8	49.8	46.2
Developing countries	9.9	8.6	8.3	8.6	5.3	5.6
COMECON/ex-socialist countries	54.2	41.8	31.9	21.9	23.8	26.1

*   I- IX months only
Sources: CSO, Ministry of International Trade Relations

If we want to review these changes from the aspect of long-term foreign economic interests, we can split the reasons resulting in decrease in two groups. Termination of exports that were oriented to production and development demand of branches and companies becoming nonviable in the partner countries, mainly related to war industry directly or indirectly. These exports were carried on with the most important developing partner countries, too.

However, input of productional branches complying with primary necessities, public consumption demand and infrastructure could mean real market opportunities. Within deteriorated financial relations on both sides and among transitional financial systems very often partners could not find the way to balance off deliveries. We may consider the problems of this area in partner countries as external factors and reasons, but the late adaptation of the domestic economic policy and institutional system is indicated by the financing difficulties in usual exports involving normal commercial risks to solvent developing countries. This way Hungarian exporters missed the markets of more processed goods offering suitable income.

The geographical structure of exports also changed significantly. The share of the European countries within total export increased from 84 per cent before the change of regime to 89 per cent in 1992, share of Asia, Africa and America dropped suddenly compared to the previous low ratio.

The figures indicate that the change of the orientation of Hungarian exports is opposite to the streamline of world economy and world market. Hungarian exporters were squeezed out in majority from the geographical region which has been developing and probably will continue to develop in the next decade most dynamically. This is true especially to China, Japan and the rapidly developing countries of the Far East. Short and medium- term prospects are unquestionably better for North and South America, than for Western Europe currently overcoming recession with difficulties.

Table 10.6
Geographical split of exports in per cent

Year	1989	1990	1991	1992
Continent				
Europe	84.2	84.9	85.0	88.8
Asia	8.6	8.1	8.8	5.9
Africa	2.0	2.1	1.4	0.9
America	5.0	4.7	4.6	4.2
Australia and Oceania	0.2	0.2	0.2	0.2
Total	100.0	100.0	100.0	100.0

Sources: KSH, NGKM

Basically two factors explain the geographical shrinking of Hungarian exports. One of them is the shrinking of decision- making period of exporters (generally, of entrepreneurs), losing their prospects. Exporting at long geographical distances is only profitable with suitable continuity, on the basis of a market and development strategy of the enterprise.

The serious financial uncertainties of the majority of companies and the ceasing of strategic activity inevitably led to geographical shrinking.

The other factor is related to the restructuring of the foreign trade system. The deterioration of big, concentrated and specified foreign trade monopolistic systems, the full liberalization of foreign trade right of entrepreneurs made the foreign trade system a lot more flexible than earlier, but newly established small organizations are not able financially or professionally to establish permanent trade relations in long geographical distances.

The significant increase of share of intermediate trade in our exports (and imports) confirms the aforementioned concept that the shrinking share of late socialist and developing countries in foreign trade turnover is related to the financing difficulties of foreign trade, not so much to the change of demand structure. Intermediate trade operated to a certain level within the foreign trade turnover of COMECON countries before the change of regime. So e.g. 6.6 per cent of our total export in 1990 was realized through intermediaries, while this rate increased above 9 per cent by 1992. 35 per cent of the export directed to the countries of the former Soviet Union was carried out by intermediaries.

Intermediaries saved serious difficulties for Hungarian exporters. Still this situation cannot be considered ideal in the long run. Intermediate trade drains away a significant part of commercial income and breaks direct relations between exporter and customer. This form of trade cannot be successful in exporting products or services requiring direct cooperation between producer and consumer demanding high value added, supplementary service.

4.

Qualitative characteristics of export structure indicate gradual relative deterioration and growing vulnerability

Ratio of exchange of Hungarian foreign trade has *deteriorated* 35 per cent within the last 20 years. The main reason for this deterioration is weakening of export structure, growing share of low world market price materials, agricultural and food products and shrinking share of higher price machinery industry products. From another perspective, this process is related to the restructured Hungarian export relations. Our relative price positions are gradually weakening in trade with developing countries so even a growing share of developing countries resulted in deterioration of exchange ratio.

Weakening of export structure is indicated by *decrease of standard added value* of export products. This tendency was especially obvious in the period of transfer to dollar accounting. Standard added value of export decreased by 3-5 per cent in 1991, and a further 2-4 per cent in 1992.

High company concentration of exports indicates that not all of the economy is export- oriented but only a relatively narrow slice of it.

Almost half of exports in 1991 was produced by companies where the proportion of export compared to net revenue was above 40 per cent. Companies where the proportion of export and net revenue was above 30 per cent produced 80 per cent of total export. If in these companies export is reduced because of financial or management difficulties, problems in market relations, hardly any exporter can substitute it with marketable products and lively market relations.

The decrease of groups of exportable products indicate weakening market positions and production background. 15 groups of products representing the biggest proportion of exports in 1989 gave 45 per cent of total exports while 15 biggest groups of products represented only 34 per cent of total exports by 1992. Unfortunately, this process is not backed by diversification based on investments and progressive structural changes realised in such diversification; that is why negative effects of the process dominate: the increased standard market costs per unit and standard development cost per unit.

Analysis of export dynamics of different groups of products indicate that the change of structure is slowing down. During 1992- 93 we could observe from half year to half year that the number of industrial and agricultural products decreased where increase could be identified compared to the period one year ago.

5.

We have to conclude because of the aforementioned that the serious shortfall of exports in 1993 was not unexpected and an extraordinary phenomenon but a tendency reflecting weakening export potentials of economy. Increase of export in 1992 could be considered as a result of extraordinary factors.

Temporary advantageous and disadvantageous factors resulted in the increase of exports in 1992. Among advantageous factors expanding liberalization of imports eased production focusing on exports, rapid decentralization of foreign trade system, establishment of private foreign trade enterprises in great numbers made identifying and marketing of smaller export basis of goods possible, which was impossible earlier because of the inflexibility of centralized foreign trade systems and because of financial reasons. The domestic shrinking of the market also increased exports temporarily. Due to liquidity obligations companies were exporting although profitability deteriorated, at the cost of utilizing equity. This process crashed at its own limits.

The equilibrium of foreign trade balance is also endangered by imports. Imports increased about 10 per cent in 1993 due to earlier wrong currency policy, lack of internal market protection, and it is indicating the deterioration of domestic production abilities. It cannot even comply with the demands of a shrinking economy.

6.

Time factor became critical in the restructuring process of the Hungarian economy.

The deterioration of foreign trade balance, more precisely permanency of causing factors, force economic policy into a not yet totally foreseeable forced direction.

The USD 3 billion foreign trade deficit of 1993 can be treated with a relatively high level of foreign currency deposits and incoming resources of foreign investment. The question is whether we can turn around the process of

deteriorating equilibrium within a time scale before growing deficit leads up
to the collapse of external financing.

7.

General ratio of development of human resources does not justify forced
retreat of Hungary from the dominating streamline of world economy.

Quantitative data characterizing inhabitants' schooling show dramatic
change in the last 40 years.

Table 10.7
Educational level of the population

Age group/school qualification, in 1000 persons	1949	1960	1970	1980	1990
15 years old and older, finished at least 8 grades	1425	2439	4185	5532	6439
18 years old and older, finished at least secondary school	356	615	1177	1866	2267
25 years old and older, graduated from university	91	103	273	448	688
In per cent of relevant age group					
15 years old and older, finished at least 8 grades	20.6	32.8	51.4	66.1	78.1
18 years old and older, finished at least secondary school	5.5	8.8	15.5	23.4	29.2
25 years old and older, graduated from university	1.7	2.7	4.2	6.5	10.1

Source: Tények könyve '93

Between 1949-90 ratio of pupils graduating from basic 8 grades increased 4
times, pupils graduating from secondary school grew more than 5 times,
students graduating from universities and colleges grew 6 times within their
age group. According to international comparisons Hungarian students'
knowledge is among the best in the world.

Modern technological knowledge spread around in the previous decades
with investment goods imported from the West even in those cases when not
all of the investments proved to be effective. Export commission works
enhanced the development of working culture and qualitative approach even if
the profits of this activity do not make further investment possible.
Unsatisfying cooperation and specialization made workers and technical staffs

inventive and many sided in solving problems within the plant. There was significant export main contractors' activity earlier that produced international experience, improved independent and complex working skills. This way Hungarian work force in general is able to comply with higher requirements. This is proved by the satisfaction of employers of joint ventures established in Hungary as well as of employees who work abroad.

According to scientific evaluation Hungarian science took the 20th place in the world ranking. This is preceding our ranking according to the number of population and the volume of economic output.

Besides these positive factors we have to face the fact that modernization effects of increased training and education could not be realised due to the limits of the social economic structure dominating the economy as well as the life of individuals during the past 4 decades. Besides a rapid development there were controversies and tensions in the education structure. Especially the professional structure and the proportion of students graduating from universities and colleges lag behind modern requirements. Additionally due to lack of management and working culture, unsuitable market and economic approach, the existing intellectual potential could not be fully utilized. So we have to conclude that *although we have reserves in human resources, these resources will not become automatically the engine of structural reform and development.*

8.

The set of economic policy criteria is controversial: on the one hand there is the challenge to catch up, on the other hand there are the market and competition limits. So a compromising and gradual economic political approach is needed: save what can be saved, and create the conditions of structural reform.

To realise both missions is extremely difficult not only because these missions are controversial due to the conflicting conditions but because the procedures so far had a direction opposite to these purposes.

The rapid erosion of the technological basis of competitiveness is a real danger for stabilization and change of structure.

Volume of capital investment has been continuously decreasing for more than a decade - with the exception of 2 years. Currently it is about 60 per cent of the level of the 80s. Indication of development can be observed in certain areas of infrastructure and within joint ventures established by investors with solid capital. In big areas of industry and agriculture investments in total do not even reach the level of capital supplement.

Serious deterioration of research and development may cause weakening of innovation abilities thus endangering structural reforms.

The seriousness of the problem is characterized by the fact that research and development expenses decreased to 1/3 of the level of the mid- eighties.

There are opinions related to it - we can hear them here in the conference - that the proportion of research and development expenditure in the previous economic system in Hungary (and in other socialist countries) was very high according to international comparisons, and this reflected the low effectiveness of this activity. We can hardly doubt this statement. However if anyone concluded that a decrease of research and development expenses to such an extent would serve the increase of effectiveness, we should start arguing about it. If the boost in the strategic development of enterprises does not create forceful drive and defined marketing orientation, shrinking human and financial resources of research and development would lead up to short-term, task-oriented problem solving - where this activity survives at all. This ensures speedy returns but this way enterprises and professions get even less involved in structural reform.

We also have to face the fact that shrinking independent research and development will deteriorate the adaptation abilities of the economy after a certain level.

This is why the most important message for economic policy is that we have to overcome current difficulties in a way not to waste the chances of future.

9.

We must find the right proportion and order of destruction and creation in economic policy to avoid deepening of decline and extension of stagnation.

Illusions were cherished about the role of private entrepreneurs. This sector that was much more significant in number and economic activity than in other socialist countries had long entrepreneurial experience. Structure and quality of their activity was mainly influenced by their earlier role, i.e. they were suppliers of big state- owned companies producing for socialist export, partly substituting import. There are less than a dozen enterprises which - taking advantage of the tax exemptions related to intellectual products, patents - have developed high technical level, internationally competitive products during the past decades and have still remained in the market. Recently tax rates and financing conditions of investments have deteriorated so this direction of structural reform gets little encouragement.

Unbiased, realistic consideration of the size of companies can be recommended in the course of structural reform. Earlier the company structure was characterised by unhealthy concentration of production activity. Much too high proportion of production was carried out by relatively big companies, cooperating middle-size and small companies were scarce and underdeveloped. Therefore, the production system was inflexible and hardly effective. From the restructuring of big companies middle- size and small companies were created. However this in itself did not heal structural hierarchy. We have to take into consideration the fact that starting smaller units established by restructuring big companies are defined by the intellectual and technological inheritance of their predecessor companies.

10.

It is the short, middle and long term interest of Hungary to reenter into traditional markets as much as possible.

First of all we have to point out that the aforementioned market expansion must be achieved not by giving up existing and newly acquired markets in developed economies, but supplementing shrunken commercial volume and weakened commercial structure.

The most important element of foreign economic and development strategy directed towards Middle and East European markets is to understand and realise the fact that trade with countries coping with development and structural difficulties, taking their special market demand into consideration in the export goods structure does not necessarily mean lagging behind, or structural retreat. If these unrealistic concepts were true, developed countries could never trade with underdeveloped ones.

The growing lag of the Hungarian production and export structure behind the leading tendencies of world economy is not caused by the fact that Hungarian economy produced and exported in big volumes industrial products complying with special demands of these countries but because the income realised in these markets was not invested in updating production, and creating technical and market conditions for competitiveness. This is the most important conclusion of the impasse of the economic development in the last decades. The Hungarian economy through its intermediary role, mainly through eastern machine exports, realised HUF 100-200 billion annual extra income - at current value - but the government budget took it away from the exporters and spent it mainly on financing community and individual consumption.

There is a long-term foreign economic - strategic aspect of the question. Concepts that consider the intermediary, servicing role of Hungary towards Middle and Eastern Europe as a possible direction of development are not without basis. Among others development of vivid, mutual business relations based on many sided cooperation is a precondition of this role. Hardly any cooperation can be imagined where we retain white-collar roles to ourselves but want to give out blue-collar ones to others.

We have to make up for historical negligence regarding Middle - Eastern European neighbours. Due to the radial cooperation structure of COMECON to the Soviet Union, parallel structures established in smaller countries, the intensity of cooperation even in earlier decades did not reach the level that would have been advantageous for all partner countries because of their geographical closeness, diversity of natural endowments. One of the means of getting closer and integrated later on can be the Central European Free Trade Agreement (CEFTA). In order to have full effects of the agreement by the turn of the century, development and cooperation concepts of the participating countries must assist and encourage establishing and deepening permanent relations among enterprises. In my opinion we have to start with the preconcept that integration of adjacent countries is a precondition for fitting into Western European integration. It would be contrary to the logic of European integration if new candidates only changed their external economic relations by replacing Eastern-oriented radial dependence by dependence on the West.

Today, business and financial innovation play equal or more important roles than technical innovation in extending cooperation, so the enterprises concerned and their banks must be encouraged to brave initiatives and persistence. It would be advantageous if the financial sector of developed countries and international monetary institutions would give more assistance than before to the internal trade of this region because this is an important condition of the economic balance of this region, and it is a universal interest.

11.

One of the most decisive factors of the structural reform of Hungarian economy in the following years can be the structural reform of the Western European industry, the resettlement of certain activities. To perceive these processes and direct them consciously is an important task of economic development and external economic strategy.

The structural reform of the Western European industry is characterized by two main interrelated tendencies. Relatively high material- and energy demanding activities damaging environment to a greater extent, and wage demanding, less competitive activities because of higher work cost, will be reduced. Regression of the past years enforced cost effectiveness so the reform process speeded up. Many countries assist investment in foreign countries related to reducing activities with tax exemption and other financial means, if in return modern activity is established domestically with high added value. This process means opportunities and dangers as well for Hungary. Regarding that this process motivates basically the technical and market structure of foreign capital investments, the Hungarian economic policy must be prepared to guard against dangers and seize opportunities.

It is dangerous if activities are established whose added value is small in the Hungarian domestic economy while their effects on the environment, infrastructure and social expenses are high. Considering the opportunities, we have to know that in cases of high labour cost mass products, Eastern and Southern neighbour countries with significantly lower wages have more chances to receive investments, but in case of processing activities demanding good technological standards and qualified skilled labour, Hungary clearly has advantage. The real question is what the direction of conditions of investments and changes of domestic economic environment is. Will joint ventures in Hungary remain lower graded subsidiaries of their foreign parent companies or is there a possibility to further develop acquired technology, management and market relations and establish developed and effective enterprises representing appropriate specialization? We can find examples of both ways in recent practice.

12.

Preparation for the continuous demand of domestic infrastructure development gives opportunity for some areas of industry to realise export-oriented development.

To seize this opportunity domestic infrastructure investments must be considered not only a factor raising demand but also a factor establishing conscious infrastructure development. This needs conscious governmental development coordination and can serve as a good example how domestic market protection by internationally accepted means can serve the development of the domestic production and export structure.

Governmental, municipal and concession infrastructure investment of about HUF 500 - 1,000 billion in the coming 4-5 years that can be foreseen and planned will give possibility for most potential domestic companies still existing in the investment goods sector to launch investments for the almost certain and specified market, they could finance these investments on a business basis, they can raise loans and capital resources. This type of conceptional cooperation between government and entrepreneurs can upgrade relevant companies for potential investors, and can create more advantageous situations for privatization. This could increase the competitiveness of our companies and assist them in winning investment markets of adjacent countries and certain faraway developing countries.

13.

A growing proportion of services has been characterizing structural reform of the economy but without updating production structure and growing income of production, the service sector cannot become the driving force of a permanent economic development.

To underline this statement I refer to the fact that although the development of services can create new demand and revenues, the realization of these revenues strongly depends on other processes of the economy. To examine this interdependence we need to split services into 3 characteristic groups.

The first group is personal services. This has an internal and an external aspect. This strongly depends on the income of the population. In a society that is characterized by standard real income decrease or stagnation, personal services cannot be expected to grow permanently and dynamically. Albeit real income decrease took place with strong differentiation of incomes and a richer stratum placed growing demand for services but the number of individuals in richer stratum and the nature of consumption of services a priori place limits for development of personal services.

A large part of the external concept is connected to tourism. Tourism contains more opportunities for the Hungarian economy than the revenue it yields today. To utilize these opportunities we have to give up certain illusions and develop consciously according to these conditions.

We have to accept that 90 million people crossing the border and about 30 million visitors do not mean that we are a great power in foreign tourist traffic, it only means that we live in a vivid spot in Europe and the economic abilities of Hungary and its neighbourhood give very strong motivation for legal and illegal arbitrage.

We also have to bear in mind that the features of Hungary are not suitable for developing luxury tourism yielding the highest standard revenue. We do not have natural endowments for it and our earlier attractiveness due to the special political status of the country has ceased.

There is significant demand for cheap and mid- expensive tourism from faraway and nearby countries. To comply with this demand cheaper hotel accommodation and related services should be significantly developed, this way modifying tourist reception capacity that was too much oriented towards high- income guests in the past decade. The situation of this profession and influential government measures do not support this direction of development.

Business and scientific tourism requires higher service level in general and yields higher revenues but its significant development is not only a question of tourism. If general conditions of business and scientific development of the country improve, business and scientific tourism can prosper giving opportunities to utilize already existing higher-level capacities.

The second group of services is strongly connected to the development of material infrastructure. Investment resources that can be spent on developing material infrastructure influence the increase of service output. However, the hopefully starting development in this area has a certain multiplying effect. The increase of service output means not only proportionally growing usage of expanding networks (telecommunication, roads, public transport), but also a great number of services can be launched based on these networks by deepening differentiation and development of the activities. But we have to note that in order to feel this multiplying effect the quality and density of these networks must exceed a critical limit.

Rapid expansion of production and business services of the third group has characterized economic structural reform of the developed countries. In order to understand the effects of this reform from the point of view of domestic opportunities we have to understand the essence of this reform. I think it is not about some external activities gaining ground but deep differentiation and specialization of production and commercial activities. In the course of this process certain business activities split up in entity, and as a result of specialization, an exceptionally high professional level and wide range of relations can be achieved. The main market of these activities is production. Product output integrates services of specialized marketing, research-development, standardization, design, quality control, financing, insurance, shipping, special legal background, customer service and many other activities demanding special knowledge and information. This means that these services are marketable if the products whose production and selling they are used for find their markets. These services can be paid for only in products whose technical - technological content allows for relatively high prices, realising high value added proportion including services. Without updating technological investments, the realisation of the value increase of services is impossible. The same holds good the other way round, technological investments do not return without the value increasing effects of modern production and business services.

Characteristic of these services is high international qualification demand. It is highly probable that the radical expansion of university- level education in developed countries in the past decades is related to this structural reform.

Economic policy has an extra responsibility in utilizing the existing intellectual capacities in the most possible way and to encouraging the establishment of flexible and differentiated enterprise systems that can provide high-level production and business services to potential users taking their specialities into consideration.

11 The problem of quality in the Estonian economy with special regard to the foreign trade

Erik Terk

My short presentation will cover five subjects. The first one concerns the specific preconditions and features of the Estonian transition. Secondly, I shall attempt to characterize the essence of the current phase of the Estonian economic transition that began in summer 1992 with our currency reform. The third subject will concern the positive results of this stage and the fourth one will deal with the negative consequences. I shall conclude with some words about the future perspectives and strategies.

There are some essential differences between the situation of the Baltic states and that of the Central European countries which used to be Socialist and enjoyed limited independence, having their own statehood. The Estonian economy was more connected to the economic complex of the whole Soviet Union. In the first stage of our systemic economic reform (it started at the end of 1989 and continued in a more decisive way in spring 1990) we only had a possibility to act within the limitations of the all-union macroeconomic framework. Of course, Estonia was attempting to act as independently as possible but we lacked our own currency and there were several other rather important limitations. For example, anti-inflationary policy was impossible before the introduction of Estonia's own currency. Before restoring our political independence in autumn 1991 we lacked many of the necessary independent economic institutions that the Central European states had. Of course, we did have some kind of banks, some kind of legislation etc, but until 1990 they were semi-independent at best. The institutions vital for every independent state such as a central bank, tax administration, customs etc. were only being formed in 1991 or operating for the first year only.

Fortunately, some results in economic reforms had been achieved already by the time political independence was gained: new private businesses had taken off rapidly, the liberalization of prices had made quite significant progress, a Western-type tax system had been created and the first commercial banks were operating.

Estonia's domestic market is very small and the Hungarian economy seems quite large compared to ours. There are only 1.5 million inhabitants in Estonia, and, consequently, it has no aiternative to export orientation. As for the advantages in our preconditions for the transition, we must emphasize that Estonian economy was quite diversified and did not depend on one or two major branches exclusively. Of course, being a Socialist economy, it was based on large enterprises, but the Estonian enterprises were not as large as those in Russia and because of this the Estonian economy survived the collapse of the big firms more easily. At the end of the 1980s and the beginning of the 1990s Westerr capital started to show interest in Estonia. It must be admitted that in many cases, Estonian was mostly seen as a preliminary step to the Russiaii market. But the interest was there anyway and some investments were made. As we compare the Western investments per capita, Estonia is one of the leaders in Central and Eastern Europe.

Now about the current stage of our economic transition. I think that our introduction of Estonia's own currency in summer 1992 was an extremely important step and many features of our present economic situation are the results of this reform. Of course, the reform itself was a package of measures, but the single most important element of that package may have been the considerable devaluation of the kroon as compared to the purchasing power in the domestic market. It gave us good competitive advantage in the Western markets.

Another element of this package was the Currency Board system and the third one was the fixed exchange rate to the *Deutschmark*. Very strict and hard monetary policy was pursued after the introduction of the kroon. Yet I would not describe this as a shock therapy in the classical sense. The reason for it is that the liberalization of prices had largely been done before the currency reform.

The shock for the Estonian economy was undoubtedly important but was not the result of the economic reform measures, but rather a result of gaining actual political independence in autumn 1991. In some months the prices of raw materials and energy sources from Russia (which had been steadily increasing anyway in 1990-91) increased as much as 20-30 times, in some cases within three or four months. The phenomenon naturally resulted in a real shock for the economy. But in the second half of 1992 it became clear that the economy would survive it, despite the steep decline. One of the results of the increasing raw material prices and the payment problems with Russia was the need for the enterprises to turn towards the West. It was favoured by the over-devalued kroon and the liberalization of foreign trade (the latter had actually been introduced somewhat earlier). The consequences of the strict monetary policy were more easily accepted by the Estonian people, they were accepted in this framework as the accompanying phenomena of regaining independence rather than the results of some government policy. The difference was quite significant.

Now, about the results of the afore described reforms. I think that 1.5 years of this policy is a sufficient period of time to draw some conclusions. The first conclusion is that this stage was generally successful. What results could be pointed out in order to support this claim?

First, we escaped hyperinflation. Of course, Estonia's rate of inflation is not low. It was 36 per cent in 1993. But there is a huge difference as compared to inflation in 1992, which was approximately 900 per cent. At the beginning of 1992 the monthly rate of inflation was approximately 70 per cent. During the first months after the monetary reform it was 20 per cent, while the current monthly rate is about 3-4 per cent.

A certain stabilization of the business environment can also be noticed from a different angle. The interest rates are falling, slowly but steadily. The interest rates of the Estonian commercial banks in 1992 were over 100 per cent and it was clearly impossible for the industry to find credit in those conditions. At present the commercial banks extend credit at an interest rate of 25 per cent. It is still high, but the tendency is positive.

A very important achievement is the change of our export structure. The share of the former Soviet Union of our exports in the late 1980s was approximately 90 per cent. At present, Russia's share is around 20 per cent and our number one trading partner is Finland, rather than Russia. Russia holds the second position, but a competition for the second place among Russia, Germany and Sweden may occur in the future.

Unemployment is not as high as was expected prior to the monetary reform. We estimated that unemployment would be as high as 20-25 per cent. Actually it is approximately 8-9 per cent. The number of workers at large enterprises has decreased (although not as much as the output), but many of those laid off have found new jobs in the spreading private business. Estonia's GDP has been growing again since the second half of 1993. Some stabilization in industry is also apparent, but it must be admitted that it follows a major decrease in industrial output. The fall of production in 1992 was 39 per cent and this is higher than the Central European average.

I have to point out that the Estonian economic policy is quite extreme in some aspects. For example, one can claim that Estonia practically lacks any economic policy apart from monetary policy and making foreign economic agreements. Secondly, I think that it would be hard to find an economy more open than the Estonian one.

We heard about Hungarian agriculture, the very limited protection and the lack of subsidies etc. In the case of Estonia the situation is even more extreme. There are practically no protectionist barriers (quotas, tariffs etc), state subsidies to enterprises are at a minimum and this also applies to agriculture. Some kinds of credits exist but their amount is quite limited and they are of little help.

It can be claimed that the Estonian economy has passed the peak of the crisis. The situation has some negative features as well. Generally, it may be said that the macroeconomic figures look more optimistic than the actual situation at the company level. Investments and technology innovation are low. The situation in agriculture is very close to a collapse.

Our export production is growing and the growth rate is not bad. But the products are generally of quite primitive nature, there is very little high-tech production with very little value added. Many enterprises operate as subcontractors to Western firms and the production is often based on Soviet-time technology. The existing human and/or technological potential is only partly utilized. The main competitive advantages are the cheap labour and the relatively well skilled careful workers as compared to several other countries with low-cost labour. The average wage in Estonia is a little more than USD 90 per month. But the prices are not comparable to those in the Western countries. While the prices of the marketable products are quite close to the world market prices, those of food and of services especially are significantly lower. The same applies to the cost of transportation, electricity or rent etc.

The trade deficit (although the export is increasing, the import has also gone up at a higher rate) is compensated by the positive balance of services. However, the export opportunities in services (shipping, port facilities, tourism) strongly depend on the international political situation.

There is a major demand for investments in infrastructure. We can use some loans of the international financial institutions for this purpose, and there are also some foreign investments available or expected in the future. The situation in telecommunications is not so bad because of an agreement with the Swedish-Finnish telecommunications companies which are restructuring the Estonian communications network. Sweden and the other developed countries of the Baltic Sea region are interested in creating an integrated network of infrastructure around the Baltic region and this project can, in principle, cover other systems of infrastructure besides telecommunications.

Yet at present the prospects for developing or even maintaining the present level of the systems of infrastructure are rather poor (energy, railways, urban transport). Increasing the price of the services would be risky (including the threat of inflation), while the sale of services does not provide enough income to modernize the systems. The strict monetary policy to balance the budget does not help to make government investments in the infrastructure. The situation is better in the case of the ports whose development has attracted the interest of foreign capital.

And of course, there are major problems with social issues and risk groups, especially with pensioners.

The income differences between various social groups are increasing and the prospects of forming a middle class are rather modest.

Finally, some words about the problems connected with future perspectives. It is realistic to presume that the type of development that started in summer 1992 will end in a few years. During this phase we have a comparative advantage in the export market thanks to the over-devalued Estonian currency, but it cannot be expected to last longer than three or four years. The prices and wages are steadily increasing and the advantages gained by over devaluation are only a temporary factor. In three-four years we shall need other higher quality exportable goods. It is not clear yet how to reach that level because of the modest investments in the technological processes, production and the whole infrastructure, the modernization of the educational system, and of equipment of technical universities, etc. But the economic growth that has started gives some hope for finding the necessary funds.

I think that some changes must be made in economic policy: a carefully considered and planned structural industrial policy must be started and the priorities must be worked out. In strategic matters the role of the state must be stronger than at present.

Table 11.1
Balance of goods and services transactions
in millions Estonian kroons

Period Item	Q3'92	Q4'92	Q1'93	Q2'93	Q3'93	Q4'93	1993
Merchandise: exports FOB	1,740	1,960	1,910	2,415	2,884	3,554	10,763
Merchandise: imports FOB	-1,564	-2,062	-1,961	-2,767	-3,226	-4,543	-12,496
trade balance	177	-103	-50	-352	-341	-989	-1,733
services: credit	724	644	791	1,027	1,304	1,311	4,433
services: debit	-483	-505	-627	-785	-906	-1,095	-3,412
services: net	240	139	165	243	397	216	1,021

Table 11.2
Main foreign trade partners in 1993

Rank	Country	foreign trade	% of Estonian export	import
1.	Finland	24.1	20.7	27.9
2.	Russia	19.8	22.6	17.2
3.	Germany	9.4	8.0	10.7
4.	Sweden	9.2	9.5	8.9
5.	Latvia	5.3	8.6	2.3
6.	Netherlands	3.8	4.1	3.6
7.	Lithuania	3.5	3.7	3.3
8.	Ukraine	2.6	3.6	1.8
9.	Denmark	2.5	2.4	2.6
10.	USA	2.3	1.9	2.7

PART IV
EDUCATIONAL SYSTEM:
KEY OF DEVELOPMENT

12 The social-economic role of education today

János Kovács - Ildikó Virág

In the 1990s, profound changes started to take place in many aspects of the European society. The accelerating unification process within the EU have brought about accelerated and wider mobility of and stronger interrelations between European people in the areas of economy, politics as well as culture.

The challenge of science and technology has primary influence on European competition, economic growth and it requires that Europe should not only be the forerunner in creating new knowledge but also has to distribute and support such knowledge so that this be applied in economic life thereby contributing to the development of the living standards of all European nations.

What requirements are set by the above process for the labour force?

The level and composition of demand will be more and more determined by qualitative rather than quantitative criteria. There will be need for a labour force with higher and at the same time more diverse education backgrounds. The number of employees in professional jobs will continue to grow. While there will be a great demand for managers and marketing specialists in business areas, the labour market for engineers, researchers, specially qualified technical experts and workers will also be lively.

The information technology and communications sector will grow more rapidly than the other areas while the products and services of these sectors will be used in all other economic sectors.

For the application of modern production processes, a working culture capable of integrating multiple skills will be essential which skills will have to be constantly renewed during a full-life career.

The proportion of employees with good communication and language skills will grow. Due to the widening mobility, it will be a must to integrate the concepts of human sciences more deeply in people's thinking so that the different cultures can recognize one another, their differences can be accepted and understood.

The analyses prepared by the EU show that the lack of adequately skilled labour force on the regional level can cause serious problems and this will remain so in the long run if accompanied by a constant or even growing unemployment level. This is a concomitant of the modernization process.

The other cause of such a lack of labour force comes from the demographic situation in Europe. According to the Commission of the European Communities (Memorandum), the demographic regression will lead to a situation by the turn of the century where annually 300 thousand less people will enter the labour market than will leave it.

This is aggravated by the fact that due to the growing quality requirements, schooling ratios are also likely to grow at every level.

Solutions for these problems have to be found partly in the education of young people within the education system but with an emphasis on training and re-training systems also in the area of adult education.

What challenges are presented by the Unified European Market for educational systems?

During the post-World War period, there emerged a conviction in the Western-European countries that education is a kind of investment whose returns are similar to those made in the economic sectors and this concept resulted in such a rapid growth in education which is labelled in the literature with good reasons as the 'education boom'.

Today, education expenditures account for 5-7 per cent of the GDP in developed countries and this ratio is only 3-5 per cent in the South-European countries. These numbers were in the 50s 2.5-3.5 per cent and 2-3 per cent respectively. Similarly dynamic growth can be observed in the field of education investments. During this period, the number of people going to secondary education has doubled and the number of students in higher education has grown ten times larger.

This process slowed down in the 70s but today the demand for education is again exploding as it is shown in the Outlook on Education Report of the OECD.

The report predicts for 1998 that already before the compulsory school-age, a great number of children will have had some kind of education. In the developed Western countries, besides the primary school, secondary education is more or less very general. This means that following the compulsory education - usually up to the age of 16-90 per cent of young people take part in some kind of further education. In most OECD countries, 15 to 25 per cent of secondary school graduates go on to a higher education institute.

Besides that, out-of-school education will also play a significant role. In some of the industrialized countries, this has already exceeded the scales of regular school education. Since, due to the demographic conditions, the labour force is active for a longer period while productivity requirements will not be eased, therefore labour force will have to be renewed from time to time. New types of adult education have already appeared. These will have special institutional and financial requirements.

1. The problems of the Hungarian educational system

The relations with the EU, even in their current lax form, have a significant impact on Hungary as well as on the so called 'Visegrad Four' group of states.

Due to the more liberalized travelling opportunities, the geographical closeness and the historical ties, these countries have not been as much segregated from Western-Europe as the other East-block countries still in the period before the change of the political system. This could be felt primarily in the human factors.

Therefore, no matter how distant full membership can be, the requirements for labour force will come up almost at the same time and to the same effect. Since the impact of education is realized with considerable delay, the necessary actions in this field have to be started right now.

In Hungary, as well as in most of the other ex-socialist countries, the development of infrastructure was undervalued as a rule, however two infrastructural sectors have always been given highest priority. These two were education and research and development.

As to the education, this was represented in the expenditures on education as well as in the schooling ratios of the population. Regarding the proportion of educational expenditures within the GNP, Hungary can be ranked among the highly developed regions of Europe. This ratio was 6.1 per cent in 1990 but a constantly high index was characteristic of the preceding years as well.

Let us list some 1990 data on the performance of the educational system. 84.9 per cent of kindergarten-age children went to kindergarten. The eighth class was completed by 94.7 per cent of children under the age of 16. 93.5 per cent of the above children went on to secondary school. 21.1 per cent went to grammar school, 27.5 per cent to secondary technical schools and 45.2 per cent to trade schools, i.e. 48.6 per cent went to schools that provide certificate of secondary education examination, in total 93.8 per cent started secondary school studies. 37.9 per cent of those with final examinations went on to some kind of higher education institute.

However, within this, 59.3 per cent of those from grammar schools and only 19.9 per cent of those from secondary technical schools went on to continue their studies. It should be noted, however, that since the drop-out level is quite high in the educational system, with these rates of further education Hungary would not get a good ranking among countries having developed educational systems regarding the number of university or college students.

On the other hand, the education-training system can be characterized by the education level of the population. In 1990, the distribution of the population above the age of 15 by their highest education level looks as follows. The number of university or college graduates was 8.2 per cent, secondary school graduates: 20.1 per cent; 14 per cent left trade schools as skilled workers or left specialized secondary schools while 35.8 per cent had primary school education. 21.9 per cent had less education than the above. This distribution projected on active earners was respectively: 11.6 per cent, 23.1 per cent, 33.5 per cent and 5.1 per cent.

Despite this relative success, the Hungarian education system still needs some changes. The reasons for this can be found in the various spheres of the society, first of all in the educational system. In fact, there are two principal areas: university and trade schools where change is essential but this change would have an impact on the entire educational system.

New social needs for the educational system

1. Needs for widening the university-level education. It became a topical problem already in the socialist era that the elite-training function of university education should be shifted to a so-called mass-scale training function. This shift has already taken place in most of the developed Western-European countries and has some preliminary indications in Hungary and the social need for this can be clearly felt.

Parallel to democratization, there has emerged a need for higher education not only to supply the economy with adequate professionals but also to satisfy some cultural consumption needs. This is the phenomenon that led to the development of mass-scale higher education in the West.

Kozma (1993) says this happens when ca. one third of the relevant generation attends university-level education.

However, despite the fact that this proportion has not even reached the tenth of the relevant population in the last two years, higher education has a better position if its other performance indices are considered. If we compare the ratio of people with higher education within 100 thousand population to the active earners, we get a much more favourable picture. If we compare this to the per capita GDP, the supply of professionals within the Hungarian economy seems to be in line with a much higher development level.

This can be explained by considering several circumstances. In the ex-socialist countries, planned economy was enforced also in the field of education, therefore the level of university education was adjusted to the needs of production. The stringent admission procedure was applied due to the fear of unemployment of 'over-supplied' professionals and with a view to cutting the education costs and this meant that applicants were strictly measured already before admission to university. Therefore, those who were eventually admitted usually graduated successfully. Thus the smaller number of students was accompanied by a smaller proportion of drop-outs. At the same time, this enabled higher quality education.

However, this principle has never been implemented perfectly. Sociological studies revealed that those who were very determined to study further - this was primarily characteristic of the children of intellectual or public employee parents - could get their diplomas.

A lot of people were able to get a diploma or a second qualification on the evening or correspondence courses throughout the various periods. The labour regulations (study leaves, work-time allowances) provided good conditions for this. In the past decade these opportunities have gradually disappeared which is well reflected in the statistics.

Considering the current unemployment prospects, it is not likely that this opportunity of getting a diploma will stay. This form has proved to be inadequate from several aspects, the diplomas obtained in this way have not reached the value of those obtained at the regular day courses. This does not mean that adult education is not needed any more but new forms have to be developed. Besides democratization and the appearance of education as a form of consumption, this is the third reason that calls for widening higher education.

There is, however, a further reason - and this is our demographic situation - which suggests that if we do not take steps towards developing higher education, then Hungary will have to reckon with serious lack of professionals by the turn of the century. From the 80s on, the number of the coming generations has been so small that the intellectual output would decrease by the turn of the century alone because of the small number of candidates for universities. (Tímár, 1993)

University studies have cost more and more for the students in the last years, although in fact there is no tuition fee. Next year, the Government wants to introduce a stricter tuition fee system. One of their arguments to support this is that they want to expand higher education. For the time being, it cannot be foreseen what impact it will have on the participation in further education. There are only preliminary studies to evaluate intentions. (Papházi, 1993)

2. The crisis of the vocational education system. In Hungary, the majority of children leaving primary schools go to vocational schools. This consists of two basic school types, the secondary technical schools giving certificates of secondary education while trade schools having a dual education system. Technicians are primarily trained in secondary schools, in the fifth class. After graduating from a grammar school, pupils may also obtain a technical qualification on two-year courses. Transfer opportunities are very rare in the secondary educational system and in fact there are only one-way opportunities. As a rule, those dropping out of the higher level schools may continue their studies at the lower level.

The economic crisis that began to unfold in Hungary in the 80s has influenced also the vocational education. It could not meet the demand that was made upon it, i.e. supplying professionals with enterprising, organizing and managing skills who are also capable of adjusting themselves to the changes of technologies. The training of skilled workers was still primarily focused on the integration in the production of large-scale industrial plants although the bulk of the production is currently shifting to medium- and small-sized enterprises.

The training of skilled workers based on large-scale industrial companies got into a crisis as these companies went bankrupt. The workshop backgrounds for the practical training have continuously shrunk as well as the demand of companies for skilled workers.

The schools reacted to this situation differently. Some of them built their own workshops, others started grammar-school classes while there were others which tried to build downwards, i.e. they opened form 7 and 8 primary school classes. Thus, today the picture is very confused and with some exaggeration it can be said that the traditional system of vocational education has collapsed.

Another problem of vocational education is that the applicants have very different educational backgrounds which is very often insufficient. The reason for this is partly found in the primary education. True, up to most recently primary education - through its unified system - provided equal opportunities for further studies but it also differentiated to a great extent, e.g. by social position or geographical conditions. Trade schools are not capable of eliminating these gaps. It is partly reflected by the high ratio of drop-outs - in fact the highest within secondary education.

It is feared that these phenomena will grow stronger in the future owing to the latest changes implemented in the educational system. We will talk about this in detail later.

Based on the available statistics, it is hard to detect the unfavourable trends, contrarily, it can be deemed positive that while the number of primary school leavers fell by 20 thousand due to the demographic wave that ended in 1992, the number of applicants to secondary technical schools fell only by 10 thousand. This means that the number of applicants to secondary technical schools fell by some per cent but the aggregate number of secondary school applicants still improved. In fact, we can observe the desirable shift that secondary education is more focused on general secondary schools and secondary technical schools.

However, these are only the application data and we cannot foresee how many of them will actually complete their studies.

Consequently, the problems of vocational education cannot be separated from those of the entire secondary education. If we do not want the number of participants in secondary education to decrease, we have to take measures to make secondary technical schools and grammar schools more generally available.

Let us highlight how this is in line with the demand for widening our higher education, i.e. to increase the number of young people graduating from secondary schools with more generalized knowledge and less specialization.

3. The changes in the requirements set for the public education system. All of the above factors have their impact on primary education. Despite the high proportion of children completing primary school, we cannot state that primary schools sufficiently prepare children for their secondary school studies. According to a study made in Budapest for 1991-92, 55-60 per cent of children are capable of going on to secondary school. If we are to expand secondary school education, we must improve primary school teaching. If we do not take adequate measures and the trend still continues, that will deteriorate the quality of the entire system.

However the greatest danger does not lie in the lack of modern teaching methods, not even in the insufficient financial resources but primarily in the changes which already took place or which will take place soon and which will cause a drastic inequality of chances for the pupils.

The equalization of social differences with the help of the educational system was a primary social goal in the past era which, although never fully realized, but could still present significant achievements with respect to the limited financial opportunities. The means of this were the schools accessible for all children near their residence, social allowances granted within the educational system (school meals, dormitory accommodation, cheap school equipment).

In the last few years Hungarian society has been differentiated by the level of welfare and income to a great extent and there are quite a lot of children whose healthy growth, physical and mental development has become endangered beyond their own fault. This is a fact today.

This process should be counter-balanced by the primary education.

What steps have been made recently in education policy?

New laws have been enacted on education and vocational training. The Education Act has extended obligatory education to the age of 16.

It should be noted that education was compulsory also up to 16 years of age previously but there is still a difference.

It is because until now young people could comply with compulsory education obligation in two ways. First, they could finish primary school by the age of 14-16 and go on to a higher school or they did not go on to learning. In this case, if they have not reached the age of 16, they would have to go to school as a rule. Previously there really were classes where the curriculum was aimed at deepening the knowledge that was taught in the primary school. However, this form completely vanished because someone who was able to finish primary school before the age of 16 - no matter with what results - went to a trade school where he spent the required years until the age of 16. Then he either dropped out or, in the better case, he obtained a usually worthless vocational qualification. That is why the drop-out ratio has been so high at trade schools.

However, the Education Act prescribes a fundamental change here which was determined by the educational administration just because of the crisis in vocational education. Since the secondary educational system will certainly be restructured, this measure can be deemed justified for managing the crisis situation. However it cannot substitute for the development of a new educational system adjusted to the new circumstances. It can remain only a single element within such a new system.

The second novelty in primary education is that the former strict structuring of the school system has been liberalized.

It has been allowed for secondary schools to expand down-wards as well as for primary schools to open secondary school classes, both usually with reference to democracy.

This can bring about considerable danger to the society in a period when it is becoming strongly segregated anyway. This can lead to the close-down of eight-class schools in villages and the former 4- or 6-class school system can return. This concern is also justified with a view to the financing system of education that was also changed at the same time.

Although from other aspects, it is also dangerous that due to these structural changes, the choice of career is made at an earlier stage which - beyond creating a very early social segregation - also makes career changes more difficult. As to the secondary schools, the limition of transfer opportunities can also be deemed problematic and its implementation in the primary school is not justified in any way, contrarily, one can bring arguments only against it.

The early recognition of talent and the management of talented children are not primarily the problems of the school structure. It can be made more effective by the improvement of the pedagogical staff and by providing the required special means for all.

It is feared that the above changes in the primary school system do not create the grounds necessary for expanding secondary and higher education.

2. The challenge of unemployment to the educational system

1. The appearance, size and structure of youth unemployment. In Hungary one has to reckon with sizeable and, according to all signs, lasting unemployment. This affects to a great extent also younger generations. The chances for getting a job are determined on the labour market at two levels; these are: the family and the school.

As we mentioned earlier, the infant and young age generations have been considerably segmented and segregated in the last few years. This is realised through the social and financial position of the parents which primarily depends on their educational backgrounds. This is further modified by geographic segregation. As an aggregate result, it can be stated that those are in the worst situation who live in an under-developed region, whose parents are under-educated and therefore usually unemployed as well.

Kindergartens are closed first in these settlements and primary schools are also primarily exposed to the above discussed dangers. Thus, schools here are the least capable of balancing inequalities. Consequently, people most affected by youth unemployment come from here.

It is very hard to give a clear picture of youth unemployment on the basis of statistics. The reason for this is that the two sources on unemployment statistics, i.e. the Labour force studies of the Central Statistics Office and the unemployment statistics at the National Labour Centre are the least exact as regards youth unemployment. To give some examples: the school system has been left by 150-160 thousand people in the last few years. In theory, these people enter the labour market. According to a calculation as of May 1993 there were 50,500 young people who have finished their schools not earlier than 1.5 years ago and who are registered as unemployed. However, this number most likely does not contain those between the ages of 15 and 19 because they are not entitled to receive unemployment benefit. Beyond that, the 7,600 people taking part in various retraining forms should perhaps also be added to the above figure. (Bereiné, 1993) According to the data from the same source, in the 15-24 year age group unemployment is well beyond the average 13 per cent. (31.5 per cent of the 15-19 age group and 15.6 per cent of the 15-24 year age group does not know anything about those who come directly from primary schools while among the rest those coming from trade schools are predominant with males in the lead.)

2. Interest conflicts between the young unemployed and other active-age generations. In connection with youth unemployment, there have emerged proposals that the reduction of the supply of other labour force could be a viable solution. One of these solutions is early retirement. What is the obstacle to this?

The retirement age is already very low in Hungary. It is a general view that it should be raised.

In the last period, only one step was taken to raise retirement age and that was to gradually raise women's retirement age to that of men which is to be implemented from 1995. In contrast to this, there began an opposite process in which ca. 50 thousand people are allowed to go to pension 5 years earlier and another 35 thousand can retire 3 years earlier. (5-year early retirement is financed by the employer while 3-year early retirement is financed from the Solidarity Fund.)

Therefore, the actual retirement date has been brought forward. At the same time, the number of employed pensioners also fell. The above described size of youth unemployment has developed parallel to the above process. We believe on this basis that early retirement cannot be expanded any longer and it cannot solve the problem of youth unemployment.

Another opinion is that the supply of female labour force should be decreased. However, under the present circumstances, only a very small part of women could use the opportunities such as part-time work or child-care allowance - even if they would like to.

The greatest obstacle to this is unemployment itself. The income of most Hungarian families is shrinking despite the usual two-earners model and due to the high rate of unemployment it is highly probable that one of the two wage earners is already unemployed No wonder, that under such circumstances women insist on maintaining their jobs. Unemployment statistics reflect that women are less affected by unemployment than men. One of the reasons for this is that the qualification structure of women is a bit more in harmony with the process that is going on in the employment structure today (i.e. a small shift to the infrastructure and deepening crisis in the industry, etc.).

From other aspects, this would adversely affect women's education. If we look at UNESCO statistics, we can establish that in the developed countries men and women take part almost in equal proportions in education. On the other hand, in less developed countries, where the education level of women is lower than that of men, their proportion is dynamically growing. Nevertheless, the greatest motivation of learning is to prepare oneself for the future job, especially in the areas of vocational and higher education.

In Hungary, the proportion of female students is equal to that of developed countries and we would derail from the European track if we changed this.

3. The existing opportunities of education for managing youth unemployment. We are convinced that there are no means other than education itself to ease youth unemployment.

The newly started 9th and 10th classes will solve the problems of the 15-16 year-olds for the time being. For those who are over 16 but do not have basic education, at least free training courses should be organised which could ensure a start of their independent life until general education is extended to the age of 18.

It would be important to pay special attention to young people whose learned profession is becoming outdated and they should be enabled to get trained for another profession free of charge, while efforts should be made to extend compulsory school-age to 18 years.

For secondary school graduates, post-secondary trainings should be organized and finally the university education should be expanded.

Unfavourable changes concerning the decrease of the technical gap,
vocational training and the situation of R&D intellectuals

1. Changes in the attitudes towards technical professions. As our previous studies showed, the technical gap, in Hungary as well as in most of the Eastern-European countries, continued to exist despite the fact that the technical intelligentsia had enjoyed a preferred status for a long time regarding both its social prestige and its financial conditions. This was also reflected in the career choice of young people. The deepening economic crises of the 80s, affecting heavy industry and metallurgy first but later expanded to the industry as a whole led to the deterioration of the situation of technical intelligentsia and consequently to the decrease in the interest towards technical careers. (Falusiné, Sz.K.)

We have experienced similar processes regarding the specialized intellectuals of agriculture whose signs were felt later, in the period directly preceding the political changes. Agriculture was deemed a success story of Hungary primarily due to the application of advanced technologies and their widespread use. This was supported by adequately qualified agricultural specialists.

However, this favourable situation was fundamentally changed by the agro-political measures taken after the political changes which - besides the adjustment to the different market conditions - were based on certain other political intentions such as the policy of compensation.

The change of the system has adversely affected the situation of most technical and agricultural professionals. This is especially magnified if compared to the situation of other intellectuals (economists, lawyers and other intellectuals). This results in leaving the profession, early retirement, unemployment among engineers and difficulties for fresh graduates in finding jobs in the technical and agricultural sector. The situation is especially grave in some crisis regions. (Tóthné, 1993, Fazekas, 1993)

These phenomena have had direct influence on the career choice of younger generations. We have already discussed what problems have been caused by this in the secondary school system. However, we can experience a similar process in university education.

This can be illustrated by the number of applicants to different universities and by the admittance rate of youths with final examinations. Since the 80s, the highest admission rates are recorded at the technical universities and colleges directly followed by agricultural faculties. While this rate is around 30-40 per cent in most universities, it is 52-59 per cent at technical universities and 35-44 per cent at agricultural institutes.

This means a declining interest together with a lower average quality of students.

If we also take into consideration that while the total number of students remained constant between 1981 and 1990 - with small fluctuations only - the number of students in technical universities has decreased significantly, by 20 per cent, and it stagnated in the agricultural faculties while at the same time it grew on the economic and arts faculties, then the truth of our statement is very much evidenced.

These tendencies have become stronger since 1991. Since education has a much delayed effect, the above conditions will influence the supply of young technical and agricultural intellectuals in 1995-97. If we also consider that today's difficulties in finding a job in the original specialization leads fresh graduates and those graduated some years ago to other professions, it is feared that by the time some progress could be made, the lack of qualified experts will pose a barrier to technical development.

2. Shifting proportions within the volume of R&D staff, quitting one's career, migration and the difficulties of supplementing labour force. New education needs due to the losses suffered. Another important factor that is essential for filling in the technical gap is the research and development activity of the country. We would not like to go into detail in this aspect as we have dealt with this topic in another lecture. We want to deal with this only as far as its changes affect the educational system as well.

The period following 1989 has been characterized by a significant decrease of research and development activities. This problem can be explored from several aspects (Kovács, J. and Molnár, Gy. 1993; Kovács, J. and Tarján, T.). It is a fact that both the number of research staffs and the total number of employees in the R&D sector has decreased. The proportion of research expenditures within the GDP has decreased, and even worse, in a period when the GDP itself has decreased. As regards basic research, the decline is slower while there is a dramatic drop in company-financed R&D activities including the R&D activities of agriculture. Social scientific research activities have been affected less than technical and agricultural research, however a regression is most likely also in that field.

It is a statistical fact that 30 thousand researchers left their jobs between 1981 and 1990, while 12 thousand (ca. one third) of the actual research and development scientists also gave up their careers.

What happened to these experts?

In general, we can say that the previous system of financing research activities has collapsed. All the transitional economies are forced to change their central budgets due to the high deficit of the budget which results from the unforeseen high costs of the prolonged transition period and is accompanied by a deep and lasting economic crisis.

This means that the resources of research coming either from the central budget or from companies have strongly shrunk.

This primarily affects the wages and income of those employed in the R&D sector. The non-researcher staff of research institutes can easily find a new job for themselves because most of them are excellent professionals in their line of work, good laboratory assistants or highly qualified technicians.

There are two directions for researchers to move: leaving the field or going abroad.

We do not yet have enough statistical data to describe its internal proportions, nevertheless, based on our estimations and personal experience, we can say that the recession is the highest among technical and natural scientific researchers.

Career leavers, although it means less capacity, cannot be deemed unequivocally negative from economic aspects. It does not mean the withdrawal of intellectual capital from the economy, except for a very few extreme cases. True, in the individual career of the given researcher it is an irreversible process, but if he succeeds it may prove how useful it is to have a multi-level, diverse educational system which each researcher has to go through (second diploma, transparency between the borders of different sciences, obtaining doctor's degree or other titles).

Working abroad cannot be judged so easily. There are in fact arguments for as well as against it. Pál Tamás gives a very detailed analysis of this question in his study (Tamás, P. 1993). Let us briefly refer to some of his conclusions. This phenomenon is probably inescapable.

This is partly due to the internal development of sciences. In a global world, it is logical that there are centres where the most excellent concepts and scientists of a given science are concentrated.

The second reason is that in the Eastern-European countries including the former Soviet Union, partly as a result of the isolation policy of the past period, a relatively high quality research capacity was created whose maintenance and utilization became very uncertain by now. This encourages researchers who are ready to move to find jobs where their work is really needed and at the same time their income and welfare conditions are more secure compared to the very low wages they presently get.

Let us note that the chances for this are largely dependent on the demand of the host country, its scientific and migration policies as well as on the supply of other regions.

For Hungary and the other Eastern-European countries, the USA has had the leading role in this aspect. It has always been the most important host country. Western-Europe is not likely to draw many people as science is traditionally based on their own staffs there. According to prognoses, the boom of the US 'scientific market' will take place in 1995-2005 and this will also affect university lecturers' positions. However, instead of the reliable average quality professionals who produce the bulk of migration today, mostly young doctoral candidates will be sought at that time.

This has clear advantages from the host country's point of view, however this migration may pose the greatest threat to the research systems of Eastern-European countries.

What does this mean from the aspects of education and the supply of new researchers?

Although Hungary has a separate research institutional system, the staff of university education and research is not radically separated. It is especially true for the training of new researchers. Although post-graduate training is currently reformed, the supply of new research and development experts depends most of all on today's leading researchers, developers and professors and the workshops formed around them.

What we can do is to keep at least these key people.

On the other hand if our researchers leave their profession in great numbers then not fewer but even more researchers should be trained. This implies that we should expand our demand for convertible knowledge and instead of reducing the so called over-supply that encourages career modification, we should establish an education system that supports transfers between professions.

This can only be achieved if university education is expanded both horizontally and vertically.

Some special requirements of a development strategy based on the infrastructure

It is a common feature of the Eastern-European countries that the sectoral distribution of labour force differs from that of developed Western Europe. The proportion of agricultural workers is high, even more people are employed in industry, consequently the number of those employed in the service sector is quite small.

On the other hand, it can be proved that the expert needs of the third sector are generally higher than those of the two productive sectors.

At the same time, as we have already pointed out, the one and only strong side of these economies is their intellectual capital, therefore it seems logical for them to prefer an economic development based on the infrastructure.

As for Hungary, it can also be argued that it has a central position within Europe which has already compelled a relative advantage in the infrastructure compared to the other countries of the region.

Beyond that, due to the changes of the political system and the market, labour force is leaving agriculture and partly industry which are now exposed to the competition with Western-Europe. The development of the third sector could be the means for absorbing this labour force, i.e. it could actively contribute to reducing unemployment.

What demand does this make on the education?

In order to enhance the role of the infrastructure, we need a highly qualified labour force with foreign language knowledge which requires the development of the educational system. Therefore the infrastructure development policy cannot leave education unaffected. Transition is going on a very narrow path where one has to simultaneously cope with unemployment, lack of capital, disappearing professions and lack of new ones.

For the education system, this means:

First of all, the different school levels should be expanded:

- extending the school leaving age by making secondary schools more general and then extending school leaving age up to 18;
- creating a mass-scale good quality university education which has already begun with the establishment of the college system;
- enhancing the convertibility of knowledge, i.e. the curriculum should be relatively general and less specialised also at this level;
- supporting computer technology, informatics and language learning at all levels of the education system;
- improving the communication skills of young people not only through teaching languages but also by learning, accepting and understanding other cultures including the languages and cultures of the neighbouring countries;
- at all levels of the educational system people have to be prepared for the possibility that they may have to change their careers - maybe several times - throughout their active life and they have to be able to solve this problem. The precondition of this is a high level of transfer opportunities at all levels of the education system.

All these indicate again that the requirements for education are pretty much the same no matter if we look at the future European trends or we want to find the solution to our new problems or we want to reduce our technical under-development.

Educational level and the newly structured Hungarian society

A significant social restructuring can be observed during the transition period in the Eastern-European countries. It is now being determined how big a share of power the different social groups will have. Under the rapidly changing circumstances the enforcement of interests seems still easy, while the power structure is less likely to change in a crystalized system. No wonder there are cut throat political battles.

We can nonetheless maintain that the outcome of this struggle is not unpredictable as the social transition follows from previous developments.

Many of us believe that Hungary has a certain advantage by the experiences and partial results it achieved in the field of market economy during the 70s and the 80s. One of the most important consequences of this was that there has been a change in the power structure.

For the purposes of promotion, professional knowledge has become more and more important while political considerations count less and less. The result is an emerging technocracy that has been capable of implementing fundamental changes in the entire development of Hungary.

In our opinion, power can be divided into three main aspects: economic, political and bureaucratic.

In the era of the one-party system, this meant a relatively simple power hierarchy as the same people stood at the top of the three elements and the subordinate layers were structured accordingly. A technocratic intelligentsia got to the top of this monolithic pyramid whose position was legitimated by their professional knowledge.

With the appearance of the entrepreneurial stratum economic power plays an independent role with its obvious influence on political and bureaucratic power. So the above mentioned monolithic pyramid has been divided at least into two. The two pyramids are linked by the middle-class whose leading group towards both pyramids is the intelligentsia.

Although in the last few years there have been significant changes in the management of the remaining state-owned companies, these have not been accompanied by a restructuring in the social layers. Therefore a technocratic group remained in power here. The new owners of privatized companies usually come from this group. Their share in power is therefore unquestionable. At the same time, the developing entrepreneurial layer acquires more and more share in power, too.

If we examine who and how properly educated people belong to the new entrepreneurial stratum it becomes obvious why this problem is dealt with in connection with education (Kovács, J. and Virág, I. 1993).

According to a study of 1991, the composition of entrepreneurs by education was as follows: 30 per cent had a diploma, 38 per cent had secondary school education, 24 per cent were skilled workers and only 8 per cent had less education than the above.

We may not attach much importance to such a study, still we can conclude therefrom that entrepreneurship, getting into the middle class and thereby acquiring a share in power will be available only to those with adequate education.

Unequal opportunities and the education

The transition to the new economic and social system is not only the era of the development of a new middle class but it also brings about social and economic polarization. According to estimates, one quarter or one third of the population is currently having a minimum standard of living and perhaps one sixth or one seventh lives at a poverty level (no matter how ambiguous the definitions for these terms are). Beyond these and the emerging middle class, there is a (much narrower) rapidly enriching, affluent class whose proportion is hard to estimate. Economists and sociologists are talking about 'wild capitalism' or '19th century capitalism'.

We cannot talk for a long time now about the need for enhancing equal opportunities but only about the need for decreasing the growth of the inequality of opportunities. This is a social and at the same time economic interest.

It is a social interest because if we cannot avoid the split of society it might endanger social stability (one of the most appreciated values of today's Hungarian society).

It is also an economic interest because the growing inequality of opportunities may reduce the basis for building and maintaining 'human capital'.

Only the accelerated expansion of the education system may offer an effective means for halting negative tendencies. The preconditions for this are given. Providing the opportunities necessary to achieve this should be given top priority.

References

Bereiné, D.I. (1993) 'Unemployment among school leavers in the Mirror of Statistics', a conference lecture: Unemployment in Hungary, Seregélyes, 1993.

Falusiné, Sz.K. (to be published) *The Intelligentsia in Hungary*, Akadémia Press Office, Budapest.

Fazekas, K. (1993) 'About the reasons for the regional differences of unemployment' *Közgazdasági Szemle*, 7-8/1993.

Kovács, J. and Molnár, Gy. (1993) 'State and future Alternatives of Hungarian R&D' a conference lecture, Sofia, 1993.

Kovács, J. and Tarján, T. (to be published) 'The role of the state during and after the transition to market economy', *Közgazdasági Szemle*.

Kovács, J. and Virág, I. (1993) 'The role of the intelligentsia in forming the middle class', *Munkaügyi Szemle*, No. 6. 1993.

Kozma, T. (1993) 'House of Professors', *Educatio*, Autumn 1993.

Memorandum on Higher Education in the European Community, Brussels, Commission of the European Communities.

Papházi, T. (1993) 'In the Focus: Tuition Fee', *Educatio*, Autumn 1993.

Sipos, A. (manuscript) *Technology Development in Hungarian Agriculture: Results and Problems.*

Tamás, P. (1993) 'A new wave of Eastern-European brain drain: the emigration chances and strategies of researcher intelligentsia', *Új Exodus*, MTA Social Conflicts Research Institute and MTA World Economy Research Institute.

Tímár, J. (1993) 'The faults and chances of education policy in mitigating unemployment', a conference lecture: Unemployment in Hungary, Seregélyes.

Tóthné, Sz.G. (1993) 'Engineers out of work', a conference lecture: Unemployment in Hungary, Seregélyes, 1993.

13 Education, training and economic change in advanced market economies

Olivier Bertrand

This paper attempts to discuss the relationship between the changes which have affected during the last decades the economy of the so-called advanced countries on the one hand and their educational and training systems on the other. It touches on the various quantitative, qualitative and institutional aspects of this relationship. As far as possible, it is based on a comparative approach and tries to identify the similarities and differences between national contexts, in order to assess whether there is a 'one best way' towards growth and development.

This is quite an ambitious project, which cannot be discussed thoroughly in such a limited contribution. This paper will attempt to throw some light on the following points:

- The relationship between competitiveness and workers' skills has been analyzed in a number of comparative researches at the enterprise level, which will be briefly summarized here.
- All countries are faced to-day with a common challenge: meeting new skill requirements. What are the factors of change and their quantitative and qualitative implications?
- Educational and training systems have reacted in very different ways to these common challenges, since they are based on specific traditions, but a number of rather converging trends can be identified in their recent evolution.

-    Assessing the process of adjustment between education and the economy requires an integrated approach and therefore a more specific analysis of some of the national situations.

1. Competitiveness and workers' skills at the enterprise level

The relationship between economic growth, productivity and competitiveness on the one hand and education on the other has been discussed at length, following the emergence of the human capital theory in the 60s. The theory has been challenged by researchers, but the idea of investment in human resources is now widespread and has had an impact on the educational development of most countries. Recently, OECD has been more interested in the issue of investment in training, with a view to improve its measurement and accounting (Miller, R. 1993).

The correlation between educational qualifications and economic competitiveness has been analyzed at the macro level on the basis of statistics and at the micro level on the basis of direct investigations within enterprises.

In a sociological perspective, the pioneering work was carried out in the 70s by the LEST in Aix en Provence and by B. Lutz at ISF in Munich, through a comparison of French and German firms (Maurice, M. et al. 1982). It demonstrated a relationship between the differences in work organization and in workers' skills. It suggested that higher qualifications of German workers, resulting from a different social and institutional context, might have contributed to a more efficient work organization and therefore to a better competitiveness of German firms. Similar conclusions were reached by a number of other comparative researches, especially between Germany and the United Kingdom.

Following a more economic approach, the National Institute of Economic and Social Research (London) has carried out a series of comparative researches on workers' skills and productivity at the firm level in the United Kingdom and in other European countries (Steedman, H. and Wagner, K. 1987). All of them led to the same conclusion: there was a close correlation between the low level of skill and qualification of British workers and the lower productivity of the firms, compared to their competitors in Germany, but also in the Netherlands and in France. These studies were also supported by comparative analyses of curriculum contents in the same countries.

These approaches, as well as the success of the Japanese and German economic systems, which give much emphasis to education and training, have contributed to an awareness of their role in work structures and firms' competitiveness. The United Kingdom and the United States have been concerned with the risk of a vicious circle between low skills, low wages/low quality and low productivity, contrasting with the virtuous circle high skills, high wages/high quality and high productivity (Marshall, R. and Tucker, M. 1992).

2. Common challenges: Facing new skill requirements

Educational systems in industrial economies are all faced with the same challenge: meeting the new requirements resulting from changing occupational structures and skill contents. These are not only the consequence of technological change. They can be approached in quantitative and qualitative terms.

Three factors of change

During the last decades, substantial changes have affected the occupational structure, the work contents and the skill requirements of the workforce in advanced market economies. This is very often related to the widespread use of so-called new information technologies. But it is an oversimplification. In fact, it is the combined effect of three factors: economic competition, technology and changing work organization.

a) The development of transport and of communication, the relaxing of regulations, the crumbling of frontiers, the internationalization of business and the faith in market forces and liberal ideology have all contributed to make competition fiercer and more widespread across countries and sectors of activity. This has resulted in a substantial shift away from the mass manufacturing of low cost goods (which tend to be produced by countries with low labour costs) and towards upgrading the quality of goods and services, striving for a greater diversification and for adaptation to a constantly changing demand, while seeking ways of reducing costs through better organization, more sophisticated management and more cost control. In this context, flexibility is the key word and emphasis is given to the production of high value-added goods and services requiring a more skilled workforce.

b) At the same time, information technologies, which initially were very rigid and centralized, offered new opportunities for more flexibility, diversity and decentralization at a lower cost. Their primary impact is the automation of a large number or simple and repetitive tasks, but they can also be used for a wider range of applications, including product innovation, marketing, management and communication.

c) In relation to these developments, the traditional forms of work organization based on Taylorian principles of hierarchy, division of labour, rigid job assignment and de-skilling were put into question, because they were no more consistent with new economic and technical requirements. The most efficient firms are now promoting new forms of organization based on flexibility, some delegation of authority and group work. They are looking for more autonomous, creative and adaptable workers.

The quantitative impact

All national statistics show a distinctive shift of occupational structures towards white collar and more skilled occupations. In the US between 1975 and 1990, the growth of executive, administrative and managerial occupations was 83 per cent, compared to 60 per cent for professionals, 55 per cent for marketing and sales occupations and less than 7 per cent for operators and labourers. In France between 1982 and 1990 it was 42 per cent for managers and intellectual occupations, 37 per cent for intermediate occupations, 31 per cent for professionals, while the number of industrial workers was actually decreasing. Projections anticipate a continuation of this trend for the coming years. In Germany, projections based on types of activity indicate a growing share of those concerned with care, advisory work, education, communication, organization, management, research and development and a decreasing share of other white collar jobs concerned with cleaning, handling, transportation, security, clerical work and sales.

These changes in the occupational structure reflect a double employment shift: between industries, from manufacturing towards services and in many cases from industries with low value added and less skilled workforce towards those with high value added and skilled workforce; within a given industry, from routine production tasks to more technical and managerial jobs.

The qualitative impact

For a given occupation or group of occupations, investigations show very often that the work contents tend to be broader and richer. This is not only because of the complexity of technologies, which require less manual and more analytical skills. It is also because workers are expected to be less specialized, to cover a wider range of functions and to understand a broader and constantly changing environment, including more diversified and complex products and services.

In addition, business firms tend to attach a growing importance to the personal characteristics of their staff. Reliability, capacity for expression and problem-solving, ability to learn, to cooperate with others, to be hard-working, to adapt to unexpected situations, to be innovative and to care about the quality of products and of services are often considered more important than purely technical skills. The problem is that these competences are particularly difficult to analyze and to assess in an objective way.

The impact on the educational attainment of the workforce

It is very difficult to assess the educational and training requirements corresponding to these personal characteristics and this contributes to an increasing blurring of the relationship between occupational skills and educational qualifications. For lack of a precise assessment and in order to be on the safe side, employers tend to recruit their staff at a higher level of education, considering that it is more likely to be adaptable to unforeseen circumstances.

This tendency is further encouraged by the increased availability of educated and trained workers, which is itself the result of two factors: a growing enrolment at the secondary and higher levels linked to a more pressing social demand and the higher level of unemployment, particularly during the recent period.

According to national statistics, the rise in the level of educational attainment of the workforce is significant in all countries. First of all, it reflects the changes in the occupational structure. But in most cases it goes beyond that: for a given occupation or group of occupations, the level of education of workers tends to be higher. It is not surprising in view of the above comments. The difficulty is that it is practically impossible to identify the relative weight of the different factors: growing complexity of work contents, rising and not necessarily justified demands of employers and increased supply of educated workers.

In a number of cases, it is quite possible that this evolution is leading from a situation of undereducation of the workforce (in the 70s) to one of overeducation (in the 90s). But it is extremely difficult to document such a statement in an objective way.

3. A variety of educational responses to the challenge

If modern economies have to face very similar challenges, they are situated in different contexts, especially from the point of view of their education and training systems, but these are themselves changing.

Different national systems

The reactions of the national systems of education and training to these challenges vary considerably, as a result of their different traditions, structures and levels of development.

Differences can be observed with reference to a number of criteria:
-    In terms of responsibility for decision-making in the field of education and training: highly centralized countries at the national level (like France, at least until 1983) can be compared with highly decentralized ones (Anglo-Saxon countries) and with those which are centralized at the state or provincial level (like Germany);
-    In terms of responsibility for the delivery of vocational training and of its relationship with general education, there are three different approaches. In countries such as Japan and the United States, most young people complete a high level of general education with little or no vocational training, as it is essentially left to the business firms. In countries such as France, most of the vocational education is provided by schools. In the German tradition, the dual system includes both education in schools and training in enterprise.
-    In terms of school enrolment ratios, very high rates of enrolment in high school and higher education can be observed in some countries outside Europe, such as the United States, Japan (nearly 95 per cent of an age-group complete high school), but also Korea (more than 80 per cent). In Europe, there are wide differences concerning the ratio of secondary school diploma holders, with more than 70 per cent in Greece and Ireland, 61 per cent in the Netherlands, around 50 per cent in France and Italy, 42 per cent in Germany, 30 per cent in the United Kingdom and 24 per cent in Portugal[1].
-    In terms of the degree of institutionalization of training and of its relationship with the labour market. In decentralized Anglo-Saxon countries, there is no national system of certification; training is highly dependent upon the labour market with a low degree of institutionalization. In Germany, the institutionalized character of training implies a more far-reaching approach, while the close relationship with enterprises guarantees their recognition of the

qualification. In France, the state has the sole responsibility for granting diplomas, but their value on the labour market is not necessarily recognized by enterprises (Campinos-Dubernet, M. and Grando, J.M. 1988).

Other criteria could be taken into consideration. If they are combined, the picture becomes a puzzle. International comparisons tend to become very difficult, since they should take into consideration:

- the institutional structure and the way the systems operate;
- quantitative developments in terms of years of schooling and enrolment ratios. The above figures confirm the need for caution with regard to the real meaning of these figures and cast some doubts on the possibility of correlating them with economic progress and efficiency;
- the curriculum contents (subjects taught);
- the quality of educational attainment, which is difficult to assess at the moment[2].

The European Commission has been faced with these problems when it attempted to define European standards of qualifications. For regulated occupations requiring a diploma, and after time-consuming studies of comparison between specific diplomas, it adopted the principle of mutual recognition between Member States for diplomas granted after completion of three years or one year of post-secondary education[3]. The work undertaken by CEDEFOP, the agency in charge of training matters at the Community level, on the comparability of qualifications for other occupations has been faced with tremendous difficulties and met with little success.

Converging trends

Despite these differences between national systems of education and training, the observation of their recent evolution indicates that in several ways it is following converging directions in many countries. A comparative study now in progress at OECD[4] and concerning more particularly vocational education and training identifies the following trends:

- extension of the duration of education and training and an increased participation in post-compulsory, higher and vocational education. As indicated above, this is partly a response to an economic demand for a more educated workforce and partly the result of a social demand;
- an attempt to relate more closely vocational education and training to the needs of industry. This is achieved through:

i) more involvement of social partners in the identification of these needs and in the planning process, at the national, regional and local levels;

ii) enhancing the role of industry in the delivery of training, which involves the development of various forms of work-based training or sandwich courses (apprenticeship with one day per week at school, or periods of work experience in enterprise); and

iii) developing various forms of partnership between enterprises or employers' organizations and universities or training institutions for specific courses or programmes.

- for the same purpose and also in order to meet a more diversified demand from students, a search for more flexibility of training structures, streams and pathways and for more breadth in the curriculum. This usually includes reducing the number of streams, which tend to be more broad-based and less specialized. There are also examples of various forms of modularity;

- a considerable expansion of continuous training provided by business in order to update the skill of their personnel and by state programmes for the redeployment of unemployed workers and of those who are threatened by the restructuring of their industry.

4. The adjusment process: national examples

In order to illustrate these general considerations, the following paragraphs refer to the example of several European countries. They do not attempt to give a comprehensive picture of their situation and evolution, but only to focus on some issues which may be of interest in this context.

The case of France

Looking at recent trends in this country requires an understanding of the specific features of its system of education and training:

- it is a school-based system, with more emphasis on education than on training for specific jobs and for entry into the labour market;

- at the higher level, there is a marked dualism between highly selective and prestigious '*grandes écoles*' and depreciated universities;

- the system used to be highly centralized, with a major role of the state, which has a monopoly for the award of degrees and diplomas (which are considerably valued by the population). The degree of

decentralization introduced in 1983 concerned essentially physical investments and their financing;
- the state has also played a role in the development of the continuous training of workers, by imposing a training obligation to firms, which can either provide training themselves or pay the cost to organizations created at the sectoral level to allocate the funds.

During the last decades, the following trends have affected this system, especially with regard to its relationship with economic developments:

a) There has been a considerable progress of schooling, both in terms of extension of its duration and of enrolment-ratios at the secondary and higher levels. In the mid-eighties, the Government set up a goal of 80 per cent of an age-group completing secondary education (baccalaureate) by the end of the century. It was inspired partly by broad economic considerations (Employers' organizations wishing to recruit a better-skilled workforce, but also the example of Japan) and partly by the social demand.

b) Concerning more specifically vocational education, substantial modifications were brought about to its structure and contents. More broad-based diplomas were created in the sixties to train skilled workers. Then, there was a rapid development of two-year post-secondary courses, either within high schools (*lycées*), or in newly created and autonomous departments of the universities, in order to train technicians to meet the new demands of industry and services.

Finally, a new 'vocational baccalaureate' was created in the late 80s to offer opportunities for further training to the holders of the first level diplomas, while meeting the needs for highly skilled craftsmen and service employees. It was also conceived as a means of reaching the '80 per cent' target, without overcrowding universities with baccalaureate graduates.

c) These changes were brought about in a context of closer coordination between the Ministry of Education and social partners, especially through consultative commissions, which provide advice on the creation and modification of vocational diplomas, on the basis of their (mostly qualitative) evaluation of the demand of the labour market. They are assisted by a research agency, CEREQ, which is placed under the authority of both the Ministries of Education and of Labour.

More long-term and broader perspectives are discussed within the framework of a Higher Commission on the relationship between education and the economy. It organizes meetings and commissions studies to a variety of research agencies and consultants.

d) Another way to bring closer training and industry has been the development of various forms of 'alternance' since the beginning of the eighties. It was initiated with the organization of short sessions of work experience within the curriculum of vocational schools. This was extended and systematized with the new vocational baccalaureate.

It has also been a policy of recent Governments to promote apprenticeship, which up to now was limited to the low-level and less prestigious occupations. According to a recent legislation, it is possible to prepare in this way all vocational diplomas and a campaign is on the way to encourage employers and young people to follow this path.

These developments call for a few additional comments.

First of all, it is interesting to observe that the target of 80 per cent of an age-group at the baccalaureate level, which looked somewhat unrealistic at the start, is likely to be reached, as a result of a pressing social demand, reinforced by the high level of youth unemployment, which contributes to an extension of the duration of studies. But doubts are increasingly expressed about the suitability of this policy. Since the population interprets the baccalaureate usually in terms of general education, most of the growth takes place in general streams, leading to overcrowded universities. Within the vocational streams, an excessive emphasis on the baccalaureate level may jeopardize the lower level, for lack of candidates, of classes and of trained teachers. Students who have obtained the diploma now would like to continue their studies; if they do not succeed, they are often disappointed with the type of job that they get, which is not at the level of their expectations.

In a country which attaches great value to diplomas and degrees, risks of frustration and overeducation are more significant. The fact that unemployment is higher among the less educated youth contributes to a push for more education, but it does not necessarily mean that a comparatively high level of academic education is necessary for the economy. It is the reflection of employers' selection practices, and also of the fact that a modern economy offers very few jobs to uneducated workers. What is required is to upgrade the level of the lower group and not of the higher one. From that point of view, the '80 per cent' target may have the effect of further marginalizing the 20 per cent left.

The case of Germany

The German system of vocational education and training is often considered as the best one and it is usually assumed that it is a major factor of the success of German industry. This is because the 'dual' system of training traditionally concerns the large majority of youth and offers them at the same time a solid educational basis, a specific vocational training which is well recognized on the labour market and a work experience which ensures a proper transition from school to employment. It is supposed to guarantee a good adaptation to the needs of industry in two ways: through a close cooperation with the social partners in the planning work undertaken under the responsibility of the Federal Institute of Vocational Training (BIBB); through the major role of enterprises in the delivery of training, which takes place in a normal work setting and is adapted to actual working conditions.

This raises at least two issues: if it is so, is it likely to remain so or is it also affected by forces of change? What are the chances of transferring the system to a different context?

Concerning the present working of the system, some questions could be raised about the differences between large and modern enterprises on the one hand and the smaller ones on the other, with regard to the quality of training and the opportunities that it opens. The first ones provide not only a practical experience, but quite frequently also an amount of additional theoretical courses. Traditionally, they used to recruit most of the trainees after completion of the course. This is not the case with small and medium size enterprises, which have only limited opportunities for recruitment and which may be first of all interested in the availability of comparatively cheap labour (as in apprenticeship schemes in other countries).

Another question could concern the relationship and the cooperation between the school, which is supposed to provide the theoretical part of the training and the firm, which is responsible for the practical part. In principle, they are complementary and well coordinated, through a detailed programme which specifies the steps to be followed and and the results to be achieved in enterprise. But in fact the coordination between the two is not always what it should be.

It could also be observed that the implication of the social partners in the planning process of vocational education makes it cumbersome, so that the adjustment with economic needs requires a very long time.

In any case, the model is changing, since a shift can be observed from its most traditional form: there has been a substantial development of training sessions in workshops set up at the sectoral level, rather than in the companies themselves, because the smaller ones do not always have the facilities and the equipment required; a considerably larger proportion of students is continuing their studies at the higher level, either without joining the dual system, or before joining, or after, in order to get a higher level of qualifications. In other words, the relative role of academic education tends to increase.

It would be too early to conclude that the system is jeopardized and, despite the fact that the difference with the French system tends to decrease, transferability in a different context is still a serious problem. Involving industry in the delivery of training supposes that it is well developed enough, that it regards it as a long-term investment and accordingly that it is willing to allocate the necessary resources to make it efficient, including particularly the availability of well-trained supervisors ('*meister*'). Otherwise, there is a risk that enterprises limit their training activities to their short-term and specific needs, or even that they tend to recruit apprentices primarily as cheap labour.

The case of the United Kingdom

Describing the training system in this country would be beyond the scope of this paper, in view of its diversity, related to its high degree of decentralization and of the numerous modifications which have affected its structure, organization and functioning during the last decades. It may be sufficient to underline that its characteristics may be seen as completely opposite to that of the French system, especially with regard to the role of the State and the degree of decentralization. The comparatively low level of education, at least after the age of 16 and until recent years[5] has already been mentioned above.

The interesting issue is the possibility of some converging trends, starting from these extreme situations. Successive British Governements have been aware of the need to upgrade the skill level of the workforce and have taken a number of initiatives to promote various programmes of complementary or remedial education for young students and workers (Youth Training Scheme, Technical and Vocational Education Initiative).

Without attempting to evaluate the impact of these schemes, they raise at least two issues. One of them is whether the challenge for the adjustment of workers' skills to economic requirements is in terms of vocational training or in terms of basic education. In UK, most recent measures have put the emphasis on the former, instead of the latter in France. The second is the role of the operation of the labour market, which appears to be in contrast with the French context: whereas in the latter country, the comparatively high cost of unskilled labour may contribute to maintain a high level of unemployment among youth and works as an incentive for the continuation of education and a later entry into the labour market, it could be the opposite in the UK.

Promoting the value and the quality of training has raised the issue of centralization and standardization. There have been several experiences in attempting to give more responsibility to a central agency for the coordination of these activities, but the decentralized approach has ultimately prevailed, together with an increasing role of local representatives of industry.

At the same time, an important programme has been carried out with a rather standardized approach: it consists in the development of 'National Vocational Qualifications'. They attempt to clarify the system of certification (up to now entirely decentralized and diversified), to propose training targets accessible to all kinds of workers and directly related to vocational objectives, and to organize the assessment in a variety of ways, including within the work context. The idea is to move away from an academic approach of training towards one which is more competency-based. It has been thought that this approach could be also followed in other countries, but it should be clear that it requires a huge investment and that there is the risk that observations are obsolete after some time.

The approach has also raised some controversies in the United Kingdom itself: training would be exceedingly geared towards specific and operational requirements, and not enough to more educational objectives; the responsibility for evaluation would be too much left to enterprise. The Agency in charge of National Vocational Qualifications has attempted to answer these criticisms, but in any case, it would seem that the system is more appropriate to the needs of adult workers than to the problem of initial education.

Concluding remarks

A few conclusions may be drawn from this brief analysis:

1. Broadly speaking, the modernization of the economy requires a better trained and educated workforce, but it is becoming increasingly difficult to assess its requirements in qualitative and even more in quantitative terms.

At the macro level, forecasting has proved risky and only broad trends can be estimated. Enterprises usually have a short-term and sometimes narrow perspective. They often have diverging views on the needs: the large ones are more interested in recruiting workers with a broad-based training, whereas the smaller ones would like to have people with a specific training who can be assigned immediately to a definite job.

2. The question is made even more complex with the shift towards a service economy. As a whole, services require more basic education and more specific training adjusted to the particular requirements of a company, but less know how specific to an occupation. It might be tempting to conclude that the traditional type of vocational training is no more appropriate and that more responsibility could be transferred, either to the system of general education, or to the firms themselves. But we have just seen the limitation of this approach. And in Central and Eastern European countries, very few of them have the adequate resources.

3. It is worth underlining that the most successful countries in economic terms (Germany, Japan, Korea) have assigned a high level of priority to training, but with entirely different systems, structures and traditions. Therefore, there is obviously no such a thing as a 'one best way' to train workers for a competitive economy. In any case, no foreign model can be simply transferred, without a considerable amount of adaptation to the national context.

4. On the other hand, the modern economic and technological context entails a number of constraints which force all systems of education and training to find their own way to constantly adapt to an everchanging situation. Flexibility and responsiveness of educational and training systems are often seen as the best response to change and uncertainty. They are often associated with decentralization at the regional, local and/or school level and they require more cooperation with enterprises and local authorities.

5. But in any case, the observation of foreign systems shows that adaptation to the market needs (supposing that they can be properly assessed) is not enough. There is always (and even more when the system is decentralized) a need for some kind of regulation and coordination of educational activities, in order:
-    to take care of the social and cultural needs and of political considerations (such as equity between regions and groups of population);
-    to take a broad view of national needs, in order to avoid duplication of efforts and exceedingly narrow programmes and also to look beyond the immediate future. In other words, there is always a need for a global strategy. This implies a lot of cooperation between various partners, a technical support to analyze a variety of data and prepare the policy options and clear policy orientations at the political level.

Selected bibliography

Campinos-Dubernet, M. and Grando J.M. (1988) Formation professionnelle ouvrière: trois modèles européens. Formation emploi n° 22. Avril-juin.

Marshall, R. and Tucker, M. (1992) Thinking for a living: Education and the Wealth of Nations, Basic Books.

Maurice, M. et al. (1982) Politique d'éducation et organisation industrielle en France et en Allemagne: essai d'analyse sociétale, Paris, PUF.

Miller, R. (1993) Connaissance de l'investissement et investissement dans la connaissance: la nécessité de repenser les systèmes d'information et de prise de décision sur le capital humain, Working paper for OECD, DEELSA/ELSA/ED(93)16.

Steedman, H. and Wagner, K. (1987) A second look at productivity, machinery and skills in Britain and Germany, National Institute Economic Review, London, November.

Notes

1   Figures provided by the European Institute of Education and Social Policy, Paris.

2   Except for the surveys conducted by the International Association for the Evaluation of Educational Achievement (IEA)

3   See the proceedings of the OECD seminar on certification held in Porto in October 1992 and Bertrand, O. and Merle, V. Comparabilité et reconnaissance des qualifications en Europe. Formation emploi, n° 43, Juillet-Septembre 1993.

4   In the framework of the VOTEC programme, to be concluded in 1994.

5   Although this depends on the way calculations are made and on the source of information.

14 Globalization in education: trends and challenges

Tamás Kozma

Abstract

The phenomenon called 'globalization' is the outcome of a series of processes that integrate systems throughout the world. Three stages of globalization have been differentiated (elitist education, democratization and universalization). The author draws conclusion from the globalization process to the reconstruction of the Hungarian educational system.

1. Introduction

The aim of the presentation

The paper deals with a phenomenon which is relatively new in the world educational system, that is, globalization. Since there are not too many talks about this tendency as such, I gather preliminary literature as well as statistical data to describe globalization. The reason to deal with globalization is twofold. On the one hand, it familiarizes us with the leading tendency that overcomes the national boundaries of the present day educational systems. On the other hand, it gives us a standard and thus serves as a frame of reference in the course of the modernization of education in Hungary.

Terms of references

Since 'globalization' is relatively unknown among experts other than educationalists, some of the terms used here should be briefly defined.

- *Globalization.* The word will be used to designate a process or series of processes in the individual systems of education that end up in similar educational solutions and thus create growing similarities in the national systems. Processes like similar elements of the *curricula*, similarities in the teaching-learning activities, similar equipment and institutions, similar ways of controlling schools, teachers and students, similarities in educational policies are falling into this category.
- *System of education.* This concept refers to a network of schools and other educational institutions which by their content (standards, requirements, goals and aims, certificates) as well as regulations are connected to each other (Green, T.F., 1980). Since I will deal with European systems, most of those ones are national systems, that is, they include all schools, training centres and higher education institutions of a given country.
- *Level (stage) of education.* The concept refers to the fact that educational systems can usually be divided into three parts. They are the primary, secondary and tertiary levels. (Equivalent to elementary, secondary and higher education but includes other activities also like post-secondary education or lifelong training.)
- *Field of study (training).* It points to three different activities in a modern educational system, such as general, vocational and higher education. In analyses like the following, the concept of 'fields' are not used frequently because it overlaps the concept of levels. However, for historical as well as administrative reasons, those levels are usually separated. I will refer to fields only if I stress that a national system includes all three.

Sources of information

Since the process of globalization has not been described in the context of the educational system of Hungary, there are only initial sources of information for it. The background of my presentation will be:

- statistics from census data as well as from school statistics;
- data from individual researches of the educational system; these data can be interpreted in a way that rejects globalization (though most of the research was aimed at describing different processes);

- data coming from the relevant literature, mostly cases of national education systems or comparative analyses of educational policy decisions. Most important of them is the initial description made by the 'Stanford group'.

Some of the data will be presented in the appendix of this paper or in the list of relevant literature. In some cases I will refer to them also in the text.

The structure of the paper

The logic of my paper is the following. Globalization as a phenomenon will shortly be described and possible explanations will be given to it. Then, the 'behaviour' of the educational system will be analyzed to show the periods through which globalization will occur in each national system. In conclusion, I give some considerations for the Hungarian system to prepare it (or, better to say, to prepare policy makers) for the coming globalization process. By this, I want to contribute to the discussion of how to reach an international standard of education in Hungary.

Everywhere in Europe (mostly in countries with central educational governance), it seems to reflect one interest only. It seems to conflict with other interests like the demand of a local society that wants to establish and control its own institutions. If, however, the local society and its government have not enough power to do so, state support is needed to secure those basic supplies. If it contradicts the theoretical vision of private provisions in education then pre-primary and primary education should be withdrawn from the impact of market and semi-market forces.

Comprehensive secondary institutions. The present debates on the new types of secondary schools in Hungary may lead to a real confusion. It reflects, as mentioned, the liberalization process around the transition when each and every institution stated its own right to decide upon programs and structure. Individual schools like individual local governments cannot see the system as a whole and tend therefore to create institutions that differ from others. A system, however, needs similarities and parallels rather than individual solutions (even if they are brilliant). The solution is therefore a comprehensive supply of secondary programs both in the form of different institutions within a reachable distance and in the form of one common institution with program variations.

One can say that an initiation like the comprehensive school has already died in Germany and in the Scandinavian systems (especially in Norway) during the late 1960s and early 1970s. On the other hand, differences are great and the situation is also different. Without analyzing the success and failure of those institutions I stick to the Hungarian reality. It shows, as early as the late 1970s, that comprehensiveness of the secondary education was already in the making. It also shows that today almost every secondary institute offering various programs (e.g. gymnasiums with 4, 6 and 8-year programs etc.) hold the clear sign of comprehensiveness. In the given regional context (especially in the south-east part of my country) I do not see alternative for satisfactory supply. Especially not in a time of growing demand for secondary schooling.

A network of community colleges. The term 'community college' may mislead those who know more about the differences of higher educational institutions in the English speaking countries. Yet, I use the term to point out the requirement of a renewed network of higher education which is also capable of incorporating post-secondary programs, professicnal trainings, probably even vocational education. In Europe, *'Gesamthochschule'* (German) or Polytechnics (British) may be the right term. In any case though, a network of colleges would be required, based on counties and their centres, and relying on the existing colleges throughout the country. Hungary has a scattered network of higher education institutions which is now falling apart with new private and semi-private institutions and church-based schools. A network would create a frame for further organization efforts and would offer the hope that the coming generations will reach higher education much easier in their own region than their parents did before.

The network of the so-called community colleges contradicts the present efforts of creating *'universitas'*, those regional universities that cover every higher education in their regions. Two explanations are necessary here. The first is that the *'universitas'* concept, that is, the regional university idea emerged from the discussions and comparative studies of the late 1970s and early 1980s. Then, social demand for higher education was much lower than today while the labour market did not exist or was substituted by bureaucratic planning of the 'labour force'. We are living in a different age today. I am certain that an expansionist policy needs more than just the regional universities that we visualized some fifteen years ago.

2. The phenomenon

Globalization

Globalization in education - as in many other fields of social and economic activities of the world society - is an emerging tendency which influences more and more national systems and covers wider and wider parts of each of the systems. Visiting schools and training centres all over the world, one can easily experience the unusual similarities of institutions, equipment and methods as well as leadership patterns, governing organizations and financing mechanisms. One can argue that schools and training centres in the industrial world are by no means similar to those of South Asia or the remote parts of Latin-America. Equipment and instructional technology as well as prepared teachers and educated parents may cause extreme differences between West and East or North and South. On the other hand, however, agricultural farms or industrial plants may differ far more than schools and colleges. The general feeling is that schools, churches or hospitals are nearly the same all over the world.

This general impression has been analyzed by John Meyer and his team at Stanford University (Meyer, J.W. et al., 1979; Meyer, J.W., 1980). After more than ten years of data gathering and analysis the Stanford group developed a theory of globalization which has the power to explain education development as the process of a system with limited autonomy (Meyer, J.W., 1992). Following the Stanford group, John Craig presents and analyzes a series of educational statistics covering a whole century of development from the Scandinavian region. His data show the process of educational expansion as an integrated element of what Meyer calls globalization process. Margaret Archer points out the stages of educational expansion in higher education in a comparative perspective (Archer, M.S., 1972; Archer, M.S., 1982). As far as East-Central Europe and Hungary respectively are concerned, the process of expansion has been described as early as at the turn of the 1960s and 1970s by researchers like János Tímár and János Kovács (Kovács, J. and Tímár, J., 1971). Following their views and statistical analyses, József Nagy gathered impressive data on educational expansion in Hungary and referred to the logistic pattern of educational growth (Nagy, J., 1970). His analysis has been followed by Katalin R. Forray and the author of the present paper showing the regional patterns of educational expansion (Forray, K.R. and Kozma, T., 1992). Yet, the connection between the 'behaviour' of the educational system and the trend of globalization was still lacking.

I therefore emphasize in this context that the statistical facts and research findings referred to can be interpreted in various ways. One interpretation might be that they reflect the initial phase of the world globalization process in education. If this is true, the well known process of educational expansion already reflects globalization as it stands in the countries of East-Central Europe.

Background 1: World literacy programs

While most of the analyses deal with the process of globalization in various parts of the world, much less have been done to explain the tendency. Meyer and his team is stressing the world literacy programs mainly because of the special interest of the World Bank towards alphabetization in the developing world. The argument goes on saying that programs like alphabetization contribute a lot to the globalization of education throughout the world. Since alphabetization needs similar basic human skills (reading and writing) and those skills require similar teaching-learning strategies, teacher training activities as well as classroom activities become more and more similar all over the world.

Alphabetization, on the other hand is a powerful process supported by production prescriptions (instructions), marketing forces (advertisements), public administration and political affairs. Literacy is deeply needed in modern life and is sometimes even artificially established, substituting traditional ways of communication with modern alphabetization during the colonization periods. Teaching and learning to read and write is, according to the Stanford group, the main force initiating the globalization process in education. Although UNESCO has reported its world-wide literacy program more of a failure than a success (depending on the rapid growth of world population throughout the 1960s and 1970s) it had one side-effect which UNESCO did not intend initially and it was globalization. Even if there is a shrinking percentage of literate people among the world population, the fact is that literacy programs have created educational environments of great similarity in every country that participated in the UNESCO alphabetization programs. While initial hopes have not been fulfilled, these similarities of the educational environment promise a future success, the Stanford group argues.

Background 2: Technological modernization

While former argumentations for globalization put the emphasis on world literacy programs, it is right to point out the extreme importance of technological modernization and mass production. Technological modernization is forced today by few innovation centres of the world where most of the modernization is created and emanated throughout the world. It is . true to high-tech as well as to more traditional still alive fields of mass production such as car industry or agricultural production. The homogeneity of innovations and their contribution to mass production create a working environment with growing similarities and decreasing individual characters. Mass production forces similar attitudes towards working, similar ways of organizing the production lines, and similar ways of controlling both the workers and their activities. In sort, technological modernization shows growing similarity around the world.

The growing similarities in production technologies require similar skills, knowledge and behaviour from the workers and the managers. Car industry if imported from the developed world to the developing world imports, together with it, a working culture that includes skills, knowledge and behaviour similar in each and every plant of the given factory, be in Spain or Brazil, Hungary and India. Not only the production skills but also the managerial activities show growing similarities, including English as the communication tool at most of the industrial giants as well as computer based administration and financial analysis. Those skills are not only similar, they are taught in the headquarters of the given industry. In this way, the teaching and learning of production skills and economic behaviours become more and more similar and contribute in a forceful way to the global character of world education. Technological modernization and vocational training are perhaps more important in this sense than literacy programs. While the latter contributes to the internationalization of (elementary) education, the former influences vocational education and training and pushes the whole system towards the same end.

Background 3: Educational expansion

While literacy programs contribute to the globalization of education in developing countries, educational expansion make systems similar to one another in the industrial world. Educational expansion is a phenomenon characteristic of societies where political and economic reconstruction took place after World War II and a rapid economic growth was followed by a period of stagnation in the 1960s. Following the political and economic reconstruction in those countries, education became free and thus part of the set of values of the societies. Secondary schooling turned to be universal during the 1950s and 1960s in most countries of the developed part of Europe, while tendencies of massification at the tertiary level started at the turn of the 1960s-1970s and became a leading trend in the course of the 1970s.

Statistical analysis of time series (see literature above), however, draw attention to the fact that educational expansion is by no means the sole product of the after-war period in Europe. Wherever secondary education became universal, elementary schooling has always had a long tradition with the population which goes back even centuries. It goes hand in hand with the introduction of the European-type education that took place nearly all over

Europe as early as in the 18th century and/or at the turn of the 18th and 19th centuries. Turning to the other end of the expansion time series, tertiary education (in the form of more or less traditional higher education) is always based on a universal secondary schooling. It seems, therefore, that the expansion of education is not only a phenomenon of a given political and economic situation of Europe and the developed parts of the world but also a phenomenon based on the history of schooling in the given societies. Educational expansion is not the behaviour of the system; rather, it reflects the steady change of the behaviour of the population towards schooling.

The changing behaviour towards schooling has a variety of explanations. Here are some of the well-known ones:

-    The rapid growth of the economies of post-war Europe raised living standards of the population. Thus, they were enabled to send their children to schools which they could not afford before or during the war.

-    The 1960s were a period of stagnation after a rapid economic reconstruction in the wake of the war. Unemployment, first after the 1929-33 economic crisis appeared in those economies. One way to reduce unemployment among young generations was an extended schooling period for them.

-    The democratization process which followed a time of authoritarian systems (nazism, fascism etc.) made the school systems available to strata of the societies which were not accepted by the former elitist systems.

-    New groups of the societies that were in marginal status before the war applied for entrance to the educational systems. Minority groups, first of all women, appeared at the secondary and (later) the tertiary levels of the educational systems.

-    The welfare state, supported mostly by the governing socialist and social democratic parties in Europe (mostly in the Federal Republic and the Scandinavian countries), abolished the market forces from the field of services like health care, housing, social policy, culture or education. It has created an over-consumption of educational goods.

-    Educational expansion is the outcome of the birth and growth of the middle class societies throughout Europe. They have a special value pattern in which education as a consumption good is highly valued. The growth of the middle class society is therefore accompanied by the growing demand for schooling which, in turn, may explain the changing behaviour of political decision making. The stagnation or retrenchment of the middle class during the 1980s may also explain the end of the expansionist policies in education.

Without following a long list of possible explanations one can state that educational expansion is not dependent on political and ideological systems. It seems that educational expansion is a characteristic change in the behaviour and value patterns of the given society (or social groups). It induces feedback from one generation to the other in the form that parents intend to give their children the same amount of education or more than they received. If this summary of explanations is correct, educational expansion has a universal social character. It generates similar demand towards schooling everywhere and thus contributes to the globalization of the supply side (schooling).

Background 4: Mass culture

In the early days, human culture had an immense amount of varieties (knowledge, patterns of behaviours and attitudes, sets of values and norms). The development of communication and the global village phenomenon created an environment where more and more elements of the human culture became similar or equivalent. In one sense a mass culture may not be as individual as the traditional patterns; on the other hand, however, the massification of cultural elements contributes to the creation of a communicating world. Here are some of the apparent elements of a mass culture today:
- A language that is known and used for international communication (English).
- The standardization of technical equipment and technological innovations at the households and in the work places (first of all: computerization).
- Similarities in the leisure time customs and behaviours.
- A universalization of cultural products and the consumption of the electronic media.

Since schooling is still the most powerful tool for internalizing the necessary communication skills in a society, mass culture is a challenge that is similar to most of the national educational systems. Common elements of a mass culture create a larger part in the national *curricula* which had its traditional contents for decades. It is a process of globalization from the content aspects of the national educational systems.

To sum up: globalization seems to be the leading tendency of educational systems today. It is backed by similar demand from the national economies, political and cultural systems. In other words, globalization is an educational answer to the 'global village' effect of the modern world. It is the leading tendency politicians and experts have to take into account in their policy actions.

3. The process

The behaviour of the educational system

The philosopher T. F. Green talks about the 'behaviour' of the educational system. Describing the system 'in motion', he analyzes the 'systemic rules of growth' (Green, T.F., 1980, pp. 90-104). What he describes in the language of systems theory can also be formulated in a statistical way. Here processes, like expansion and/or globalization can be represented by a logistic (S) curve.

The logistic curve has been developed to represent the unique character of growth in living systems. Unlike the 'uniform growth' (Green, T.F., 1980), the logistic curve shows three different periods of growth within the whole process.

a) In the living systems, growth or any other kind of changes are introduced by a period of stagnation. In this period, forces towards change are cumulating but for a long time the growth may not even be visible. The end of the first period is the first point of inflection.

b) Here the second period is started which is a period of rapid growth (or other types of change). In this second phase, growth and other changes become not only visible but also seem to be unlimited. It is the period of becoming a fashion, whirling as an unlimited achievement or a process which for ever will grow and thus will rapidly change the entire system. The second phase is also closed by the second point of inflection.

c) After the second point of inflection, the third phase starts which is again a period of stagnation. Here the growth reached its peak. The change went through, all the demand has been met. Here, the process of growth ends.

The logistic curve, what it means, how it can be applied and interpreted is properly known by experts of various living systems. There is less talk about the cyclical character of an S-curve. That is the character by which the period of saturation is, by turn, an introductory phase of a new growth. It is clearly reflected in the analysis of the behavioural changes of the society towards schooling. Once the primary level of schooling has been reached, the growing demand for secondary education starts. Once it is almost universal, the expansion of the tertiary phase begins. Globalization like other changes in the 'behaviour' of education (or, rather, in the behaviour of the surrounding society) can be described by a series of logistic curves. In the following section, I describe the globalization process with the changes in one of its major elements, that is, expansion.

Introductory period: Elitist education

In every phase of expansion (be it at the primary, secondary or tertiary levels) the introductory phase is the period of elitist education. Here 'elitist' means a selection policy where entrance is closely controlled and by which education is provided not for the whole population but only for the highest stratum of it (the socio-cultural elite). It is true of the elementary education where literacy is the privilege of the few, it is also true of the secondary education with its highly selective grammar schools throughout Europe. It is especially true of the higher education where universities in many countries of Europe (including those of the Eastern part of the Continent) remain ivory towers.

M. Trow in his first analysis for the OECD calculates the elitist phase of education as a system accepting less than 15 per cent of an age cohort (Trow, M.A., 1974). If it is agreed upon, higher education in Hungary, as in the other East-Central European countries is still at this phase. It is worth mentioning, however, that the elitist period of (higher) education is based on a growing period of secondary education. It is true also to Hungary where the massive growth of secondary school entrance (senior level) started in the first third of the 1970s. The entrance to this level of education is above 90 per cent of general school leavers (83-86 per cent of an age cohort). The structure of the Hungarian secondary education means, however, that only 40-45 per cent of an age cohort receives graduation after its secondary schooling (*Abitur*).

Rapid growth: Democratization in education

What the second phase of the logistic curve represents (rapid growth after the first point of inflection) is called democratization in the history of education. 'Democratization' in this context means changes in the selection policy by which new social groups get chances to participate in education. In the field of higher education Trow (Trow, M.A., 1974) talks about massification and suggests that 15-30 per cent of an age group should be accepted by tertiary education. Democratization, however, means more than that. It opens up schools for all which schools have traditionally been selective and addressed themselves to the social elite only. It also means a universalization of general education which was targeted at those who would later participate in higher education or become professional administrators (the bureaucrats).

Massification of secondary education started in 1973 in Hungary. Between 1973-78 the percentage of secondary school entrance emerged by 16 per cent. One can argue with the impact of an earlier demographic wave. However, the growth of entrance followed and it reached 83 per cent of an age cohort during the mid-1980s. Characteristic is the shift of interest from professional education and vocational training towards general secondary education (upper level). Between the early 1970s and the late 1980s, traditional apprenticeship education shrank down from 50 per cent of the secondary school students to 35 per cent of them. At the same time, gymnasiums (grammar schools) became so popular that 25 per cent or more apply for it (from the former 18 per cent). Professional secondary schools, once the favourites among working-class parents have been stabilized around 30 per cent or lost interests depending on their geographical location and professional programs.

All in all, the period of the 1970s and early 1980s proved to be the period of democratization in the Hungarian education (upper secondary level). It followed the massification of primary education in the early 20th century and the democratization of the lower-level secondary education after World War II. This is represented by the growing part of the S-curve of the Hungarian educational system. These processes are preparing society and education for the massification phase of higher education which may take place in Hungary after the year 2000.

Closing period: mass education

Each of the growing periods ends up in a phase of fulfilment and new stagnation. In the life of an educational system it is the period of mass education. 'Massification' as a word may not be accepted by experts outside the educational circles. Inside them we understand what it means. It designates a period when education is offered for all. It goes hand in hand with free education, universalization and standardization.

Massification of lower level secondary education occurred after World War II in Hungary. In 1945-46 political forces established the 'general schools' that is, elementary and lower-level secondary schools under one roof. It followed a general trend of post-war Europe (*Gesamtschule*, comprehensive schools) but with a special political stress. General schools were boosted to substitute selective secondary education for the 10-14-year olds and thus to contribute to the 'democratization of culture' (later: the 'cultural revolution'). Whether or not it reached that objective, the system of general schools prepared society for the growing demand for upper level secondary education. Once a new generation of parents stepped into the educational arena with at least general school graduation, they immediately required more education for their offsprings. It is the explanation of the rapid growth period of upper secondary education in the decade of the 1970s.

As far as higher education is concerned, massification (that is, 30 per cent or more of an age cohort within tertiary education) is a long term goal only. Yet, it is not unrealistic. Comparative data show that the developed societies of Europe have already reached that level or will reach it soon. If Hungary does not change its higher education policy in a substantial way, this level will not be reached during the 21st century.

4. The challenge

The process of globalization in East-Central Europe

The globalization process was hindered during the Soviet influence in the Eastern part of Europe. Yet, changes in the behaviour of the population towards schooling took place long before the 1989-90 transition. In my regional analysis of higher education (Kozma, T., 1993) I differentiated between two types of sub-regions.

Sub-Region A: Territories with State Education. Sub-region A consists of territories where education has long been established and controlled by the state (a central government). In those territories, elementary education was prescribed and sanctioned by administrative means. They have also had a traditionally established secondary education system for around two centuries. During those centuries, middle classes have been established and social demand for education has cumulated. In these areas, educational systems face growing numbers of applicants. The social and political elite incorporated education in their value patterns and higher education became a commodity competitive with others. Here both the social demand and the political power of the middle classes are strong enough to force educational expansion even in the course of financial restriction and welfare state retrenchment.

Sub-region A in Eastern Europe consists of the Northern part (Finland and the Baltic republics), parts of present Poland, Czech Republic, Slovakia, Hungary, Slovenia, Croatia, Voivodina (Serbia), Transylvania (Romania), parts of Greece, the European part of Turkey, and goes down to Lebanon and Israel. It would be easier to speak about countries if the present borders had been stable for centuries but they were not. Instead, various central governments influenced those territories and integrated those territories into different larger European units (like Sweden, Prussia, and Austria). The Eastern part of Europe still shows clear signs of that historical tradition as the new waves of conservatism or minority movements represent them.

Sub-Region B: Territories with Non-State Education. Other territories were organized and administratively controlled by new central governments only a century later. The Balkans were liberated under the Turkish empire only towards the end of the 19th century. Parts of Poland as well as the Baltic republics were under Russian control again and again from the 17th century up until recently. Countries and states like the present Moldavia or the Ukraine, Albania or the present Bulgaria, Bosnia and Hercegovina have been formulated only after decisive wars.

Educational developments started a century later in those territories and their secondary schooling was still under reorganization during the latest decades. Their middle classes could not gain political power or if they did they did not incorporate (higher) education in their social and political priorities. Here general secondary schooling is still ahead of the respective administrations.

Education in those areas fulfils the role of enlightening and flagship; a place where intellectuals may gather and gain power to decide on their own questions. Autonomy of institutions in those areas is the political target of those intellectuals and state policy-makers. Institutions are more of a political than an administrative question for the policy-makers.

System requirements

Globalization has already started in Hungary, as I stated before, and if it is kept as a standard for long-term policy making for education, then some conclusions have to be drawn. Among them, system requirements are probably the most essential ones.

Hungary needs an educational system which has been harmonized with other European systems. The present system of education is a mixture of various school types and programs at the secondary level. It is an outcome of the liberalization period right after the transition and the still dominating system of education before the transition. Experts may not agree upon the 'right version' of schools and programs at the secondary level. Yet, they may easily agree on the requirement of a unified system that allows students, parents and teachers to move from one institution to the other. They may also agree on the importance of a national *curriculum* (or at least a frame) that makes a way for such mobility. The system, once re-unified (in one form or another) has to be in harmony with the systems of Hungary's neighbours to be able to send and host students to and from those systems.

In perspective, general education has to be expanded until the end of secondary schooling. This harmonization dictates an expanded general education. Hungary has a ten-year school obligation today (6-16 years of age), and a general education that covers eight years. History of schooling shows that the general education programs developed and filled the role of professional and vocational training during the last century. General education in most developed countries covers twelve years instead of the earlier ten-year programs. In some cases, however, general education is also a part of the post-secondary programs. It does not mean universal education (neither its general nor its professional or vocational forms). It means, on the contrary, alternatives with always the same accreditation.

Vocational education, in various forms (including apprenticeship) has to be postponed till the end of the secondary education (post-secondary stage). Vocational education, both in the forms of professional education and apprenticeship training, creates a part of the obligatory school years in Hungary. It means therefore that as early as at the age of 14, students are required to choose their profession or vocation (around 55 per cent of an age cohort). Although general education creates a part of professional schooling, it seems that good vocational education needs more than that in the future. History proves the same. Fifty years back most trainings could be started at the age of 10 or 12, right after 4-6 years of elementary schooling. Today the requirement is eight years of general education or the equivalent. Tomorrow this requirement might be ten years or more.

Higher education has to be expanded by incorporating post-secondary stages and by creating introductory courses with general education. The next step of educational expansion is, without question, the tertiary level. Today, higher education is offered to 10-15 per cent of an age cohort, depending on what is called 'higher education'. If vocational education is postponed after the secondary schooling, the capacity of the tertiary level has to be expanded by at least 30-40 per cent in the future. It does not mean the expansion of university and/or college education in their present forms. Instead, it means new forms of post-secondary programs and new types of higher education institutions.

Institutional network

An institutional network that fits to the system requirements would also support the process of globalization. It can be understood as the system itself in its spatial dimension. Rethinking the network requirements might help understand the conclusions of the requirements of the educational system itself. Here are the most important requirements of an institutional network that would support educational expansion and thus the globalization process.

Basic supply of primary and pre-primary education. Present discussions on school autonomy may overshadow the simple fact that parents with young children under and around school age need a basic supply of nurseries and schools. Other discussions on the financing of education may confuse the public about its responsibility for primary education. It is important to state therefore that a basic supply of pre-primary and primary education is a social, cultural and political requirement. It is also important to stress that globalization in all its forms needs public financing of those institutions.

The ongoing discussion on school autonomy is mostly initiated by teachers and experts, though the question of autonomy has a far-reaching impact. The second explanation has a delicate character. Yet, an expert may not escape the fact that the present debate on higher education expansion and regional universities is a debate between the 'academic oligarchy' and university management on the one hand and the central budget on the other. It seems today that university administrators are the strongest supporters of regionalization. They apply and/or develop an argument for educational expansion in order to gain more financial support from the central budget. Thus, they are by no means open to the grassroots demand for post-secondary and introductory higher education to be deployed closer to the public in geographical terms.

Content. Globalization needs not only systems and structures. It needs equivalencies also. The Hungarian education has to offer diplomas and certificates that are acceptable in other labour markets while it has to be able to accept others' certificates and diplomas. More important than that is the requirement for the teaching/learning process as well as its objectives (the 'content' side of an educational system) which would prepare the young generation for the international (European) division of labour. What does that 'content side' mean?

New information such as the use of an international language, the ability to live with a technical environment and the attitude to create a democratic community. An international language is the necessary requirement for stepping into the global age. There are ongoing discussions about language-teaching with suggestions to prefer one language to the others. Those discussions may not realize the pure fact that English has to be taught and it cannot be a subject of parental choice or foreign policy considerations.

As far as the new technical environment is concerned, I refer to computerization. It represents, though does not cover the new technical environment around us. Education should be the vehicle to convey new technologies to society.

'Democracy' in the present context means a (political) culture which is acceptable in the international community and therefore is required if any of the new democracies wants to step into any form of globalization and internationalization. There are too many considerations about how to start with democracy education. The fact is, however, that democracy as a culture can and should be taught in schools since we teach and learn other elements of the culture too.

New methods of teaching and learning which cope with the modern face of the young generation and support the renewal of school climate. Visiting schools in our region would end up with the impression that their climate has been preserved from the early 20th century. Traditional one-way communication, stress on memory achievements, sharp distinction between teachers' and students' roles create a rigid, selective and competitive climate in the successful schools of the Eastern part of Europe. One can argue that it provides the students with skills and knowledge easily sold on the international market. The fact is, however, that those schools still train the elites of their societies rather than the general public. Further, it is also true that the young generation with their changing sub-cultures do not want to live with that elitism. Aggression and unrest in schools and higher education is one clear sign of their protective attitudes towards the present ways and means of schooling; one-way student exchange and brain-drain is another, painful one.

The changing behaviour of teachers throughout the system to manage the new social groups in the former elitist education. Few of the teachers and professors have realized that globalization in education may require a substantial behavioural change. The reason is simple. If new groups enter the system, they will have new educational needs. As more and more youngsters are accepted in the general programs of the secondary education, the 'gymnasiums', once being elitist in style and climate should turn to be 'populist'. In other words, teachers should teach and not preach because the families of the students themselves may not necessarily support the school and parents will not be able to help their children with additional teaching support. Painful as it is, the same is true to the teaching and learning process in higher education. While there is much stress on knowledge production (research) in higher education, the fact is that institutions at the tertiary level have to turn into teaching-learning institutions. Activities called 'research' have also been professionalized and industrialized. If they finds home in higher education, they are relevant to the post-graduate phase. Also, they need a diversification of higher education and learning by which research centres would also be authorized to give higher education graduations.

5. Summary

1 The paper deals with a phenomenon which is relatively new to the educational systems of East-Central Europe. The phenomenon called 'globalization' is the outcome of processes which integrate systems throughout the world. The reasons for such integration are manifold (economic drives, social pressures, cultural activities of international agencies, mass media etc.). The most relevant process of similarities is educational expansion.

2 Three stages of globalization have been differentiated (elitist education, democratization and universalization). Statistical evidence supports this description (S-curve). Further analysis shows that the stages are bound to each other and the whole process has deep historical roots.

3 If globalization is a general tendency and will be taken by policy-makers as a frame for harmonization with Europe, some conclusions can be drawn from it. These are:

- Hungary needs an educational system that copes with special international tendencies;
- It needs an institutional network that can accept, more than today, a student wave (educational expansion);
- The renewal of the content of education is also a necessity both in objectives and teaching-learning processes.

Bibliography

Archer, M.S. (ed) (1972) *Students, University and Society: A Comparative Sociological View*, London, Heineman.

Archer, M.S. (ed) (1982) *The Sociology of Educational Expansion*, London, SAGE.

Forray, R.K. and Kozma, T. (1992) *Társadalmi tér és oktatási rendszer (Social Space and Educational System)*, Akadémiai Kiadó, Budapest.

Green, T.F. (1980) *Predicting the Behavior of the Educational System*, Syracuse, University Press.

Kovács, J. and Tímár, J. (1971) 'A munkaerő és az oktatás távlati tervezésének módszerei néhány európai szocialista országban.' (Long-term planning of labour force and education: Some methods in the European socialist countries) *Szigma* 214-31, 303-12.

Kozma, T. (1993) 'The expansion of education in Eastern Europe: A regional view', *Higher Education in Europe* 18, 2: 85-96.

Meyer, J.W. (1980) 'The world polity and authority of the nation state' in Bergesen, A. (ed) *Studies in the Modern World System,* Harper&Row, New York, pp. 109-37.

Meyer, J.W. et al (1992) 'World expansion of mass education 1870-1970', *Sociology of Education* 65, 3 : I 09-35.

Meyer, J.W. and Hannan, M.T. (eds) (1979) *National Development and the World System: Educational, Economic and Political Change, 1950-70,* The University of Chicago Press, Chicago.

Nagy, J. (1970) *Az iskolafokozatok távlati tervezése (The Long-Term Planning of School Levels),* Tankönyvkiadó, Budapest.

Setényi, J. (ed) (1993) 'A felsőoktatás modernizálása' (Modernization in higher education), *Educatio* 2, 3: 1-170.

Trow, M.A. (1974) *Problems in the Transition from Elite to Mass Higher Education,* OECD, Paris.

Trow, M.A. and Nybom, T. (eds) (1991) *University and Society,* Kingsley, London.

15 The role and problems of education and vocational training in Hungary in the period of the social transformation and the modernization of the economic structure

János Tímár

The transition from the state-controlled system to market economy sets higher standards for the education, the professional knowledge and skills of labour force. Education and vocational training play a decisive role in creating the required intellectual background. My lecture is to give some information of the special problems and new tasks that may arise in connection with this topic.

My starting statement is that as a result of the development of education and vocational training in the last four decades, the formal education level of the population as well as the quantitative supply with professionals is high in international comparison and its quality is sufficient in many areas. However, the shaping market economy conditions and the modernization of the economy require serious changes in people's attitudes and skills as well as in the quality and character of their knowledge. This requires a comprehensive modernization in the educational and vocational training system as well as in the content of education and the methodology of teaching.

When developing education and vocational training, we have to bear in mind that due to the demographic developments in Hungary, the size of younger generations is constantly decreasing, sometimes with great fluctuations which significantly affects the development of education and vocational training.

The other type of problem is in connection with the internationally known phenomenon that behind the significant success of the intellectual elite and a solid average general knowledge, there is a layer of the population which has a very low level of knowledge. This is a consequence primarily of the existence of handicapped social groups, the negative effects of which can be either conserved or, at least partly, counter-balanced by education influencing in this manner also the intellectual background.

The basis of this development is the public educational system. The present Hungarian public education is based on the 8-class, unified, general and compulsory school that was introduced almost half a century ago. This non-selective education has for almost a quarter of a century been extended to the entire population between 6 and 13 years of age and the proportion of children completing the school or studying further is around 94-95 per cent.

The number of applicants to the three main types of secondary schools stabilized by the 80s. One quarter of children went to the grammar school and one quarter to the secondary professional school, both of which provide final examinations while almost half of them went to the three-year, dual-type vocational school. In the last three years the proportion has shifted towards the two types of secondary education and vocational schools fell back. The main reason for this is that the number of compulsory general school finishers has constantly fallen due to the demographic regression. On the top of the demographic wave, in 1989, 171 thousand children finished primary school, this year the number will be around 136 thousand, while next year only 118 thousand, but from 1997 on there will be only 110 thousand children finishing basic education.

The regression of vocational schools is also in connection with the fact that the labour demand of the industry and agriculture fell to the minimum due to the deep economic crisis of recent years.

As an aggregate result of the outdated teaching methodology and the unfavourable environment, the average proportion of pupils dropping out from the three types of secondary education jumped from the 28-29 per cent of the 80s to 34 per cent by the early 90s and the educational level and qualification structure of school leavers has deteriorated.

As a consequence, if the proportion of those going on to secondary school and those ending their studies is not changed in the forthcoming years then the number of youngs with final examination would soon fall from today's 60 thousand below 50 thousand and the number of university applicants would inevitably decrease. In order to prevent this predicted danger first of all the structure of public education and the teaching methodology should be fundamentally reformed.

Hungarian professional debates and the international experience have shown that an equalizing 'elementary' school should be the first grade in creating the modern new school system. The second grade would be a still equalizing general and unified lower secondary school which would already have a career orientation function. These two grades could constitute the 10-class basic education prescribed by the new Hungarian Education Act.

These would be followed by the upper secondary school, the third grade of future public education. The structure of this differentiated and selective education should be flexible enough so that children should not drop out in mass scales - as the current practice is - but they should be enabled to exit through various gateways or to transfer to the wide-ranging out-of-school specialized vocational training courses.

The new type upper section of the secondary school could integrate the present two types of secondary schools by eliminating the great differences between today's grammar schools and the specialized or overspecialized professional secondary schools.

In the main subjects of grammar school *curricula* (literature, languages, exact sciences, natural sciences, etc.), 'specialization' could be introduced which would enable deepening knowledge but still not exceeding the extent of professional basics. This would reinforce the grammar school's function to prepare for the university, but at the same time it could support the professional specialization of those not going to higher education as well as in finding their jobs.

The common *curricula* of the presently over-specialized professional schools could be integrated in much less specialized subjects. This would enhance the role of professional secondary schools in higher education and the more flexible basic vocational education would make it easier for those not going to higher education to adjust themselves to the rapidly changing labour demand. The preparations for the modernization of the professional secondary education go on successfully with the support of the IBRD.

Although the new Education Act is not in contradiction with the above described development concept, it still does not meet the requirements as it intends to realize the 10-class school model that was proposed several decades ago while maintaining the old school types. Due to the flaws of the new Education Act, this Act and the law on vocational training, too, do not reckon with the fact that the rapid growth in the share of secondary education pupils - partly an inescapable consequence of the demographic trends - will make it impossible to maintain vocational training in today's public education system. In the future, specialized vocational training should be based primarily on secondary school graduation and it would provide a more differentiated training regarding its length, content and methods - while reinforcing its dual feature - to those finishing secondary school and not willing to study further.

The primary obstacle to the implementation of this education policy is that the three Educational Acts, the Public Education, the Vocational Training and the Higher Education Acts enacted last year were prepared without a comprehensive education policy concept, isolated from one another and without any coordination. The flaws of the Public Education Act are especially conspicuous inasmuch as it deals with a lot of unimportant details while it does not give any guidelines in vital questions of the education policy such as the school structure, instead, it shifts all responsibility on to local governments. In this way it legitimated the spontaneous process of the last few years under which grammar schools started to expand the 4-class secondary school 'downwards' thereby creating 'new' 8- and 6-class secondary schools.

The makers of education policy do not seem to realize that this tendency is not the result of a well-grounded pedagogical and sociological concept but rather it is motivated by the sharpening competition between schools for getting a higher share from the constantly decreasing number of children. However, the downward expansion of secondary schools dangerously segregates the primary schools of small villages and suburban areas; it drains the majority of 'good pupils' from these schools and limits their opportunities to develop 'upwards'. The necessary and reasonable expansion of secondary school attendance would require just the opposite.

The modernization of the content and methodology of education and training is an organic part of the educational reform. Developed on the basis of the Prussian traditions, the Hungarian pedagogy is strongly concentrated on factual knowledge; only those pupils can acquire the formally required great pile of knowledge who are sufficiently prepared by their family and social backgrounds. The others start to lag behind from the beginning and the gap will only grow throughout the years.

In this way, present education does not mitigate but rather reproduce social inequalities by qualifying functionally illiterate pupils not capable of studying further as 'successfully finished'. The change of this intolerable situation and the development of skills and knowledge demanded by market economy and modernization requires up-to-date education philosophy and methods. This would significantly lessen the segregation and frustration of children coming from undeveloped environments, encourage their learning and further studies. This is not only essential for the principle of equal opportunities which is a pillar of democracy but also it is required to be able to extend the basis of secondary and higher education which is a must.

The assumed great-scale quantitative development of higher education and the enhancement of its quality can only be achieved if - according to my estimation - the proportion of secondary school pupils to go on with their studies would increase from the current 50-55 per cent to 75 per cent while the proportion of those with final examination should grow from the current 40 per cent close to 60 per cent.

It follows from the above that while the present education policy regards the introduction of 10-class basic school as the long range strategic goal - with almost 30 years' delay - the future trends would necessitate the gradual development of the 12-class school and the goals and ways of developing public education and specialized vocational training as well as higher education should also be drawn up in line with this. However, the education policy should not let local spontaneous interest enforcement campaigns determine whether secondary schools should expand downwards or primary schools should expand upwards or today's primary schools and secondary schools should be organically integrated.

Compared to secondary schools, there are less but similarly serious problems in higher education. There is no doubt that the number of students should be increased. Instead of the previous general and compulsory admission tests, it would be more reasonable to reinforce continuous selection by the examinations which alone would necessitate a larger number of students. Finally, this would be reasonable also because it would decrease labour supply and if higher education produces labour force more in harmony with the demand of the market then it could even reduce unemployment.

The development of higher education can be finally motivated and established by the anticipated long-term labour needs of the national economy. Such indicative prognoses were regularly made in Hungary between 1963 and 1974 and similar studies are prepared now in most of the developed market economies - although with more modern methods. The Labour Ministry has started to prepare such a prognosis on the basis of a very sophisticated model taken from the United States but finishing the job would take too long on this path. In the current situation, it would be more reasonable to apply the available simpler models that lead to fast results. Only the future prognoses can give an authentic answer to the problem of the distribution of students by types of institutions and specialization which is a much discussed topic.

New proposals have been submitted recently for the development of higher education. Their great value is that in this case the leaders of higher education themselves set down progressive guidelines which were previously opposed by many critics. The new development concept states that the structure of higher education should consist of several grades, the average training period should decrease, flexibility and free choice should be enforced in the *curricula*, the role of universities should be increased in research, etc. However, beyond the problem of the number and distribution of students, no significant progress has been made in other areas such as clarifying the future function and methods of distance or correspondence courses.

There is sufficient teaching staff for the development of public education, and vocational training, moreover, in international comparison this is even a bit over-sized. The situation is similar in higher education where there are neither central nor local performance standards. Despite that, the majority of the teaching staff is overloaded which is partly attributable to the fact that the majority of them are women who have other burdens in connection with the family and the household and secondly, due to the relatively low earnings, undertaking extra work is widespread.

Adequate financing is a precondition for the development of education. In Hungary, more than 80 per cent of the current expenditures of school education is provided by the state budget. The ratio of educational expenditures within the GDP grew from 3.4 per cent in 1973 to 5.6 per cent by 1990 and it is very high also in international standards, being around 7 per cent in these days. The fast growth of educational expenditures is primarily in connection with the fact that the GDP has decreased in the last few years, the growth rate of investment and energy prices are well beyond the average, the number of employees in the education sector has grown and the number of students in the more expensive secondary and higher schools rapidly increased. Therefore the increase of the ratio of educational expenditures within the GDP only indicates that education has had a bigger share within decreasing funds, but it might mean that the real value of educational expenditures has nonetheless fallen.

Due to specific reasons, among the cost factors of education, the wages costs and the social benefits paid to students turned out to be the 'toughest' items in the last couple of years. The real value of material expenditures and investments in education has significantly decreased which carries especially high risks. The development of education requires not only well-qualified and efficiently working teachers but also the establishment of well-equipped, modern institutions.

Our brief review may reveal that the development of an intellectual background to support the progress of our national economy and the entire society is a manifold and complicated task. The successful achievement of this urges today first of all the preparation of a comprehensive strategy of education policy which has been missing for a long time now, because only this can provide a firm basis for the efficient development of education and training that are fundamental in enhancing the cultural level and qualification of the population.

PART V
SOCIAL BACKGROUND: CULTURE, LAW AND STATE

16 The failure of the Soviet-type system and obstacles to transition: collective action in the transformation of an economic system[1]

Bruno Dallago

1. Introduction

The transition from a Soviet-type system to a 'post-socialist' one is a dynamic and not completely predetermined process, whose duration, sequence and final outcome depend on many and various factors[2]. By transition, in fact, is meant the complex of transformations necessary for a country to change its economic and socio-political system from (mainly) centrally administered to one in which market coordination plays a dominant role. The process is not entirely predetermined[3] in that the path of transformation and its final result, i.e. the future state of the economy and the society, cannot be determined from the outset. Various factors, in fact, restrict the choice of the path and the final goal and these factors cannot be freely chosen nor can they entirely be controlled by the promoters of the transformation. A major influence is exerted by starting conditions (path dependency), pre-existing institutions, the diversity of the agents (individuals and organizations) and their different goals, exogenous factors. The dynamic nature of the process means that during transition the agents and factors involved interact and mutually influence each other through time, leading to compromise solutions that were unintended or unforeseen at the very beginning, or to the prevalence of one part (one agent or group) to the damage of others. This may open the path to a reaction by the losers, thus leading to distortions and even a break in the transition process.

Given the dynamic nature of any transition process, the static comparative approach conventionally used when comparing different economic systems is unsatisfactory, especially in the case of a comparison between the old Soviet-type system and the future market economy envisaged by transformation projects and policies. In order to understand transition and make a thorough assessment of its possible outcomes, one has to carefully evaluate the forces that destroyed the old system and the reasons why this occurred, the process leading to the implementation of a new economic system and the forces and factors that encourage this transformation and hinder the transition process.

In this paper I shall seek to give a general interpretation of the transition process, with particular regard to the obstacles that impede it. My analysis is based on the observation of all economies in transition, although this term is an extreme simplification which is only justified by the existence of a relevant set of common starting features of these countries (they formerly shared a similar economic, political and social system, namely the Soviet-type system, although individual countries displayed significant differences) and problems they must contend with (all these countries are undertaking transformation of their economic systems in an attempt to achieve some type of market economy). However, there are also many and deep differences which explain why the process of transition, its goals and implementation vary so widely among countries. For a mere question of length, these differences will be disregarded in this paper.

In the next section I outline the general features of the Soviet-type system, looking briefly at its ability and failure to promote collective action aimed at pursuing systemic goals. In section 3, I consider economic reforms attempted since the 1960s and interpret their lack of success as due to a failure to implement reformist collective action. The fourth section deals with the processes which led to the start-up of transition, considering key changes which occurred both within the countries considered and in the outside world. Then, in section 5, I examine the nature of transition as a process involving different elements (agents, institutions, goals and strategies, exogenous factors, initial conditions). The obstacles to transition are analysed in the following sixth section: the most important of them being the difficulty of promoting collective action not only finalised to (re)distribution, but above all to change the economic system and to prevent free riders from profiting from the ample opportunities offered by transition. Finally, section 7 considers the two principal stages of transition - the initial one preparing for change and change proper - in order to show how this lack of unity in the transition process is relevant to explanation of the obstacles to transition. The paper closes with some remarks on the prospects for transition.

2. The Soviet-type economic system

The old system[4] can be modelled as a two-player game involving the government (the Communist party, the Government proper, central planners, the Central Bank, and the like) on the one hand, and executors, i.e. enterprises and people (workers and consumers) on the other[5]. Society was simplified and fundamental links were vertical. Since, thanks to prevailing state ownership of production assets and central planning, the government was supposed to possess perfect knowledge of the situation (all information was centralized) as well as the power to enforce its decisions and since economic agents (individuals and organizations) were all part of the same machine with (supposedly) no competitive interests, with identical objectives pursued with the same intensity and the same quantity of resources[6], the government was able to define and implement a preference function unique and common to all agents.[7]

The declared aim of the government was to 'build socialism' - by which was usually meant to pursue accelerated growth in order to improve the country's standard of living and to strengthen its defence, and to keep distributive equity. To achieve this aim, the government had to induce enterprises and workers to obey its orders, and it had to determine consumers' choice. Provided that material and moral selective incentives[8] were well chosen and targeted, enterprises and workers were willing in principle to implement the government's decisions. The coincidence, in the model, of the goals of the two agents was an outcome of the centrally administered system that was facilitated by the fact that quantity always dominated over quality: accelerated growth could be pursued without requiring enterprises and workers to achieve major quality improvements. A quiet life, as the effective though undeclared aim of enterprises and workers, could be pursued at the expense of the quality of production and, in particular, of technical progress[9]. As long as potential resources were not fully utilized, this was not in conflict with the government's interests either, given that pursuing quality and technical progress would have jeopardised the stability of the two-player game and was all could be reached in a system lacking, for its very nature, strong positive and active selective incentives[10]. Neither could distribution, which usually engenders discord and conflict among social forces, threaten its stability, because it was not part of the game; it was defined by the government before the game began and imposed upon the players.

The old system was based on powerful selective incentives, both negative and positive, but in any case mainly passive: it favoured the government by assigning it great and substantially uncontrolled property rights in the productive process, which included the power forcefully to impose the implementation of its political priorities to economic agents. However, it also granted undeniable advantages, such as full employment, social mobility[11], modest productive performance, social security, free medicare and education, to the large majority of the population. In brief, it granted everybody a stable, although modest, way of life - provided that they accepted low productive requirements and a dictatorial or paternalistic[12] political system.

Against this background, one of the agents (the government) found it easy to promote collective action on its own initiative; collective action which was (mostly passively) accepted by the other agent (the executors) or was imposed upon them. The powerful but mostly passive selective incentives which coupled coercion (e.g. the duty to have a job, or working for free on 'socialist Saturdays' in order to fulfil plan objectives) with moral and material private benefits (e.g. a sure wage, free education, privileged distribution of goods and services, a 'profit') left no choice to individuals and enterprises but accept, at least formally, to play the role assigned to them within the collective game. In fact, duties were subdivided by enterprise, establishment, department, team, and even individual worker through the central planning system. Moreover, the private costs of collective action were low and difficult to avoid (a passive attitude was mostly required) and some room was left for individual action (e.g. changing jobs, except during the War Communism period[13]) which did not conflict with collective goals.

Therefore, the Soviet-type system appeared to rely formally on a social contract[14]. However, this contract was only partially based on the mutual, direct interest of the agents and their moral involvement in pursuing the system's goals, a consequence of popular participation in revolutions - in the Soviet Union, China, Cuba, Vietnam, Yugoslavia - and partially democratic elections - in Czechoslovakia - which opened the way to the introduction of the Soviet-type system. However, one can easily argue that people did not want the system that was *actually* implemented and as a consequence they had to be compelled to participate in the game according to the rules established by the government (the Communist Party and/or the Soviet Union as the war winner power).

Until radical reforms first and transition then were put on the agenda, the most relevant problem for static (i.e. not spontaneously evolving) collective action was the possibility that people could avoid private costs imposed upon individuals by collective action (e.g. to work at a minimum accepted standard) while enjoying the advantages made possible by the existing system (e.g. a secure job) or taking undue advantage of other opportunities (e.g. stealing on the job). The real reason for this situation was the lack of effective active selective incentives, both positive and negative, such as voluntary exchange, profit and competition[15]. As a consequence, passive selective incentives had to be strengthened as much as possible and the daily implementation of the social contract had to be forced by one of the parties (the government) upon the other (the executors: workers, consumers and enterprises)[16] in order to reach acceptable results.

There were two areas in which the failure of collective action - and, as a consequence, of the economic system - was particularly striking:

-        the elaboration and implementation of the central plan as the key operational document embodying the collective preference function, and

-        the second economy.

Dirigiste planning comes about in a situation characterized by the state ownership of capital and often also of land. The central planner issues orders targeted at specific agents (enterprises) which are administrative units responsible for implementing these orders and subject to a system of (mostly passive) selective incentives which dispenses rewards and punishments according to their success in fulfilling them. Markets are limited to those of consumption and labour and are instruments of distribution, not of allocation and even here their role may be limited.

The dominant role of a politico-economic elite (the government) and the passive role of firms, workers and consumers, which do not have fundamental conflictual distributive goals *ex post*, somehow manage to engender a joint vision of economic activity. This also makes it possible to establish a production equilibrium which is both intersectoral and intrasectoral. Yet dirigiste planning also suffers from the serious problem of non-truthfulness, and this undermines the basis for collective action. There are, in fact, powerful motives for executors (in particular, enterprises) to transmit false or distorted information to the government. The predominant situation of shortage in the economy and the consequent uncertainties over the allocation of resources, as well as the irrelevance of costs for enterprises and the system of rewards and punishments to enterprises according to their success or failure in fulfilling the plan, induce them to act in such a way to reduce private costs while enjoying collective benefits. As a consequence, they conceal part of their effective production capacity, underestimate the costs of new investments while overestimating the necessary inputs, build up hidden reserves of inputs (both labour and materials), and keep obsolete machinery as a form of insurance against the possible raising of plan targets or against increased shortages. The information available to the government planning bodies consequently does not correspond to reality, and this has deleterious effects on the formulation of an optimal collective preference function and obstructs collective action aimed at its fulfilment.

However, in dirigisme it is only the duty to fulfil the plan that induces enterprises to produce and which guides their behaviour - if one excludes the second economy. If planning fails to work, the only alternative is administrative intervention outside the framework of the plan. And this is what inevitably happened in the Soviet-type economies, with the outcome that government bodies were over-burdened with an enormous amount of everyday work of control and intervention in addition to planning real and proper, and in the absence of a market which, as well as enabling the economy to function autonomously, provides automatic feedback on both the behaviour of firms and the consequences of administrative intervention. The final outcome was the increasing bureaucratization of the economy and the government's scramble to keep up with events, instead of anticipating them and dominating them. All this not only made government action more cumbersome, complex and inefficient, but significantly complicated the lives of enterprises, giving them further bargaining power in their dealings with the government[17].

The basic problem was therefore not so much the difficulty of producing and transmitting information - which was attenuated by progress in communications and data processing - as the existence of irreducible problems deriving from the non-co-operative strategies of planners (government) and executors. As already noticed, the fundamental reason for this was that the government was also a player in the economic game, thus preventing it from the possibility to establish and enforce the rules in a neutral and exogenous way.

The second area where collective action strikingly failed to function is that of the second economy. This term was used by Grossman[18] to refer to all economic phenomena that were 'ideologically alien to the Soviet system'. In particular, 'the second economy comprises all production and exchange activity that fulfils at least one of the two following tests: a) being directly for private gain, b) being in some significant respect in knowing contravention of existing law'. Since these two aspects often coexist in the same activity, the second economy constitutes a field for (almost) boundless free riding in Soviet-type economies.

In principle, all the capital in Soviet-type economies is socialized (that is, it is owned by the state or by co-operatives) and all labour is supplied to the socialized sector. This, as we have seen, is the basis on which collective action can take place. However, it is relatively easy for numerous individuals to evade private costs (such as being at work and actually working, increasing productivity in order to implement plan objectives, pay due care to the socially-owned goods and assets) while continuing to enjoy the advantages deriving to them from the participation in collective action (a steady wage from a secure job for workers, free education and medicare and cheap basic goods for consumers, a predetermined profit and lack of competition and bankruptcies for enterprises, and so on). Moreover, the prevailing passive nature and the effective weakness of selective incentives means that the government is unable to prevent people from also privatizing the goods and services deriving from collective action: unlawfully earnings from one's job (e.g. extracting under-the-counter payments from customers, speculating on goods in shortage), stealing collective goods, work time (through absenteeism), and capital (used for some private activity, possibly underground). These phenomena blur property rights[19], make the pursuit of the goals of collective action even more difficult and reduce the efficiency and organization of the system, which in turn creates further incentives to take advantage of the second economy[20].

These failures of the Soviet-type system provide further confirmation of Mancur Olson's finding that the larger the group (in this case the whole society), the less likely it is to undertake collective action in pursuit of its common interest[21]. This is even more so when the general institutional framework and relative incentives are ineffective in promoting collective action, as in the Soviet-type system. In this case, society acts as a latent group with weak common interests, while in the second economy small special interest groups prevail. They have strong common interests and are effectively organised to pursue them. Hence they are often able to prevail over the collective interest in matters relating to their particular interests[22]. One may therefore conclude that the basic reason for the ineffectiveness and inefficiency of Soviet-type economies was that the pursuit of general interest was the (loose and weakly defined) duty of a huge latent group. In the economy and society many special interest groups existed whose interests were contrary to the general one. The latent group was led to pursue the general objective by the government, which on the one side had only passive selective incentives to that end and on the other was itself a large and composite group having many characteristics of a latent group. In fact, within the government various special interest groups existed, that were in charge of (and therefore interested in) pursuing specific goals: planning, the management of a specific industry or region, credit, foreign trade, etcetera. The general judgement of the activity of these groups, and therefore the present and future situation (career, income, sometimes even freedom and physical safety) of people working in them depended upon the performance in the pursuit of the specific goal of the group and not the general goal of society. As a consequence, the nature itself of the economic and political system pushed these groups within the government to privilege the pursuit of specific goals at the disadvantage of the general interest.

3. Economic reforms: a failure of collective action

As long as the economic system is in conditions which are well structured and repetitive from the cognitive and decisional perspective, its functioning is guided by the routines which distinguish individuals and organizations. In such circumstances, individuals and organizations afford a sequence of choices which form a repetitive procedure that can be easily memorized and organized and give rise to automatic responses to repetitive variations in external conditions[23]. If this behaviour is successful, the role of rational calculation within organizations and among organizations in the market - and as a consequence the complexity of decisions - is substantially restricted, thus leading to decrease transaction costs and reduce the possibility to commit decisional mistakes.

Following Nelson and Winter, routines can be defined as consisting of 'all regular and predictable behavioural patterns of firms [and also within firms and other organizations]... [In the economic evolutionary theory] these routines play the role that genes play in biological evolutionary theory. They are a persistent feature of the organism and determine its possible behaviour (though *actual* behaviour is determined also by the environment); they are heritable in the sense that tomorrow's organisms generated from today's (for example, by building a new plant) have many of the same characteristics, and they are selectable in the sense that organisms with certain routines may do better than others, and, if so, their relative importance in the population (industry) is augmented over time.'[24] Routines, therefore, also govern collective action and they ensure that it is repeated in the future as it was performed in the past.

Although routines tend to preserve the essential features of the system, they may change, since the system sometimes has to deal with new problems caused by changes in the environment[25]. If these changes are sufficiently profound and long-lasting, they often give rise - after a more or less long period of time and either spontaneously or by design - to new institutions which devise new routines more suitable for the new situation. However, also in economic systems as in organisms and in microeconomic organizations, the system's control processes seek to resist mutations in its routines[26]. A change of routines, in fact, threatens the basis itself of collective action because it privileges certain participants while penalising others by altering the interpersonal and inter-group distribution of costs and benefits.

This resistance to change raised by economic systems is well illustrated by the history of economic reforms in the countries of Central and Eastern Europe and their substantial failure. Because of the features briefly discussed in the previous section, the Soviet-type system lacked microeconomic mechanisms able to bring about change on a continuous and vast scale, that is to innovate and introduce new routines. Therefore, the system had to rely almost entirely on intervention from the centre, as the sole instrument able to promote collective action for the accomplishment of the system's goals and to push individuals and organizations to adapt to external changing conditions. Institutional change was almost wholly the result of 'top-down' interventions which, by their very nature, could not be continuous, but only discrete. This fact inevitably conferred political and administrative significance to every institutional change, provoking strong resistance and impeding the evolution of the system.

Changes in the environment were brought about by the transformation of the world economy, and also by the partial success of the Soviet-type economies in their early stages. The prolonged growth of the economy had led, in the absence of significant technical progress, to the full employment of resources and the exhaustion of extensive growth resources, and mounting pollution. This happened in a world in which technical progress and production quality acquired rapidly increasing importance, relative prices changed following oil shocks and other modifications in the economy, and while the countries of Central and Eastern Europe - economically weaker - were caught up in an economically debilitating arms race. The increasingly demanding domestic market, especially in quality terms, could not be supplied adequately and this fostered unsatisfaction of consumers.

The slowdown in economic growth registered during the 1960s, and which was the consequence of the above problems, made it obvious that the functioning of the economic system had somehow to be changed and conducted to the development of new routines. This led to the formulation and implementation of economic reforms in all the countries of Eastern Europe during the latter years of the 1960s and then again in the 1980s[27]. The principal aim of these reforms was to give renewed dynamism to the economy by introducing certain changes, without, however, substantially transforming the economic, political and social system[28]. In spite of some relevant difference among individual countries, the most significant changes were the following. The management of the economy was partially decentralized, in the sense that enterprises acquired autonomy in non-strategic investment decisions and in establishing certain relationships among themselves. The price system was partially liberalized and the system of obligatory plan indices was in part abandoned. The government relied mainly on indirect instruments (the so-called regulators, such as the interest rate, the management of subsidies out of the state budget, taxation, the centralization of a proportion of profit rather than of all enterprise income) to fulfil its economic plans, the targets of which were formulated in value and were not - at least formally - obligatory for enterprises. Important changes were made to the central administration of the government, where its functional organs - in particular the ministry of finance and the central bank - enlarged their functions and powers at the expense of the industrial and sectorial ministries and also of the central planning bodies[29]. All this led to a transfer of property rights from the government to enterprises, as well as among the various state organs. At the same time the aims and conditions of collective action changed too: enterprises were no longer obliged merely to be executors; they now had to operate (partially) as independent agents. This entailed the change of selective incentives with a greater reliance on moderately active incentives.

Despite a certain amount of progress, the economic reforms of the 1960s were nevertheless a failure[30], because they were unable to generate steady collective action which had change of institutions and the creation of new routines as its goals. The reforms, in fact, promised the collective advantage of a more effective and efficient economic system and greater well-being for all in the medium-to-long term, but they imposed private costs in the short one that were considered to be higher than the anticipated value of the advantages by the determinant special interest groups within the government and the executors. These private costs consisted in greater work effort by individuals, the loss of property rights and other privileges for organizations, and greater uncertainty for everybody[31].

Losses mainly affected the middle levels of the state administration and of the sole party in power, and also, despite the reformers' assurances, numerous managers (except for those running the most efficient enterprises). In the face of uncertain advantages in the future, managers partially lost their guaranteed and privileged positions in the enterprise; they were forced to cope with increased uncertainty now that they no longer received obligatory orders from the centre; and they became responsible for their enterprise's performance and therefore incurred a certain amount of risk. This was a situation in conflict with their traditional motivations, in particular their desire for security and for a tranquil social and psychological work environment[32]. At the same time, the new selective incentives for managers (a closer ratio between income and the economic results of the enterprise, and increased decision-making power in production matters) were not enough to offset their greater personal costs. This created a coalition of forces opposed to change.

Also the new role of the government became a further obstacle for the success of reforms. Lacking an exogenous judge of the performance of enterprises (the market), the involvement of the government in the daily management of the economy increased further. Having limited the issue of orders (in some way having the nature of hard rules), the government opened the way not only to the traditional bargaining with lower level organizations concerning the general guidelines of the economy and the planned targets for ministries and enterprises, but also the regulators. This created a situation that often compelled the government to resort to central intervention, thus invalidating the substance itself of economic reforms.

These factors, together with policy mistakes and contradictoriness of the reform measures, interacted in blocking reformer collective action and impeding the change of routines, thereby causing the economic reforms to fail[33].

4. Goals, conflicts and the start of transition

The failure of the attempted economic reforms of the 1960s only delayed the onset of problems to the 1980s. Since it proved impossible to adapt the economic system to changes taking place in the domestic economies and in the external environment, economic performance declined to a critical extent. As a consequence, a new wave of reforms were introduced in the 1980s, although the reformers (usually a coalition of politicians, technocrats and intellectuals) immediately realised that their measures would have to be much more radical than they had been in the 1960s. Ultimately and largely unwillingly, collective action managed to achieve a fundamental goal: destroying the old Soviet-type system and initiating transition to a new one allegedly based on the market. It is therefore necessary to understand why this second wave of reforms also failed and why - unlike the first wave - it paved the way for systemic change.

These developments can only be understood if one considers the following: after the death of Stalin in 1953, and even more so after the implementation of the first wave of economic reforms in the 1960s, rapidly growing consumption and overcoming the West in production and consumption alike were openly promised to citizens. The former fundamental goals of the system (building socialism, industrialization, and later also defence) therefore slowly withered away, without any decisive change in institutions and the system performance taking place. At the same time, the economies and the societies grew increasingly open towards the rest of the world. A certain differentiation among countries and a limited liberalization in the political sphere emerged as the Soviet grip on them weakened following *détente* with the West, and particularly during the 1980s and even more so after Gorbachev rose to power. All these developments occurred while the efficiency of the economic system was in relative decline and amidst increasing quality and technical backwardness of these countries relative to the developed economies of the West.

This increasing openness to the West combined with relative backwardness and with persistent cultural links progressively influenced the attitudes and expectations of the peoples of Eastern Europe. When the traditional external constraint, i.e. the threat of Soviet intervention, then began to fade, popular expectations acted as the catalyst for collective action which sought to change the institutions of the economic system[34]. Individuals began to assign increasing importance to consumption, political freedom and freedom to travel to the West, ignoring the fact that improvements in the structure and the level of consumption *first* required improvements in the production process, there comprising the work effort.

As long as two different systems pursue different objectives, as was the case until the first economic reforms, the stability of the relatively less developed system is easier, especially if the two systems are isolated from each other[35]. And this situation may continue as long as conflict with the other system does not develop into an open clash and if it does not impose economic, political and social costs so high that fulfilment of the system's objectives is impeded. The diversity of objectives, in fact, protects the system against comparison with the other. Instead, its stability depends directly on its ability to achieve its declared objectives and to exclude the pursuit of alternative objectives.

However, if two systems pursue the same objectives and if one of them starts from more unfavourable initial conditions, the latter encounters greater difficulties in justifying its existence, both internally and externally. It may survive in stable form only if at least one of the following conditions is satisfied:

-    it is more efficient than the other in at least one aspect of importance for the system's objectives; for example, if a catching-up process takes place. This was apparently the situation in Eastern Europe until the late 1950s, but this effort could not be further sustained when extensive resources were exhausted, due to systemic aversion to technical progress.

-    it remains economically, socially and culturally closed to the other system and there is a monolithic political power of sufficient strength not constrained by significant demands for democracy. This was the situation of the Soviet Union until the first *détente* and China until the mid-1980s.

-    there are internal or external extra systemic features which are stronger than systemic ones: i.e. there is close internal social and political cohesion (nationalism, defence of a revolution, religious goals, etc.) or else a strong external constraint (danger of war, strong international tensions, the threat of invasion, etc.), like in the Soviet Union after the October revolution up to the death of Stalin, or Cuba.

If objectives are identical, but pursued on the basis of different institutions, the problem arises of the relative effectiveness and efficiency of different institutional arrangements and of different strategies. In fact, different institutions may have different degrees of effectiveness and efficiency in diminishing costs, controlling free-riding, pursuing objectives and the like[36]. The conditions listed above have different significance and different consequences for the development of the system. The most favourable situation occurs when the system starting from the most disadvantageous initial position manages to be more efficient and effective in at least one important respect[37] which ranks high in the society's preferences (for example, by securing a higher rate of growth, or full employment, or an egalitarian distribution of income, or by maintaining a zero inflation rate). In this case, the question which of the two systems is more effective and efficient can only be resolved on the basis of the specific preferences of the members of each, the existence of trade-offs between different objectives, as well as of the importance of individual objectives in the overall performance of the economy and in competition between the two systems.

However, certain conditions may compromise the achievement of objectives over the long period and therefore bring about the failure of the system. Such is the case, for instance, of the closeness of the economy or a dictatorship, which decrease competition, the active participation of individuals to public life and hinder the democratic control of government decisions. On the other hand, if the disadvantaged system is unable to achieve this partial superiority, it will become unstable and susceptible to change (e.g. through imitation) or disruption (through a revolution).

Both cases are relevant to explain the failure of the Soviet-type system and transition. As was said above, although failing to implement a relevant evolution of the economic system, the reforms led to a change in the objectives pursued; namely, their progressive convergence towards the objectives typical of the economically more advanced Western capitalist system. The most important among these were the growth of private consumption, the nominal emphasis on technical progress (the so-called technical-scientific revolution), and political democracy[38].

In parallel, the traditional objectives of the Soviet-type economic system which were the basis of the (forced) social contract (full employment, price stability, equity) progressively lost ground, either because they were formally achieved, or because their pursuit and maintenance created more problems for the economy than they resolved in cases where there were trade-offs with other objectives. For instance, full employment and equity in personal income distribution substantially contributed to weaken incentives to work and labour productivity, and price stability - in the given institutional settlement leading to soft wage policy and soft budget constraint for enterprises - had its counter-item in spread shortages.

Finally, one should not neglect the important fact that those who had most to gain from the pursuit of these objectives (for example, unskilled workers and pensioners) were also those least aware of the systemic nature of these objectives and, above all, those least able to influence the power coalition in its decisions concerning the timing and form of transition. They thus constituted the social base least necessary for transition and therefore the group least able to impose its demands. Hence one readily draws the conclusion that this group of people was destined to pay the highest price for transition while being simultaneously the least actively involved in the process of change.

By adopting the same objectives as the other system (consumption, technical progress, etc.), the countries of Eastern Europe sought to give their economic system a competitive posture, but started from unfavourable conditions as regards both the effectiveness and efficiency of the economic system itself and the environment and politics. We may cite their lower level of development, their exhaustion of extensive resources, their relative isolation from the more developed countries, the ineffectiveness of their international economic relationships, largely obsolete capital stock, the pervasiveness of the bureaucracy and of administrative procedures, scant innovation by enterprises and the low quality level of their production, the impediment to change represented by the second economy[39]. However, the economy's inability to evolve meant that changes were not made to the institutions in parallel with the altering of objectives, so that collective action could not be mounted to achieve these new objectives. This led the Soviet-type system into an impasse.

The results achieved in economic development, which led to the increasing differentiation of society and of the economy, closer contacts with the democratic Western countries, attempts to consolidate the political system by conceding greater space to social pluralism, weakened the control exercised by the communist party and by the central administrative apparatus; that is to say, the nucleus of the old power structure which, by using powerful, although mostly passive selective incentives, was able to promote or impose collective action. In the meantime, however, the resistance raised by the old institutions had impeded the development of the alternative (market) institutions which would have provided a new basis for collective action. A situation was thus created in which the former system was weakened and partly disrupted, but the new one could not develop.

All the factors which would have permitted the coexistence of two different systems pursuing the same objectives progressively declined in the countries of the East, until the changes introduced by Gorbachev removed the last one of all: the threat of foreign restorative intervention. In conclusion, although these developments were stimulated by the external environment, they were at the same time and to an equally significant extent engendered by the features themselves of the Soviet-type system that had developed in these countries or had been imposed on them from outside.

5. The nature of transition

These events fostered the development first, and then the success, of forces and a powerful coalition of interests which initiated transition[40]. To assess this process thoroughly, five elements basic to the development of a market economy must be examined. They are discussed in this session, and they are reconsidered in the conclusions to interpret transition and obstacles to it. The five factors are:
- the individual parties involved together with their organizations (agents);
- institutions;
- the goals, ideas, projects, preferences, expectations which mould the different strategies pursued with the means and instruments available (goals and strategies);
- external factors;
- initial conditions.

These elements are largely similar in all the economies in transition, due to the long lasting implementation of the Soviet-type system. There are also, however, substantial differences, due to historical factors and natural and cultural features and to different levels of development and dimension and openness of the economy. I now briefly examine these five basic components:

1. The parties (agents)

The starting of transition has largely been a pragmatic-constructivist process, the result of a set of deliberate decisions taken by some agents[41]. The agents of the coalition of forces which promotes transition (the winning coalition) vary somewhat from one country to another, and the same is true for losers. They are determined first of all by initial conditions, including non economic factors.

One may distinguish four major agents in the transition process:
a)   workers/consumers;
b)   private investors and owners, entrepreneurs in the private or public sectors and top technocrats, there comprising the managers of state

privatization agencies, private and state investment funds, banks, stock exchange and the like (owners);

c)   state administrators (administrators), including former politicians and the administrators (managers) of state-owned enterprises;

d)   new politicians and political parties (politicians)[42].

The situations of the four groups are highly differentiated. Two of them, the 'owners' (the agents sub b) and the 'politicians' (sub d) have emerged as the clear winners: they have acquired new property rights through the process of privatization, free elections and the formation of new governments. However, their situation requires more careful examination, since, although the owners have already gained property rights, they have also incurred a number of potentially very substantial private costs.

Two of these private costs are of particular importance: the cost of acquisition, and the cost of restructuring. The former may be high when ownership rights can only be acquired on the market: this, for instance, is the solution preferred in Hungary. On the other hand, they may be low, as in the case of the free distribution of former state ownership (e.g. the voucher system in former Czechoslovakia and its successor states) or the restitution of expropriated property to its former owners (in various countries). In the two latter cases, private costs are mostly administrative in character: the necessity to learn the new system, to submit applications, and the like. In any case - provided that owners utilize their ownership rights to derive a profit and do not merely speculate on the changing value of real estate - they must face substantial restructuring costs. These consist of both the direct disbursement of money in order to finance investment, and the absence of profit in the short run until restructuring is complete. However, a proportion of new owners who have acquired their property rights through free distribution or restitution may simply resell them, pocketing the profit without incurring any restructuring cost.

Politicians find themselves in a mixed situation: compared with the old politicians, the new ones have lost a considerable amount of property rights and now they are submitted to the risk of adverse results from free elections. Nevertheless, as individuals they are on the winning side (in the sense that they have acquired property rights), since (most of) them were ordinary intellectual workers in the former system and therefore had few property rights.

The losing side comprises workers and administrators. Their situations too, however, are differentiated. As a group, the administrators have lost the most, and they have no chance of regaining the substantial property rights removed from them by transition, provided it continues and is successful. The administrators, in fact, can only hope that transition comes to a halt (and reverts to the former system) or that a populist coalition largely based on administrators will take over. Therefore, one can expect administrators as a group to try their best to interrupt or to deviate the process of transition, seeking to form a coalition with the workers. This eventuality cannot be ruled out: indeed, developments in some countries seem to be moving in precisely this direction. This is the case, for instance, of many Soviet Union's successor states, Balkanic states and partially also Central European states (in particular, Slovakia and also Hungary and Poland). However, individual administrators may still play a substantial role in the new administration and in managing the residual state enterprises[43].

The situation of workers is somewhat different: as a group, there is no doubt that they have lost substantial property rights, in particular their tenure rights in the labour market. They must now contend with substantial and increasing unemployment and higher quantitative and qualitative labour standards. Their other lost privileges include many services, like cheap or free vacations at their enterprise's holiday resort and free or cheap kindergartens. On the other hand, all workers are also consumers, and as such they have gained some advantages (wider choice and better-quality goods), together with disadvantages (lower real incomes due to inflation or unemployment, and the introduction of new taxes). The main advantage accruing to consumers, however, lies in the long run: if transition succeeds, they stand to gain from the substantially improved situation brought about by the improved performance of the economic system. As individuals, though, there are significant differences among workers: some of them (skilled workers) can already benefit in the short run (e.g. by earning higher real wages and finding better opportunities for employment), while for others (unskilled workers, younger and elder workers, workers belonging to some minorities) the long-term prospects are rather bleak as in the short run. This heterogeneity of situation renders the workers' group the most likely to voice dissatisfaction or protest, but hardly the active promoter of action aimed at stopping or reversing the transition process - provided, obviously, that this heterogeneity persists and that the group of workers acquiring property rights, or not losing a substantial amount of them, continues to be large. However, workers could easily join an opposition coalition led by the administrators.

The fundamental organizations in which the actors behave are the enterprise and the state. Both undergo substantial transformations during transition[44]. The enterprise must become autonomous, and the state must refrain from interfering in productive activity with orders, bargaining and soft financing. These changes are necessary regardless of predominant property rights. By their very nature, organizational changes take a great deal of time. In the meantime, the enterprises which remain (temporarily or permanently) the property of the state must not be controlled by the party (or parties) in power and they must not have any further access to the resources of the state budget. The situation preferred by the majority of countries seems to be the transformation of enterprises into joint-stock companies, and the transfer of their management either to state privatization agencies or to one or several state management bodies, or to public or private investment funds. Moreover, the previous monopolistic structure of the economy must give way to competition. The methods used to achieve this end are antimonopoly administrative measures, the liberalization of foreign trade, and privatization. As altready noticed, the state should concentrate progressively on its normative role. It should indirectly procure the resources with which to finance its activities through taxation, but in reality budget deficits substantially and rapidly increased in almost all countries.

2. Institutions

The relevance of institutions is stressed by the fact that an economic system is the set of all the institutions relevant to economic life which pursue in a socially co-ordinated manner the goals of economic activity[45]. In a normal situation, the institutions serve to build this unity of intent and therefore to lay the basis for collective action. In fact, the ultimate goal of an economic system is to create collective action which pursues the system's objectives as expressed in its collective preference function.

Institutions are normative models which define what within a particular society is perceived as appropriate, legitimate or expected forms of behaviour or of social relationship. They are therefore a set of norms[46], rules of behaviour, habits, roles, repetitive patterns of thought and action (routines), which constitute a stable structure of social relationships and which, by influencing the formation of preferences, induce the members of a particular society to behave in a uniform and therefore predictable manner. Therefore, every economic system is characterized by a certain degree of coherence among the institutions of which it is composed[47]. In this way, the danger of conflict is substantially reduced, and so too is the uncertainty that derives from such conflict. This contributes to reduce transaction costs in economic activity.

Institutions are based on a series of organizational structures, mechanisms, laws, attitudes, behaviours, traditions, and prohibitions, in which they find actuation and which are the constitutive elements of the economic system. Therefore, institutions guarantee the survival, operation, and growth of the economic system. However, when the external environment changes or the conditions of the economy are modified, institutions may change (either in a pragmatic-constructivist or organic-evolutionary way) leading to the development and the transformation of the economic system. When the transformation of the economic system is the result of a pragmatic-constructivist process, as in transition, the change of institutions is first the result of a set of deliberate decisions and their following implementation taken by the agents who want to change the economic system (the winners or a winners' coalition), under the constraints put by the opposition of losers, resilience of old institutions, external factors and initial conditions. However, also within a pragmatic-constructivist change, organic-evolutionary processes have a relevant role.

The key institutions and their organizational forms during transition are:

A) Property rights. The component of transition that has provoked most debate and which, in word and by official declaration, has been given the greatest importance, is privatization. In reality, however, matters have gone otherwise, and the results so far achieved have been rather modest, in particular concerning privatization of state owned enterprises[48]. Privatization has been pursued because it is believed indispensable to the development of a market economy - because private enterprises are regarded as being more efficient than state ones, and because the government wishes to free itself from the management of enterprises and believes privatization to be the most efficient method to separate enterprises from the state budget. It is necessary, moreover, to develop a legal system which defends property rights, enforces contracts and reduces transaction costs. The latter are key elements in the construction of a state of law.

B) The main aim of transition is the development of real market economies. Once *dirigisme* has been abandoned and its instruments dismantled, and once the decision has been taken to move towards a market economy, certain institutional changes must be implemented. and their relative legal and organizational instruments must be adopted. Administrative intervention by the government must be kept to a minimum and the main policy instruments become indirect instruments and regulation (monetary, fiscal and income policies) based on clear and fixed rules and appropriate legal, administrative and social reforms. All these changes are necessary in order to encourage the development of basic markets: i.e. of goods, labour, and capital. For the goods market to develop, it is necessary to liberalize - rapidly or gradually according to political and technical choices and to the economic situation - both the domestic market and foreign trade. This liberalization is required to reduce distortions in the price system and improve the allocation of resources. In the labour market, hiring, dismissals and union bargaining must be liberalized, with the simultaneous introduction of the necessary social shock-absorbers (for example, unemployment benefits). As regards the development of a capital market, the banking system has to be restructured and the old single-bank system eliminated. The minimum requirement is that competitive commercial banks should be created which are entirely independent of the central bank. Other financial intermediaries should also be introduced: for example, investment funds and a stock exchange and a commodities exchange. The final measure necessary for the development of a capital market is the liberalization of entry by foreign capital.

C) Money and prices. An essential component of the market system is a price system determined by the market together with the active role of money. The liberalization of prices was one of the first measures adopted in most countries when transition got under way. For this to lead to the complete activation of the role of money in the state sector as well, in the sense that it influences the decisions of enterprises, the transformation of enterprises and the state must be completed. It is worth noting, in fact, that the macroeconomic stabilization policies adopted by all countries, albeit with varying degrees of rigour, have been largely frustrated in the state sector by the behaviour of enterprises. These in fact have resorted widely to mutual indebtedness - thereby effectively abolishing money from their exchanges - and to decapitalization in order to overcome restrictions on credit and state subsidies, and they continue to pursue their traditional objectives while lobbying to induce the government to change its attitude.

D) Passage to a market economy entails a radical change in motivations and in incentives. Once direct control is largely abolished, new indirect selective incentives must be introduced, which are enforced through the market but also sanctioned by clear and fixed legal rules, not influenced by bargaining over the same rules. This applies principally to managers and enterprises although it also concerns workers. The key motivational factor for enterprises and managers must be profit, which also becomes the key discriminatory factor among enterprises. To this should be added the regulatory role of competition and the threat of bankruptcy. As regards workers, their jobs and wages are no longer a right and are therefore no longer guaranteed. Wages become a key incentive to the labour supply and to work effort, since it is tied to marginal productivity. Trade union bargaining becomes a fundamental feature of the new system in which trade unions are democratically legitimated by the support of their members.

E) As a consequence of the changes listed above, the budget constraint of enterprises becomes harder[49]. Enterprises must pay closer attention to their profitability on the market, especially if they have been privatized. More sagacious management of the state budget, with a drastic reduction of subsidies to enterprises, a new tax system (e.g. based on the principle of value added) and the transformation of the banking system (the prerequisite for more rigorous credit management) - these are all factors which lead, within the government and in the credit sector as well, to a reversal of the situation that distinguished the old system. They induce the rapid conversion of an economy limited by resources into one limited by demand. Shortages disappear and their place is taken by the unemployment of resources (especially labour), a phenomenon which, in the first phase of transition, is rapidly on the increase[50].

These processes are going on in all Central and East European countries, although substantial differences exist concerning the stage of implementation and the specific solutions adopted.

3. Goals and strategies

Each agent in the economy has one or more goals, either explicit and openly announced or implicit and sometimes even unconscious. To implement those goals, agents elaborate strategies, develop coalitions, act and use instruments. The final goal of transition is the implementation of an economic (and socio-political) system which differs substantially from the former Soviet-type one and is based on the market. However, beyond this rather common general agreement, agents differ markedly as to which specific system they wish to see implemented. Five major systems can be envisaged: liberism, liberalism and social market economy, mixed economy, populism. By liberism is usually meant a system run by owners (as defined in paragraph 5.1 above), in which the role of the state is reduced to the minimum and economic activity is undertaken as far as possible through an unconstrained market based on private ownership. A liberal economy - a relevant variant of which is the social market economy[51] - is a market economy based on neutral and hard rules established by the government via politicians with the aim to avoid abuses and grant *ex ante* equal opportunities to all the market players. The state reduces as much as possible its involvement in the economy outside its normative role: it does not intervene directly in production, but may assume an important role in distribution in order to achieve equity and to pursue other social objectives through the wide-ranging use of indirect instruments of economic policy. In a mixed economy also, administrators and particularly managers assume a relevant and direct role in production as well. Finally, populism is a system in which new politicians run a coalition comprising administrators and workers, whose goal is to defend the privileges of workers and administrators by restricting the role of the market and by trying to control the fundamental components of the economy, including the imposition of political control over state enterprises, and thereby hampering the transformation of the economic system towards a market system.

Each agent concerned, according to its interests and beliefs, has different preferences regarding the goals of transition. The actual choice will depend on the strength of coalitions among the agents seeking each goal, mutual relationships among coalitions and trade-offs among goals. However, other factors, such as initial conditions and intellectual and scientific debate, may also put constraints and have important consequences. Moreover, each goal can be pursued by means of different strategies, including those selected by the interests of the predominant coalition.

There are two basic strategies: 'shock therapy' and gradualism. The advocates of the former[52] maintain that only the rapid, even brutal, implementation of the fundamental components of transition (i.e. the transfer of property rights, macroeconomic stabilization, the reorientation and restructuring of foreign trade, demonopolization, the introduction of bankruptcy and unemployment) can ensure successful transition that becomes irreversible because changes rapidly reach a critical mass[53]. This, they argue, minimises transition costs, as well social and political opposition, because a shock strategy concentrates costs into a limited period of time. However, the proponents of this strategy often forget that it implies that shock is necessary only in the short run: after a short while, they assume, the results will be such to repay everybody for the costs and sacrifices involved. This presupposes that the shock compels agents in a transition economy to react in the way that they supposedly behave in a well-established market economy and conceals the danger that if the optimistic expectations aroused by shock therapy are not rapidly satisfied, they may exert a destabilizing effect which may lead to the predominance of a populist coalition. This is a relevant danger nowadays in various Central and East European countries.

The supporters of gradualism[54], instead, contend that the nature of processes involved and the specific situation of these countries can only permit gradual transition to a market economy. They cite various reasons for this view: the attitudes, expectations and behaviour of people (workers and consumers) and enterprises must be radically changed before the goals of transition can be achieved; new laws must be passed before the introduction of any economic measures; these countries lack the necessary resources (particularly capital); shock therapy might destroy the commitment and resources of potential entrepreneurs and create social instability which could halt transition; the state sector - which is bound to remain dominant for some time in the future - must be restructured and not only repressed; incomes and consumption should be somehow sustained in order to prevent the total breakdown of the domestic market and social unrest. However, this approach, too, conceals a number of dangers and shortcomings. Gradual transition reduces pressure on the former power-holders (administrators) and may give them time to reorganize and to hamper the process; it also reduces the pressure on enterprises and workers to change their attitudes and behaviour to market-oriented ones; long-drawn-out changes without substantial results may reduce social support for transition, increase apathy and, eventually, become socially destabilizing; the economy may become disorganised and property rights disrupted further if the old Soviet-type system is destroyed and the new market system is still far from being effective. Such dangers are real also in those countries which have adopted a relatively orderly and substantially gradual approach to transition, like Hungary.

4. External factors

These factors derive from the environment external to economies in transition. They operate largely independently of the will of the countries concerned, but exert a substantial influence over the various processes involved. The external factors influencing transition are of two kinds. Both categories comprise factors which act positively on transition, in the sense that their existence render it easier (positive factors), and factors which hinder transition and render it more difficult (negative factors).

The first kind of factors comprises those that existed before the onset of transition and derive from the external features of the Soviet-type system, the histories of the countries which adopted it, and their relationships with countries which have different systems. Here two main types of negative factor are comprised: economic and non-economic. The former consists primarily of the long isolation of these economies from the world market, which makes it more difficult for enterprises to adapt to the new situation created by transition. They lack, in fact, the relevant experience and skills. The latter mainly comprises the unfavourable external political environment which increased the isolation of these countries from the rest of the world (particularly its most developed regions) and imposed substantial economic and political costs upon them (the arms race).

Other external factors are largely the consequence of transition itself and came into being with its start-up, but have rapidly consolidated. These factors can be divided between negative and positive. Among the former, two phenomena in particular should be borne in mind: the collapse of CMEA and the disruption of traditional trade links, and stagnation on the world market. Whereas the former makes the reorientation and restructuring of the foreign trade of economies in transition of vital and sometimes desperate importance, the latter makes this reorganization more difficult to implement - as well as the equally important growth of exports and imports as a key component in the restructuring and modernization of the domestic economy (imports of technology and energy, and exports to finance imports, repay foreign debt and sustain domestic production and employment).

However, there are also positive external factors, the most important of which is Western support for the process of transition and the countries implementing it, and the greater willingness of Western countries to accept (some of) the Central and Eastern European countries into their supranational organizations (like the European Union) and to open (to some extent) their domestic markets to exports from transition economies.

5. Starting conditions

As I have already stressed, the goals chosen and the strategies implemented, and therefore the final outcome of transition, also depend on pre-existing factors. Some of these derive from the historical features of the countries, or from the characteristics of the Soviet-type system. Others result from the first stage of transition or have been activated by it. Truly pre-existing factors are both negative and positive in nature. Belonging to the former category are all those factors which rendered the pre-existing situation unfavourable to the development of a modern market economy. Among them were the essential features of the Soviet-type system: a soft budget constraint, political interference in the economy, monopolies, aversion to technical progress, consumer dissatisfaction, mostly passive and ineffective incentives, environmental and technical failure, accelerated growth to catch up. Other economic factors are the mistaken policies pursued in the past (soft money, populist policies, reform failures), the lack of capital, certain second economy activities (like speculation and black market) and the role of criminal organizations (such as *mafias* in the Soviet Union). To these one may add a number of important non economic factors, such as the absence of institutions able to sustain a market economy, the lack of democratic traditions in various countries (political failure), and cultural attitudes and historical factors often averse to the development of the market, such as the lack of a strong historical tradition favourable to private ownership in Russia.

Positive factors include all those achievements of the old system which improved the economic and social situation in a certain respect (usually equity and opportunities for people), but which, precisely because of their success, now mean that the population is unwilling to accept sacrifices during transition, increasing social differentiation and a meritocratic system. However, they supply important human capital for the achievement of transition. Among these positive factors, mention should be made of egalitarianism, high social requirements, the absence of unemployment and social security, a high level of education, and extensive social services. Certain activities in the second economy (such as private entrepreneurship) are also positive in their effects. Finally, one should remember that, because of certain features of the old system, the population is usually rather tolerant of (or apathetic towards) and willing to accept (although mostly passively) decisions taken by the government. This may provide *de facto* valuable support for transition.

A number of other factors stem directly from implementation of the first phase of the transition process. Examples are the introduction of macroeconomic stabilization programmes, the dismantling of the old institutions and laws (and the failure rapidly to replace them with new ones), the explosion of nationalist conflicts and conflicts between central and regional/republican governments[55] and political disruption, sometimes triggered by the disappearance of centralized control over society and the introduction of a more democratic system.

6. Obstacles to transition

In spite of careful preparation and wide planning, transition has encountered great and often unexpected difficulties in all the countries concerned. This is not only proof of poor knowledge of the true situation in these countries and the effective complexity of transition, but also of the existence - which was not acknowledged in due time - of major obstacles to transition.

These obstacles to transition provided an important example of the difficulties encountered by collective action in a dynamic environment characterized by non-continuous choices. In transition, individuals and organizations cannot choose from among a continuous range of strategies. Their choice in fundamental questions is instead discrete, with alternatives grouped at non-continuous intervals (e.g. concerning the number of enterprises to be privatized) or polarised, with extreme alternatives in terms of 'yes' or 'no' (e.g. privatize or keep state property, many parties or only one). In these cases, co-operation is less likely than when choice can be made from a continuous range of strategies[56].

First of all, this may be a problem of path-dependency and irreversibility which makes the final result depend on the initial state and therefore on the history of the system and of the country in question[57]. In this case, the starting conditions are of crucial importance.

Change may also be impeded or halted by uncertainty over its outcome and over the advantages of the future system. This regards both uncertainty over the future state and the probable emergence of undesirable consequences. This second form of uncertainty adds to the first. Uncertainty is further increased by the restitution policies pursued in various countries and by the political and sometimes even judiciary persecution of people who held administrative posts in the former system.

A third obstacle is the costs entailed by transition from one system to the other, costs which may, or appear to, be so high that change is blocked. Consider, for example, the conflicts between social groups defending opposing interests that invariably accompany every change[58], or the economic or social disorder that inevitably arises until the new rules and institutions have been experienced and internalized. This applies both to change which is expected to be protracted (for instance, the economic reforms of the 1960s in the countries of the East) - in which case lower costs must be borne for a longer period of time - and to change which has a more immediate impact. This does not mean that change is impossible in all cases because of uncertainty and transition costs; but it does entail that only some strategies of change are likely to succeed. These strategies should reduce to the minimum the number of individuals and organizations damaged by the change, and they should increase to the maximum the number of those who benefit from the change.

One should also bear in mind that, in contrast to the former system, during transition the 'game' concentrates primarily on distribution, mainly through the privatization of existing state ownership and the redistribution of political power[59]. This provokes a clash among the different and contrasting interests of various coalitions and renders collective action all the more difficult, so that it proves impossible to create collective consensus on the goals to be pursued. Whereas the old system had rather weak and usually not openly organized privilege groups and they were formally (although not always substantially) subordinated to the officially established social goals, these are now able to dominate the situation: by lobbying activity, they can bring about the rapid reallocation of resources, thus creating diffused opposition and slowing down or halting economic growth.

Finally, the collective action necessary to achieve the best system can be impeded by a lack of co-operation[60].

As we saw earlier, the transformation of an economic system requires collective action which imposes individual costs (e.g. greater and better work effort, retraining, changed attitudes and behaviour, unemployment, loss of privileges) in exchange for certain gains (higher incomes, more freedom, ownership rights).

However, the distribution of both (private) costs and (collective) advantages varies among individuals and organizations: they have different probabilities of affording costs and obtaining gains, and they attach different intensities to them. A further element to consider is that most individuals' and organizations' costs are concentrated in the present, and their gains are distributed in the - sometimes distant and poorly defined - future. Also, different individuals and organizations have different preference and objective functions and different expectations concerning the outcome of collective action and attach different intensities of preference for gains and different dispreference for costs to individual events. Finally, it should also be considered that knowledge about the transition process (strategies and measures to be taken, results and implementation, etc.) is asymmetrically distributed among individuals and organizations and different individuals and organizations have differing influences over decisions.

In reality, there exist organizations (trade unions, political parties, associations, etc.) which help to resolve these problems, although their contribution will not necessarily be sufficient. Moreover, in periods of rapid and profound change like transition, these organizations too enter crisis and in part lose their influence.

All these facts not only obstruct the development of collective action, but they create ample opportunities for free riding and for the development of adverse coalitions in an uncooperative environment. Free riders are concentrated in the winners' coalition (see below): for example, many politicians and state managers may be interested in transition only or mainly to gain personal advantages in the distribution of property rights.

7. Stages of transition and coalitions

Transition can be divided into two stages:

1. A change in the political structure

This came about rapidly and successfully, and for a variety of reasons. On the one hand, the former power-holders lost their domestic political basis and their Soviet backing. In this new, weaker position they hoped to keep and to strengthen their power through democratic elections or agreed to give up partially their power as a part of an agreement reached with the social and political opposition during 'round table' meetings in the hope of keeping the role also after the political change was implemented. In any case, the elites in power were unable to form a privileged group and to pursue collective action, also because often one section tried to take advantage of the other's weakening position by entering *de facto* in alliance with the opposition. On the other hand, opponents were able to form an effective privilege group under the leadership of those who stood to gain the most or were led by strong ideological and moral motivations (intellectuals, new politicians, prospective owners). The majority of the population was passive, i.e. they formed a latent group, although they backed those calling for systemic change, in the conviction that they would gain a great deal as consumers without losing as workers or in terms of social security.

2. First stage

However, this first stage automatically rendered society more complex and led to the creation of the main groups that I illustrated above:
a)   workers with a subgroup of the unemployed,
b)   new private owners and entrepreneurs,
c)   administrators, including former power-holders and managers of the state-owned enterprises,
d)   new politicians and political parties.
This growing complexity made it more and more difficult to implement the collective action required by transition at the systemic level. In fact, no general agreement could be reached among largely incompatible (concerning the goals of transition) agents and no universally accepted civilian authority proposing and implementing the rules of the new co-operative game could exist in a highly dynamic situation. And in fact the only such authorities (the Church and the army) were external to the economic and political game and could only guarantee the most general rules of the game and contracts, sometimes being themselves split between the two great coalitions.

The above mentioned players tend to form two - effective or only potential - coalitions in opposition to each another, a situation which may lead to damaging populism. The two coalitions are as follows:
a)   The winners' coalition: a reform-minded state made up by part of the new politicians and new or potential private owners, including state managers who found a way out and managed to find a relevant role in the new system and enrich themselves[61]. Sometimes, this coalition is actually primarily interested in maximizing or increasing its payoff from redistribution.
b)   The losers' coalition: administrators, including former politicians, workers (at least those with little or no specialization or operating in

sectors bound to shrink), the unemployed, managers of state owned enterprises to be privatized, former black-marketers and all those who gained substantially from shortage, artisans who formerly lived off shortage. This coalition is mostly interested in blocking redistribution of property rights and political power, from which they can only lose.

When a game is destined to be played repeatedly, the rational solution is co-operation between the two coalitions[62]. The essential condition for this to occur, however, is that both parties should possess substantial power of retaliation. But in our case, the game (transition) is played only once and is profoundly asymmetric. In fact, coalition a. (the winners) exercises great retaliatory power over the (individual members of) coalition b. (the losers): they can fire, persecute, privatize by using a system unfavourable to members of coalition b., etc. At the same time, the losers' coalition possesses no weapon (in the short and medium term) with which it can threaten the winners with retaliation except for strikes, protests and emigration, rather unlike on a wide scale in a still unsettled social and political situation. Their only effective retaliation applies in the long run: the overthrow - either by democratic elections or through revolt - of the winners' coalition.

However, for a few years since transition began (the 'period of grace') it is likely that coalition b. does not in fact exist, or else it is so loosely-formed that it has no effect and power. In fact, it consists of individuals (social groups) who dislike each other and do not wish to cooperate because of previous experience in the old system and fear of unfavourable social, economic and political consequences in the new situation. They may even be ready to cooperate with the winners in order to overwhelm certain losers other than themselves. Nor do they have any strong interest in common, except their opposition to the winners. Most losers believe that their real goal is not to overthrow the winners' coalition - thereby transforming themselves into winners - but to enter the winners' coalition individually, as a group or an organization. This is the more so if (as is usually the case) individuals, groups or organizations within the losers' coalition have different probabilities of being coopted into the winners' coalition. Thus the losers' coalition is often only potential, and will only acquire concrete form when individual and group mobility from the losing to the winning coalition is blocked or when social tensions become very powerful and when the winners' coalition lacks co-operation among its components.

The winners' coalition may also use various means to co-opt large components of the losers' coalition into its ranks, in order to avert retaliation or to block their (potential) co-operation. One of the most powerful of these means is privatization in the form of free or cheap distribution. However, this strategy may be dangerous for the winners' coalition, because it must relinquish one of its most powerful instruments of retaliation, namely selective privatization. In fact, if it takes place case by case, it may arouse the interest of the judiciary, foster political opposition by those who were excluded and have negative consequencs for the state budget. If it happens on a general basis, it must be based on general and open rules, that greatly deprive the government of its selective power.

8. Conclusion

As we have seen, the predominance of a distributive game leads likely to stagnation or a decline in economic performance and - if the losers' coalition is strong enough to defend (some of) its privileges - also to inflation. It is also likely to have negative consequences in social and political terms. The most probable outcome will be stagnation, social contrasts and conflicts. This may increase the distance between the two coalitions and favour the development of a co-operative attitude within the losers' coalition - and perhaps weaken co-operation among the winners. Should this happen and should a different winners' coalition with different transformation goals and strategy addressed to development and not only to redistribution fail to take the place of the old one, the prevalence of the distributive game may become permanent. The losers may win by forming a populist coalition and halt transition as it was envisaged by the former winners or more likely change its path. Indeed, there are already some examples of this development.

Until the game is only distributive, it is very unlikely that winners seek co-operation with (a large part of) the losers. In fact, their different preference functions cannot be reduced to only one, consistent function and this prevents a co-operative development[63].

However, co-operation between the winners' coalition and a (substantial component of the) losers' coalition can develop more easily once economic growth has begun. Therefore, one relevant element in determining the outcome of transition consists of the long term features of the transition game and in particular of the strategic meaning of distribution within it.

The only possible positive outcome is that distribution frees so powerful and formerly repressed energies (in particular entrepreneurial energies) to overcome the above mentioned disadvantages of the distributive game. In fact, this is one fundamental conviction of those who push to base transition on redistribution of property rights and political and social power. However, schumpeterian entrepreneurs are not the result of a simply redistributive ('zero sum') game, but are firstly the product of 'creative destruction', namely of a dynamic game, whose goal is the production of something new (a higher profit reached through technical progress, new markets, new organizational solutions, etc.). Only in such an environment is the schumpeterian entrepreneur capable of becoming the engine of development. Moreover, Western experiences with privatization show that even in a market economy privatization does not bring relevant changes in the performance of privatized enterprises, unless other dynamic changes take place too, in particular greater competition[64].

However, if the goal of transition is to start the development process along a new path - and it is within this strategy that redistribution takes place as a necessary, although not sufficient step - the outcome can be quite different. Redistribution (in particular privatization of former state owned enterprises) is undoubtedly a necessary step, but priority should be given to other goals and should be a part (probably not even the dominant component) of a more complex privatization strategy based less on pragmatic-constructivist components and more on organic-evolutionary elements. In fact, it should give priority to the rapid and sound development of new private enterprises and to a more effective and efficient functioning of commercialized (but still largely state-owned) enterprises.

Only in this way are new energies actually freed and the role of schumpeterian entrepreneurship is maximised. Moreover, a great relevance should be assigned to the pursuit of competition and harder budget constraint for all enterprises, there comprising those which, although commercialized, are still (temporarily or permanently) in the ownership of the state. This is to say that priority should be given to the transformation of the attitude and working of all enterprises and privatization should be considered in this perspective.

This brings us directly to the factors that play the determinant role in moulding transition and determining its outcome. The following discussion will be centred on the fundamental factors already discussed in section 5.

First, the final outcome of transition will depend on the specific type of agents in the economy (and politics and the society), the character of the most active among them, the nature of coalitions they enter in and the goals these coalitions pursue, the relationships among different coalitions. As already said, the most favourable situation exists when the dominating agents play a schumpeterian role within coalitions interested in implementing a new development path within which redistribution has a secondary role functional to development. More precisely, when redistribution is seen as a means to get rid of dead-weight administrative control over the economy, introduce competition and harden the budget constraint. In this situation, the dominant coalition is made of agents interested (by their characteristics, but first of all by the systemic rules) to get more power through a dynamic process, i.e. by playing a dominant role in the transformation of the economy and the society, and to become richer by getting a substantial share of the marginal (increased) income. In such a way, they also establish their moral right to be the new ruling elite, by showing that they were able to accelerate the growth and start the new development of the economy and the society. Also, such a situation permits to reduce the number of losers, limiting them to the former ruling elite and possibly only to the high ranks of the ruling party and state administration. In such a way the development of a strong coalition adverse to transition can be prevented.

However, in most cases redistribution has been utilized as a powerful means toward easy personal enrichment and as a way to replace the old ruling elite as the right of the winners. This process was accompanied by the hope that redistribution would be enough to start a new development process simply by creating 'new' owners. However, these are sometimes new only as persons (but often they were actually members also of the old ruling elite), but their behaviour and attitudes (institutions they embody) are too often very much the same as in the old system. As a consequence, social relations in the economy are hardly changed, i.e. modernized in a market sense.

Moreover, the stress put on redistribution has been at the disadvantage of other changes: the development of new private enterprises, competition, hard budget constraint of private and state owned enterprises and this hampers the development of a market economy. The consequence is a drastic fall in production accompanied by a dramatic increase in unemployment. The political concern for the destabilizing effect of these consequences leads to increasing state budget expenses which - in a period of decreasing revenues - result in substantial budget deficits, one of the fundamental causes of high inflation. And in fact, the distributive solution has many aspects that render it rather similar to the situation existing in relatively rich developing countries, in particular those of Latin America. It leads to a polarized society which, after the success of the political transition, offers too few opportunities of social mobility, thus increasing the possibility of the formation of adverse coalition.

Second, the outcome of transition is favourable in creating a dynamic market economy, the more rapid the formation of new market institutions and of structures where they find expression is aiming at finding new solutions and ways to increase private rewards (profit or else) through the growth of production and/or the decrease of costs. This is by necessity a long, although progressive process, because it requires substantial changes in the behaviour, attitudes, preferences, expectations of economic and social agents. However, policy decisions can substantially accelerate (or hinder) their development. In fact, the formation of new institutions (entrepreneurial behaviour and hard budget constraint, active role of money and prices, new motivations and incentives, property rights, etc.) is by necessity a prerequisite of the full development of a market system, although the liberalization of direct dealings among enterprises and of prices substantially helps also the formation of new institutions. The development of new organizations, the approval and implementation of new laws and rules, the introduction of competition, the imposition to enterprises of a harder budget constraint, etc., are all fundamental steps that can substantially help the development of new market institutions and the formation of groups and coalitions embodying and implementing the new institutions.

Once again, an exclusively or predominantly distributive game can only hinder the development of new institutions and strengthen the old, administrative ones, centred on the attempt to enjoy the public goods resulting from collective action without paying the necessary private costs imposed by the transformation. In such a situation, institutions are neither effective nor efficient in decreasing production costs and/or increasing production and the overall income distributed to the society, thus enlarging the size of the market and improving its qualitative requirements. Instead, they can be very effective and efficient in pursuing a distribution of existing resources more favourable to dominant agents (the winners' coalition).

Third, goals explicitly chosen and strategies implemented by the winners' coalition can either help or hinder the development of a market economy. Here it is not only a long run question of the choice among more or less incompatible models of market economy: liberism, liberalism, social market economy, mixed economy, populism, or else. In fact, the choice is not simply a political question, because it is submitted to various constraints that limit substantially the actual choice and influence the development of a given market system.

Historical, cultural and other social factors limit - together with external and technical factors and initial conditions - the strategy of transition. In fact, the choice between shock therapy and gradualism is largely constrained and no such thing as shock therapy and even gradualism at a general level can exist. Moreover, the idea of a shock therapy behind the stabilization programs implemented during transition in various Central and East European countries was based on the (often implicit) assumption that agents - and primarily enterprises - react in a unique, rational market way to policy decisions and their implementation. This is like to say that institutions do not matter or can change overnight.

Now we have plenty of evidence that this assumption was wrong coming from the experience of Poland, Russia and other countries that tried to implement a 'shock' transformation. This is not to say that only a 'soft' approach should be used in any case: examples where a rigorous, rather fast approach should be implemented include macroeconomic stabilization and the approval and implementation of the legal and administrative framework necessary to transition and, first of all, the clarification of property rights and the establishment of the basic conditions for fostering new entrepreneurship (like removing administrative constraints and implementing the proper credit conditions and taxation). The latter is not the same as privatization: the only way to implement it rather rapidly is via free distribution. However, also in this case privatization risks are only formal and not substantial - as many aspects of the Czech and Slovak experiment may induce one to think- and in any case many other questions (like recapitalization and restructuring of enterprises) remain unsolved.

However, as already observed, only a distributive game can be implemented via a (*quasi*) 'shock therapy'. In a development strategy, the shock approach can only concern some legal and administrative and also a few macroeconomic preconditions (there comprising some distribution). The development itself - and primarily the development of new institutions and organizations - can only be an incremental, gradual (evolutionary) process.

Fourth, external factors are only partially favourable to transition, options differ through countries and most countries have been unable to take advantage of the favourable ones. So, the disruption of CMEA affected the worst those countries that were the most dependent on it and those that used to export goods unwanted on other markets or were heavily dependent on Soviet energy. Also badly affected were the countries less skilled in doing business with the West. Also Western assistance presents varying opportunities and has different consequences for individual countries. It is not only a question of geographical and historical-cultural vicinity or strategic interest of Western countries in helping some countries more than others. It is also a question of institutions, goals, strategies and agents: the closer these elements are to those typical of a market economy, and the more favourable they are to start and sustain a development process, the more effective Western assistance can be[65].

Fifth, also initial conditions vary sensibly through countries and contribute to explain the type of agents dominating the transition game, institutions, the goals and strategies chosen. Here fundamental are historical, cultural and social factors remembered above. Other relevant factors are the actual way in which the Soviet-type system was implemented. Under the latter aspect, the countries which are the most advantaged clearly are those where a relevant economic reform was implemented and proved rather successful in promoting the transformations of institutions and rendering agents (both enterprises, administrators, workers and consumers) more skilled and sophisticated (Hungary) and where the management of the economy was characterized by the successful pursuit of domestic and external equilibrium and the imposition upon enterprises of a rather rigorous financial discipline (Czechoslovakia). On the other side, the existence of domestic and international tensions (promoted by nationalistic conflicts or else) may substantially hinder transition, because - in the most favourable case - they usually lead to a distributive game also at a regional level wasting human and material resources.

If one considers the five factors briefly discussed above and analyzes the situation of individual countries in transition from that perspective, it clearly turns out that they have different probabilities of success and that their future economic (and social and political) systems can substantially differ. This also stresses that different goals should be given priority in different countries and different strategies should be implemented. In any case, the great danger is given by the supremacy of a distributive coalition among strong and determined special interest groups over agents more interested in the development of the economy and society. Here comes the fundamental, new role of the state during transition as a powerful agent capable of starting, together with existing and potential shcumpeterian entrepreneurs, the formation of a leading coalition aimed at starting a new development path and overcoming distributive coalitions and also comprising the huge latent group of agents interested in development. It is needless to say that in order to play this role the state itself must be substantially transformed and modernized so as to serve the development of a modern market economy.

Bibliography

Adam J. (1989), *Economic Reforms in the Soviet Union and Eastern Europe since the 1960s*, Macmillan, London

Amann R., Cooper J.M. (1982) (eds.), *Industrial Innovation in the Soviet Union*, Yale University Press, New Haven

Amann R., Cooper J.M. (1986) (eds.), *Technical Progress and Soviet Economic Development*, Basil Blackwell, New York

Aslund A. (1990), *How to Privatize*, mimeo, Stockholm

Axelrod R. (1984), *The Evolution of Cooperation*, Basic Books, New York

Bacharach, M. (1977), *Economics and the Theory of Games*, Westview Press, Boulder, Co.

Barry N. (1993), 'The Social Market Economy', *Social Philosophy & Policy*, Vol. 10, No. 2, Summer, pp. 1-25

Becker G.S. (1983), 'A Theory of Competition Among Pressure Groups for Political Influence', *The Quarterly Journal of Economics*, Vol. XCVIII, No. 3, August, pp. 371-400

Berliner J. (1976), *The Innovation Decision in Soviet Industry*, MIT Press, Cambridge, Mass.

Bradshaw M.J., Hanson P. (1994), 'Regions, Local Power and Reform in Russia', paper presented at the conference on *Local Governments, Economic Development, Conflicts. Regional Experiences in Russia and Italy*, Trento, 11-12 February 1994 (to be published in R.W. Campbell [ed.] *Issues in the Transformation of Centrally Planned Economies. Essays in Honor of Gregory Grossman*, Westview Press, Boulder, Co, forthcoming, 1994)

Breton A. (1989), 'The Growth of Competitive Governments', *Canadian Journal of Economics*, vol. XXII, No. 4, November, pp. 717-750

Brus W. (1964), *Il funzionamento dell'economia socialista. Problemi generali*, Feltrinelli, Milan

Chavance B. (1992), *Les réformes économiques à l'Est de 1950 aux années 1990*, Nathan, Paris

Csaba L. (1991) (ed.), *Systemic Change and Stabilization in Eastern Europe*, Dartmouth, Aldershot

Dallago B. (1990), *The Irregular Economy*, Dartmouth, Aldershot

Dallago B. (1992a), 'Convergence, Evolution and Disruption of Economic Systems', in B. Dallago, H. Brezinski, W. Andreff (1992), pp. 123-148

Dallago B. (1992b), *Measurement of the Private Sector's Contribution*, The World Bank, Socio-Economic Data Division, Washington, D.C.

Dallago B. (1993a), *Sistemi economici comparati*, La Nuova Italia Scientifica, Rome

Dallago B. (1994a), *Second and Irregular Economy in Eastern Europe: Its Consequences for Economic Transition*, in *Economic Statistics for Economies in Transition: Eastern Europe in the 1990's*, Bureau of Labor Statistics and Eurostat, Washington, D.C.

Dallago B. (1994b), *Some Reflections on Privatization as a Means to Transform the Economic System: The Western Experience*, in H.-J. Wagener (1994a), pp. 113-143

Dallago B., Ajani G., Grancelli B. (1992) (ed.), *Privatization and Enterpreneurship in Post-Socialist Countries: Economy, Law and Society*, Macmillan, Basingstoke

Dallago B., Brezinski H., Andreff W. (1992) (eds.), *Convergence and System Change. The Convergence Hypothesis in the Light of Transition in Eastern Europe*, Dartmouth, Aldershot

Dietz R. (1992), 'From Command to Market Economies - an Exchange Theoretical View', *WIIW Forschungsberichte*, No. 185, July

Ece (1992), *Economic Survey of Europe in 1991-1992*, Economic Commission for Europe, Geneva

Ece (1993), *Economic Survey of Europe in 1992-1993*, Economic Commission for Europe, Geneva

EE (1991), 'The Path of Reform in Central and Eastern Europe', *European Economy*, no. 2 (special issue)

Eggertsson T. (1990), *Economic Behaviour and Institutions*, Cambridge University Press, Cambridge

Egidi M. (1994), 'Competition and Learning within Organizations and Markets', paper presented at the Fourth Trento Workshop of the European Association for Comparative Economic Studies on *Centralization and Decentralization of Economic Institutions: Their Role in the Transformation of Economic Systems*, Trento, 28 February - 1 March

Eidem R., Viotti S. (1978), *Sistemi economici comparati*, Il Mulino, Bologna

Elster J. (1985), *Making Sense of Marx*, Cambridge University Press, Cambridge

Grancelli B. (1988), *Soviet Management and Labor Relations*, Allen & Unwin, Boston

Granick D. (1987), *Job Rights in the Soviet Union: Their Consequences*, Cambridge University Press, Cambridge

Gregory P.R., Stuart R.C. (1980), *Comparative Economic Systems*, Houghton Mifflin, Boston

Grossman G. (1963), 'Notes for a Theory of the Command Economy', *Soviet Studies*, XV, No. 2, pp. 101-23

Grossman G. (1967), *Economic Systems, Prentice-Hall*, Englewood Cliffs, New Jersey

Grossman G. (1977), 'The 'Second Economy' of the USSR', *Problems of Communism*, 26, Sept.-Oct., pp. 25-40

Grossman G. (1979), 'Notes on the Illegal Private Economy and Corruption', in JEC (1979), pp. 834-855

Grossman G. (1981), 'La seconde économie et la planification économique sovietique', *Revue d'études comparatives est-ouest*, June, pp. 5-24

Grossman G. (1987), 'The Second Economy: Boon or Bane for the Reform of the First Economy?', *Berkeley-Duke Occasional Papers on the Second Economy in the USSR*, No. 11, December (Also in C.O. Kim, S. Gomulka, eds., *Economic Reforms in the Socialist World*, forthcoming)

Hanson P., Pavitt K. (1987), *The Comparative Economics of Research Development and Innovation in East and West. A Survey*, Harwood Academic Publishers, New York

Hauslohner P. (1992), 'Gorbachev's Social Contract', *Soviet Economy*, vol. 3, No. 1, pp. 54-89

Hodgson G. (1988), *Economics and Institutions. A Manifesto for a Modern Institutional Economics*, Polity Press, Cambridge

JEC (1979), *Soviet Economy in a Time of Change*, Joint Economic Committee, U.S. Government Printing Office, Washington, D.C.

Karol K.S. (1971), 'Conversations in Russia', *New Statesman*, June, pp. 8-10

Kornai J. (1980), *Economics of Shortage*, North-Holland, Amsterdam

Kornai J. (1986), 'The Hungarian Reform Process: Visions, Hopes, and Reality' *Journal of Economic Literature*, dicembre, vol. 24, n. 4, pp. 1687-1737

Kornai J. (1992a), *The Socialist System*, Princeton University Press, Princeton

Kornai J. (1992b), 'The Postsocialist Transition and the State: Reflections in the Light of Hungarian Fiscal Problems', *American Economic Review*, Papers and Proceedings, Vol. 82, No. 2, May, pp. 1-21

Kornai J. (1992c), 'The Principles of Privatization in Eastern Europe', *De Economist*, Vol. 140, No. 2, pp. 153-176

Kornai J. (1993a), 'Postsocialist Transition: An Overall Survey', *European Review*, Vol. 1, No. 1, pp. 53-64

Kornai J. (1993b), 'The Evolution of Financial Discipline under the Postsocialist System', *Kyklos*, Vol. 46, No 3, Fall, pp. 315-336

Lipton D., Sachs J. (1990), 'Privatization in Eastern Europe: The Case of Poland', *Brookings Papers on Economic Activity*, 2, pp. 293-333

March J.G., Simon H.A. (1958), *Organizations*, John Wiley, New York

Marer P., Zecchini S. (1991) (eds.), *The Transition to a Market Economy*, 2 vols. , OECD, Paris

Marwell G., Oliver P. (1993), *The Critical Mass in Collective Action. A Micro-Social Theory*, Cambridge University Press, Cambridge

Murrell P. (1990), ''Big Bang' versus Evolution: East European Economic Reforms in the Light of Recent Economic History', *PlanEcon Report*, no. 26, 29 June, pp. 1-11

Nelson R.R., Winter S.G. (1982), *An Evolutionary Theory of Economic Change*, The Belknap Press, Cambridge, Mass

Nuti D.M. (1986), 'Information, Expectations and Economic Planning', in AISSEC, *III Convegno scientifico annuale*, Nuova immagine editrice, Siena, pp. 231-250

Nuti D.M. (1994), 'The Role of the State in Post-Communist Economies', paper presented at the Fourth Trento Workshop of the European Association for Comparative Economic Studies on *Centralization and Decentralization of Economic Institutions: Their Role in the Transformation of Economic Systems*, Trento, 28 February - 1 March

Olson M. (1965), *The Logic of Collective Action*, Harvard University Press, Cambridge, Mass

Polanyi K. (1980), *Economie primitive, arcaiche e moderne*, Einaudi, Turin

Pryor F. (1973), *Property and Industrial Organization in Communist and Capitalist Nations*, Indiana University Press, Bloomington

Richet X. (1989), *The Hungarian Model: Markets and Planning in a Socialist Economy*, Cambridge University Press, Cambridge

Roland G. (1990), 'Gorbachev and the Common European Home: The Convergence Debate Revived?', *Kyklos*, vol. 43, no. 3, pp. 385-409

Stigler G.J. (1974), 'Free Riders and Collective Action', *Bell Journal of Economics*, vol. 5, n. 2, pp. 359-365

Targetti F. (1992) (ed.), *Privatization in Europe. West and East Experiences*, Dartmouth, Aldershot

Taylor M. (1987), *The Possibility of Cooperation*, Cambridge University Press, Cambridge

Voszka É. (1994), 'A redisztribúció újraéledése' (The revival of redistribution), *Közgazdasági Szemle*. Vol. XLI, No. 1, pp. 1-13

Wagener H-J. (1992), 'Pragmatic and Organic Change of Socio-Economic Institutions', in B. Dallago, H. Brezinski, W. Andreff (1992), pp. 17-37

Wagener H-J. (1993) (ed.), *On the Theory and Policy of Systemic Change*, Physica-Verlag, Heidelberg

Wagener H-J. (1994a) (ed.), *The Political Economy of Transformation*, Physica-Verlag, Heidelberg

Wagener H-J. (1994b), 'What Type of Capitalism is Produced by Privatization?', paper presented at the Fourth Trento Workshop of the European Association for Comparative Economic Studies on *Centralization and Decentralization of Economic Institutions: Their Role in the Transformation of Economic Systems*, Trento, 28 February - 1 March

Webster L. (1992a), *Private Sector Manufacturing in Poland: A Survey of Firms*, Industry and Energy Department Working Paper, Industry Series Paper No. 66, December

Webster L. (1992b), *Private Sector Manufacturing in Hungary: A Survey of Firms*, Industry and Energy Department Working Paper, Industry Series Paper No. 67, December

Webster L. (1992c), *Private Sector Manufacturing in Czech and Slovak Federal Republic: A Survey of Firms*, Industry and Energy Department Working Paper, Industry Series Paper No. 68, December

Wiles P.J. (1977), *Economic Institutions Compared*, John Wiley and Sons, New York

Winiecki J. (1986), *Why Economic Reforms Fail in the Soviet System: A Property Rights-Based Approach*, Seminar Paper n. 374, The Institute for International Economic Studies, Stoccolma

Zamagni S. (1991), *Il rapporto tra stato e mercato e la teoria dell'intervento pubblico: un riesame critico*, Quaderni del Dipartimento di Scienze Economiche, Università degli Studi di Bologna, Bologna, No. 109

Notes

1   The research on which this paper is based has been financially sponsored by the University of Trento and the Italian Ministry for the University and Scientific Research. The Author thanks Professors Horst Brezinski (Technical University Freiberg), Robert Campbell (Indiana University) and Vittorio Valli (University of Turin) for their helpful comments and suggestions on an earlier version of this paper. However, the responsibility for remaining errors rests solely with the Author.

2   The reference of the analysis are the countries of Central and Eastern Europe, excluding the case of former East Germany, because of its too peculiar features.

3   That is, is not a pragmatic change in the Austrian sense. On this cf. Wagener, H.J. (1992).

4   On the Soviet-type system cf. Grossman, G. (1963) and Kornai, J. (1992a).

5   Indeed, in reality other players had constantly or for a shorter period a relevant role and complicated the game. One relevant example is given by republican and regional governments in the Soviet Union. For some times (e.g.

during Khruschev's period) the economy was even organized along a territorial principle. Also one should consider that during its historical existence, the basic characteristics of the Soviet-type system underwent relevant changes and a progressive differentiation among countries also took place. However, these complications will be disregarded here, because they would need a longer presentation without substantially changing the shape of the model.

6   In principle, the quantity of resources allocated to producers was a function uniquely of the planned quantitative level of the target, measured at the centrally established prices. Supposing that these were equilibrium prices, this meant that all the enterprises received the same quantity of resources per output unit. However, in reality there existed a number of priority sectors (military, energy and other heavy industry) that enjoyed priority in the allocation of resources, both at a physical level (in a shortage economy) and via prices that strongly deviated (upward) from equilibrium prices. This actually meant that enterprises in these sectors received a higher quantity of resources (also usually of better quality) per output unit than comparable enterprises in non priority sectors.

7   It should be noted that a great weakness of this system was that the government not only (weakly) established and enforced the rules of the economic game, but was actually a player. Therefore, the role of the state was not *super partes*, thus preventing the possibility to establish and enforce the rules in a way that was neutral and exogenous to the economic game. Nor any effective external 'government' of the economy existed (as now happens, e.g., for European Union members) that could impose hard rules upon national governments. As a consequence, also the role and duty of economic actors and their relation to the state was unclear. This opened the way to an enormous bargainig activity between agents and the state and within each of them, and to a ludicrous room for free riders. In turn, the establishment of neutral rules and their enforcement was strongly hampered, the assessment of the economic performance of the agents extremely difficult, if not impossibile, and planned incentives weak if not useless. The state lost the effective possibility to discriminate between efficient and inefficient agents and to foster technical progress. Finally, this made the spontaneous evolution of the economic system extremely difficult and slow, if at all. In Kornai's (1980) terminology, the adaptation of enterprises took place in the control sphere and not in the real sphere, as in a market economy.

8   A selective incentive is defined by Olson, M. (1965, p. 51) as.

> '..an incentive that operates, not indiscriminately, like the collective good, upon the group as a whole, but rather selectively toward the individuals in the group. The incentive must be 'selective' so that those who do not join the organization working for the group's interest, or in other ways contribute to the attainment of the group's interest, can be treated differently from those who do. These 'selective incentives' can be either negative or positive, in that they can either coerce by punishing those who fail to bear an allocated share of the costs of the group action, or they can be positive inducements offered to those who act in the group interest.'

Examples in Soviet-type economies were material and moral rewards, administrative punishment, full employment, lack of opportunities for work and investment outside the state and cooperative sector.

9   On technical progress in Soviet-type economies Cf. R. Amann, J.M. Cooper (1982), (1986), J.S. Berliner (1976), P. Hanson, K. Pavitt (1987).

10   By positive selective incentives I mean a selective incentive that rewards the agent to whom it is directed, provided that the agent complies with the requirement(s) of the government or any other body that has control over the selective incentive. Conversely, a negative selective incentive consists of a punishment for a given action implemented by the agent concerned. A selective incentive can also be active when its obtainment depends on a purposeful action of the agent concerned, who has to look for the best (or acceptable) way to pursue the objective of its activity. A selective incentive is said to be passive when the agent to whom it is addressed only has to obey explicit or implicit orders to enjoy the reward. The best example of an active selective incentive is profit, while free medicare is a passive one, being enough to be born in a given state to have right to it. Other selective incentives are in between: e.g. hourly wages and rents are mostly passive, piece wages and financial participation of workers in their enterprise-s profit are moderately active, competition and the menace of bankruptcy is an active and partly positive selective incentive, the menace of dismissal can be considered a moderately active negative selective incentive, taxation on inheritance a substantially negative and passive selective incentive.

11   This was historically substantial - at least for the first period of the implementation of the Soviet-type system - both upwards and downwards. It should be noted that the latter, although representing an actual menace (sometimes even to their life) for the upper echelons of the *nomenklatura*, it also opened important opportunities for those who aspired to leading positions.

12   Paternalism is defined by J. Kornai as the kind of system in which the state takes care of every aspect of the life of its citizens in an authoritarian relationship similar to that between parents and children. Under paternalism, protection and mutual dependence are mixed together. Kornai distinguishes five pure cases of paternalism. Cf. J. Kornai (1980, pp. 575-83 of the original Hungarian edition).

13   On the role of the softness of the labour market and of the substantive rights of workers in the Soviet economy, cf. D. Granick (1987).

14   The interpretation of *perestroika* as a social contract can be found in P. Hauslohner (1992). I due this observation to H. Brezinski.

15   'Voluntary exchange enhances both participants' welfare. On the other hand, a planning act p alludes to planning acts x, y, z etc. Its rationality is only secured if the activity triggered by p is reconciled with all the other imaginable consequences.' Cf. R. Dietz (1992, p. 9).

16   '..la difficoltà ultima risiede nel fatto che una teoria della cooperazione o del contratto fondata in chiave esclusivamente strategica costituisce un'illusione, dal momento che la cooperazione con gli altri può venire fondata razionalmente solo secondo il metro di misura dell'accordo contingente degli interessi e non in chiave deontica come obbligazione di principio vigente per tutti. Ma stando così le cose, l'obbligazione alla cooperazione non può venire fondata neppure mediante

accordi perché se nella teoria dei giochi si astrae in modo coerente dai presupposti di un'etica deontica dei principi, allora anche il dovere morale del rispetto dei patti dev'essere ricondotto agli interessi strategici contingenti dei soggetti che stringono l'accordo. Ciò però significa che gli individui, quando seguono la sola razionalità strategica, possono stipulare il contratto anche con 'riserva criminale', nutrendo cioè il proposito di infrangere il contratto alla prima occazione buona.' S. Zamagni (1991).

17   On these problems and for a comparison with planning in a market economy, cf. D. M. Nuti (1986).

18   Cf. G. Grossman (1977), (1979), (1981). Cf. also B. Dallago (1990). The term was first employed by K.S. Karol (1971). However, its use became widespread mainly as a result of the work of G. Grossman, who also made a fundamental contribution to study of the subject.

19   These give rise to informal property rights:.

> 'By informal property rights we mean legally unsanctioned and even illegal, yet in reality effective, control over assets for private profit or other form of access to future streams of informal/illegal income and consequent wealth.'

(G. Grossman, 1987, p. 2.4.). See also ECE (1992).

20   The analysis conducted by G. Grossman is particularly sharp on this point:.

> '...the second economy and its concomitants create powerful vested interests, which in turn may exert substantial conservative influence on social policy and change, especially in periods of officially sponsored reforms. While not the same as the vested interests deriving from the official (formal, legal) positions, rights, privileges, and property holdings of individuals and groups, the two are mutually related and reinforcing.'

(G. Grossman, 1987, p. 2.2.).

21   'The larger a group is, the farther it will fall short of providing an optimal supply of any collective good, and the less likely that it will act to obtain even a minimal amount of such a good. In short, the larger the group, the less likely it will further its common interests.'

M. Olson (1965), p. 36.

22   'Since relatively small groups will frequently be able voluntarily to organize and act in support of their common interests, and since large groups normally will not be able to do so, the outcome of the political struggle among the various groups in society will not be symmetrical.. The privileged and intermediate groups often triumph over the numerically superior forces in the latent or large groups because the former are generally organized and active while the latter are normally unorganized and inactive.'

(M. Olson, 1965, pp. 127-8). See also G. S. Becker (1983), pp. 385-386. A latent group

> '...is distinguished by the fact that, if one member does or does not help provide the collective good, no other one member will be significantly affected and therefore none has any reason to react. Thus an individual in

a 'latent' group, by definition, cannot make a noticeable contribution to any group effort, and since no one in the group will react if he makes no contribution, he has no incentive to contribute. Accordingly, large or 'latent' groups have no incentive to act in order to obtain a collective good because, however valuable the collective good might be to the group as a whole, it does not offer the individual any incentive to pay dues to any organization working in the latent group's interest, or to bear in any other way any of the costs of the necessary collective action.'
(M. Olson, 1965, pp. 50-1).

23   Following this reasoning in the case of individuals within organizations, March and Simon (1958) arrive to represent formally a routine as a program and model procedural rationality. See also M. Egidi (1994).

24   R.R. Nelson, S.G. Winter (1982), p. 14.

25   By 'environment' I mean all the factors exogenous to the economic system, apart from economic policies, which influence the results achieved by the economy. The most important components of the environment are: resources, i.e. the features of the natural environment and the endowment of productive factors possessed by the economy at the beginning of the period considered; the level of economic development; the preferences and behaviours of microeconomic agents; factors external to the economic system such as the behaviour of other systems and countries and relationships with them; the dominant or official ideology, ethics, politics, the legal system and religion; the consequences of fortuitous and unpredictable events like natural disasters, wars, strikes. Cf. B. Dallago (1993a), pp. 144-5.

26   'However, in functioning complex systems with many highly differentiated and tightly interdependent parts, it is highly unlikely that undirected change in a single part will have beneficial effects on the system; this, of course, is the basis for the biological proposition that mutations tend to be deleterious on the average.. It is not surprising, therefore, that the control processes of (surviving) organizations tend to resist mutations, even ones that present themselves as desirable innovations.'
R.R. Nelson, S.G. Winter (1982), p. 116. Cf. also G. Roland (1990).

27   For a description of these economic reforms cf. for example J. Adam (1989), B. Chavance (1992), J. Kornai (1992a).

28   W. Brus (1964) gives a good description of the original spirit of the reforms.

29   It is important to note that the central planning office had its own operational and sectorial organs, and a transfer of functions and power took place among these as well.

30   The only, and important, exception was economic reform in Hungary. Introduced in 1968, this reform had long-term beneficial effects on the Hungarian economy, although it failed to overcome the limits intrinsic to the Soviet-type economic system. Cf. J. Kornai (1986), Richet (1989).

31   In some cases - Hungary for example - the introduction of limited unemployment was mooted in order to stimulate and to discipline workers. The

proposal was rapidly abandoned following protests by the trade unions and opposition by the party in power.

32   On the motivations of managers and on work relationships in enterprises cf. B. Grancelli (1988), J. Kornai (1992a).

33   The partial exception of the Hungarian reform can be explained by the political consequences of 1956. The events of that year forced the government, and in particular the party in power, to introduce substantial changes (e.g. the abolition of obligatory stockpiling in agriculture) already in 1957, to act decisively in favour of change, and to introduce selective incentives that were more effective than those of other countries. Besides the dominating reformer attitude of the government, the early start granted ample possibilities to test the changes introduced and modify them whenever necessary.

34   This interpretation is obviously less valid for the ex-Soviet Union. Here endogenous factors were of much greater significance in explaining events: particularly relevant were, for instance, interethnic conflicts and conflicts between central and regional/republican governments. Among exogenous factors the extremely high cost of military competition with the United States and the support provided to certain ally countries were of major importance.

35   In the following I summarize B. Dallago (1992a).

36   Cf. A. Breton (1989).

37   In this case, one must obviously consider the complementarity and incompatibility among objectives. It may happen that greater efficiency and effectiveness in accomplishing one or a few objectives will prove illusory in the long period from the point of view of the system's stability. Consider, for example the cost that the privileges guaranteed to workers imposed on the Soviet system in terms of efficiency, in the absence of effective selective incentives capable to foster labour effort.

38   As a matter of fact, these factors were considered to be relevant in the supposed convergence of the two systems. However, the traditional approach to convergence did not carefully consider that a change in goals can also have disruptive consequences on the economic system. On the convergence hypothesis cf. B. Dallago, H. Brezinski, W. Andreff (1992).

39   Cf. B. Dallago (1994a), G. Grossman (1987).

40   For a general introduction to transition cf. for example L. Csaba (1991), EE (1991), J. Kornai (1993a), P. Marer, S. Zecchini (1991).

41   On the ways in which an economic system can be transformed cf. H-J. Wagener (1993), (1994a), (1994b). Obviously, this is not to say that a pragmatic-constructivist change is a rapid change. The rapidity of the change, in fact, depends not only on the will of the agents, but also on other factors, there comprised the resilience of old institutions.

42   I disregard here the state because it is supposed to assume a purely normative role and therefore it should not be considered an actor. In reality, however, the situation is quite different. On the role of the state during transition see D.M. Nuti (1994).

43   A substantial number of them were able to jump to the winners' group becoming private owners through privileged privatization solutions (the so-called *nomenklatura privatization*) or entering the group of politicians.

44   See J. Kornai (1992b).

45   Definitions of 'economic system' vary among authors according to their theoretical approach. For G. Grossman (1967, p. 12 of the Italian edition) an economic system is the set of institutions which the social economy employs to achieve its purposes. For R. Eidem and S. Viotti (1978, p. 13) an economic system may be defined in broad outline as a network of institutions and agreements aimed at the utilization of scarce resources. Again, P. R. Gregory and R. C. Stuart (1980, p. 12) define an economic system as a set of mechanisms and institutions which take and implement decisions regarding production, income and consumption within a given geographical area. F. Pryor (1972, p. 337) asserts that an economic system includes all the institutions, organizations, laws and rules, traditions, beliefs, attitudes, values, taboos, and the patterns of behaviour that derive from them, which directly or indirectly influence economic behaviour and its results.

46   By norms is meant the social and technical relationships (parameters) whose quantitative and qualitative values are fixed - either exactly or approximately - by tradition, by habit, by the government, by freely arrived-at contracts among the social partners, by supranational and international bodies, by technology, and by the structure of industry. They may concern, for example, working hours, the method for calculating prices, the tolerated level of pollution, the forms and means of payment, the permitted forms and instruments of competition, and so forth.

47   Cf. in particular G. Grossman (1969), G. Hodgson (1988), and also K. Polanyi (1980). For a comparative study of economic institutions see P. J. O. Wiles (1977).

48   For comparative analysis of privatization in the course of transition, see B. Dallago (1992b), B. Dallago, G. Ajani, B. Grancelli (1992), ECE 81992), (1993), J. Kornai (1992c), F. Targetti (1992).

49   On the actual situation see J. Kornai (1993b).

50   On the concepts of budget constraint, economy limited by resources and by demand, and economy of shortage and unemployment, see J. Kornai (1980).

51   Norman Barry (1993, pp. 11-12) defines the social market economy.

'...in two aspects. First, it must be seen as a normative account of an economic 'constitution', i.e., a system of social relationships that describes not merely the private property, free exchange system, but also those moral, legal, and political rules without which it is not sustainable...'

Second, the doctrine must be seen as the set of welfare and redistributive measures that happened to emerge in the later development of the West German economy.

52   Cf. for instance A. Aslund (1990), D. Lipton, J. Sachs (1990).

53   On the concept of critical mass in collective action see G. Marwell, P. Oliver (1993).

54   Cf., among others, J. Kornai (1990), P. Murrell (1990).

55   On this very important aspect of transition, especially in Russia and other post-Soviet states see M.J. Bradshaw, P. Hanson (1994).

56   Cf. M. Taylor (1987), p. XI.

57   There are two versions of the notion of path-dependency on past development, one deterministic the other stochastic. The first asserts that convergence between two economic systems which start from two different initial systems towards the better system may be blocked in certain directions and encouraged in others. In the stochastic version, specific and unforeseen events occurring during the process of change may have an enduring influence on it.

58   If the former system is defended by a minority (for example, by agents of the state), a compensation policy can be introduced which induces them to accept the change. This could result in a higher Pareto optimum. However, it is obvious that this solution would be optimal before the change occurs. Once the minority has lost its power, the optimal solution is to cut off the compensation. Expecting this kind of behaviour to occur, the minority may rationally prefer the existing situation, unless a well defined contract is agreed on by the parties involved (e.g. during 'round table' meetings) and enforced by an independent authority (e.g. the Church). Cf. T. Eggertsson (1990), G. Roland (1990), J. Winiecki (1986).

59   See É. Voszka (1994).

60   See, for example, R. Axelrod (1984), M. Bacharach (1977), J. Elster (1985), M. Olson (1965), G. J. Stigler (1974). This situation can be described in terms of the prisoner's dilemma. Although all those concerned want collective action to take place, individually they prefer to abstain from it. Change normally entails conflict, and this incurs private costs, while the benefits of collective action are public goods. Consequently, individuals who do not cooperate can enjoy a free benefit, which is greater the larger the group in which the change occurs. This is the well known problem of the free-rider. These forms of behaviour and their effects are reinforced by the behaviour of the political parties that give rise to an electoral cycle and by the underground economy. Collective action, as a consequence, may not take place.

61   It is interesting to note that a World Bank survey of private manufacturing firms carried out between May 1991 and January 1992 in Central Europe (Poland, Czechoslovakia, Hungary) found that the large majority of the new private entrepreneurs were managers of state owned enterprises before transition started. Another substantial part came from people who held leading positions in the government prior to transition. Cf. L. Webster (1992a), (1992b), (1992c).

62   Cf. R. Axelrod (1984). Axelrod's contribution considers the case of games which are repeated an infinite (or very great) number of times. In such a situation, it turns out that strategies that are cooperative since the beginning lead to greater payoffs in the long run than opportunistic, uncooperative strategies. However, in actual terms the basic question is why and how a cooperative solution should take place. Although in principle this can develop spontaneously among rational or socially educated individuals or organizations, in actual terms such a spontaneous development is made difficult by the threat of free riders taking a short term advantage from an opportunistic, non cooperative attitude. It appears that a cooperative solution in a repetitive game can only be the result of an explicit agreement among the individuals and organizations involved - delegating to some external body selective incentives to control free riding - or, more easily, can result from public intervention.

63   This lack of cooperation between the two coalitions explains why the winners are ready to implement 'experiments' and 'recipes' (often coming from abroad): social activity (transition) is not driven by the pursuit of compromises, but by 'pure', 'supreme', 'just', 'rational', etc., goals (in a 'pure', etc. way).

64   For a review of the literature cf. B. Dallago (1994b).

65   It should be noted that, in order to be effective, Western assistance has to take into consideration the specific set of institutions of individual Central and Eastern European countries and formulate on this basis specific assistance policies overcoming egoistic short-run domestic considerations. A strategic component of such policies should be a more generous opening of Western markets to Eastern products.

17 Japan from isolation to the position of world economic power

István Kiglics

1. Introduction

I have been in Japan several times, spending there a few years on research. The image I got first about the country has gradually changed, deepening, reflecting the accumulated knowledge gained during the passing years. Nevertheless a part of my first impressions have remained almost unchanged. The pieces of information I collected later on could only refine them. These impressions can be characterized with such words as *isolation, openness, faith, unfaithfulness* or one might say *betrayal.*

What do these words mean?

Let me interpret them with the following examples. As for the *isolation* or the *closed door policies:* Since about the beginning of the 80s Japan has had to cope with a growing trade surplus. In order to avoid a trade war with her partners of international community (USA, EC) she had to control export with 'voluntary restrictions'. Meanwhile the same partners are complaining about the closed doors and the impenetrable Japanese market conditions, whereas the Japanese companies are taking over a bigger and bigger market share in almost every corner of the world, coming to a dominating position in several fields of commodities (consumer electronics, cars, etc.) as well as on the capital market.

This conspicuous contradictory situation is pushing the Japanese officials always into defensive position. Ten years ago, in 1984, during my first stay in Japan, a government official in the Economic Planning Agency (EPA) tried to describe the speciality of Japanese economic management taking it in contrast with the Hungarian one under communist regime at that time. According to his opinion, unlike the Hungarian economy, the Japanese economy is a perfectly free, market economy, based on private ownership, to which the government has no access to control.

To shed light on this statement I would like to quote an article found in The Times two months ago[1]. According to it the Japanese government disclosed a liberalization program by which: 'A total of 10,942 regulations concerning distribution, welfare and financial structures, will be reviewed with at least 1,000 targeted for abolition.' In another part of the same article a MITI official was quoted as saying: 'Manufacturing companies are being told that ... they should no longer rely on being supported by government'.

From these characteristic examples it is obvious that the way the Japanese behave towards the rest of the world is a peculiar mixture of the closed doors toward others, i.e. not to let them enter into their domestic market, they favour their own country and penetrate any market wherever they can.

Turning onto *faith*[2]: in January 1972, 28 years after World War II, a Japanese soldier was found in the jungle of Guam hiding in a cave[3]. As he had not heard about any surrender, he considered himself as a member of the Imperial Army, and it was difficult to persuade him to return home. Even today you may find that a similar phenomenon in today's society is not an exceptional one. One working for a company may feel obliged to be faithful to it not only in work but as a consumer as well. Not only him, but his wider family also will support the company involved by purchasing its product.

Europe, dominated by Christian culture, would feel puzzled to perceive the Japanese behaviour toward religion. According to a survey of the Ministry of Education conducted in 1985[4]: among the 120 million inhabitants, 112 million declared themselves Shintoists (the aboriginal religion of Japan), 89 million Buddhists, and about 16 million belonged to other religions. Summing up these figures we will get a figure which is about twice as big as the number of the whole population. Knowing this, one would not be surprised to learn that most Japanese are usually born to be Shintoists, marry also by Shintoist rites, parallel with Christian procedures as well, and finish their life as Buddhists. Similarly, this sequence of religion can be observed within the same year and within the same person. Moreover, according to the same survey, the Japanese did not find this fickle, volatile habit to be strange.

These are contradicting behaviours. Faith and disciplined responsibility is on the side of - as they say - *one's own circle* (means family, company, country, emperor), and the reverse, a sort of freedom in action and obeyance toward *the outer circle* which may have some sort of controlling, directing or just very influential by its power[5] (can be of religions, Gods, economy or another civilisation). It might create a machinery, firm on achievement of *its own goal* and very much adaptive in *absorbing outer effects* at the same time.

2. Achievements and environment

These characteristics might be only mosaics on the surface of a nation's culture. However the achievements should make us think twice of those mosaics. The country, which at the time of the collapse of *shogunate*[6] was still on the technological level of a medieval country, within 125 years has succeeded not only in catching up with the developed countries at a dazzling speed, but in some fields has set the pace for further development.

Between the second half of the 19th century and World War II, Japan's average real growth rate in terms of GNP had been 4 per cent/year; from 1946 to 1970 it was practically between 9-12 per cent/year. After the oil crisis the Japanese growth rate gradually slowed down, but it was almost always higher than that of any other industrialized (even not industrialized) country except for some NICs after the second half of the 70s. As a result, Japan's share in world production in terms of GNP increased[7] from 3 per cent in 1960 to 10 per cent in 1980, while in the same period the USA dropped back from 33 per cent to 22 per cent, and the rest of the OECD countries climbed from 26 per cent to 31 per cent.

Table 17.1
Growth rate comparison

Real GDP growth rate (5-years average, %)		Real GDP growth rate/year (%)		
		Country	1975-79	1980-84
1960-65	10.0	Japan	4.7	3.9
1966-70	12.0	USA	3.2	1.8
1971-75	4.7	W.Germany	2.8	1.0
1976-80	5.1	U.K.	1.8	0.7
1981-85	3.9	S.Korea	9.9	5.3
		Taiwan	10.0	6.7

Source: Japan 1991 An international comparison

This long lasting, exceptionally high growth should require some sort of explanation to the driving force and energy source behind it. The way Japan completed this achievement might also provide some lessons worthwhile to our attention.

The energy resources cannot be of foreign origin. After the long period of isolation, Japan was forced to open her doors under unfavourable[8] treaty conditions dictated by foreign countries which Japan could get rid of only after a considerable period. The poor natural resources and lack of arable land[9] could not help either. The only available resource was the abundant and persistently growing human force, and its challenging accumulated ability: *culture*[10].

Japan produced this growth as a capitalist country but there was no other capitalist country to produce such an achievement. Therefore we have reason to believe that in achieving this success Japan should use *other (recognisable) social energy resources* besides the one the capitalism could contribute with.

Japan followed a typical 'catching up strategy'. During the Meiji reforms, when Japan opened up for the rest of the world, her culture, civilization was quite remote in many ways. People had to cope not only with the technological gap, but also with the overwhelming civilization gap in order to survive the colonization attempts and join into a strange world. Japan was so successful in fulfilling that historical task that nowadays the developed economies have to follow the pace set by their diligent ex-pupil.

3. Isolation and its outcome

The main reason why the 'black ships'[11] could force a whole country to abandon the isolationist policies is the technical backwardness. This fact should not lead us to the conclusion that the country had to embark upon a modernization program with an all-out underdeveloped environment. The rigid isolation policy was less unfortunate than it might be thought. There were some merits gained out of it. The isolation itself could not be kept for about 250 years defying everything inside and outside the country without a refined, well organized information and controlling machinery. The traditions of it are still living and working in some sense of the word.

The country was obliged to exploit its own resources, spiritual - reflected in arts - as well as material. The severe natural environment, the extremely limited import possibilities (caused by isolation) forced the country to cope with the problem of food supply on her own. The outcome was positive to a certain extent: on the one hand, there was a vivid flow of goods, even with some element of commodity exchange market, even an increase of population, while on the other hand, a unique culture resembling in some element other, mainly Eastern cultures, but as a whole exceptional (in terms of effective use of inner energy resources).

When coming to power the founding *Shogun*[12] secured the social position for his servants, i.e. *samurais* by upgrading them to the leading caste of the society, furnishing it with privileges. At the same time he morally obliged them to learn, creating in this way a new class which could become the leading force of the country intellectually as well.

For the inferior castes like merchants, he also established schools to learn at least the basic knowledge essential for them, i.e. reading, writing, and the basic calculation methods and supplied them with standardized teaching manuals all-over the country. These schools were linked with Buddhist temples (*teracoyas*).

In this way a considerable literate population had been created (to compare it with the peculiar writing system and the conditions of contemporary Europe one can evaluate it as an achievement). What is more important:

- this emerging merchant class could become the driving force of the economic (and cultural) development,
- there was created a businessman basis which abandoned land cultivation specializing in the role of a go-between across the society and accumulating considerable fortune by supplying the growing number of town population[13]. Practically this was also the origin of the internationally well known corporation empires of our time[14].

The Buddhist temples were functioning not only as educational institutes, but as administrative organs and ideological bases as well. Each family (and its members) had to be registered there (*kokuseki*[15]), by which the *Shoguns* were able to control not only the population, but also the tax collection.

After the long lasting civil wars in the previous centuries, the *Tokugawa Shogunate* established rigid control over the country and every person available, all the armaments[16] were confiscated regardless of the owner's social status (great nobles, peasants or artisans)[17]. This police state fixed the hierarchy more rigidly than in any neighbouring country[18], a tradition which can be identified as a speciality of Japanese society and person-to-person relationship even today. This strictly centralized and firmly ruled, controlled environment, its continuous refinement and its drill for centuries *created a well disciplined society*, ready to accomplish anything charged with, or imposed upon it.

The country and its society melted together and were standardized under conditions which were pretty different from the ideas of Franklin's constitution or Rousseau's France, from the enlightenment. Inside, it was *well organized* and in comparison to the contemporary Europe *well educated* (in the sense of mass education) *eager to absorb* anything to break out of her obstacles and take it as an additional chance, even fuel for further advance.

4. The way of catching up

The catching up phase began with a unique imperial power transfer which made it possible to replace the obsolete *shogunate* with the ambitious imperial system without causing a substantial shock to the country. Formally the emperor was always in a reigning position[19]. Therefore the new structure did not bring anything new at the top. Furthermore, the emperor got back into power with some help from foreigners, so he could remain in controlling position for the sake of his country. Therefore he and his country could avoid being overtaken by colonization attempts. by the abolition of the rigid *shogunate* control. With the encouragement of the emperor, the elevator had been opened up for the ambitious personalities of the new era, toward the new social and economic positions.

The war-lords and their followers[20] formally lost their earlier privileged status (with the abolition of castes), but got in turn another one. The emperor managed to find them demanding jobs to serve for the sake of all, to fulfil the role of saviour of their country. As they were not only soldiers, but, as we mentioned before, they represented the intellectuals as well, they could ascend to the leading positions of the new establishment. They became the rank and file, the leaders of the new bureaucracy, and the new entrepreneurs of industries besides the merchants.

To eliminate economic backwardness the emperor also established the basic institutions of the western type economy (banks, government offices, etc.), spent large sums of money on industrialization, the establishment of factories, then privatized them after their stabilization. New western type educational institutes had been set up and the best selection of professors, engineers available were invited. At the same time a number of capable and promising people were sent to different countries (Europe and the USA) to the best educational institutes and industrial laboratories to study there for years (a method still extensively practised throughout the country). After returning back they became the leaders of universities, industrial organizations and the administration as well. The new leaders introduced the European type legal system, elaborated the first European type Constitution.

In spite of the enormous changes, Japan had not been forced to give up her identity, such attempts were always rejected either formally or informally[21]. The changes were controlled by themselves and not by outsiders. Japan could manage this position even after the World War II during the American occupation.

To stick to this hard line paid well. The country leaders could always set the pace for changes and decide the selection and form of things to be introduced into the traditions of the Japanese society and economy. They determined the elements of foreign institutional, legal, industrial system, which best fitted the environment, or was most suitable to serve the goals and ambitions of the country. Of course, there are examples after World War II that show that certain things were imposed on Japan[22]. Although there were some changes due to this, Japanese behaviour has not changed much for 44 years. Japan has not become an American type state of the rule of law. The legal cases in USA usually end up in court, in Japan they are still settled traditionally outside it[23].

5. Catching up stages and today's status

It is not an all-round success story. However it has messages to analyze and take. All the 3 stages began with a sort of institutional and legal reform following certain models. The real driving force and its strategic goal was however something different: the security of the country, the preservation of sovereignty at any expense. It was in a rush to build up a military state[24]. After giving it a trial and getting some confidence it had exceeded the original goal. Afraid of foreign colonization attempts and making its utmost effort to avoid it, the country turned out to be a diligent follower of her masters, seizing territories in neighbouring countries and establishing her own colonies there. Japan ended up in a bloody war with a dramatic defeat in the end.

The surrender and its consequence, the occupation by aliens was an almost unbearable shock for the country. From another point of view this produced a sort of breakthrough, openness and further energy resources and a sort of driving force.

In a country which was very keen on defending its interests, its sovereignty even at the expense of cutting itself off from the rest of the world, when it was needed, in a country which never experienced such an incident in its entire history, in a country exhausted from the bloody war, most people came to realise the deadlock of the course they got on.

Therefore the people were ready for some sort of changes in military affairs, the political system, ownership structure, etc. Although there were a number of changes, they did not very profoundly influence the underlying factors of the society. Their *spirit of Her remained uninjured*, on the contrary: *rather stimulated*. The core of changes is to be found *in the instrument* of completing the original strategy: to become a strong country, but with a switch from the military to the economy. *The goal did not change*: The country in fact became more reinforced and convinced of the importance of defending its interests.

For that reason the *'kyohei'* was dropped, the right war was denounced[25], but the *'fukoku'* remained. The country made every effort to come out from the trap, using all resources, concentrating them for the same purpose: to build a strong and successful economy. On the way to implementing it, the leaders did not release the grip on society either in the political or economical sense[26].

Every available financial resource was collected from the people and channelled effectively toward production and to services backing up and fuelling the need for production i.e. productive infrastructure.

The healthy spirit and the heavy concentration on the economy yielded an outstanding growth, an 'economic miracle' meanwhile it left the society and welfare affairs far behind. The gap between the domestic social infrastructure and the one existing in the advanced countries (in terms of industrial development) created a potential tension. It could not come to the surface. The reason is probably hidden behind other aspects of isolationism. While the economic entities were set free to move on the world market and were even supported in various ways by the government, the freedom of movement for the citizens was very much limited.

The exchange rate was in favour of company profit making[27], setting the price level high on the domestic market[28]. While the working conditions were favourable in terms of lifetime employment, they were rather suppressed in terms of income level.

The weekend leisure time (not to mention the longer holidays) is very limited even now. The employees cannot leave work for more than 3-5 days. The Japanese work the most and have the least leisure time yearly in comparison to other industrialized countries. In terms of the whole population, the percentage of Japanese who travelled to foreign countries amounted to 3.9 per cent in 1980, and 9.7 per cent in 1989, while foreigners coming to Japan in the corresponding years rose to 1.3 per cent, and 3.0 per cent[29]. It is obvious that most of the population have no personal experience or contact with the rest of the world[30].

However the expansion of the Japanese capital and commodity export increases the number of employees obliged to work and study abroad. These people come into close contact with other cultures, working and living conditions. Their influence gradually appears in the Japanese society and business circles as well.

The amendments of laws, the slow erosion of traditional practices in political life (a shift in the behaviour of the people in the election and its outcome in results, the growing demand for reforms), the liberalization attempts, and growing demand from inside and outside the country, shows that something is changing in the society as well. *Japan is approaching the third stage of her catching up process*, which might be the *social stage* toward the *welfare state*.

6. Closing remarks

The achievement Japan can show after 125 years of fierce struggle is exceptional. Even more remarkable is the development after World War II, often quoted as 'the economic miracle'. This success inspired a number of researchers to try and find the secret driving force behind it. However, the most convincing is that Japan is not only attracting researchers from the leading industrial countries, but also has successful followers among NICs.

Both the explanation of the EPA official, and the arguments being widely heard in Eastern Europe concerning the transformation period and its problems would bring me the same message: the cold war had significant effect on the people's mind on both sides, which does not help us to find the real explanations. To have a clear view we need a bit greater distance in time.

After experiencing the fall of the Berlin Wall, a symbolic termination of a failed catching up experiment[31] and parallel with it a successful one (i.e. Japan), one should come up with some conclusions. These are not the sort of statements popularly expressed by certain circles, as say 'the winner is capitalism and the loser is defeated communism'. Thinking over the Japanese example, I would rather tend to think about something else: *we do not know who the real winner is*. Fierce and short-sighted political confrontation does not help, even misleading us in finding the real driving forces behind economic development.

What innovative points could the Japanese model show us about the core elements of extraordinary economic success, of producing a performance enabling them to override her own obstacles to leaving behind her previous teachers?

Perhaps it suggests to us that the catching up process is manifold, having legal, economic, social, etc. aspects, and in spite of the enormous difficulties it is manageable with a proper strategy. These phases can develop parallel during the process, and can be run at different speeds, with certain priorities and sequences. From another point of view, it certainly indicates gradualism, taking into consideration the limits of resources and determining some priority in different fields.

Japan is not only an example for successful catching up, but is also - as it has always been - the 'commander in chief' regarding the control of advance in the society and economy, a good example for adaptation to a different environment with the preservation of one's own cultural values.

Bibliography

Clayton, D.J. (1975), *The years of McArthur*, Houghton Mifflin Co., Boston
Goedertier, J.M., *Japan, a historical and biographical dictionary*, Tokyo Printing Ltd., Himeji
Kiglics, I (1989), *Japán: Múlt a holnapban*, Pszichoteam, Budapest
Kiglics, I. (1992), *Nihon to Hangari no mineika ni tsuite* Fukuoka Unesco Association, Fukuoka
Kiglics, I (1986), 'Hivatalnok a japán kormányintézményekben', *Tervgazdasági Fórum* 1986/4
Japan Almanac 1975, The Mainichi Newspapers, Tokyo
Japan: An international comparison; Keizai Koho Center Tokyo 1986, 1991
Nakamura, T. (1983), *Economic growth in the prewar Japan*, Yale University Press
Nakamura, T. (1981), *The postwar Japanese Economy*, University of Tokyo Press
Tonomura, T. (1986), 'Bipolarity in Japanese Religious Feelings', *Japan Quarterly* 1986 Apr.-Jun
Reischauer, E.O. (1977), *The Japanese*, C.E. Tuttle Company, Tokyo

Notes

1   Japan's economy needs a bitter pill to cure 'foreign disease' (The Times, 1 December 1993)
2   I would rather prefer to use the word 'faith' instead of the usual 'loyalty' mainly to counterpoint it with 'fickleness, volatility' behaviour of Japanese people toward multiple outside factors one can belong to or depend upon.
3   Japan Almanac 1975 (The Mainichi Newspapers, Tokyo).
4   Tonomura, T. (1986) Bipolarity in Japanese Religious Feelings (Japan Quarterly 1986 April - June).
5   One of the most frequently used Japanese expression is: 'shikata ga nai' means 'there is nothing to do against it'. Can be heard in any situation: order given by of one's superior, accident, government actions, etc.
6   *Officially*: from 1868 when the last *Shogun* resigned, *practically* from 1853, when U.S. Commodore Perry broke through the long lasting isolation of

Japan with his 'black ships'. Soon after in 1854 the first U.S. - Japan trade treaty was signed.

7   Ex-Soviet Union came down to 15 per cent - 13 per cent, rest of Eastern Europe 4 per cent - 5 per cent, China 5 per cent - 4 per cent accordingly. (Japan: An international comparison; Keizai Koho Center Tokyo 1986, 1991)

8   Withdrawing rather than supplying resources.

9   The tiny, hilly country has only 15 per cent arable land of her total territory, which is even further limited by the population with among the highest density in the world. Limited energy resources exhausted soon gave impulse to colonization attempts toward neighbouring countries.

10   In this case I consider the expression: 'culture' in the wider content of the word, including not only arts, but also industrial, legal, social, etc. aspects of it.

11   Commodore Perry's frightening warships, as it is usually quoted in Japan.

12   The *Shogunate* dates back to around the 12th century, but we consider only the last period of it (1601-1867), as it was an epoch - making system. It has a remarkable effect from various points of view on the today's Japanese society. It was founded by Tokugawa Ieyasu, so the name of this time can also be identified as *Tokugawa* period, or *Edo* period (named after his headquarters).

13   The existence of this population created a new consumer for cultural goods, generating a market, giving incentive to further development in this area. Thanks to this environment the Kabuki theater arose, the popular version of woodblock printing (Hokusai, Hiroshige and their followers), which stimulated even the impressionism later in the 19th century. Means: a lot of things the Westerners identify today as typical Japanese.

14   These are the Sumitomo, Mitsui, Mitsubishi.

15   Inheriting to our time a unique population statistics for hundreds of years back.

16   Which stimulated the development of a new fighting technique, using only one's own body (*karate* = empty hands).

17   Only the *samurai* class was authorised to have weapons also under strict control. Some of the famous stories of this period arose from this situation. (The story of 47 masterless *samurai* [→*ronin;* see note 20].)

18   China and Korea also had such cultural traditions, but had never been so much untouched by foreign influence as Japan.

19   The Emperor reigned over the *Shogun* and formally even nominated the victorious one emerging from inner fighting, meanwhile he was always in inner exile remote from the power centre. The power was always in the hands of *Shoguns* who in turn never questioned the throne.

20   With *Samurais*: warriors, the leading caste and backbone of the *shogunate*, obliged with absolute loyalty toward their master, even at the expense of their life. In return they were furnished with outstanding privileges over the society. The masterless *samurais* are almost in outcasting position. They are the *ronins*.

21   Although the emperor in the last century introduced the western type footwear and clothing for the business world, everything out of it remained traditional. The Japanese people prefer to use at home and in their 'intimate sphere' (means private, personal, family, etc.) the *geta* and *yukata* the traditional

version of what they had to wear outdoors. They feel relaxed to change into it at home, for that reason, these things are standard elements of service in hotels as well. The public bath is not exceptional, but if one has a private bathroom it is equipped and used in the Japanese way.

22   The Constitution amendment is a typical example of that. It was (at least it is a frequently cited argument in Japan) mainly translated from the American one and forced through by the occupational army headquarters. On the other hand, it is said, that they 'refined' it during the translation, and what is more remarkable, was seldom used at least soon after it come into force. Nowadays it is sometimes applied, but far more seldom, than in the USA or in Europe.

23   Two disasters, two cultures, two remedies (US News & World Report 26. August 1985)

24   The widely propagated slogan of that time was *'fukoku kyohei'*, means 'rich country, strong army'. It can be interpreted in many ways, but evaluating it now, the ultimate goal was rather the 'strong army' than rich country.

25   It is included in the Constitution. Although in the last 10 years there has been some sort of changes in this field as well, I would not expect it to turn back to the position before World War II.

26   The conservative leadership in politics continuously remained in power after the war (as they were before the war) having linked tightly to business circles, and it dropped out government positioning only in 1993 for the first time, but still is in a very influential position. Meanwhile in the economy: the big family conglomerates, the *'zaibatsus'* were dissolved by the occupation forces, but they regenerated soon after the end of the occupation in a slightly different shape. At the same time a unique economic organization structure was created with the *'keiretsu'* as a substantial element. The big firms could manage tight control over the entire economy.

27   The exchange rate against the USD in 1970 was 360 JPY/USD, in 1993 was 106 JPY/USD. The first change occurred after the 'Nixon shock' in 1972, but the breakthrough, the substantial change came in the second half of the 80s, when it came down from 240 JPY/USD, making foreign travel available for the wider public (at least in terms of money).

28   For certain commodities, articles (rice, meat, beef, etc.) multiple times higher than abroad. But sometimes it is the same for electronics as well, even if it is made in Japan, not to mention goods manufactured abroad.

29   In comparison: data for Hungary at the corresponding time, behind the 'iron curtain': in 1985 about 56 per cent of the Hungarians travelled abroad, and in 1989 more than 140 per cent of the population did the same. However the percentage of foreigners visiting Hungary was about 140 per cent in 1985, and 250 per cent in 1989.

30   The telecommunication and movie can not be regarded as complementary.

31   Note that: Socialism in its ambitions has also a manifold character in politics, society and economics as well. One feature was obviously a sort of catching up attempt. As, Kruschev's long term plan in the 60s to overcome the capitalist countries by the 80s, or for example the Chinese Mao's 'Big Jump' including, - attempt which both have the same aspirations.

18 Attempts at closing up by long range regulators in the Carpathian Basin

Miklós Banai and Béla Lukács

Abstract

At the end of the migration period the Carpathian Basin (and the whole region of Eastern Central Europe) did not belong to the Western civilization, but was the Westernmost part of the steppe cultures. However, the state of the Carpathian Basin accepted (Western) Christianity in 1000, and started to introduce laws to conform to Western standards. Then started a close-up process by long-range regulators. This process is followed in the present paper.

1. Introduction

Prof. J. Kovács has introduced the concept of long range regulators as the governors of the social-economic processes of the different societies in different civilization periods (Kovács, J. 1990). He identifies five long-range regulators in the modern age. These are:

1.   Public sector, the ratio of the public to private sectors.
2.   The system of education.
3.   The system of research and developement.
4.   Technical development, innovation.
5.   The system of planning based on forecasting.

In the following paper we try to formulate the close-up strategies in a region of Europe, called Eastern-Central Europe, in terms of long range regulators. As for the results, some characteristics of societies will be discussed; from ca. 1850 including quantitative data (employment, production, GDP/capita, etc.). The data are taken mainly from the bibliography (Berend, T.I. and Szuhay, M. 1973; Ciepelewski, J. et al. 1974; Ocherki..., 1960) and also from handbooks not referred to. For a more detailed quantitative review, see our former paper. (Banai, M, Kovács, J. and Lukács, B. 1993)

In summary our main theses are as follows. In our approach we separate two *historical* long range regulators. These are:

I.   The legal system of the civilization.
II.   The culture of the civilization.

The five long range regulators of modern age listed above had evolved from these historical long range regulators. The long range regulator 1 follows from the historical long range regulator I, and regulators 2, 3, and 4 had evolved from the historical long range regulator II, while the long range regulator 5 has evolved from both as a superposition.

By the study of the history of the different civilizations one can say that the two regulators I and II determine the evolution of a civilization. Roughly speaking the legal system of a civilization determines the 'kinematics' of that civilization, while the culture of that civilization determines the 'dynamics' of that civilization.

In the second chapter of this paper we show that in the last one and a half thousand years one can observe three distinct civilizations that existed up to World War II in Europe. These are as follows:

-       the civilization of West Europe evolved from the unification of Roman law and German private land ownership in a culture dominated by Roman Catholicism;
-       the civilization of East Europe evolved from the unification of Byzantine law and Slav village community land ownership in a culture dominated by the Greek orthodox Catholicism;
-       the civilization of East Central Europe: in this civilization the culture was dominated by the Roman Catholicism and the legal system is also based on the Roman law but it lacked both the German private land ownership and the Slav village community land ownership.

The closing-up attempts of East Central Europe to West Europe always meant a closing up to the legal system of the West especially in the property law.

After World War II, East Central Europe was dominated by the Soviet Empire and the basis of the East European civilization (law and culture) was introduced by brute force in this region. In recent years, after the fall of the

Soviet Union in 1990 East Central Europe has started to recover its own civilization and formulated a medium scale closing up strategy to the Western civilization.

In the third chapter of this paper we try to formulate the necessary quantitative conditions of this closing up in the framework of a simplified growth model. According to the results of this study, for Hungary to catch up the per capita GDP of Portugal (the less developed country of the EU) in 2005 it needs external financial resources between USD 8 to 16 billion distributed on the ten-year interval in a progressive manner from a lower amount to a higher amount at the end of the period. The lower external resources (the bottom USD 8 billion) are based on the assumption that the hidden economy can be successfully legalized, while the higher external resources (the top USD 16 billion) are estimated if the hidden economy cannot be succesfully legalized.

2. The region from historical viewpoint

The topic of this paper is the present and future of the close-up strategies of the Carpathian Basin. This Basin (except a strip on the South) is defined by geographic realities. However it is a part of Eastern Central Europe, and such pseudo-geographic terms as Eastern Europe, Central Europe etc. have rather doubtful and ill-defined meanings at the end of the 20th century, and therefore first we have to define the region to be investigated, and, furthermore, we have to show evidence that it is indeed a coherent region with some common social, economic etc. laws and behaviour.

Some parts of the Eastern Central European history (e.g. some steppe connections) are rather exotic for Westerners. So the Appendix gives brief notes of histories of important steppe nations. Unfortunately the fine details of such histories are often in Hungarian, not translated. The same holds for the history of the Basin.

First we define our region, and then we try to give the evidence for coherence. Here East Central Europe will be the self-governing or self-determining part of a roughly vertical strip on the map, from the Adriatic Sea to (or almost to) the Baltic Sea. The borders are: the Holy Roman Empire of the German Nation on the West; the borderline between Catholicism (later all the filioque successors) and Greek Orthodoxy on the East; the Adriatic and the heartland of the Balkan (or again the religious borderline) on the South and the Hanseatic and Prussian territories at the Baltic Sea on the North. Now we are going to show that this region, defined not quite from an economic point of view, was indeed a semi-coherent region in the last thousand years, however all its borderlines were of course fluctuating and semi-permeable.

For the western border it is worthwhile to note three facts, two negative and a positive one. First, the region never belonged to the German Empire, therefore it did not share the legal system of the Empire, furthermore, it never had a complete and multi-layered hierarchy of feudal vassalage. The reason will be given immediately. Second, the substrate population here was not the free German warrior-farmer (subjugated only later on the West) with his own primordial piece of individual land. Third, in contrast to the Greek Orthodox territories in the East, private ownership of lands and individual rights of at least the ruling classes were fully established from the first millenium AD. These three initial conditions predetermined a unique historical development for the region.

The lack of a multi-layered hierarchy of vassalage comes from the war tactics of the Eastern mounted warriors, occupying East Central Europe during the migration period. As excavations show, in the sixth century still both German and Eastern societies had three different groups of the population. In the Lombard law the hierarchy levels were the lance-bearing freemen named arimanni or barons. The wealthier members of this class had a complete armament of lance, shield, sword, helmet, etc., expensive and hard and long to learn to use; the poorer members had incomplete armament, but always at least a lance. Another group which still belonged to the army but was unable to hand-to-hand combat, was the aldiones, who were archers. The third group is the skalks, who were slaves without the possibility and right to fight. A full-property owner is a person who can defend his own property, therefore it seems that the original private owners were the barons; among them a definite social stratification can be observed. The Pannonian Lombard graves indicate that the freemen outnumbered the half-free archers. The contemporary Gepids, after long previous Hunnish rule, show the opposite ratio. (Bóna, I. 1976)

Originally the Avars, replacing the Lombards in Pannonia on Easter Monday, AD 568, had also the discrimination between heavy and light armaments, but in their army the archers were also mounted. It is possible that in this time they still had a hierarchy of rights, but their legal system is practically unknown.

During the subsequent centuries, however, the social evolution diverged. To the west of a fault line roughly along the Vistula and Danube the half-free archers became insignificant (but remember Robin Hood, who led archers and tradition is ambiguous if he was a poor nobleman or a commoner), and the most efficient subclass of warriors became the heavy mounted knight, which type of fighters needed enormous training and investment; around and below them the light mounted and the foot warriors became dependent on them. The economic and legal reflection of this evolution can be seen in the legal texts from the empire of Charlemagne, where poor freemen are continuously offering the ownership of their own lands to the wealthy for defence and for getting rid of the duty of going into battle. So the natural result is the hierarchic society of more and more partial rights of greater and greater numbers of population.

East of the fault line, on the open steppe, the evolution went in the opposite direction. The few heavy cavalrymen vanished, except that some such armament remained in formal use in ducal families, and at the end of the Migration Period, conveniently put to the occupation of Hungary by the Magyar tribes in 896 AD, the Eastern armies were composed almost purely of light mounted archers. In addition the steppe conquerors were at least partly nomadic, so they could change the locations of their communities if needs be. Therefore land-ownership was more or less temporary, while the property rights of cattle and horse were well defined. As a natural consequence, when these migrating peoples stopped at the west end of the Eurasian grassland and had to settle down, ownership was got by the numerous and more or less equal light mounted archers. Their relative number at the first millenium AD must have been remarkable, since even at the end of the Middle Ages, after centuries of economic inhomogenisation, the ratio of nobility is around 10 per cent in Poland and Hungary, and definitely higher in Croatia.

So at the first millenium the full-right class of Eastern Central Europe is numerous, and legally equal. (The first elaborate document of the Hungarian constitutional evolution, the Bulla Aurea from 1222 AD, only seven years after the Magna Carta, definitely states the unity and equality of nobility; naturally an ideal whence reality deviated, which was just the reason to demand a royal law.) Below them we find the subjugated population in which the Germans were rare exceptions (as e.g. the Easternized Gepids in Eastern Hungary). Excavations do not indicate private ownership of land below the warrior class; there is no trace of unification of privately owned small estates here at the first millenium, which would be the parallel of the evolution in the Empire. Rather, the new lands were first taken by the whole army, and later distributed by the leaders among the numerous free warriors. So here evolution started from a homogeneous unity towards the spread of the notion of private ownership in a bigger and bigger part of the society.

This East Central European territory gets Christianity from the West, from Rome. At the first millenium the Christian Church of Europe is still theoretically undivided; the Rome-Constantinople dualism comes from the dual administration of the Roman Empire after Theodosius the Great. In different parts of this region the predominance of Roman influence has different reasons.

In Poland originally the converting activity could come only from the West. Namely the Kievian Russia took Christianity only in the second half of the 10th century, at which time the archbishopric of Gniezno was already founded.

Hungary contained two earlier Roman provinces (Pannonia and Dacia), and parts of the Barbaricum between and above them. Dacia was completely evacuated by Aurelianus in 271 AD, therefore no ecclesialistic organization survived. As for Pannonia, the territory was always administrated from Rome until the defeat of Avitus, 455 AD, when it became lost forever for the Western Empire. (For the lack of any Greek influence in Pannonia Romana see the dream of Emperor Probus, in which the ghost of Apollonius of Tyana spoke to him in unnatural Latin because he did not expect a Pannonian to understand Greek.) (Fl. Vopiscus) Anyway, Pannonia is very near to Rome, and in 795 it temporarily became incorporated into the western empire of Charlemagne.

As for Croatia, remember that the so-called Southern Slavic ('Yugoslavian') nations are mainly of Western origin. The German name of Slovenians is Wend, which indicate an original location in the neighbourhood of Venice. The Serbs and the Lausitz Wends (Sorbs) must be closely related according to their common own name Srb. Finally the similarities between Serbian and Croatian languages indicate that the ancestors of the Croatians must have also been located in the Elbe region. For all the present knowledge both ancestral tribes were pushed to the East by the settling Avars returning from Thuringia between 562 and 568. Since these Slavic groups were settled down on both sides of the demarcation line of Theodosius, the Eastern groups were subjugated by the Bizantian Empire about 630, at the weakening of the Avar Khaganate (when the dynasty of the founder Baian became extinct); by definition Croatia is the territory which remained under Western influence (and later both neighbouring nations were employed for defending the borders of the two regional centres against the other neighbour). The name *'chrvat'* (Croat) comes from a Sauromatian tribe, i.e. the Croatian nation was organized by Sauromat leaders. Figure 18.1 shows Europe just before the end of the *Avar Chaganate*. (Formally the Frank dominions became an Empire five years later.)

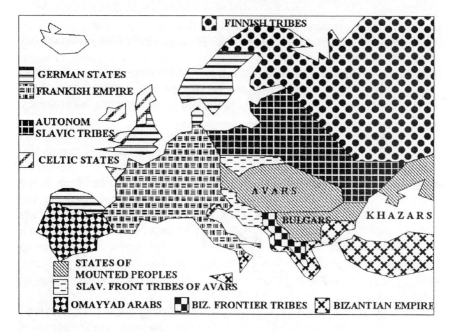

Figure 18.1   Europe in 795

But the whole administration, and specially tax-collecting of the Western Church was based on the individual owner, either from Roman Law or from German customs. So when Christianity became accepted, the Church not only established a heavy Western legal and ideological influence but also taxed the families individually. This helped to spread the clear definition of pieces of land belonging even to subjugated families, therefore helped the individual family husbandry even without legally owning the land.

In 1054 occurred the *Great Schism* between Rome and Constantinople, existing even now, and thenceforth the cultural ties to the Bizantian East were severed. In the whole Roman region the Church was in symbiosis with the State (while on the East the Church was subjugated), therefore the prohibition of ecclesialistic connections acted against other connections as well. Therefore from 1054 practically no cultural influence came from the Bizantian region. This definitely does not mean closed borders. True, the Carpatians shielded Hungary from the East, and a consequence is that in later times Hungary got Bizantian incursions not from the East but from the South. But Poland was without any natural border on the East. Indeed, 896 is only a theoretical end of the Migration Period; latecomers, as for example Petsenegs, Cumans and Osetian Jazones crossed the Eastern border of the region as late as the early 14th century, but these new groups were incorporated and assimilated into the societies of the region, giving special local colours but not altering the foundations of these societies. Figure 18.2 is Europe in 1076, just when King Zvonimir of Croatia succeeded in freeing his country from Byzance. Observe that the three Roman Catholic countries east of the German Empire roughly continue the territory of the mounted peoples on Figure 18.1, except that Bulgaria went to Byzance. There was a short period in 864 even there for trying to make agreement with Rome.

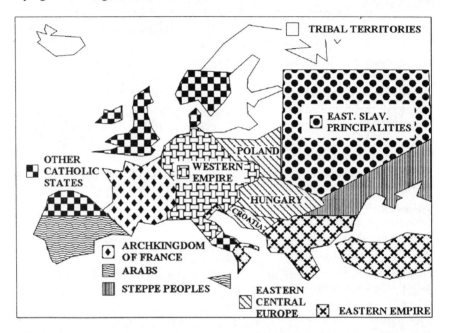

Figure 18.2   Europe in 1076

The first close-up stage in Hungary was the acceptance of Christianity, and privatization of a part of state property to warriors and local leaders. (Győrffy, Gy. 1977) (There was a second wave of privatization during Andrew II, in the first half of the 13th century, leading to dominance of private estates over those of the State.) After that the ruling class was accepted by the Western feudal lords and knights as their peers. As a proof, note that the Eastern borders of the common Western heraldics were the eastern borders of Poland, Hungary and Croatia; for example in Russia the rules of heraldics were imported by Tsar Peter the Great in the late 17th century, who founded the so-called *Geroldmaisterskaia Kontora*, an office of evidently German name. So this close-up strategy was politically successful; the society started to converge to the western ones even at the bottom levels.

This convergence was helped in some territories by Western immigration. This process was, however, quite different in the three medieval sister countries. In Poland, the so-called *Drang nach Osten* is still a point of discussion: but, no doubt, about the first millenium German population moved into the North of the later Kingdom of Poland, establishing there a German substratum. Later, a military Order (The Teutonic Knights), having evacuated the Holy Land, went to the so-called Prussia (after a short interlude in Hungary), and colonized the territory before the Poles. This was followed by a massive German immigration, and this is the reason that we have serious doubts to extend the region under investigation up to the Baltic Sea. (We are not too interested in political or linguistic histories but rather in evolution of societies.)

Otherwise a number of Polish cities were founded by German burghers who remained the dominant element for centuries there. But in Central and Southern Poland no substantial German population could be found outside the cities.

In Hungary the story was different. Pannonia belonged to the Frank Empire and later to its eastern successor state for almost a century. Although her German population was very sparse, it seems that the western fringe of the territory had a Franko-Bavarian strip, and this population remained undisturbed at the conquest of the Magyar tribes. Afterwards Hungarians were continuously raiding Western Europe for two generations and without any doubt a substantial number of Western captives were brought into Hungary who may have contributed to the farming and artisan population. After the first millenium the Kingdom of Hungary received Western immigrants, and in the 12th century King Geyza II organized the first large scale implantation of Saxonians, who went first into the south-eastern part of the Basin (Siebenbürgen Saxons) and later also to the north-eastern one (Zips). These groups were farmers, and the settling process was organized from the Hungarian side.

At the same time some families of the German nobility sought fortune in Hungary, and became incorporated into the Hungarian ruling class. The cities were founded, refounded or extended by Italian, French and German immigrants. While the survival of Roman elements is utterly improbable until the foundation of the Hungarian state, a rather unexplained fact is the survival of the wine culture of the Balaton Highland, initiated by Emperor Probus in the 3rd century.

Croatia did not have these massive immigration processes. However, at her Adriatic coast she had a chain of cities continuously from late West Roman times, with a Neolatin population, whose language (extinct from 1898) is called Dalmatian. (Some time in the *Renaissance* period these cities switched to Italian.) This coastal region gave Croatia an organic connection to the developed world even without any immigration.

As for higher culture and economy, also some definite convergence was seen, the Hungarian currency followed Bavarian style from the first millenium, and in the first half of the 14th century Hungary and Croatia (in an English-Scottish style personal union between 1091 and 1918) immediately followed the leading Italian states in the use of reliable golden coinage. As a special explanation, note that in this time the economic, cultural and innovative centre of Europe was in Northern Italy, just in the neighbourhood of Croatia and Hungary. The region was definitely *not* peripheric in this time.

During this period Hungary is always in a balancing position between the imperial superpowers of Germany and Byzantium. Note that this properly appears in the title of Archiregnum, i.e. a kingdom without any imperial overlordship; the parallel is the Kingdoms of France and England. (Indeed, the Holy Crown of Hungary came directly from the Pope, and it is closed above, compared to the open crown of Croatia.) On the North, Poland had no neighbour on her east comparable to the German Empire, and on the south Croatia was in connection only with the Byzantine superpower. After the temporary evaporation of the Greek Orthodox superpower in the Fourth Crusade (1204) Hungary (in personal union with Croatia) tried to fill in the vacuum on the Northern Balkan. It is not trivial if these territories became parts of East Central Europe or not; e.g. Bosnia was Roman Catholic but with a strong Bogomil or Kathar heresy, but here we deliberately ignore the question, because later the 500 year Ottoman occupation once again removed these lands from the region.

It is interesting to observe the repeated recurrences of unifying tendencies within the region. Hungary and Croatia got a common king in 1091 and this status (slightly more than a personal union) remained unchanged until 1918, but during this period always two nations existed with two parliaments. The border between the two states was a matter of common agreement, but changes were rather exceptions. As for Croatia+Hungary and Poland, the first personal union happened in the 1370s under a Hungarian king, and in the next century it was repeated three times backwards. Still the Hungarian-Polish border is practically constant from the 11th century; from 1918 it became the Czechoslovakian-Polish border, and from 1993 the Slovakian-Polish one, but it is still unchanged. Therefore foreign dynasties from within the same region do not mean colonialization or territorial losses, there was no danger in asking help for the country attacked from outside.

Between 1450 and 1500 a serious change happens in the position of the region. The centre of world commerce and innovations leaves Northern Italy and goes to the Atlantic shores. The reasons are manifold, but the final cause is the discovery of America; thenceforth the Mediterranean Sea lost its primary importance. Afterwards the region belongs to the periphery, gets only indirect pull from the centre, and at the same time starts to have to defend itself against the Ottoman invasion. Croatia and Hungary get the invasion frontally, while Poland is more or less a secondary theatre of war for the next two centuries. Figure 18.3 is Europe in 1491.

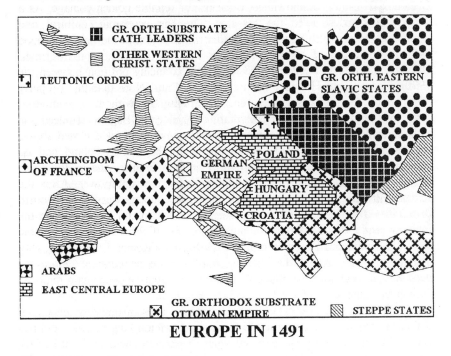

EUROPE IN 1491

Figure 18.3   Europe in 1491

In the next two centuries the Ottoman Empire is a substantial factor in the region. There is a continuous border fighting in the middle of Hungary and Croatia, while Poland is continuously attacked on her southeastern periphery. Since Northern Italy is also a theatre of war from 1494, the southern part of the region can hope for support only from Poland or from the West, the German Empire. The Polish support could not stop the Ottoman advance, and from the middle of the 16th century the Ottoman Empire keeps the southeastern half of Croatia occupied, and also a third of Hungary which strip runs roughly vertically in the centre.

However still the eastern and western boundaries of the region are intact. On the East, the border is still the Eastern Carpathians, not occupied, and further up the border of Russia is roughly the River Dnieper. (Our guess is that the eastern border of our region is somewhere to the West from the Dnieper, but it is rather hard to draw a definite line there.) In the eastern parts of Poland and Lithuania (in personal union) the population is then composed of Greek Orthodox peasantry, with Catholic landowners, tax collectors and warriors, a number of Armenian and Greek merchants, and in the Zaporozhye, some Orthodox free warriors known as Cossacks. We would rather avoid discussing the economy and sociology of that area. The western border deserves some discussion. From 1526 Hungary (together with Croatia) is in personal union with the Archduchy of Austria, practically with the German Empire under the Habsburgs. Still the western border continues to exist (and unchanged up to 1920), Croatia and Hungary do not join the Empire, keep their own legal systems, and the societies continue to give different answers to the challenges. E.g. in the first wave of reformation half of Germany converts to Lutheranism, Austria herself remains Catholic, but the majority of Hungary becomes Calvinist. (One of the reasons is, of course, that Luther made some pro-Ottoman speeches, so his teaching was not too attractive in a fighting situation for Hungary in distress.) At the same time Poland and Croatia remain Catholic; our guess is that the reason is to clearly distinguish themselves from Greek Orthodox neighbours of very similar languages. Hungary and Croatia gets some financial support for the continuous fighting from the neighbouring parts of the Habsburg estates, and the frontier is stopped in the heartland. Two centuries of fighting disturbed the economic development, but it seems that this factor was only one amongst a few. As mentioned, the centre of the European economic life is no more in Northern Italy; what is more, the silver and gold mines of Hungary (not occupied) become secondary in comparison to those in America. As the scarce surviving data show, in this time Hungary only partly participates in the inflationary tendencies of the West. At the same time she does not follow the development of industry, but specializes in food production for Western customers. The same is true for Poland.

At the same time the Ottoman occupation disturbs the internal commerce in Croatia and Hungary, but does not stop it. The demarcation line does not develop into a true border. Hungarian and Croatian laws remain valid for the non-Moslem subjects of the Ottoman Empire in the occupied areas. The Ottomans tolerate even taxation for the rightful landowners and for the enemy states. Occupied cities of Hungary get their law books confirmed from the King of Hungary, who is incidentally the German Emperor. Guilds in the occupied area keep legal and commercial contact with brother organizations of the free areas.

Still the continuous fighting and the agricultural specialization have a consequence unique in Europe, which is sometimes called 'the second serfdom'. In these centuries the peasants are gradually being freed from personal dependence on the West, and to a lesser extent in the Empire. At the same time in our region there is the very populous warrior class with a real function, and there is a need to organize the mass commerce of wheat and meat to the West. So they take this role too, and again subjugate the peasants, who cannot be independent because they need defence against the invaders. It seems that the more important factor is the agricultural specialization, because the subjugation is stronger in Poland, not occupied, and the weakest in Croatia, where the Ottoman danger is the strongest, but the territory is not too good for mass production of food.

Poland loses large territories on the East from the middle of the 17th century. However it is not too clear if these territories were really the parts of Eastern Central Europe.

From the beginning of the 18th century the Ottoman Empire ceases to influence the region. Croatia and Hungary remain in personal union with each other and with the Habsburg lands, but they continue to keep their identities as well. During the 18th century both countries, but mainly Hungary, are getting German immigrants to the depopulated territories, and the wounds of the previous two centuries start to heal up. At the same time Poland has no intrinsic connections to the German Empire, but is more and more the object of Russian political and military influence.

At the end of the 18th century the region loses territories on the northeast. This is the 3rd partition of Poland. Thenceforth up to now, except for 20 years between the World Wars, the former Eastern Poland belonged to Russia (from 1991 to the Ukraine). Henceforth Eastern Central Europe reduces to Croatia, Hungary still (in personal union) and the so-called Galicia or Southern Poland, belonging to Austria until the end of the First World War.

The Napoleonic Wars do not disturb too much this reduced region. Hungary even enjoys some prosperity from food production for the armies. From 1815 the reduced region is at peace, and has the possibility to try to close up to the more Western parts of Europe. Indeed, in Hungary then starts the so-called Reform Age.

The 'reform age' of the Carpathian Basin

Emperor Francis I lost the throne of the German Empire in 1806, when the western German territories were occupied by Napoleon. From that time the Habsburg rulers used the title of Emperor of Austria, although there was no state called Austria. From this time the connections of the 'Austrian' and

Bohemian territories became weakened with the Western half of the Empire. However in principle the Empire itself was not dissolved, therefore we continue to regard the Austrian and Bohemian lands as parts of the Western Central European region. In 1815 Austria got back Galicia, and acquired Dalmatia (taken previously from Venice by France.) Galicia was claimed by Hungary in 1772 when Austria took it; Dalmatia also was claimed via Hungarian or Croatian (or both) arguments: she was continuously disputed between Croatia (or Hungary) and Venice from the Fourth Crusade, and earlier (back to 1076) had belonged to Croatia. So both Galicia and Dalmatia were governed from Vienna, but did not belong in any sense and by any right to the Empire. Therefore we must consider both territories as parts of Eastern Central Europe.

Now remember that close-up *strategies* imply some organization and planning. If individuals learn techniques from more advanced regions, such an activity may or may not be successful, may or may not result in some close-up, but it is not a close-up strategy. We concentrate on strategies. But the formulation and execution of a close-up strategy and programme needs some kind of a political body, which can make decisions and can enforce them at least to some extent. In other words, some kind of a parliament is a precondition. The optimal case would be an independent country, but in the period just considered no part of Eastern Central Europe was independent in the sense as used in the last century. Galicia and Dalmatia had some '*Landtäge*', which were responsible for taxation and education in some restricted sense. However the only parliaments with full sovereignties were the Hungarian and Croatian ones. For example, the Hungarian parliament offered the taxes, made laws (valid if signed by the King of Hungary, incidentally the same person as the Emperor of Austria) and the government of Hungary was the Chancellery of Hungary (strangely enough in Vienna). So the Hungarian Parliament was definitely in the position to formulate and execute a strategy for developing the country, even if it could not enforce directly the acts on the government. (The situation was slightly similar to that in England during the reign of Charles I.)

Indeed, the Hungarian Parliament did formulate some steps for closing up. Some laws created between 1825 and 1844 were parts of such a strategy. They wanted to change or manufacture some long-range regulators of the national economy. We can classify these into the following groups:

1) Education, Research and Development, etc. Introduction of the majority language into legal life. Effects: extension of culture to a large part of population; minority frustrations on the periphery.

Organization of a network of industrial training schools. Wanted effect: increase of the level of industrial skills; however the law was not signed by the King.

Establishment of the Hungarian Academy of Sciences. Effect: the state starts to organize research, industrial development and import of ideas from developed countries.

2) Modernization of the legal system (of economy). Creation of separate Hungarian laws for finance (credit) etc. Transformation of the feudal ownership of lands into a Western-type property. Effect: market of lands; ability for investment into agriculture.

Freedom for establishing factories independently of the guild membership of owners or employees. Effect: weakening of guilds.

3) Infrastructure. Licences and tax reductions for channel and railway conductions. Decision for a permanent bridge on the Danube. Effect: the first bridge across the Danube in east-west direction, therefore permanent connection between the eastern and western parts of the Basin.

Planning and starting of river regulation. Effect: prevention of regular floods on the Great Hungarian Plains, therefore new agricultural land and safer traffic.

While these steps had only a limited effect on closing-up, Hungary was able to do this autonomously, having her own legislative body. Other parts of the region were able to implant only the educational regulators at best. This continuous legislative activity was interrupted in 1848 by the Austrian-Hungarian war; in 1849 Hungary was defeated, the Hungarian Parliament dissolved, and no part of the region was self-regulating until 1867.

The age of dual monarchy

In 1867 the Austro-Hungarian or Habsburg or Danube Monarchy was rearranged according to an agreement between the Austrian and Hungarian leading political groups, and in 1868 there happened a subsequent agreement between Hungary and Croatia. Thenceforth the situation was as follows.

To a first approximation the Monarchy consisted of two independent states, loosely called Austria and Hungary. In this context Austria means Austria proper, Bohemia, Trieste, Slovenia, Dalmatia, Galicia and Bukovina (the last one should be classified to Eastern Europe). The Hungarian half consisted of Hungary and Croatia. In Austria the constituent lands had no home rule; however they had local administration and a limited autonomy in education and culture. There was a sovereign Imperial Parliament in Vienna for all the Austrian lands.

In Hungary there was a Hungarian Parliament as well as a Croatian one. However a great number of issues were common matters and in them the decisions were made by a common body containing the whole Hungarian Parliament together with some Croatian delegates. Education, culture, law, economy and administration were separate in Hungary and in Croatia.

However to the second approximation there were some common matters between the two halves of the Monarchy, namely defence and foreign policy. For these matters both Parliaments sent delegations (with Croatian delegates as well as the Hungarian delegation) to make decisions. In addition the two halves agreed in customs union for 10 years, which agreement was repeatedly renewed until the end of the First World War.

Therefore:

- East Central Europe as a whole was not a self-governing or self-regulating unit, because Galicia and Dalmatia were ruled by Austria. However note that the 1881 Linz Programme of the German parties of the Austrian Imperial Parliament suggested the reorganization of the double monarchy by transferring Galicia and Dalmatia to the eastern half. The suggestion was not accepted; however afterwards Galicia got limited autonomy, while there was a continuous increase of influence of local Croatians compared to local Italians in the administration of Dalmatia. At the same time Hungary continuously demanded the transfer of Dalmatia to Croatia.

- The core territory of the region, the Carpathian Basin, i.e. Hungary with Croatia, was in principle self-governing in all questions relevant to economic development. The customs union was an agreement, and if great needs be, free not to be renewed. However practically the existence of this union established a coupling in economy.

- On the East Croatia had a limited possibility to regulate her own closing-up via the educational and cultural regulators, and to a less extent, Galicia had the same possibility.

The situation will be demonstrated on the Hungarian strategy of close up by long-range regulators. The example has been chosen on the ground that until the First World War in the region Hungary had the widest possibility to determine her own regulators. Before this review two technical notes are made:

- The jurisdiction process of Hungary results in laws named after the year and a Roman numeral followed by a 'tc' which indicates the sequentional order of the law in that year. For reference we mention these numerals. For details see: Berend, T.I. and Szuhay, M. 1973; Hanák, P. 1975.

- As told earlier, the term 'Hungary' needs a nontrivial definition. As a rule here for cultural, and partly for legal, issues, Hungary stands for Hungary proper, not including Croatia. On the other hand, for financial and foreign issues 'Hungary' is Hungary and Croatia.

While this needs some attention, one cannot help, because this complication originated just from the special position of the Central Eastern European lands, territories and countries.

Regulators 1: Laws

As told earlier, the legal system of Eastern Central Europe did *not* originate from that of the Western Empire or any Western state. In addition, the medieval legal system here survived until the middle of the 19th century, therefore modernization of economy and society needed legal changes. (However, note the quantitative differences between the Hungarian system and that of e.g. the *Ancien Regime* in France. In Hungary:

- no chain of vassalage existed, so each noble was equal, directly depending on the Crown;
- the percentage of nobles was 10 per cent of the neighbourhood;
- some local groups were more or less self-governing, and their territories free of the medieval landlord system. As a result, the share in voting power for the Parliament was higher in 1830 in Hungary than in contemporary modernised France. The biggest steps of this process followed each other as listed below:

1848. tc (a whole sequence): Establish legal equality of all male citizens, including taxation according to common principles[1].

1872. VIII tc: Disbands the guild system. Henceforth economic activity is free for everybody.

1881. XLIV tc: Supports the home industry. Freedom from taxation for 15 years if the factory is sufficiently up to date, either existing or under construction. This law substitutes the custom laws for which the Hungarian Parliament had no authority, such questions belonged to an Austro-Hungarian body of delegations of equal number (and the Hungarian delegation must have contained Croatian delegates of prescribed number too).

1890. XIII tc: Widens the above preferences.

1907. III tc: Gives the possibility for such support in any industrial establishment if economic reasons suggest.

At the beginning of the new century, complete legal equality of male citizens is an established fact in Hungary; earlier preferred or dispreferred classes, religions and other groups have been equalized, with some exceptions in the voting power, and with special legal regulations for big lands of feudal origin. This situation is comparable to contemporary Great Britain, except that the percentage of the population with voting power is lower, somehow between 6 and 10 per cent. Industry and finance are completely free.

Regulators 2: Monetary, fiscal etc. regulations

> *1848:* Customs agreement with Austria on the basis of greatest preference.
> *1850:* Austria unilaterally forces customs union.
> *1864:* Stock market is established in Pest (one of the precursor cities of the later capital Budapest).
> *1867. XVI tc:* Establishes customs union with Austria for 10 years, renewable.
> *1867:* Hungary accepts that she will not erect a central state bank.
> *1878:* Reorganization of the Austrian central state bank on dualistic basis.

Generally these regulations were made as external agreements. As told above, neither Hungary nor Austria had the right to regulate her own external relations and defence: these issues together with the finances supporting them were common issues of the two independent states Hungary and Austria, determined by the mixed delegations of the two Parliaments (or three, including the Croatian one), and in the lack of any 'federal' government the administration of these issues was done by the offices of a common foreign ministry, a common ministry of defence, and a common ministry for the finances of the foreign affairs and defence. (In addition, the ministry of finances for common foreign affairs and defence governed the Territory of Bosnia, whose position between Austria and Hungary was rather obscure. Until 1908 the same ministry administrated the Novipazar Sandjak, belonging to the Ottoman Sultanate, given by the Berlin Conference to Austria and Hungary for administration, and separating Serbia and Montenegro. This task ceased by the peaceful reoccupation of the Sandjak by the Sultanate.) Neither part of the Austro-Hungarian complex had its own monetary system, and had no right to introduce it. Separate customs territories were possible in principle, but only after a long and difficult process of not renewing the customs unions. Until the end of the First World War no separate customs territories were established.

Regulators 3: Infrastructure

The whole Eastern Central European region was behind the West in the middle of the 19th century for the development of the so-called infrastructure including roads, railways, embankments, etc. The Hungarian government strategy was to concentrate the available financial resources here, because an improved infrastructure would result later in higher incomes, consequently taxes. Infrastructural investments just after 1867 were high, while in this period their profit was negligible. After a quarter century the share of this area went down much in the investments, but the profit increased. The explanation is that the first quarter century was necessary to reach the level of profitability in development.

While these investments were by no means purely made by the state, the state had a great possibility to regulate them, and in this area the Hungarian (Croatia included) sovereignty was complete.

The first process was to promote investments into railway building. Up to 1875 this was achieved by indirect means, namely the Hungarian Parliament guaranteed a fair profit for 10 years for anybody who got the licence to build a line. From 1876 the state treasury started to buy up the private lines, by which the Hungarian State Railways became the biggest employer of the country, and railwaymen became state employees similar to soldiers, customs officers etc. This new status of the Railways led to frictions between the Hungarian and Croatian authorities about ruling the network. This indirect or direct investment activity definitely helped the close-up in the density of railway lines.

The next step was the building of artificial waterways and other regulations of natural waters; from 1878 the state started to organize the building of the so called Ferenc Channel between the two great rivers, the Danube and Tisa and backwards in the area which is now the Vojvodina. Henceforth some laws promoted the activities as follows:

> *1879. XXXV tc:* Regulates River Tisa. The total length of the meandering river was reduced to 60 per cent by shortcuts. Result: floods became less frequent, new lands became available for grain, and in the same time fishing was reduced. A large part of the river became available for steam ships.
>
> *1888. XXVI tc:* Prescribes the regulation of Danube at the so-called Iron Gate between Romania and Serbia. It was based on a multilateral agreement. At the Iron Gate the river was very narrow, therefore the stream was too strong for shipping upwards. The regulation made the Danube an efficient international route to the Eastern seas.

1895. XLVIII tc: Orders the regulation of the Danube within Hungary. With this the entire Hungarian section of the Danube became available for steamers.

1897. XVI tc: Nationalization of the telephone system of Budapest.

1898. IX tc: Establishes the Hungarian Oriental Shipping Company.

Regulators 4: Education, Research and Development, etc.

1868. XXXVIII tc: Orders education for everybody up to the age of 15.

1872: Erecting the second university of Hungary in Clausenburg.

Later laws tried to solve the problem of a centralized education system in a multilingual country.

The Carpathian Basin at the eve of the First World War

In 1900 Budapest became a big European city comparable to Vienna, or to Munich not only for its size but also for the general level of industrial, civilizatory and artistic level. For the English-speaking reader we can recommend the review book 'Budapest 1900', by John Lukács. Here we stop for a moment just before the First World War. For such a stop and overview the most convenient year is 1910, when in the whole Austro-Hungarian

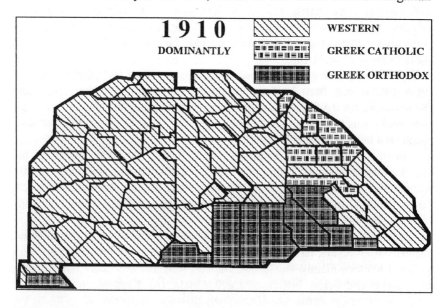

Figure 18.4   Religions in Hungary and Croatia in 1910

Monarchy population counts were made according to common principles[2]. In some pie diagrams one can compare the structures of employment of the four more or less independent countries of the region (Hungary, Croatia, Galicia and Dalmatia) to other countries of all regions of contemporary Europe.

Figure 18.4 shows the distribution of various religions in Hungary and Croatia in 1910, from an East-West cultural viewpoint. No doubt, in that time religion strongly influenced the everyday way of life. From the above viewpoint three blocks of religions will be distinguished among the seven religions individually handled in the population counting process in the Basin.

Western: Includes Roman Catholic, Calvinist, Lutheran, Unitarian and Israelite.

Eastern: The Greek Orthodox religion.

In between: The Greek Catholic Church, with Byzantian rite but accepting the *filioque* dogma and Roman leadership.

All other religions counted as Others, remained in each county under 0.1 per cent individually and 0.3 per cent together. (The Basin was divided into 72 counties, 63 Hungarian and 9 Croatian ones.) A block is considered 'dominant' on Figure 18.4 if in a county it is the biggest. Then Figure 18.4 shows that in 1910 in the biggest part of Croatia+Hungary it was dominant to belong to the West either directly (Block 1) or indirectly (Block 3). The Eastern substrate was characteristic only in an Eastern wedge based on Serbia and showing to the North. This wedge was partly a product of the 150 years of Ottoman rule.

Within the Western group Roman Catholics were an absolute majority, but mosaic-like one could find counties of Lutheran and Calvinist majorities as well. No bigger unit with Unitarian or Israelite majority existed; for both the highest ratio was between 20 and 25 per cent, in a Szekler county in Transylvania for the first, and in Budapest for the second.

Hungary was a multilingual country, and language is not a topic of this paper, not being among the important long-range regulators. So we only note that in Hungary proper (i.e. without Croatia) the biggest language group was the Hungarian (Magyar) with 54.5 per cent. Croatia had some 65 per cent of Croats and 25 per cent Serbs. Religions correlated with languages; in some cases strongly, in some cases weakly. In Hungary Roman Catholics were mainly Magyars, Slovakians, Germans or Croatians. Calvinists were almost exclusively Magyars, Lutherans mainly Slovakians and Germans, Unitarians exclusively Magyars, Israelites mainly Magyars and to a less extent Germans, Greek Catholics mainly Ruthenians and Romanians and Greek Orthodoxes Romanians and Serbs. In Croatia the correlation was rather strong: Roman Catholics were Croatians, and Greek Orthodoxes were Serbs.

Figures 18.5 and 18.6 display the employment structure in Eastern Central Europe in 1910, compared to that in the rest of Europe. Eastern Central Europe is then characterized by a high enough share of agriculture, however with non-negligible industry and commerce. Note that within Eastern Central Europe the structure is 'more Western' or 'modern' in the two countries not belonging to Austria, so not governed from the West (of Central Europe). Since it is extremely improbable that Austria would have 'exploited' the poor countries of Galicia and Dalmatia, we must see the result of a close-up strategy, possible in the Basin due to the sovereignty of the Parliament of the Basin (which we cannot name, because it had no name of its own), but impossible with simple *Landtäge*. The employment structure in the Basin was transitional between East and West, but not unlike to the South. In Eastern Central Europe Hungary showed the 'most modernized' structure, similar to that of Italy. This similarity would be preserved until c. 1965.

The post-war changes

In 1914 the First World War started. At its end, between 1918 and 1920, serious changes happened in the region. Briefly they can be summarized as follows:
-   The Austro-Hungarian Monarchy was dissolved.
-   Hungary shrank to the centre of the Carpathian Basin. Her peripheries went to states outside the region.
-   The personal union of Hungary and Croatia was dismantled and Croatia went to a state outside the region.
-   Poland had been restored, however with a substantial Eastern and some Northern parts, which may or may not have belonged to the region of Eastern Central Europe.

As a consequence one may say that between the World Wars the region was represented by two national economies, that of a new, smaller Hungary, and that of the new, greater Poland. It is doubtless that all of the territory of Hungary belonged to the region, while Polish data contain the contributions of the new territories. Therefore henceforth comparison to other parts of Eastern Central Europe is impossible. We, furthermore, must continue the study with a lesser Hungary, so some data are not comparable even for Hungary before and after 1920, because of the substantial changes in area and population.

The period between the World Wars was a general stagnation for all of Europe. No close-up strategy was possible for Hungary until the Great Crisis, because long years were needed to reorganize the national economy according to the new numerous customs borders. As a single example, the Hungarian grain mills, concentrated in Budapest at the great railways centres of lines

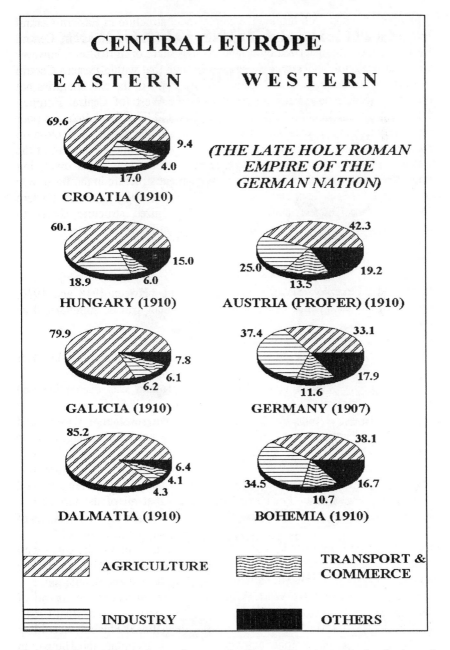

Figure 18.5   Shares in employment in Central Europe at the beginning of
the 20th century

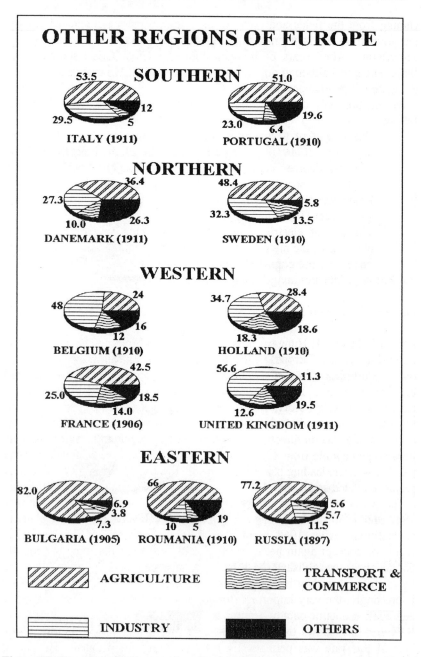

Figure 18.6   Employment structure in other regions of Europe at the beginning of the 20th century

coming from the fields and going to the Western markets remained without the grain from the southern lands. Therefore some factories simply became superfluous. After years of reorganization the Greet Crisis started which shook Hungary, although not as strongly as the West. However she was able to regain her relative position.

We mention only three characteristic changes between the World Wars as follows:

- The weight of agricultural population continued to decrease: from 60.3 per cent (1910) to 50.8 per cent (in 1930); the weight of industry and commerce continued to grow. Roughly the Hungarian employment structure evolved parallel with that of Italy.
- In industry the employment share of small enterprises decreased from 47 per cent (1910) to 39 per cent (1938).
- The use of electricity increased rapidly and so strongly that the decrease of the area did not result in a perceptible jump-back, as can be seen on the graph at the end of this paper.

All of these changes are generally considered 'modernization'.

The socialist period

After World War II Hungary soon became a part of the economic community centred in Eastern Europe. In that time some modernization continued to go on; 'modernization' was a slogan of the Eastern ideology. However, at least between 1949 and 1968, modernization was not regulated by long range regulators, but by orders based on natural quantities of some products regarded as 'modern'. Consequently the employment structure continued to change in the general direction of modernization, although the lag behind Italy became perceptible from 1965. For electricity the increase continued roughly parallel with the leading part of the world. However the weight of the tertiary sector remained small, and there appeared an increased lag in the GDP/capita.

The period of planned economy can be divided into two parts. Between 1948 and 1968 the economy was directed by commands based on plans or superstitions. After 1968 regulations became 'indirect', so the long-range regulator concept again became very useful, and from that time the country continuously reestablished the Western connections, thus deviating more and more from her Northern, Eastern and Southern neighbours. However, interestingly, the very important turning point in 1968 cannot be seen in the aggregate economic data of Figures 18.7 and 18.8.

Figure 18.7 shows the (net) investment rate in the period. Before World War II this rate was permanently between 8 and 10 per cent. The forced close-up is demonstrated by the sudden jump to a higher value, and even more by the continuous increase of the rate. Until the end of the 70s the planned economy was able to maintain an exponential growth of GDP (Figure 18.8), however at the cost of forcing more and more investments. Even so, the exponential growth broke down at the beginning of the 80s, and then the investment ratio started to return to a moderate level similar to the inter-war times before planned economy. So the close-up strategy of Hungary's socialist period ended somewhere in the first half of the 80s. (Bogár, L. 1989)

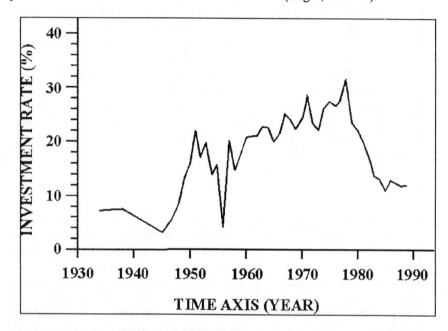

Figure 18.7   Net investment rate in Hungary
Note: Observe the high and growing investment rate in the socialist era. After
         1982 this rate returned to its pre-war values.

We give Figures 18.9 - 18.11, which compare raw iron production, electric consumption and GDP/capita for Hungary and USA, roughly during a century. One can see that

-        In iron production Hungary's lag was slightly growing until the First
         World War. Between 1940 and 1970 the Hungarian increase was
         relatively faster.
-        In electricity the Hungarian and American developments were parallel
         between 1920 and 1980. No close-up is seen, but no increase of the
         gap either.

In GDP/capita the USA started from an initial level at 1867 four times higher than Hungary, but Hungary was able to keep this initial ratio roughly constant. However from 1931 the Hungarian currency is not convertible, and from 1948 the currency rates became purely arbitrary. So Figure 18.11 stops at that year.

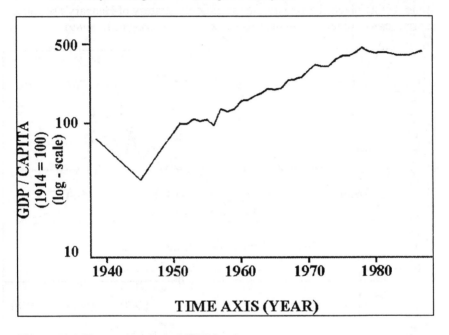

Figure 18.8 Home consummed GDP/capita
Note: 1914 = 100

However, in the last 200 years the main desire in the Hungarian soul is not the close-up to distant USA but the catch-up with neighbour and sister country Austria. So Figure 18.12 is the ratio of the two countries' GDP/capita. After the First World War both data series are rather uncertain, but sophisticated estimates do exist. We use the data of Tarján and Molnár (Tarján, T. 1993; Tarján, T. and Molnár, Gy. in this volume), and, indeed, our Figure 18.12 is almost a transformation of one of the Figures of Tarján and Molnár in this volume. For the GDP ratio some corrections are needed.

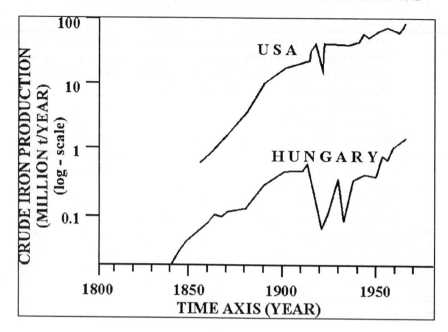

Figure 18.9   Crude iron production in USA and Hungary

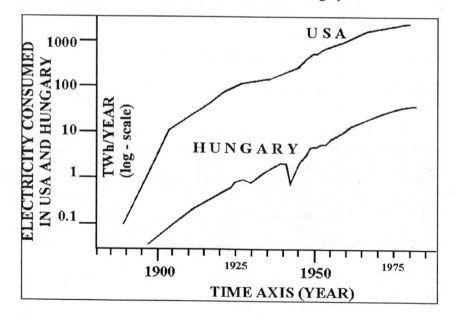

Figure 18.10   Electricity consummed in USA and Hungary

Namely:
- between 1921 and 1937 Hungary's NNP is converted to GDP by a constant factor 1.55 to reproduce the average ratio known for 1925-34;
- after 1945 existing ratio estimates are used (for these two items see the study of Tarján, T. [1993]); and
- the Schilling-Pengő parity was ca. 0.80 in 1937.

Now the moral of Figure 18.12. The long and systematic efforts of the Parliament of the Basin resulted in the increase of the ratio from 0.58 to 0.70 until 1913. After the First World War the increase continued, ended with 0.86, so catch-up was not impossible for the first time since the Middle Ages. The socialist era broke this trend, but in its first half returned only to the ratio of 1913 (the last peaceful year of the Double Monarchy) and stabilized there. However after 1973 the ratio drops steeply, and at the end of the socialist era Hungary is back at a relative position similar to that at the beginning of the Reform Age in 1825, 165 years before. In 17 short years she slipped back as much as was the slow climb-up of 88 years before the First World War.

However mere 17 years is nothing in the ages-old race of the two countries. What can be lost by mishandling in relative position, can be won back as well in comparable time *by appropriate strategy*.

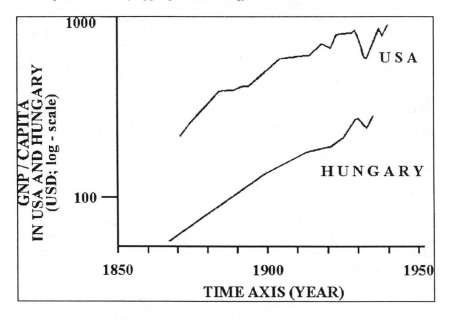

Figure 18.11   GNP/capita in USA and Hungary

3. The forecast of the present closing up attempt of the region by means of a generalized Kovács-Virág dynamic one sector economic model

In this chapter we briefly present a quantitative approach of predicting the outcome of a possible closing up strategy of the central European civilization to the west European civilization. In this study we have determined the lower and upper limits of the 'cost' of the closing up growth path for Hungary.

In our paper (Banai, M. and Lukács, B. 1989) we formulated a generalization of the Kovács - Virág dynamic one sector economic model (Kovács, J. and Virág, I. 1981) and gave solutions optimalizing the consumption function.

One can slightly modify this model to obtain quantitative predictions about the time horizon of the present closing up attempts of our region.

The basic equations of this modified one sector economic model are:

$$dK/dt = qsY - \lambda K \qquad (18.1)$$

$$Y = gK \qquad (18.2)$$

where:

s	the savings rate, is a function of the time: $s = s(t)$,
λ	is constant (depreciation rate of capital stocks),
g	the efficiency of the capital, is a function of the savings rate and the time: $g = g(s, t)$; and
q	the investment to capital multiplicator is a function of the time: $q = q(t)$.

We have specified the form of capital efficiency in our former paper (Banai, M. and Lukács, B. 1989) as follows:

$$g(s) = \beta s(1 - s)^{\gamma} \qquad (18.3)$$

where:

γ	is a constant in time (around 4 in Central Europe according to quantitative analyses); while
β	can depend on time, especially through technology.

In evaluating the generalized Kovács - Virág model we specified the time dependence of investment to capital multiplicator and the capital efficiency in the following manner:

$$q(t) = \frac{q_0 T_q + q_1 t}{T_q + t} \qquad (18.4)$$

$$g(t) = \frac{g_0 T_g + g_1 t}{T_g + t} \qquad (18.5)$$

We note that with the explicit time dependence in the saving rate, in the capital efficiency and the introduction of the time-dependent investment to capital multiplicator enables the model to describe transition processes, a phenomenon characteristic of an economy being in a closing up state.

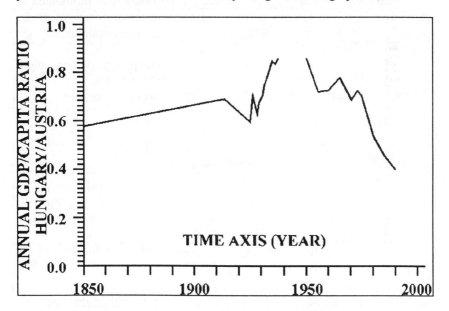

Figure 18.12   Hungary's race to catch up Austria since 1850
Note: It is remarkable the gradual close-up until 1938, the slide back and stagnation until 1973, and the later decline.

Numerical analyses (not cited here) give the following values for the parameters in equations (18.4 and 18.5). The Hungarian value of β_0 was 3.53 y^{-1} at the end of the 80s, while the contemporary Italian value was higher by some 2/3. The q value of the average of the 35 years up to 1986 was 0.84 in Hungary, while the corresponding West German value was 1.36. Therefore the initial and final values of a reasonable close-up path are:

$$\beta_0 = 3.53, \qquad \beta_1 = 5.76,$$
$$q_0 = 0.84, \qquad q_1 = 1.36;$$

what remains is the values of the characteristic times of changes in (18.4 and 18.5). We were looking for a path of optimal total consumption in 15 years, which ends at the half of the present Austrian GDP/capita.

The results are as follows. The path cannot end at the target GDP/capita if either of T_q and Tg is larger than three years. So, fast privatization and technological renewal are needed.

Loans without real interest rate (e.g. a new Marshall project) may help. If investments can be finished two years before paying back, then the desired path is marginally possible with the characteristic times 10 years for complete technological changes and 4.5 years for privatization + efficient stock market.

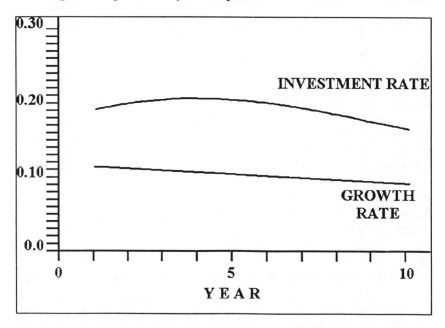

Figure 18.13   A 10 years path optimalizing total consumption and enhancing GDP by 2.7 for an economy with the average data of Hungary

Note: Time scales: new technology 5 years, privatization 5 years, gestation 0 year. Details in the text.

We have also calculated growth paths of optimal total consumption in 10 years, which end at the Portugalian GDP/capita in 2005 (assuming a 3 per cent average growth rate for the Portugal economy in the next 11 years). We calculated two paths, one of them applies the assumption that the hidden economy is can become legal at the start of the growth path, while the other assumes that it is cannot become legal. In the first case the parameters T_q and T_β take the values of three years and four years, respectively, on the growth path, while the average half gestation time takes the value of 1.9 years. In the second case $T_q=T_\beta=5$ years and the half gestation is equal 0 years. Then one can calculate the cost of these growth paths to be implementable, and obtains that the lower limit of the needed cost-free external source is about USD 6-8 billion (used 2/3 of the amount for the legalization of the hidden economy at the starting period of the growth path) and the upper limit is about USD 16-18 billion partitionated for the 10 years in a slowly growing manner. Figure 18.13 shows the investment rate and growth rate on these paths.

References

Banai, M. and Lukács, B. (1989) KFKI-1989-68

Banai, M., Kovács, J. and Lukács, B. (1993) in: Carpathian Basin: Evolutionary Stages. KFKI-1993-21, p. 84

Berend, T.I. and Szuhay, M. (1973) *A tőkés gazdaság története Magyarországon 1848-1944*, Kossuth, Budapest

Bogár, L. (1989) *Kitörési kísérleteink*, Közgazdasági és Jogi Kiadó, Budapest

Bóna, I. (1976) *The Dawn of the Dark Ages*, Corvina Press, Budapest

Ciepelewski, J. et al. (1974) *A világ gazdaságtörténete a XIX. és a XX. században*, Kossuth, Budapest

Fl Vopiscus Syracuseanus 'Divus Aurelianus', in Historia Augusta

Győrffy, Gy. (1977) *István király és műve*, Gondolat, Budapest

Hanák, P. (ed) (1975) *Magyarország története, III-IV*, Tankönyvkiadó, Budapest

Kovács, J (1990) 'Regulative Planning' in Kovács, J. and Dallago, B. (eds) *Economic Planning in Transition*, Dartmouth Publ. Co., Aldershot, p. 33

Kovács, J. and Virág, I. (1981) Közgazdasági Szemle, 28, 675-686

Ocherki novoi i noveyshci istorii SShA. Izdatelstvo Akademii Nauki, Moscow, 1960

Tarján, T. (1993) Közgazdasági Szemle 40, 815

Tarján, T. and Molnár, Gy.: in this volume

Notes

1   This decision did not completely eliminate prerogatives of nobility. E.g. all noblemen retained their voting power, while commoners got it only above a certain level of income. Reason: existing rights were not confiscated.

2   The data of the 1910 census were published in volumes for the whole Double Monarchy. Specially for the Hungarian data: Magyar Statisztikai Közlemények, New Series, Vol. 42, Budapest, 1912

Appendix

Keywords of the history of some steppe nations

Here some historical data are collected for the convenience of Western readers about steppe nations almost unknown in the West but mentioned in the present text and present in the everyday historical memory of the Carpathian Basin. This Appendix has its own bibliography, the references are - exceptionally - cited by reference numbers. The nations, tribes, peoples etc. are alphabetically ordered here. See also the short explanations in [1], which paper will not be explicitly cited henceforth.

In some cases the Hungarian literature is the most detailed (among the steppe nations Hungary founded the first Academy of Sciences) and often is not translated into Western languages. This we cannot help.

After the entry the most common name used in the Basin in singular is given in brackets.

When looking for an item in literature, note that in Hungarian, Chinese and Japanese names family name comes first (at least when the text is also in one of these languages).

For brevity, if not indicated otherwise, dates are meant in AD. A number of shorthand notations is used, namely: E.=East(ern), S.=South(ern), W.=West(ern), N.=North(ern), P.=Prince, K.=King, Kg.=Khagan, R.=River, c.=about (in time), ct.=century, bw.=between. 'Basin' means Carpathian Basin, and 'obscure' is to be read as 'still a matter of argumentation'. ~ stands for the entry.

Avars (Avar)

Possibly the zhuan-zhuans of early Chinese chronicles [2]. C. 500. ruling in the Altai (now Kazakistan and S. Russia). Defeated by the uprising Turks led by Kg. Bumin (and by the mythical Grey Wolf) in the first half of March, 552 [3]. Led by Kg. Bayan to W., in 565 defeat the Thuringian K. Sigebert I at the R. Elbe (FRG). Thence turn back with Slavic tribes (probably Serbs, Croats and pre-Slovaks) and enter the Basin in 567 [4]. Anti-Gepidic coalition with the Lombards; take the Gepid lands in 567, and, by a Treaty of 200 Year Friendship, the Lombard lands on the Easter Monday of 568. Second unification of the Basin. (For the first see Huns.) 630: extinction of the Bayan dynasty. Steppe territories E. of the Carpathian lost. First in history the Basin is a self-governing unit (with border guard tribes on the outer slopes). 680: reorganization of the state after immigration of new tribes (probably Onogurs from the First Bulgar state) led by P. Kuber [5], [6]. 791: Frank attack, completely unsuccessful and disastrous [7]. 795: internal struggles exploited by Count Erik of Friuli. Avar Pannonia is subjugated by Franks. 805: E. half of the state subjugated by Kg. Krum of (Danube) Bulgars [5].

The subsequent fate of ~ is obscure. Until 822 (or 840) names of Christian Avar Khagans are known. (E.g. Theodorus and Abraham.) They were subjects of the Frank Emperor so must have belonged to the Roman Church. ~ probably were assimilated by the incoming Magyar tribes. Arguments exist for and against linguistic similarity bw. tribes entering the Basin in 680 and 896 [6].

The exact time of the settling of Serbs and Croats on the Balkan is a matter of argumentation. Some scholars believe it to be pre-Avar, in which case ~ could not have had a role in it. However it seems to have happened in the Avar era [5], [8] and the 6 Croat leaders of the migration mentioned by Konstantinos Porphyrogenetos all have Turk names [9] which, in any possible time, could not have been anything else than Avar (or related). See also [10], and for reconstructed previous locations, [11].

Bulgars (Bulgár)

Alliance of tribes organised N. of the Black Sea by Irnak, son of Atilla, just after 454. Later ruling the Lower Volga region. K. Kovrat, c. 635-665 baptized in Byzantium. K. Batbayan subjugated by the W. Turk (later Chasarian) Chaganate in 668 [5]. His 4 brothers with peoples emigrate. P. Kotrag founds Volga Bulgaria. P. Asparuch founds Danube Bulgaria. P. Kuber goes to the Avars. P. Altsek goes to Ravenna.

Since Bulgarian belongs to a special subgroup of Turkish languages (the r-group), inheritors of Bulgarians can be recognised among Turkish peoples. Danube Bulgaria has survived. Volga Bulgaria existed until ct. 13 and her successor people and state is the Chuvash Republic of the Russian Federation (Middle Volga, near Kazan). The old Turkish words of the present Hungarian language are of r-Turk, so probably Bulgarian.

Chasars (Kazár)

Successor state of the W. Turk Chaganate, core territory among the Volga, Don and Mtn. Caucasus, Sarig Sin (White Wall, in Russian times Tsaritsin, later Stalingrad) keeping the narrow gateway between the rivers. The 7 Magyar tribes lived on the W. periphery of the Chaganate bw. 750 and 830; in 830 the Magyars picked up 3 rebel tribes of the ~ (the Kabars). Mixed population in the Chaganate; the leading ~ Turkish. Defeated but not subjugated by P. Sviatoslav of Russia in 976, then decaying until the Mongolian invasion in ct. 13. Assimilated into the Golden Horde c. 1240. For some details see [12].

As for culture, the Chaganate was a focal point of influences of Byzantine, Arab, Steppe and Varaegian (Middle Swedish) cultures. In c. 750 Begh Bulan accepts the Old Testament religion in Karaitic form (i.e. without Talmud), the common part of Judaism, Christianism and Islam [13], [14], [15], [16]. The extent of conversion is obscure, but Karaitic communities survived in Krimea and Lithuania, the latter speaking Kipchak Turk. C. 840 Kg. (or Begh) Obadia accepts Judaism. In the Chaganate also Christianism and Islam were widespread [12].

The Kabar rebels of ~ entered the Basin with the Magyars in 896, transferring thither some Chasarian culture. Khasdai ben Yitzhak ibn Shaprut, Prime Minister of the Cordoba Chaliphate contacted K. Joseph of the ~ c. 955. In the answer K. Joseph mentions Bulgarians and Magyars (or maybe Onogurs?) as previous Chasarian tribes, having gone to the Danube. For the most detailed surviving text of this letter, found by Abraham Firkowicz, see [17]. It gives various details of cultures in Chasaria.

Cumanians (Kun)

Kipchak Turks fleeing from Mongols into the Basin in 1240, led by K. Kuthen. Now in Europe the Cumanian language is spoken only by the Lithuanian Karaims. In Hungary free subjects of the Crown. Local Cuman autonomy dissolved in 1872.

Gepids (Gepida)

East German tribe, subjects of the Huns, leading the uprising against Huns in 454. Then rulers of the E. half of the Great (Hungarian) Plains, E. of the R. Tisa. From c. 520 bitterest foes of the Lombards. In 567 defeated by Avars and Lombards [4]. Still in existence along R. Tisa c. 950.

Later fate is unknown. Assimilated by Magyars, Slovaks, or, maybe, Saxons (Zips).

Huns (Hun)

Possibly the Hiung-nus of early Chinese chronicles [2]; maybe of mixed Turkish-Mongolian origin. At the end of ct. 3 BC triggering the erection of the Chinese Great Wall. BC 209-175: Kg. Mao-Tun. Starting to W. in ct. 2 AD. Crossing the Volga (led by Balambér) in 375; immediately subjugating the majority of Goths and triggering the Migration Period for Europe.

Great King Attila (433-453) rules an empire from France to Central Asia. For details see [18], [19]. Under his rule the Basin was first united in historic times (and as far as it can be known in any time at all). However this united Basin was not self-governing then but a part of a huge empire. He dies in 453, and in the following year the empire breaks up in a revolt led by Ardarich of the Gepides. ~, led by Irnak, son of Attila, retreat to N. of the Black Sea.

The later fate of the ~ is somewhat obscure. A state of the Black ~ is in existence in 681 when Bishop Israel of Georgia is fairly successful in converting them to christianity [20]. Hephtalits subjugating N. India in ct. 6 are called also White ~. According to Gumilyov [21] Asian Huns in the Hosi region (China) survived until c. 500, and then their Asina clan went to Avars, thence Turks, founding the Turkish state. The Bulgarian states may be of Hunnish origin. The Szekler tribes (speaking Hungarian) in the S-E. part of the Basin traditionally originate themselves from the ~. The founder dynasty of the Hungarian state from 896 regarded itself as descendants of Attila the Hun.

Hungarians (Hungarus, Uhor)

Up to 1920 the common word for subjects of the Basin (except Croatia) with no relation to language. Since 1920 the term has a narrower meaning: the subjects of Hungary (dominated by Magyars) in the centre of the Basin plus Magyars anywhere. In Slovakian, however, the equivalent word úhor means Slovaks plus Hungarians together.

When applied to language it always means the language of Magyars.

Originally the word meant the Onogurs of the Basin in the ct. 8-9, and went continuously to the new state and nation after 896 in W. use.

Jazones (Jász)

Iranian horsemen, entering the Basin in ct. 14. Nearest relatives are the Osets along the Russian-Georgian border. In Hungary free subjects of the Crown. Local Jazonian autonomy dissolved in 1872.

Magyars (Magyar)

Dominant population of the Basin from 896, and especially of the present Hungary. In first historical notes alliance of seven tribes, of whose names five are Turkish (probably Bulgarian or relatives), two Finno-Ugrian.

First reconstruable location S. of the Ural, c. 500 BC. Possible connections with Huns moving to W. Later on the periphery of the W. Turkish and Chasarian Khaganates until 830. Then moving to the W., and stopping to migrate up to now in the Basin c. 900.

Since Old Testament religions were well known in the Chasarian Khaganate, and the territory (especially the Krim Peninsula) was within the radius of the (Eastern) Christian missionarism, ~ can have known elements of medieval 'European' culture before reaching the Basin; but definitely not in their Western form.

Magyar tribes unified the Basin third time (for first and second see Huns and Avars).

The language of ~ is called Hungarian in the W. The present form of this language is mainly Finno-Ugrian, i.e. a member of a family whose most W. language is Finnish, and most E. ones are two Ugors (see later). However there is a strong layer of Bulgarian (or r-) Turkish words. Nearest kins (without the Turkish words) are two small languages, the Manysi or Vogul (6000 speakers) and the Hanti or Ostyak (20000 speakers) just E. of the Ural, at the confluence of R. Ob and R. Irtis. Hungarian, Ostyak and Vogul constitute the Ugrish subfamily of Finno-Ugrish family.

Onogurs (Nándor)

Alliance of ten (Bulgarian) Turkish tribes (on = 10, ogur = tribe, Bulgarian word form). Some ~ lived in the Basin in ct. 8-9. Assimilated to Avars, Bulgarians and Magyars. For more details see [5], [6].

The W. term 'Hungary' comes from the name of ~. Contemporary W. historiography did not observe the reorganization of the Basin in 896.

Petchenegs (Besenyô)

Alliance of 8 (common or z-) Turkish tribes. Until 889 E. of R. Jajik (Ural). Pushing Magyars to the W. just before 896. Some ~ entering the Basin c. 950, later assimilated to Magyars. The ~ remaining E. or S. from the Basin contributing later to the formation of Walachians and Moldovans ('Romanians') [21].

Sauromatians (Szarmata)

Iranian horsemen, from ancient Hellene times, relatives to mythical Amazons. (Distinction bw. Sauromatians and Sarmatians ignored here.) At 500 BC in the Volga region. Five big tribes of ~: Alans, Aorsi, Jazyges, Roxolani, Siraces [22]. Aorsi mixed with Alans from ct. 1, and Siraces always outside the Basin. For the other 3 groups:

Jazyges enter the Basin c. 20, and occupy the Great Plains bw. Pannonia and Dacia. Some Roxolani join them during the Jazyg-Roman War (ends in 176). The Basin Sarmatians become more or less the allies of Romans. Their last king mentioned is Babai, killed by Theoderik of the Ostrogoths [23] c. 469. His subjects assimilate to neighbours.

Alans divide into branches in ct. 2 BC with different fates [22]. E. Alans are dominated by Huns from 200, participate in Hun movements and some go as W. as France. Some Alans are independent in the Caucasus up to 450, may meet with Magyars (or with Onogurs), and can be seen until ct. 13. 3 other groups are Antae, Choroates and Serboi.

Antae are in Moldavia after 200, where divide into two branches. One goes to W., settles in later Poland (Zakrzew graves). This kingdom is subjugated by Attila of the Huns c. 440. The other group remains in Moldavia until the retreat of Huns to the E., and afterwards (c. 470) extends its rule to Kiev.

This kingdom is subjugated by Avars at the end of ct. 6. 'After AD 500 the Serboi, Choroates and Antae (Alanic tribes) are gradually absorbed by the Slavs over whom they reign.' [22]. So the Serbian and Croatian nations seem to have been founded by Sauromatians. Note that within the Indo-European family of languages the nearest kin of Slavian group is Iranian, to which Sauromatian belonged. The possible successor states of Antae may be Poland and Ukraine, but with one remark. The later Poland was formed by N. (Polyan) leaders occupying S. (Wislyan) territories. Now, the latter ones around Cracow are called also White Croatians. White Croatians were allies of the Hungarian state from 896. Their

Cracow territory was continuously incorporated into the Polish state from 962 by K. Mieszko of Poland. In Bohemia the Slavnik clan of White Croatians (centre in Libice) concurred for high power with the Premisl clan of Czechs (Prague) but became exterminated c. 995 [24].

In mediaeval Polish historiography Sauromathians as organisers of the Polish state was commonplace.

A convenient steppe timetable of migrations can be found in [25].

As for the possibilities of Western influences in culture and legal system on peoples prior to entering the Carpathian Basin, one can conclude as follows:

1)   Huns moved too fast to get any Roman influence. They lived together with Germans for decades, but these tribes were Eastern Germans, at which no clear data for private property of land etc. are known.

2)   Avars remained outside East Roman or Christian territories until the Carpathian Basin. In the Basin they may have got Western influence, but until the end of the 8th century no wish can be seen on the Avar side to converge to the West. Since in 795 Erik of Friuli was able to occupy Pannonia after that the Western Avar chief (the tudun) have changed sides, it is possible that by then convergence was a program in some groups of Avars. The Christian Khagans and cross motives in Avar graves are signals. If so, there was a pre-phase of convergence by long-range regulators c. 800. However the Christian Avar statelet was not quite self-governing.

3)   As for Magyars, various pre-Basin Christian influence may have existed. Note that Nestorian Christian missionary activity is proven in 781 as east as China by the Chang Ngan stele [26]. Also, Old and New Testament teaching could very easily be picked up in Chasaria and their devotees must have been among the Kabar tribes joining the Magyars. However there 'Christian' did not mean 'Western' at all. It was Byzantine, or even more eastern variety. (Georgia and Armenia were Christian from the beginning of the 4th century.) Still, such pre-Basin influences were important because they made the conversion to Western Christianity of Pannonia much easier.

Bibliography for the appendix

[1]   Bóna, I. (1976) in 'A magyar régészet regénye' Panoráma, Budapest, p. 105

[2]   Deguignes, J. (1756) *Histoire général des Huns etc.* Paris

[3]   Ecsedi, I. (1979) *Nomádok és kereskedők Kína határán*, Akadémiai Kiadó, Budapest

[4]   Bóna, I. (1976) *The Dawn of the Dark Ages*, Corvina Press, Budapest

[5]   Todorov, N. and Dinev, L. (1968) *Bulgaria. Historical and Geographical Outline*, Sofia Press, Sophia

[6]   László, Gy. (1973) in 'Évezredek hétköznapjai' Panoráma, Budapest, p. 164

[7]   Bóna, I. (1973) in 'Évezredek hétköznapjai' Panoráma, Budapest, p. 141

[8]   Giurescu, C.C. (ed.) (1974) *Chronological History of Romania*, Editura Enciclopedica Romana, Bucharest

[9]   Mikkola, J.J. (1927) Archiv f. Slav. Philologie 10, 158

[10]   Alföldi, A. (1934) Eurasia septemtrionalis antiqua. 9, 302

[11]   *Atlas zur Geschichte*, Band 1. VEB Hermann Haack, Gotha/Leipzig, 1981

[12]   Magomedov, M.G. (1983) *Obrazovanie hazarskogo kaganata*, Nauka, Moscow

[13]   Kohn, S. (1881) *Héber kútforrások és adatok Magyarország történetéhez*, Athenaeum, Budapest

[14]   Dubinski, A.: private communication

[15]   Kobeckaite, G. (1990) Vilnius 1990/4, p. 103

[16]   Koestler, A. *The Thirteenth Tribe -The Khazar Empire and Its Heritage*, Random House, N. Y.

[17]   Harkavy, L. (1875) Russ. Rev. 7, 79

[18]   Thompson, E.A. (1948) *A History of Attila and the Huns*, Oxford University Press, Oxford

[19]   Németh, Gy. (1940) *Attila és hunjai*, Magyar Szemle Társaság, Budapest

[20]   Kalankatuaci, M. (1912) Patmutiwn Aluanic asxarhi. Tiflis

[21]   Rásonyi, L. (1970) in Phil. Turc. Fundamenta III, Wiesbaden, 1970, p. 1

[22]   Sulimirsky, T. (1975) *The Sarmatians*, Thames & Hudson, London

[23]   Schmidt, L. (1934) *Geschichte der deutschen Stämme bis zum Ausgang der Wölkerwanderung. Die Ostgermanen.*

[24]   Győrffy, Gy. (1977) *István király és műve*, Gondolat, Budapest

[25]   Bérczi, Sz. and Szabó, L. (1993) in *Carpathian Basin: Evolutionary Stages* (ed. Lukács, B. et al.), KFKI-1993-21, p. 72

[26]   Toynbee, A. (1979) *A Study of History*, Weatherwane, N. Y.

19 The transformation of the legal system in Hungary with special reference to human rights

Tamás Földesi

1.

Eastern Europe was confronted with a unique task in 1989. Perhaps it was the first occasion in history when the economic and political system had to be changed at one and the same time as well, in a way that there had been no model for such a double test. The West was unprepared for the domino-like, sudden collapse of both the soft and hard dictatorships. Naturally, it had been impossible to deal with such problems legally and discuss possible solutions.

In my lecture I shall discuss a third sub-system which however, is equally closely linked with the economic and the political, namely the transformation of the legal system. In order to understand why the fundamental transformation poses a major problem whose solution is a decade long process, one has to start out from the role law had played in Eastern Europe in the four decades before 1990.

As a consequence of several international and domestic causes, the East European countries naturally had a well-established state and legal system but this differed from the idea and practice of a state governed by the rule of law (hereinafter referred to by the German '*Rechtsstaat*' for brevity). Both the state and the law were subordinated to the ruling one-party system (hence the term party-state) and for this reason, law - in contrast to the '*Rechtsstaat*' - did not function as a limitation of power which had to be observed by the political party (parties) but as a means used for political goals and which could be set aside according to the political will. (See the long range of examples, from whipped-up trials to the widespread corruption and the privileged, often above-the-law position of the members of the nomenclature.)

Three phenomena in particular sharply revealed that law was in an unworthy situation in these political systems.

First: although the East European countries had a constitution (with insignificant alterations, they took over the 1936 Stalinist constitution), this did not function as basic law. The Constitutional Court was an unknown institution in most of the East European countries and anti-constitutionality, as a legal term, was almost missing from the legal vocabulary.

Second: the legal system was not primarily based on law, the mostly sham-Parliament which rarely met passed 3 or 4 laws a year. Rules and regulations having legal force constituted the majority of the regulations and no small part of these was not in a hierarchical order - sometimes lower level regulations were in force as against higher level ones. In addition, as Elemér Hankiss pointed out, an unofficial, second or third law was issued which played an increasingly strong role in the regulation of economic and other relations. This too, indicated the crisis of the legal system.

Third: understandably, human rights did not have the place in this legal system which they duly have in the '*Rechtsstaat*'. The situation of human rights was rather ambivalent in the East European countries. On the other hand, in each East European country one could find - even if not the complete - catalogue of human rights because under UN provisions only those states could be members which had codified human rights. In line with this, the East European political systems officially recognised human rights, regularly celebrated 10 December, Human Rights Day. More than that, in the controversy with the West it was frequently underlined that human rights were genuinely observed in Eastern Europe.

On the other hand, it is a basic fact that the one-party system is incompatible with the rights of political freedom and human rights because it stems from the essence of the one-party system that it fails to provide an opportunity for the right to organise oneself and form associations. The lack of the right to create any other real parties means an evident limitation on the freedom of opinion and press because non-existent parties cannot have their own press and the opposition too, does not have the possibility of freely expressing its ideas etc. As a result only the economic, social and cultural rights were put into practice to some extent and the East European countries were anxious to stress that these rights were given priority among human rights. (Földesi, T. 1990)

This ambivalence found its manifestation not only in the fact that political human rights were in fact not implemented in East European countries but also in that the political regulation was fundamentally different from that in the democratic states. The differences were clear in at least three forms. First: in the constitution of each East European country a general clause was attached to the political human rights under which these could be applied lawfully only in line with the interests of socialism. In practice, this formula meant that any action by the opposition could be declared anti-socialist and thus was banned or punishment was imposed on that basis. The second difference concerned the 'soul', that is the guarantees of human rights. Because, in contrast to most parts of law, human rights mediate the interests and the will of the people to the state and for this reason, their implementation largely depends on whether there are adequate legal guarantees against the violation of human rights by the state. These legal guarantees, as for example, the Constitutional Court or Public Administration Court were subsequently non-existent. The third difference was the failure to recognize human rights as basic civic rights. The ideology behind it was that the citizens of the socialist state did not need basic civic rights against their own state. (Földesi, T. 1989)

But there were other examples: the legal system differed basically from that of the *Rechtsstaat*. The social relations were not only overpoliticized, but *overregulated* as well, because the political system believed: every social problem could be solved through legal means.

Therefore the legal system contained a large number of irrational elements, and many decrees were frequently changed thereby causing legal uncertainty, depriving the law of one of the main advantages, of its predictability.

Similarly the problem of the *justice* of the law was a neglected question, because the notion of justice has been an unfavoured concept for Marxism.

2.

I shall try to describe the changes the Hungarian legal system has gone through in the past four years compared to what was stated above. For the political parties involved in the peaceful change of system, change was to be the creation of the '*Rechtsstaat*'. The axis of this rule of law had to be the *Constitution* in line with the traditions of Continental Europe. Clearly, the former Constitution was unsuitable for this function and for this reason, there were two alternatives open: to elaborate a new Constitution, or to radically change the existing one. For specific historical reasons which I do not want to discuss in detail, the decision was in favour of the latter solution[1].

The fundamentally transformed Constitution lays down the basis of a democratic pluralistic state system. Already in its first points it lays down the banning of forced organization and exclusive ownership of power, and stresses the principle of establishing parties freely. The most important provisions of the Constitution include the acceptance of the organizational framework and operational principles of the democratically elected Parliament, the establishment of the Constitutional Court, the creation of the institution of the Ombudsman to defend the rights of the citizens, of the international and ethnic minorities, the revival of the State Audit Office, the setting up of the system of local self-governments which is basically different from the system of councils and the much more multifarious and richer summary of human rights. (Constitution)

However, the Constitution has not only been renewed in its content but its role in the legal system has also changed fundamentally. Because Parliament can only pass laws which are in harmony with the Constitution, perhaps one of the most significant functions of the Constitutional Court is to provide a normative control of laws prior to and after enactment, in other words it examines whether or not the laws are in harmony with the Constitution. This idea has not remained a dead letter and in the three year existence of the Constitutional Court it has met several such requests and in a number of cases the study ended in the need to withdraw or modify the law.

One of the most basic elements of the transformation of the legal system is that in contrast to the previous era, the most important social relations have to be controlled *by law*. Parliament has to make laws in 8 months and as a result, this Parliament, elected in May 1990 made roughly 100 new laws each year. But before giving a short analysis of these laws, I have to discuss a closely related process which was a precondition to making those laws. This is *deregulation,* whose essence is that a competent committee reviews the existing laws and proposes to annul a large number of them. The decision concerning deregulation is naturally taken by bodies that have the authority and competence to do so. However, deregulation does not only cover the annulment of certain legal regulations but in some cases also that of specific parts of given laws. This is how lots of provisions of the Penal Code and the Civil Code have been changed. For example, the parts of the Penal Code on political crimes which bore the features of the one-party state can be grouped in this category.

Within the legal system, regulations which played an outstanding role were those aimed at the transformation of the economic system. These primarily included the laws concerning privatization. Act No. 1 of 1992 should be mentioned in the first place which is about the decrease in the role of the state and also Act No. 54 of 1992 which regulates the forms and procedures of privatization. Other laws in this group include those serving the establishment of new institutions, for example the Stock Exchange or the regulations concerning bankruptcy that had been almost completely unknown in the previous system (Act No. 49 of 1991). The laws relating to compensation constitute a separate category which has created a significant economic rearrangement. Act No. 22 of 1992 on the Labour Code has a significant impact on the economic transformation.

Tax laws involving incentives as well as a brake have also played an important role in the economic changes. One has to state with regret that these laws have set norms that have changed very much from one year to another, a fact which has had a negative impact on economic stabilization.

Laws concerning the cooperatives have played a significant role in agricultural changes: however, there are very diverging evaluations concerning their social impact especially with regard to the deep crisis of agriculture in Hungary in the past few years.

But not only concrete laws were passed, but the main principle of law-making has been changed as well. During the socialist regime the ruling principle was: everything is forbidden, which is not allowed. In the present it changed to the contrary: everything is allowed, which is not forbidden. Of course the latter gives much more freedom to citizens.

3.

One of the most pronounced changes within the transformation of the legal system that has an impact on various fields can be detected in the legal regulation of *human rights.* In this regard, one can distinguish two different, though not disconnected periods. The first phase begins with the changing of the Constitution to which a number of laws adjoin, where given regulations are linked to one or another human right laid down - understandably - only briefly in the Constitution. If one compares the earlier Constitution first adopted in 1949 and amended in 1972 with the one passed in 1990 then it can be said that although human rights are included in both of them, the *volume, nature* and *depth* of the regulation are basically different. The regulation of human rights in the earlier Constitution was based on an ideology under which there were no human rights in general, only bourgeois and socialist human rights existed. The fact that the so-called socialist human rights were very different from the internationally accepted human rights, as for example from those laid down in the 1948 UN Declaration, or the 1950 European Convention on Human Rights was not considered a weakness but on the contrary, it is their merit. In contrast to this the drafters of the paragraphs on human rights of the 1990 Constitution (I myself also took part in that work) started out from the fact that, in essence, human rights are not specifically dependent on the social system, there are human rights without attributives, and their models are the previously mentioned international documents. As a consequence, the traditional, first generation rights to liberty are in the forefront, ranging from the right to life, gathering and assembly, while in the earlier Constitutions the so-called ECOSOC rights were at the top. Naturally, the new Constitution does not contain any restricting clauses. In addition, in the new Constitution such human rights are also included which were not by coincidence missing from the previous ones. One of the most important ones of these is the freedom of movement which had no place in a country that accepted the 'Berlin Wall' and which was separated from the West by the ' Iron Curtain' even if this eroded significantly in the soft dictatorship of the 1970s and 1980s, and where emigrating to another country was a grave crime. Similarly, (Földesi, T. 1993) the right to petition appeared in the new Constitution which was alien to the society in the previous regime because ensuring the collective right to launch a petition would have meant the provision of the possibility for the opposition to collect signatures and other forms of organization. The formulation of several human rights reflects basic changes in content. These include for example, the right to seek refuge which in the earlier Constitution was very limited and was guaranteed only for those who had agreed with the principles of communism, while the new Constitution ensures the right to seek refuge to all those persecuted for racial, ethnic, religious or political reasons and undertakes the duty of not returning the person to the country where he has suffered persecution. These regulations are in harmony with the norms included in the International Agreements on Refugees of 1951 and 1967. (Goodwin-Gill, G.S. 1983)

The part of the amended Hungarian Constitution concerning the rights of ethnic minorities can be regarded as very progressive in Eastern Europe because this is the only law to lay down that national minorities are also groups of people constituting the state. This is in contrast to the widespread practice which regards only the majority nation as one to form the state in line with the idea of 'one nation - one state'.

In their formulation, the regulations of human rights in the Constitution and the related laws often react to those dangers threatening human rights which unfortunately, were implemented in the previous system. From this point of view, a typical example is Act No.4 of 1990 on the freedom of religion and conscience. While in the former regime the churches and religion were an undesired but tolerated phenomena and had very limited freedom, Act No.4 of 1990 lays down in its introduction that the religions and churches play a positive role in society, preserve and create values. In a similar fashion, in the former system of East European political practice, the State Church Office supervised the churches and their autonomy was limited to the minimum. By contrast the new law provides that the establishment of such an office would be against the law.

From the point of view of the implementation of human rights, the system of guarantees is of fundamental importance and its creation already began in the first stage. Three institutions are of major significance in this regard. First, the Constitutional Court which in Hungary does not deal with human rights grievances of individual citizens, except if a provision of a law applied against them is also against the Constitution. But by defending the Constitution as a whole so the Constitutional Court has a guaranteeing function. In addition, Act No.20 of 1990 created the Public Administration Court which has the primary function of remedying human rights violations of the citizens committed by the public administration. The third organization of guarantee is the Ombudsman. The Council of Ministers decided on the creation of this institution under the provisions of the Constitution in the autumn of 1990 but unfortunately, the Ombudsman and their deputies have not as yet been elected by Parliament.

The second phase of regulating human rights in Hungary began with Hungary's joining the Council of Europe in 1990 which included the acceptance of the European Convention of Human Rights and the provision that Hungarian citizens whose human rights had been violated and who had not obtained redress from domestic courts, are free to seek legal protection at the European Court of Human Rights in Strasbourg. True, the ratification of Hungary's membership only came at the end of 1992 which means that citizens can make use of that right only in the future, that is they can appeal to the Strasbourg Court with grievances that they suffered after Hungary's accession to the Treaty.

Hungary's membership in the Council of Europe is of major significance for human rights regulation. First of all because the European Commission of Human Rights and its Court primarily take into consideration the European Convention of Human Rights and the relevant case-law when deciding on complaints. In case the domestic legal system differs from the European Convention of Human Rights to a lesser or greater degree, it may happen that masses of Hungarian citizens would win court cases against the Hungarian state which would involve a serious loss of prestige. Against this background it is fully understandable that the Ministry of Justice organized research in the spring of 1991 covering the whole of Hungarian law to find out how and to what degree all Hungarian rules of law in force and the practice applied in its cases differ from the European Convention on Human Rights. I myself was involved in this work and the summarizing study by Károly Bárd and Tamás Bán provides a detailed analysis of the need for changes of law concerning human rights that are rooted in the historical and traditional differences of Hungarian law. (Bán, T. and Bárd, K. 1992)

(Let me note that the practice of the European Human Rights Commission and Court is far from being rigid or dogmatic that would disregard the individual countries historical development and specific characteristics from the freedom of religion to the ban of obscene writings because a number statements and rulings indicate that there is a smaller or larger scope for movement within the norms of the European Convention on Human Rights in which only the differing specific features of the individual countries can be realised. Just one example: in Germany, for instance, there is compulsory religious education but if the child's parents or being above 14, he, himself requests exemption, he will get it, while in Hungary and in many other countries, religious education is not compulsory.) (Schanda, B.)

The requirement that Hungary is now expected to adjust its legal system to the standard of European human rights is seemingly just an external compulsion. Starting from the 1950s all European countries which have been members of the Council of Europe for decades, unlike East European countries, have gone through this process which has had a very positive result, namely the gap between their legal systems has narrowed : this has had a number of economic and other advantages in the European Union. In this way, there is every reason to assume that this process is useful for Hungary not only because the number of cases at the Strasbourg Court will be significantly smaller but because this is a means on the road leading to Europe, as it is Hungary's determination to join the European Union as soon as possible.

I will now discuss a few modifications of laws whose immediate source is the European Convention. Perhaps, the most significant of these is the No.23 ruling of the Constitutional Court of 1990 on the *abolition of the death penalty*. As it is well known, the original Convention on Human Rights did not then contain this ban and the ban on the death penalty was only included in what is called the 6th supplementary protocol. Although the former Hungarian legal system regarded the death penalty as exceptional, the Penal Code contained more than 20 cases where capital punishment could be imposed. It is worth noting that the abolition of the death penalty did not belong to legal regulations for which there was a strong social demand.

According to opinion polls a very significant proportion of the citizens still think that capital punishment should be applied for the most serious crimes even though the abolition of the death penalty means that in this regard Hungary also accepts the more humanized European norms. Issues that require further changes in the law include several fields of penal law. Among these, one can mention the principle of the presumption of innocence with which the conduct of the lawsuit is not in full harmony when the judge asks the accused instead of the contrary model of the prosecutor, and the defence lawyer. It is highly doubtful whether the sentence based on lack of evidence (which is an established form of Hungarian penal law) can be harmonized with the presumption of innocence. A fundamental requirement of the European Convention of Human Rights is the right to court proceedings within a reasonable period of time, but this requirement is absent from both the Hungarian Constitution and the Hungarian legal system. It seems, the legal procedures by which dangerous, mentally ill people can be placed and kept in asylum will have to be changed. The present regulation, for example, leaves the continued hospitalization to the full discretion of the given team of doctors and the court has the right to examine if the procedure had been legally, correct, a practice which is completely different from that of the European Human Rights Commission and Court.

The ban on what is called '*ex post facto law*' which is also included in the amended Constitution may pose an essential legal political problem in Hungary. In each of the East European countries it is the source of a great problem of how to judge those political crimes which were committed in the past 40 years and to which many people fell victim. One of the basic problems here is that when these crimes were committed, the law did not consider them as crimes (plus many acts have since become statute-barred). The ban on '*ex post facto law*' lays down that no one can be called to responsibility for acts that were not punishable at the time they were carried out. The 20th century legal practice has one exception from the principle of '*ex post facto law*', namely war crimes and crimes against mankind are punishable even if these were not regarded as crimes in the given country at the time they were committed. On this basis the Hungarian Parliament adopted a law in 1993 under which in 1956 there was war in Hungary and for this reason, the crimes committed in 1956-57 and 1958 can now be punished. It is an open question, however, that if some people who were then responsible are sentenced and turn to Strasbourg, will the Strasbourg Human Rights Commission and Court accept that indeed, there were historical conditions in 1956 that can be judged in this way.

From this short description it is clear that during the transformation of the Hungarian legal system, the change in human rights regulation is of outstanding importance. This, just like the transformation of the legal system is a process whose test will be provided by Strasbourg by evaluating the harmony between the Hungarian human rights regulations with the European Convention on Human Rights.

Finally, a few words about one problem which originates in the specific conditions of the Hungarian change of system. When the rules of Parliament were shaped in 1989 and 1990 on what kind of majority is needed for a law, then a very large circle of laws was determined for which not a simple but a

66 per cent majority was needed. (The background to this regulation was the fear that perhaps, the then ruling party would have such a majority which could be counterbalanced by only a one third minority forming the opposition.) As a consequence of this rule of voting, a number of laws have been rejected because, while they did receive a simple majority of votes, they failed to receive 66 per cent due to the lack of support of the opposition. As a result, the transformation of the Hungarian legal system is rather defective here and there. The unfortunate fate of the law on electronic media belongs here. Up to now it has not been adopted despite the fact that due to the absence of that law, the control of Radio and Television is still unresolved. At the same time, there are several legal regulations against which the opposition raised its voice in a wellfounded manner but which have been passed with a simple majority of votes. But since it is highly probable that after the 1994 elections a coalition different from the present one will form the government, there is good chance of basically modifying many laws adopted in the period between 1990 and 1994. However, this analysis of the transformation of the legal system would not be complete without discussing to what extent the changed legal system has been realized and become effective. It is all the more important because in contrast to the former system, the '*Rechtstaat*' rests on the basic principle that law is implemented and does not remain on paper. In general, I can say that the changing legal system has stood this test. On the basis of free elections, a pluralistic political system has emerged. Parliament has worked very intensely even if many people criticise - not without foundation- certain features of its work and tone. The Constitutional Court and the Public Administration Court have been similarly active. The freedom of religion and press and other liberties are realised even if there have been attempts to limit the freedom of expression. In conjunction with the laws on privatization, the proportion of the state and private sectors has significantly changed and several hundred thousand people have received compensation. The guarantees protecting the rights of imprisoned and detained people function. The courts and the Public Prosecutor's Office operate independently of party political principles. At the same time, the changing legal system has a few weak points where compliance with law and the realization of law is far from being perfect. In this regard I would mention first of all the laws on taxation where the problem is also caused by the fact that in Hungary, the failure to declare a smaller or bigger part of income - especially in the entrepreneurial sphere - has become a habit and, as a result, not only the state economy suffers a loss of billions of forints of income but huge inequalities emerge as taxes are consistently deducted from declared wages and salaries.

Summary: the evolution process towards a *Rechsstaat* is *contradictory*. On the one hand we can see a great development in the transformation of the legal system to the needs of the 'social market economy', but on the other hand we still have much to do, from better law-making to the just application of the law.

Bibliography

Földesi, T. (1990), 'The unity of Human Rights in Western and Eastern Europe. Meditation about Human Rights', *Rivista internazionale di filosofia del diritto* 1990/1.

Földesi, T. (1989), 'Az emberi jogok' (Human Rights) Kossuth Kiadó, Budapest.

A Magyar Köztársaság Alkotmánya. (The Constitution of the Hungarian Republic) 1990/29. Törvény.

Földesi, T. (1993), 'The Right to move and its Achilles' heel the Right to Asylum', *Connecticut Journal*, 1993. pp. 293-297.

Goodwin-Gill, G.S. (1983), *The Refugee in International Law* 1983. pp. 27-34.

Bán, T. and Bárd, K. (1992), 'Az Emberi Jogok Európai Egyezménye és a magyar jog', (The European Convention of Human Rights and the Hungarian Law) *Acta Humana* 1992/6-7.

Schanda, B. *Vallásszabadság a magyar jogban,* (Freedom of Religion in the Hungarian Law), PhD Dissertation. pp. 20-24.

Notes

1   This decision clearly had drawbacks. These include that certain people who are dissatisfied with the work of the Constitutional Court question the legitimacy of the Constitution arguing that in essence it is still the old, and not a new Constitution. But this is a basically wrong view, not only because at least 85 to 90 per cent of the text of the Constitution is new but primarily because it lays down the principles of a completely new political system.